Stories for the American Freemason's Fireside

Also from Westphalia Press

westphaliapress.org

The Idea of the Digital University

Gems of Song for the Eastern Star

Bulwarks Against Poverty in America

Crime 3.0

Treasures of London

Anti-Masonry and the Murder of Morgan

Avate Garde Politician

Understanding Art

L'Enfant and the Freemasons

Spies I Knew

Baronial Bedrooms

Lodge "Himalayan Brotherhood" No. 459 C.E.

Making Trouble for Muslims

Philippine Masonic Directory ~ 1918

Ancient Masonic Mysteries

Collecting Old Books

Paddle Your Own Canoe

Masonic Secret Signs and Passwords

Opportunity and Horatio Alger

Careers in the Face of Challenge

Death Valley in '49

Bookplates of the Kings

Lariats and Lassos

The Boy Chums Cruising in Florida Waters

Mr. Garfield of Ohio

The Wisdom of Thomas Starr King

Freemasonry in Old Buffalo

Original Cables from the Pearl Harbor Attack

The French Foreign Legion

War in Syria

Social Satire and the Modern Novel

Naturism Comes to the United States

The Essence of Harvard

New Sources on Women and Freemasonry

The Genius of Freemasonry

A Definitive Commentary on Bookplates

Designing, Adapting, Strategizing in Online Education

James Martineau and Rebuilding Theology

Gunboat and Gun-runner

Memoirs of a Poor Relation

Bohemian San Francisco

Espionage!

Stories for the American Freemason's Fireside

by Mrs. C.W. Towle

WESTPHALIA PRESS
An imprint of Policy Studies Organization

Stories for the American Freemason's Fireplace
All Rights Reserved © 2014 by Policy Studies Organization

Westphalia Press
An imprint of Policy Studies Organization
1527 New Hampshire Ave., NW
Washington, D.C. 20036
info@ipsonet.org

ISBN-13: 978-1-63391-079-9
ISBN-10: 1633910792

Cover design by Taillefer Long at Illuminated Stories:
www.illuminatedstories.com

Daniel Gutierrez-Sandoval, Executive Director
PSO and Westphalia Press

Rahima Schwenkbeck, Director of Marketing and Media
PSO and Westphalia Press

Updated material and comments on this edition
can be found at the Westphalia Press website:
www.westphaliapress.org

Catharine W. Barber

STORIES

FOR THE

AMERICAN FREEMASON'S

FIRESIDE.

By Mrs. C. W. TOWLE,
OF ALABAMA.

CINCINNATI:
AMERICAN MASONIC PUBLISHING ASSOCIATION,
114 Main Street.
1868.

TO THE

MOTHERS,

WIVES,

SISTERS, and

DAUGHTERS

OF THE

𝕱𝖗𝖊𝖊𝖒𝖆𝖘𝖔𝖓𝖘 𝖔𝖋 𝕬𝖒𝖊𝖗𝖎𝖈𝖆,

THIS VOLUME

Is Cordially Dedicated by

THE AUTHORESS.

PREFACE.

THE STORIES which compose this volume were originally written for a Masonic magazine. A popularity, as unlooked for as it is gratifying, demands for them now a more permanent form. To the "Brethren of the Mystic Tie" they are commended. May their firesides be enlivened by them. May prejudice against a noble and ancient fraternity, whose only object is "to do good and ensue it," be by their instrumentality removed; and may those to whom this book is particularly dedicated be led, by its perusal, to believe that, in casting despite upon that institution whose workings these stories illustrate, they are warring with a friend.

If these objects be attained, I shall not have written, nor they have read, in vain.

C. W. T.

LAFAYETTE, ALA., 1868.

CONTENTS.

STORIES

FOR THE

FREEMASON'S FIRESIDE.

———⬦◇⬦———

MOLLIE CROSS, THE BLIND GIRL.

————

CHAPTER I.

" I'm blind !—oh, I'm blind !"

"AND so, Mollie Cross, your father is to be married
again, I hear," said Mrs. Brittain, as she dipped her hands
into the hot suds with which Judy the servant girl was
washing, and then drawing them out again, wiped them
on the corner of her checked cotton apron, "your father
is to be married in a few days to the widow Morrison."

The little girl to whom these words were addressed sat
upon the edge of a huge granite rock overhanging a
stream of water which went hurrying and dimpling, dashing and foaming, bubbling and singing away through a
beautiful piece of meadow land, and finally emptied itself
into the clear and sparkling waters of the Chickitohatchie,
just where the mill of Tom Williams stood, with its ceaseless clatter, keeping

> " The miller and the miller's son
> So busy all the day."

It was a picturesque spot, and little Mollie Cross made
a picturesque feature in the landscape. Her white bare
feet just touched the surface of the water—her little round
face wore an innocent expression—her dress was drawn
up by one chubby dimpled hand, so that the edge of it

might not touch the surface of the stream, and her curls, short but golden, whenever she moved her head, as she often did with a dainty sort of grace, nestled around her bare throat and shoulders, as if they loved their abiding place.

"I'm afraid," continued Mrs. Brittain, after a moment's pause, "that Mrs. Morrison will not make a very good step-mother; and then her five boys are such rough ones; the oldest one, Jefferson, I hear has taken to drink of late, and the second one swears awfully. It's only yesterday that Judy here heard him cursing Jim Williams, the miller's son, all into ribbon strings, and just for nothing at all, she says. Well, it's a sad pity if it is so, but she's rich, that Widow Morrison is, and that's what's captivated your pa. I shouldn't ha' thought as sensible a man as William Cross has always shown himself to ha' been could ha' been led into any such a match; but strange things happen in this world, and widows when they try can bewitch almost anybody."

The little girl did not reply; on the contrary, she bent her face down in the direction of the stream, and a shade of sadness came over it, like a cloud over a sunny landscape.

"There was my uncle, Fred Parker," continued the indefatigable Mrs. Brittain, "as smart a man as ever was born, rich too, and genteel, who took it into his head to wed his housekeeper, Mrs. Spinkney, a widow woman forty years old, without property or without family connections of honor; and in spite of all that could be said to him, he married her. His children were enraged beyond measure, but it did no good—have her he would; and now the minx rides in her carriage, while many of her betters hobble through life on foot. Then again, old Grandsire Tompkins did the same thing, only he took a young and good-looking Irish girl for his second wife; he was about seventy-three, and she not quite nineteen; but as I before said, strange things happen in this world every day. But cheer up, child, don't be despondent; though it does seem to me that Colonel Cross might have done better, and ought to have done better, than to have taken widow Morrison with her five rough boys, especially when he knew that you, his only child, was so dependent for happiness upon the kindness of those about you, for you never have seen, and it isn't probable you ever will see."

"No," said the girl in a plaintive tone, now raising her fair young face, so that a full view could be obtained of her sightless orbs, "I'm blind; father knows it well—I'm blind! I never saw, when she was living, my own dear mother's face—never saw the blue-arched sky overhead —the bright sun—the fragrant flowers—the green meadow—the mill-house beyond—and the gleeful birds that warble upon the banks of the river, as if determined to sing down the tuneful water. I never saw *you*, Mrs. Brittain, though you have been our housekeeper always, and I have loved you from my earliest infancy—never saw Judy yonder—never saw dear old Brindle, the cow, though coming daily to the stream to drink, and lapped meal out of my tiny hand a thousand times—never saw Nanny the goat, with her two pretty little kids, though they frisk about me all day long—never saw Giss, the pet deer— never saw moon nor twinkling star; all around me is dark, drear, and endless night. *Yes, I'm blind!* and the girl put up her faultless hand and drew the fingers across the orbs, as if something like a crystal tear might have sprung into them, which she was anxious to brush away.

"Well, never mind that," said Mrs. Brittain soothingly; "it's a sad thing to be without sight, I've no doubt, but you're not to blame about it, child—so don't cry. Your afflictions are nothing to what little Peter Parker's were, my uncle's child. He was deaf, dumb, and lame, and that stepmother of his wasn't the kindest in the world. I've heard her scolding him many a time, though it's what might have been expected. But uncle Fred would marry her—that he would, in spite of all that could be said to him. I was very indignant myself about it, though I was at that time a mere slip of a girl. But here comes that bird of Paradise, Kate Devens; she will cheer you up, I know, for you think there is nobody in the world like Miss Kate."

As Mrs. Brittain spoke, she looked towards a tall interesting girl, who came tripping over the green sward toward the washers. She was slightly built, and above the medium height; her hair was very black, her eyes large and full, such as we see in lovely pictures, and her dress of white muslin, sprinkled with scarlet dots, became her admirably. She held her sun-bonnet in her hand, for the sun was in a cloud, and she did not stop until she reached Mrs. Brittain.

"Is little Mollie Cross here?" she asked abruptly; "I have come to take her home with me. O yes! there she is without shoes or stockings, dabbling her feet in the water. Mrs. Brittain, isn't that a dangerous place for her? She might slide off into the stream, you know, and being blind, couldn't save herself. I wouldn't leave her there long at a time, were I in your place. But where are your shoes, Mollie, and your bonnet? you must put them both on, and go home with me," and as the girl spoke, she reached down with both hands, and lifted the blind child to her feet on the bank.

Mrs. Brittain bustled about after the child's shoes and stockings. They were found at last, and safely tied on. Next came the search for her bonnet. That was taken from a green loop where Judy had hung it, and Kate stooped to tie it under Mollie's chin; as she did so, she espied a tear upon the blind girl's cheek, and was struck with the mournful expression of her face. She stopped a moment, and looked at her anxiously without saying a word.

"It's the marriage," said Mrs. Brittain apologetically. "Mollie is a little sad about those five big Morrison boys —that's all; I cannot blame her—it's natural you know, miss. I'm truly sorry that Colonel Cross, at his time o' life, hasn't exercised more discretion; but the widow Morrison is rich they say, and the colonel is somewhat involved. She's rich, and that has had a deal to do in the affair."

A bright blush stole to the pale cheek of the girl—she bent her head very low over Mollie's bonnet-strings, and for the first time in her life felt glad that the child was blind—so sightless that she could not discern her emotion. The bonnet-string might have been in a troublesome knot —Kate Devens was a long time in getting it right. When she did raise her head, there was a bright red spot upon both cheeks, and her hands trembled so that Mrs. Brittain took notice of them.

"You haven't got over that spell of the fever yet, I declare Miss Kate," she said. "Walking so fast has flushed your face, and made you tremble. If I were in your place I'd get a bottle of Sanders's Strengthening Bitters; they are capital, and would set you up in no time. Don't forget, when Jim Williams goes to town next week, to send for a bottle. They keep them at Gilbert's. If I can think of it, I'll send for them myself. There's nothing like them for a tonic. But speaking of the wedding—do you know when it is to come off?"

The girl shook her head, and bent very low to be sure that the knot was out of the bonnet-strings, while the garrulous Mrs. Brittain continued:

"I've heard so many tales about it, that really I don't know *what* to believe. Some say that they are to be married in the village church—some say that they are going to have a grand party at Mrs. Morrison's house— some say one thing and some another. But I dare say the colonel would tell you if you were to ask him. He lets you get nearer to him than almost any body else."

Something like a spasm contracted the corners of Kate Deven's pretty mouth, but she turned away so hastily that Mrs. Brittain did not see it, and she grasped Mollie's hand tightly, preparatory to the walk.

"I really don't know anything about the wedding, Mrs. Brittain," at length she said in a voice of forced calmness. "I wouldn't ask Colonel Cross about it for anything in the world. I hope that if he marries Mrs. Morrison, she will aid him in retrieving his affairs, and will make him happy, and that our dear little Mollie's anxiety is unneces-

sary—but we must go now—good bye, Mrs. Brittain—
good afternoon, Judy—and the girl walked away, leading
the blind child affectionately by the hand.   Mrs. Brittain
shaded her eyes, and stood looking after them until they
were quite out of sight.

"Humph!" she exclaimed, turning towards the wash-
tub, and then she was silent.

"It's my opinion," said Judy, "that the colonel likes
Miss Kate a'most as well as he'll ever like the widow
Morrison."

"And it's my 'pinion," rejoined Mrs. Brittain, "that
Kate Devens likes Colonel Cross a'most as well as she'll
ever like any body else, but that's none of our business,
neither here nor there—the colonel is not agoing to marry
her, for reasons best known to himself, and she is not go;
ing to marry the colonel, though for Mollie's sake I wish
it was to be so.   The child thinks a powerful sight of her,
and well she may, for there is nobody so gentle and tender
with her, though I did not expect it of Miss Kate after it
leaked out that the colonel was going to marry the widow
Morrison.   It shows what a good-hearted creature she
is.   Well, as I've long had a way of saying, this is a
strange sort o' world.   Things that ought to happen
won't happen, and what ought not to be *will* be, and who's
to blame about it?   Why just nobody at all, Judy;" and
having delivered this oracular piece of wisdom, Mrs. Brittain rolled up her sleeves, and went to washing, as she
was in duty bound to have done an hour before.   Here
we will leave her, and in another chapter introduce our
readers to another scene.

CHAPTER II

"Away with weakness!
Let me prove my manhood now."

In a spacious and handsome apartment, a vigorous man,
aged perhaps forty-five years, sat on the afternoon mentioned above.   That man was Colonel William Cross.
His hair was slightly sprinkled with grey—his face was

a little seamed with time, but still he was very handsome. In stature he was above the medium height. His eye was dark and piercing, and his whole aspect showed great ·pride, love of popular favor, much force of character, and an indomitable will. His frame was well knit and powerful, his eyebrows were heavy; he was entirely unlike Mollie, the little blind fairy, who called him "papa." He was evidently an intelligent man. Books, newspapers and pamphlets lay scattered about, but just now none of these occupied his attention. Yet in his hand there was something small and light—it was a locket, and he laid it upon the table, and bent over it with an earnest face, and murmured words which perhaps he would not have spoken had anyone been in the room to have overheard him.

"I must give this back to Mollie," he said aloud—"this likeness of Kate Devens; it will never do for me to keep it now, and yet somehow I hate to part with it. I wonder if Kate knows that I have it? I don't believe she does. She gave it to my poor blind child, and I easily enough persuaded Mollie to let me keep it for her. I love to look at this face. How unlike the widow Morrison's. Here there is softness, gentleness, amiability, and sensibility. How beautifully the bright brown hair shadows the pure white forehead; a noble soul looks through those gentle eyes—a soul made to laugh in the sunlight of prosperity, and weep amid the shadows of adversity—a soul that, like the huma bird, can soar and seldom touch this mean, mercenary earth; and this emanation from Divinity itself —this thinking, hoping, loving human soul *might* have been linked to mine by almost indissoluble ties—its rich treasures of thoughts, sentiments and emotions might have been poured first into my ears— its griefs might have been mine to have soothed—its joys to have shared—its love to have cherished and returned. But it is over now. Kate Devens must go one way in life, and I, with the widow Morrison whom I have chosen, must go another."

The man, when he had thus spoken, closed the locket hastily, and starting up, began to stride across the floor with long and uneven steps.

"I have deliberately made my own path," at length he
said, "why shrink now from flinging my full length shadow upon it? Harriet Morrison is rich. I shall get all
that I have bargained for—a handsome house, plenty of
servants, acres of choice land, five strapping boys, and a
wife—yes, a wife—flaxen-headed, blue-eyed, and homely.
But she keeps a splendid establishment; my friends will
call it a fine match, a noble match; they will be elegantly
entertained when they call on me, and the world will say
that I have married well. It will be trumpeted to the east
and the west that I have formed a very desirable connection, and I suppose that really I ought to feel comfortable
and happy. Yes, I ought to give this locket back to Mollie;
shut the eyes of heart, soul and body to Kate Devens'
beauty, wit, sweetness, and intelligence, and become a model husband. I will try to do it. I will go out and see
Craggs & Elliott, my going-to-be wife's lawyers. They
have the art of praising up her dividends, and making
me feel particularly happy."

Gentle reader, do you pause here, and condemn my
hero? Do not do it. He was like all mankind, a mixture
of good and evil, though, as a general thing, good predo-
minated in his character. He had become somewhat involved. Debt, that incubus which fastens upon so many,
had laid its hold upon him; he saw but one way of extri-
cating himself, and that was by making an advantageous
match. He was proud-spirited; the widow Morrison had
sought and flattered him; self-interest urged him on; and
an engagement had been achieved almost before he was
conscious of what he was about. It was only when Kate
Devens crossed his path, with her sweet pale face, and little Mollie, his blind darling, clinging affectionately to her
hand, that he felt particularly gloomy in view of his coming nuptials. He had never addressed the girl; she was
a long way his junior, but somehow he liked her, and the
conviction had fastened itself on his mind that she was not
devoid of a certain degree of affection for him. But it was
now too late to retreat honorably, had he wished to have
done so; indeed, when he came to think the matter over

closely, he did not wish to break off with the widow Mor-
rrison. His debts must be paid, and Kate Devens' property was small compared with that of Mrs. M.'s.

So he gave the locket to Mrs. Brittain, whom he met
coming with a pile of dried clothes in her arms, and told
her to be sure and return it to Mollie on her return from
Mosswood Cottage, to which Kate Devens had taken her;
and then going out, he sought the snug little office of
Craggs & Elliott, and was soon forgetful of the soliloquy
which he had held over the locket in his parlor that afternoon. Ten days afterwards, the village church bell rang
merrily. There could be no longer a doubt in Mrs. Brittain's mind relative to the time and place of the wedding.
Colonel Cross was to be married that morning; he was
even then on his way to the altar. The establishment at
Elmwood was broken up. Colonel Cross had paid Mrs.
Brittain her wages—sent his servants to Mrs. Morrison's
house, and was soon himself to enter under the roof as
nominal lord and master. Little blind Mollie was to live
there too. Mrs. Brittain could not repress a sigh when
she thought of Jefferson and Jack, the widow's two oldest
boys.

But there was now no time for gloomy reflections. So
she closed the doors and shutters at Elmwood—left the
keys in the hands of a near neighbor, to be given to the
new proprietor who was expected in a few days to take
possession of the house, for the colonel had sold every
thing, even the old household furniture, so familiar to Mollie's touch, and which the child so dearly loved. Crowd
after crowd, in holiday array, was pouring down every
avenue and lane, wending their way to the church. There
were wreaths of flowers in the hands of the young girls,
with which they purposed to strew the roads on the
return of the bridal party from church; there was laughter and merriment, and much hurrying forward, lest every
seat should be early crowded, and a sight of the ceremony
be lost to the latest comers. Mrs. Brittain caught the
spirit of the scene, and hurried on too. It was well she
did, for the house was filled to suffocation. There was

only one vacant place from which a view of the couple standing at the altar could be obtained. She pressed forward to it, and found herself standing face to face with Kate Devens, who held, as usual, little blind Mollie's hand tightly clasped in hers. The girl was leaning against a pillar in the church, near the chancel; her face was flushed at times, and then pale again, as Mrs. Brittain had seen it many times before; a beautiful serenity lay upon brow and feature—a calmness and peace, such as is born only in great and noble souls, overspread her whole countenance. Quietly she watched the priest in his white surplice and the clerk standing beside him. Then her eyes wandered to the couple standing before them—the colonel, tall, straight, and with a prouder air than ever, and by his side a small figure, not elegant, but common-place enough, except that the white brocade in which she was dressed was very stiff, and the bridal veil thrown over her flaxen hair very costly. The face beneath was an ordinary one, not very much wrinkled by age, not very objectionable in point of complexion, but the eye was vacant, and the expression upon the features meaningless. Mrs. Brittain thought, and said afterwards, that the scene was somewhat like an eagle wedding a goose, but Mrs. Brittain may probably not have been an unprejudiced observer.

The ceremony began, and proceeded quietly enough to the end, only when the usual interrogation was made, "do you take this woman for better or for worse?" and the colonel, in his strong tones, answered "I will," little Mollie grasped Kate's hand convulsively, and in her emotion hid her sightless eyes in the folds of her dress. Kate laid her soft white hand gently upon the blind child's head, and looked down upon her half-reprovingly. Congratulations soon began. The villagers, headed by Craggs & Elliott, pressed up to shake hands with the bridegroom, and the ladies kissed the bride—but poor Kate Devens never moved. When the ceremony was over, she stopped for a moment to shake hands with Mrs. Brittain, and quietly passed out, still leading Mollie by the hand. The little girl seemed glad to reach the fresh air. She stopped for a moment upon the steps, and when she resumed her walk, tottered feebly.

"Oh, Kate!" said Mollie, "is the sun shining brightly to-day—I cannot see—I do not feel it—on the contrary, I feel chilly as though it was in a cloud."

"Yes, dear, it shines—why do you ask?"

"Because I've heard Judy sing time and again,

'Blessed is the corpse that the rain rains on!
Blessed is the bride that the sun shines on!'

It rained on my own dear mother's corpse—I think that she is blessed—and I would have the sun shine brightly to-day upon my father's bride. Does she look pleasant and loveable, Kate?"

"Yes, she looks well pleased to-day," said the girl; "I dare say she will be very good to you, Mollie."

"Perhaps she will be, but I have a presentiment of evil —I wish my own dear mother was alive, or that I could live with you always, then I should fear nothing. By the way, is not this the grave-yard gate that we are passing?"

"Yes."

"Well, go in with me, Kate, and lead me to my mother's grave. Let me kneel there, and say my prayers. I shall feel happier then—almost as well as though I could see. I *shall* see in Heaven, shall I not, Kate? See the pearly gates, and the golden streets, and, what will be best of all, my own sweet mother's face. I shall love better, I am sure, to look upon that than upon all the ranks of God's shining angels—upon the martyrs, or upon the Apostles; even the four Elders, dressed in white before the great Throne, about whom you read to me last night out of the Bible, will not be, I am certain, as beautiful in my freshly opened eyes, as will the sweet one who sang soft lullabies at night over her poor blind little Mollie's crib. Oh, Kate! she seemed to me to be an angel even then. I do not think that she needed much changing to be ready for Heaven. Let me pray that I may meet her there."

The girl opened the black, heavy church-yard gate, led
the blind little one along the grassy walks and among the
white marble monuments towards the grave of her mother.
It was a touching sight to see the slight figure of the child
kneeling upon the tomb that covered her parent's dust,
with her hands clasped tightly upon her breast, and her
sightless orbs turned toward Heaven.

"Gracious Father," she said aloud, "remember the
helpless and the blind. Thou hast promised that when
father and mother forsake us, *thou* wilt take us up. Fulfil
that precious saying. Thine arm is strong—those who
lean upon it will never stumble. Thy love is infinite—
those who drink at the fountain need never thirst. Gracious Father! bless the little blind girl who prays to thee
to-day upon her mother's grave. Take her soon to live
with all of you in Heaven, where there are no tears nor
fears for the future—where no grief makes the heart
heavy and the eyelids red."

Kate Devens had before betrayed no emotion that
day, but she wept now as if her very heart would break.
"Mollie," she said, "leave your mother's tombstone, and
go home with me. Stay there until you get reconciled to
the idea of living with your new mother, but do not, I
beseech of you, pray to die. I am not quite sure that it is
right to do so In God's own good time death will come.
His fiat bade us live at first. By and by he will claim our
spirits. This life surely will not be the end of us. I am
not certain that it is our beginning. If at His fiat we live,
certainly He will nurture and cherish the existence He has
given! Think of the ravens that He feeds, the lilies that
He clothes! If He cares for the grass that now is, and
to-morrow is cast into the oven, surely He will care for a
helpless, tender and gentle, blind and motherless girl. If
you do right, you have nothing to fear."

The blind child got off the grave's head, and shook
carefully the folds from her dress. The face had grown
beautifully calm—the peace of which the Saviour made a
parting bequest to all his weary, tried and tired followers
fell upon her sensitive spirit like a healing balm, and she

took hold of Kate's hand without saying another word, and walked towards Mosswood Cottage as quiet as a little lamb that has seen "the green pastures and still waters" by which it is yet in peace to feed.

Brittain soon overtook them, for she was going henceforth to live with Kate's mother at the cottage, and was now on her way to her new place of service.

"Well!" she exclaimed, as half-breathless she came up, "it was a very pretty show, to be sure. The colonel looked amazing stately. I've not seen him look so well before since his wife died. Yes! I believe I have too—the day the Masons paraded, you know, Miss Kate. The colonel was a sort of head man among them, and looked monstrous fine I thought in his — what do they call it ? I can't remember the name of them fixins."

"In his regalia I suppose you mean."

"Oh, yes! that's the word I was trying to think of; in his regalia. And the bride looked better to-day than I ever saw her before—but her two oldest boys, Jeff and Jack, did you see them at their wild pranks in that pew behind their mother ? I declare that it was as much as I could do to keep my hands off of them, as much as ever I could do, to save my life. Them boys will harrass the colonel to death, and make him grey-headed before his time. But it is his own doings. He'll have nobody to blame but himself; but bless my soul, Miss Kate, you have been a crying." Here the garrulous housekeeper stopped for want of breath, and Kate, not knowing what reply to make, very wisely forebore answering at all, but walked in silence to Mosswood Cottage.

CHAPTER III.

"I must say, my dear," said Mrs. Cross, a few days after the scene narrated in the last chapter, "that your little daughter pays very little respect to her new mother ; she has not so much as spoken to me since my marriage. I saw her in the church on our wedding day, and thought that after the ceremony was over, some one—you perhaps

—would present her to me, but I was mistaken. She
was led away by that tall Miss Devens, who seems to be
her self-constituted guardian; and I have not seen either
of them since, though nearly all of our friends and neighbors did us the honor of calling on us next day."

"My little girl is blind," he said. "She could not see
you, and consequently could not come to you without
being led. It was, I must acknowledge, my duty to have
sought her out, and presented her to her new mother; but
I was too happy in being made your husband to think of
anything but the treasure I had won. So you will pardon
me, I am sure, my love."

"But I took particular pains, previous to our marriage,
to have you properly made acquainted with my fine little
ones: Jefferson and Jackson, Hamilton and Monroe, and
even darling, dumpy little Franklin, the rogue, was
brought to see his future papa."

The colonel bowed. He distinctly remembered the
introduction—indeed, it was hardly probable that he would
forget it; Jefferson had eyed him sharply, and then whispered amiably to his brother, "that he looked like a fine
old coon, only a little stern, and he was apprehensive might
object to pony racing, card playing, and children fighting
on Sundays—he hoped not, however." Monroe had managed to spill a whole glass of wine upon his immaculate
shirt bosom, while he had the boy perched upon his knee,
questioning him about his books and dog—and thereat
there was a great titter among the juveniles. Hamilton,
who was somewhat of a genius and philosopher in his
way, stole his gold-framed spectacles—and when found
had forced out one of the eyes, which he was using for a
sun-glass, striving in vain to make a pipeful of tobacco ig-
nite in the sunshine. Little darling, dumpy Franklin was
a bloated, ill-natured child, who screamed when carried
into the presence of his new parent, as though a whole
menagerie of wild animals had been let loose upon him—
every one of which was eager to tear him limb from limb;
he finally kicked himself from his nurse's arms, ran away
into the kitchen, and the colonel did not at that moment

remember to have seen him since. Oh! yes, the newly married man remembered, *distinctly*, having been introduced to his step-children—he remembered, too, having wished there was not so many of them, or that they were a little better behaved, but the future Mrs. Cross had smiled complacently upon all their pranks, and affirmed continually, that seldom had a mother been so blessed before—every one of her children was a treasure—a model—a specimen of perfection; and the future husband had afterwards reasoned in this wise, "if Mrs. Morrison is so kind to her bad boys, how will Mollie's gentle ways and affectionate nature win upon her—she will surely worship my poor little blind one."

Mrs. Brittain had once, it is true, in her blunt way, hinted something about Mollie's happiness being destroyed among bad children; but he paid little attention to the hints and suggestions of his housekeeper—he went his own way, and never troubled his head about her opinions relative to anything.

"You were introduced to all of my boys," continued his new wife in the observation referred to above, "and it is now my wish to have your daughter brought to me. I will try and have her properly taught everything that she can learn."

"You forget that she is blind," replied the colonel, "and consequently can learn but few things. Miss Devens has been very patient with her, and has taught her the alphabet by means of raised letters; she can also sew a little, I believe. She will never be able to do much, but she is gentle and teachable, and somehow she is infinitely dear to me. I have sometimes thought that I loved her better than I should were all her senses perfect; she was also a pet with my wife—her own mother—Maria worshipped the child."

It is a hazardous business for a man or woman, married the second time, to mention the name of their former companion. In this instance it brought clouds to the bride's brow; she nibbled the end of her fan nervously, and at length said, "I shall never mention to you the name of

Mr. Morrison—why pray, my dear, should you torment me with tales of the former Mrs. Cross? You must know that it is very unpleasant having her name mentioned in my presence."

"No! I didn't know it tormented you," said the bridegroom, looking up. "I'm sure I didn't mean to annoy you. I have no objection to your mentioning Mr. Morrison's name, if you choose to do so; but if you don't like to hear about Maria, why, I shall make a point of not mentioning her—that's all."

"Well, the child, when is the child coming home?—that is what I want to know. Is she going to live with that tall Miss Devens always?—if so, you had better have married *her*."

A flush passed over the colonel's high stern brow; "I will send for Mollie this afternoon," he said hurriedly, and took up his hat and went out.

The new wife, who, by the way, was an excellent housekeeper, not having any body to talk to, began carefully inspecting the parlor furniture, to see if the servant had done her dusting well that morning. The investigation proved that the work was highly satisfactory. "Never mind," she said to herself, "I'll teach her to leave dust enough on the tables to write her name in;" and she immediately proceeded to the kitchen, where Fannie, the house-girl, got such a berating that she scarcely knew what she was about.

"You wretch!" exclaimed the estimable lady, in a high passion, "you think because I have so much company now-a-days to engross my attention, that you can slight your work without my finding it out—but I'll teach you, miss, that you are mistaken—take that—and that—and the bride bestowed with her hands sundry blows upon the domestic's ears, which made them ring soundly for an hour afterwards. In the midst of this affray Jack made his appearance, holding the struggling, dying body of a chicken, from which he had cruelly torn both legs in a scuffle with Teff.

Mrs. Cross paused. "My son," she said, instantly, in a

calm tone, "you ought not to mangle those chickens in that way; you will, I am afraid, destroy every one in the coop."

"Well, make Jeff let me alone, then; they aint his chickens, you know, and he is always meddling with them."

"I haint got no father—you know I haint, and I wont mind any body who pretends to be—if Jeff does, he's a fool. That's all I got to say about it," and the hopeful youth threw the chicken on the floor, and flung himself out of the door in high dudgeon. Mrs. Cross turned a moment to give orders for dinner, and then she went in nd drummed awhile on the piano. Afterwards she took a gold thimble from its morocco case, and stitched away upon a collar for Jefferson. She was thus engaged when the colonel again returned.

"My love, you certainly forgot that there is a hat-rack in the hall," said the new wife, glancing towards the table, without replying to his remark. "It looks so bad to see hats standing about on the tables and chairs; I hope you will not, henceforth, forget to leave yours as you come in. It's what I've learned all my family to do. Jackson and Jefferson never bring their caps into the parlor—they would sooner think of leaving them in the street."

"Certainly—certainly," said the colonel, bowing and resuming his hat. "I'll leave it in the hall; I forgot the rack altogether."

"And so you have sent for Mollie," continued the woman, as the colonel returned and resumed his seat. "I hope the child will be teachable and good, and I will try to get on well with Jackson and Jefferson, Monroe and Franklin. If she does, she'll find a pleasant home here. But that tall Miss Devens! I don't somehow like her looks, and I hope she will never think of interfering at all with the girl."

"Kate, I dare say, will never interfere," said the colonel. "She has long been an intimate friend in my family, and such I beg leave to hope she will continue."

"Well, I don't object to the girl's visiting here, not at

all. I'll go into the parlor and entertain her as I would anybody else, but I shall not like Mollie to stay with her for days, and even weeks, as she has been in the habit of doing. You will of course put a stop to that."

The colonel did not make a ready reply. Just then, to his unspeakable relief, the door bell rang, and the conversation was interrupted.

CHAPTER IV.

MOLLIE sat, on the afternoon on which the messenger despatched after her reached Mosswood Cottage, in the little honeysuckle covered perch, on a low stool at Kate Devens' feet, and rested her head upon her knee. The girl's lips were parted in song. She sung the old family tunes that little blind Mollie loved—poetry which spoke of rural scenes—of violet covered banks—of gurgling rivulets, and wild birds hid amid the brakes—of flying clouds —of crystal showers and green fields. The little blind one's heart swelled within her. "Shall I never see all these beautiful things?" she murmured to herself. " Earth, it seems to me, must be a Paradise of loveliness—but it is hid from my poor eyes. I sometimes hear the rivulet singing, and Mrs. Brittain says it is bright like silver. What does that word '*bright*' mean? They say the sun is bright—that silver is bright—that water is bright, and sometimes papa says that his little blind daughter's face is bright? Are these things all alike? Is my face like the sun? Surely it cannot be like the water which turns Tom Williams mill-wheel—I feel at times greatly puzzled. Oh! that I could see! I found yesterday a flower—its perfume was sweet like the air of Heaven; I thought that it must be very beautiful; but when I carried it to Kate, she said, ' Oh, no, that is not a beautiful flower, Mollie, although it is a fragrant one. Beauty is something which addresses itself to the eye—fragrance to the organs of smell. You are blind, and, therefore, can have no conception of the beautiful.' She was right; *I am blind!* Mrs. Brittain has pitied me a thousand times.

My own dear mother, I am told, wept when she first discovered my poor orbs were sightless. Oh, it is a sad—sad thing to be blind !" And the little girl nestled her pale face close down in the folds of Kate Devens' robe, as if her heart would break.

Kate laid her white hand gently upon Mollie's forehead, and smoothed away the bright soft hair. " Why do you weep so, Mollie ?" at length she asked.

" I weep because life to me, dear Kate, must be one eternal night. The heavens, with all their blazing heraldry of stars—the earth, with its flower-scents, and violet banks, and flowing rivers, its temples of art and its tro phies of genius, must ever be to poor little Mollie Cross a sealed book. Others can look into it and read the tracery of God's own hand—others can go abroad fearlessly and roam over the flowery fields, and explore nature, and drink in life and health at every bounding step. I creep onward in darkness—day succeeds day, but it is all a moonless, starless, Egyptian sort of night to me. I shall never see anything on earth—never see your own sweet face, my darling Kate—never see my mother's grave. where I knelt the other day and prayed—never see Mrs: Brittain or my new mother—never see anything until I stand disrobed of the flesh, a sainted spirit among shining ranks of seraphim, close by my mother's side, near where falls the shadow of the Great White Throne.

The little girl's grief was so touching that Kate wept in spite of every effort at self-control. She flung her arms passionately around the child, and imprinted kiss after kiss upon her pure forehead.

" God's ways are not our ways," at length she murmured in a soothing voice, " and yet *His ways are right and just and true.* We are happy amid the numberless ills of life, Mollie, only when we know, feel and realize this great fact. What we know not now, we shall know hereafter. We shall see then that the discipline of the Heavenly Father's hand was needed ; each of us, like a noble boat, made to breast the waves, must be well tested in regard to our strength and virtue, ere we are freighted with the shining glories of a happy immortality, and launch out upon the shoreless ocean of Eternity.

Mollie continued to weep, and Kate continued her remarks. "Every situation, my dear child, has its annoyances and its disturbances. The only way is to patiently endure the ills which fall to our lot; fearlessly, promptly and resolutely discharging the duties devolving on us. You are a little blind girl; there are responsibilities incumbent upon me which can never possibly devolve upon you. There are duties devolving upon you, which can never possibly, as long as I am gifted with sight, be mine. I am called upon to act—you to patiently endure. And so it is throughout the role of our existence here—and believe me, Mollie, life's cares and engagements, its pleasures and its pains, its duties and responsibilities, are much more equally distributed by our Heavenly Father's kind and bounteous hand, than we are, at first sight, inclined to suppose."

"But it must be a great pleasure to see," said Mollie. "Such a delight to watch, even a growing plant. First, I am told there is a tiny seed, next the emerald leaf, then the expanding stalk, and soon afterwards the bud and flower. I have yearned to watch this growth of vegetable life; it seems to me that those who can see, can enter into the laboratory of the Almighty—can watch the operations performed by His almost visible hand. Here in this honey-suckle-crowned porch, you can daily be delighted with fresh unfolding manifestations of His presence, which I can never behold. Oh! my dear Kate, you may strive as you please to comfort me; still, it is a sad, sad thing to be a poor little blind girl."

Just at this moment Mrs. Brittain's heavy step was heard in the hall.

"There is a man here," she said, sticking her head into the door, "who wants Mollie Cross. Her father has sent for her."

"I don't believe I can go, Kate," she said. "I don't believe I can go," and she clung with her thin white hands to the folds of Miss Devens' dress. Kate gently disengaged her hand, and again smoothed back her hair. She looked into her sightless orbs, from which tear after tear was stealing fast, and again wept herself afresh. Mrs. Brittain stopped a moment to survey the scene.

"It's a shame," she said, "that you two have to part. If I had my way about things, you should always stay together—that you should. I don't like the idea of Mollie's going to live with Jack and Jeff Morrison. I don't know what Col. Cross was thinking about, I'm sure, when he married a widow with half-a-dozen rough boys. But it's the way with the world. Folks will reverse the old adage, and leap before they look."

Mollie got up, shook the curls back from her brow, and began groping her way with both hands towards the room usually occupied by her aunt Kate.

"Where are you going?" asked Mrs. Brittain.

"Going to pack my trunk and carpet-bag. My father has sent for me—I must go home."

Kate now arose and followed her. "Mrs. Brittain," she said, "you will see that the young lady's things are packed away. Come with me, Mollie, into the flower-garden." Hand in hand the two friends wended their way into the cool and quiet recesses of Mosswood garden. Jasmine and cactus and pink were in full bloom along their path ; but Mollie could not see these floral beauties, and Kate was too sad to heed them. When they came to an arbor, they paused and sat down upon a bench. Then Kate spoke to Mollie high words of hope and trust. She spoke to her of the "life that now is, and of that which is to come." Life's high and holy duties came out and stood in bold relief even before the eyes of that unfortunate blind child. Life's mission, that thing which cannot be insignificant even to the most lowly and humble, seemed to her in that hour to be a sacred thing ; and when she again arose to depart, her face had assumed the serenity of an angel's.

CHAPTER V.

Mrs. Cross was still busy upon Jefferson's collar, when
Mollie, with a timid, hesitating air, entered her presence.
The step-mother did not welcome her blind child very
warmly. She did not throw her arms around her neck
and kiss her, as Kate would have done under similar circumstances; she did not even kindly clasp her hand, but
deliberately laid down her work, and taking hold of the
child's shoulder, wheeled her around, so that she could
gaze straight into her blind eyes.

"It's very strange, Col. Cross, that this girl can't see,"
she said at length. "Her eyes look sound enough. Are
you quite sure that she is as blind as she makes herself out
to be."

"Yes," said the colonel, "hopelessly blind. She has
been blind from her birth."

"And she can't go without being led, can she? It must
be a great bother to always have to be a leading her everywhere. I suppose I shall have to keep a servant expressly
for that purpose."

"Where she is familiar with the house and furniture,"
said the colonel, "she manages to grope her way ex-
tremely well; but here, where everything is strange to
her touch, it will be necessary to lead her about awhile.
Yet she is a gentle, peaceable little thing, my dear, and
will not give you any unnecessary trouble, I am sure."

"Can you sew?" queried Mrs. Cross.

"Not very well," replied the little girl, now speaking
for the first time. "Kate Devens tried to teach me, but
I couldn't learn. I couldn't feel where to place the point
of my needle; so, after awhile, Miss Kate gave it up."

"You will manage, I dare say, after awhile to hem the
servant's aprons, and sew straight seams in their other
clothing. I, at any rate shall do my best to teach you,"
said Mrs. Cross, resuming the collar. "You can take off
your bonnet now, and make yourself at home, for this *is*
to be your home in future; and I shall expect you to stay

in it too. I shall not, by any means, approve of your running over to Mosswood Cottage every other day, as I've
been told you've been in the habit of doing."

Tears sprung into the little blind girl's eyes, as she turned
away and tried to untie her bonnet strings. She twitched
at them for a long time. They had now really got into a
hard knot, and Kate's kind hand was wanted to undo
them; but alas! that was missing.

It was not long before Jefferson and Jackson, Hamilton
and Monroe, came racing in to see, as they boisterously
affirmed, "the show." They stared at Mollie long and
rudely, and tittered behind their hands, while she, in at-
tempting to deposit her bonnet on the bed, dropped it to
the floor, and then groped her way, as best she could, to a
low seat not far from Mrs. Cross's feet. These hopeful
youths afterwards emigrated to the woodshed, where they
amused themselves for awhile in planning pranks, to be
played off at some convenient season on the little helpless
one who stood to them in the sacred relation of sister.
Sometime they hoped to have it in their power to burn
her hands by thrusting them into the blaze of the candle
—sometimes to decoy her to the front steps and then throw
her down—sometimes to scare her life out of her, by leading her into the wood back of the house and leaving her
there alone for hours. Indeed, Jefferson affirmed that
nothing had ever before promised so much fun as the coming among them of that piteous little one.

Grave theologians tell us that man is by nature totally
depraved. No one looking, at that moment, into the diabolical faces of the juvenile Morrisons, would have felt
much like disputing the proposition. Alas! poor Mollie.
Unless kind angels are sent to guard thee, what is to become of thee in future? But need fears be entertained for
one who, on her mother's grave, had kneeled and prayed
thus: " Gracious Father, remember the helpless and the
blind. Thou hast promised, that when father and mother
forsake us, *Thou* wilt take us up!"

No! The experience of every trusting heart enables its
possessor to affirm in the end, that the Lord is *not* unmind-

ful of those who, weak, frail and fragile though they may
be, hide themselves under His mighty wing. Yet, it cannot be denied that the little girl suffered.

Mrs. Cross, true to her promise, tried to teach her to
sew, and sometimes scolded her most unmercifully, when
she failed in her task. Once or twice she boxed her ears,
as she would by no means have boxed Jefferson's or Jackson's, had they killed every chicken in the coop, or left
their caps in the parlor, or raised Cain generally throughout the whole establishment.

Sometimes, also, the boys succeeded in playing their
pranks off upon the little sightless one; but they gradually
learned to fear her father. There was something about the
colonel's stern face which, now he was no longer the lover,
but the husband and father, awed the most headstrong of
them into silence and fear. Jefferson did not entertain a
doubt about his objecting to pony racing and chicken
fighting on Sunday. He was very careful to conceal all
such amusements from the old gentleman's eyes, and Hamilton let the gold framed spectacles rest undisturbed,
whenever they chanced to be deposited upon the mantelpiece.

But the colonel was not always in the house; indeed, he
went about a great deal. Mrs. Brittain said that his new
home could not be the most pleasant spot in the world to
him, else he would not be away from it so much; but Mrs.
Brittain (as my readers have already discovered) was
something of a gossip, and looked a good deal into her
neighbors' affairs.

Kate Devens, soon after the colonel's marriage, went
into a distant part of the country, on a visit to some of her
relatives, and was seldom heard from.

We have stated somewhere in the course of our narra-
tive that Col. Cross contracted his second marriage with
an eye to relieving himself of pecuniary difficulties, into
which he had been unwillingly led. Judge of his astonishment when he learned that Mr. Morrison had made a
will, in which it was distinctly stated, that in case his widow married again, his boys were to inherit all his estate.

Not one cent of it could be touched by her present husband.

To Col. Cross this was a soul-thrilling discovery. It
was a dark day when it was revealed to him. He betook
himself afterwards to his library, and paced the floor with
a hurried tread. Without, the rain came down in torrents.
Within, his little blind girl sat at her stepmother's feet,
trying to accomplish her task in sewing ; but her sightless
eyes would not enable her to guide the shining needle
aright, and her way along the seam was marked by scarlet
spots of blood, which had been picked out of her tiny fingers, by the sharp point.

Every now and then, the harsh reprimand of the cruel-
hearted woman, whom he called " wife," came to his ears
through the door which stood ajar. Jeff and Jack were
in high dispute over some marbles in the hall. Hamilton
and Monroe, detained indoors by the rain, were in all kinds
of mischief, and Franklin had cried himself hoarse after
some forbidden fruit. Taking it all in all, Col. Cross's establishment, just at that moment, somewhat resembled
Bedlam. The cloud upon his brow was as thick and black
as that which overspread the skies without.

"And I have sacrificed peace, love, a quiet home, and
almost everything that makes a man's life desirable—have
I? for *this*," he said gloomily. "I have gained nothing,
it seems, by this union, but on the contrary have lost
everything. My little motherless blind one is made to
execute her task through blood and tears. My house is
full of riot and disorder, all occasioned by those bad boys.
My wife, whose money was her chief, almost her only recommendation, is penniless. My creditors are no nearer
being satisfied than before. That meddlesome old housekeeper, Mrs. Brittain, was right, when she intimated to
me all is not gold which glitters.

Just at that moment his foot hit a locket, which had
dropped from Mollie's pocket to the floor. The clasp was
loose and the lid flew open. Was there reproach in the
sweet young face which looked into his ? Oh no ! Kate
Devens was too gentle to upbraid, even by a look, one who

had, perhaps unwittingly, won her love. The last time he had seen her, she was at his bridal. Her face was serene even then. Perhaps, after all, she did not care so very much for him. Perhaps, when he was a lonely widower, living at Elmwood, he had flattered himself too much, by supposing that she liked, possibly *loved* him. He wondered if he could have married her; and while he thus wondered he stooped over, and picked up the picture.

"Yes!" whispered something deep down in his heart. "So sure as there is truth in woman, this face might now have gladdened my fireside, and brightened the existence of my poor little Mollie. But it is too late! too late!

CHAPTER VI.

Two years after the scenes which we have narrated in the last chapter, there was a funeral procession slowly winding its way along the street through which Colonel Cross had once before moved a mourner. Again he was on his way to the silent home of the dead: again the sable hearse preceded him, and the pall-bearers moved with measured tread beside the long black coffin. Who slept within it? Not little blind Mollie, surely. The badges were too wide—the coffin was too long—the crowd too dense—the mourners too careless. Little Mollie still lived.

Could it be that the strong, cold woman, who had so recently stood a bride at the altar in the little church, now left in the distance behind the crowd, had paid the last debt of nature, and bowed low before the destroyer. Yes; the hard face which had so often frowned upon the sightless child, was now rigid upon the pillow of death. The hand would never again be raised to strike; the heart was still within the cold bosom; dust was about to mingle with dust—ashes with ashes; and the soul had gone to its final account.

Colonel Cross, of course, moved as chief mourner. Close beside him sat Mollie; but the boys had seats with their near relatives, who were anxious to assume their guardianship and obtain the management of their property.

How looked our hero, the colonel? A little older perhaps than he did when we last saw him pacing the library floor, but not one whit graver or sterner. The woman, whose remains he was following, had never sought, by one act, to endear herself to his heart. She had not made his fireside pleasant—she had not been an affectionate mother to his child—she had not striven to aid him in the discharge of those debts which pressed, at times, like an incubus upon his spirit.

But, nevertheless, those debts were now all paid. The colonel himself could hardly tell how it had been done. Masonic friends had aided him a good deal; he had been very economical and very energetic. When he found that nothing was to be hoped for, outside of his own exertions, he bent all of his energies, time and talents, towards the accomplishment of this one object; and to the astonishment of all who had any insight into his affairs, he succeeded in freeing himself from the demands of creditors.

About this time his wife fell sick, and eventually died. Her relatives, as we have before intimated, claimed her boys, and the colonel was left again with no tie to bind him but Mollie. His heart yearned, as it had never done before, over the little creature, who had so nobly striven with abuse and wrong—who had, in numberless instances, overcome evil with good, and patiently borne with what could not be helped. Kate Devens' lessons had not been lost upon her. Her little face was paler than before—her form slighter perhaps, but taller than when we last saw her; yet it was evident to all who looked upon her, that affliction had done for her, as it does for most of us, a wholesome work.

Mrs. Brittain thought so, as she came up and clasped her warmly to her heart, standing almost upon the brink of the new made grave, and she whispered then in her ear, " You must go back with me, darling, to Mosswood Cottage. Miss Kate has been looking for you ever since she got home. But we heard that that woman there (pointing to the coffin) was sick, and that you were groping your way about her room, and waiting upon her as well as you could. But she's gone now, and there's no excuse. You can go home with me as well as not."

The little blind girl did indeed return to Mosswood Cottage with the faithful old domestic, and when she met Kate Devens, she threw her arms around her neck and wept passionately. Kate, too, cried, and Mrs. Brittain afterwards assured Judy, that " it was the *affectingest* sight she ever saw in all of her born days. Those two ought never to have been separated. She always said it—she always knowed it. Now that cross old widow Morrison was dead, (Mrs. Brittain somehow never learned to call her Mrs. Cross,) she hoped Mollie would be permitted to stay at Mosswood Cottage, for surely Miss Kate made it the *cheerfullest* spot on the whole earth. It was enough to do one's heart good to hear her sing, and to see her gliding about the house with such a kind, thoughtful look upon her sweet young face."

Perhaps Colonel Cross thought so too. Certain it is, he often went to see Mollie, and while visiting Mollie, he could not well keep from looking at Kate. The blind girl, about this time, missed a certain locket from among her possessions, and was much puzzled to know what had become of it. She asked Mrs. Brittain about it, and that worthy old housekeeper laughed in her sleeve, while she affirm d that she knew nothing about it. She asked Kate if she had seen it, but Kate blushed and said "No." Finally, she asked the colonel if he had seen it, but he would not enlighten her in relation to its whereabouts, and for a long time, Mollie was greatly troubled at her loss. But one day Mrs. Brittain espied it in the colonel's hands. She whispered this fact to Mollie, and for the first time in her life, the little blind girl guessed a great and wonderful secret, viz., that her father loved Kate Devens almost as well as she did herself.

But the fair young mistress of Mosswood Cottage was not left to guess over the secret which had so rejoiced the little blind girl's heart. The colonel made a formal declaration of his attachment, and Kate joyfully became his third wife.

Does some romantic girl throw down the paper at this announcement and declare that she will never stand third in any man's affections? So be it. We reply that our gentle heroine could not have been happier, had she been the first to wear her husband's name.

AN ECHO FROM THE HEART.

How wildly did I love thee once,
  But thou art all forgotten now,
I had even lost thy voice—thy smile,
  The expression of thy noble brow.
But in my dreams last night thou came,
And clasped my hand, and spake my name.

Thou cam'st to me o'er troubled years,
  Thou cam'st thro' sleep's dim mysty realm,
And in my soul the flood came back,
  The tide that once could overwhelm;
But when sleep fled, my soul grew calm,
And now thy memory hath slight charm.

I wonder that love can forget—
  Such love as once I bore for thee!
Both true and tender, strong and deep,
  Wild as the dark tempestuous sea.
I wonder that both time and space
Have blotted out thy form and face.

'Tis well! sleep on, tempestuous love!
  Ne'er wake in dreams or life,
Sleep on for aye, and let me live,
  Unburnt by passion's fearful strife,
In the bright world beyond Time's shore—
There let us meet, and part no more.

KITTY SEYMOUR AND THE FREEMASONS.

"MAMMA, I want to join the Freemasons."

The speaker was a slight fair girl of fifteen. Her face for a full half hour had worn a shade of serious thought, and her mother, every now and then, had cast furtive glances at her child, wondering what theme of weighty import thus engrossed her mind. Mrs. Seymour could not now forbear smiling.

"Is that what you have been so gravely pondering, Kitty?" she said. "I thought, from your abstract air, you were musing upon some question in theology, or solving some abstract problem in mathematics; or perhaps striving to untie one of those Gordean knots, which are always occurring in the tangled web of human life. Instead, you have been puzzling your little brain, it seems, over what is, in fact, of little or no importance."

"Why, mamma! I am entitled to *one* degree, to say the least. Wasn't my father, Col. Wm. Seymour, a Mason, and don't Henry and Joseph all belong to the lodge? Now what shall hinder me from becoming one too, pray?"

"Nothing, Kitty, nothing in the world; but what good will it do you? That's what I want to know. I don't see why people should spend time and strength in running after something which is not going to benefit them, or theirs, in the least. I always look to the utility of an undertaking. It may be well enough for *men* to join the lodges. I was quite willing, too, that the boys should meet upon the level and part upon the square, as they have it, but as for you, Kitty! Nonsense! What good would these little side-degrees do the loved, protected, caressed, and only daughter of the late rich and honored Col. William Seymour? No, no, Kitty, I object," and Mrs. Seymour shook her stately head, until the rich lace

and white satin bows trembled upon her cap. Kitty bowed
her head over her embroidery, and mused on for the next
half hour in silence.

"Mother," at length she said, looking suddenly up,
"I've got my heart quite set upon this affair ; I want to
join the Freemasons. If it don't benefit me, it will, at
least, do me no harm. My father once laughingly told
me, that when I got old enough to keep a secret, I might
take a side-degree, and I am sure that I am old enough for
that now."

Just at this moment a loud laugh was heard at the
drawing-room door, and Charles Seymour entered.

"Old enough to keep a secret, Kit," he said, throwing
his hat down, and seating himself by her side on the sofa.
"Was woman ever old enough for that, sis ? I should
like to see her do it. She would be a specimen of antiquity—worth preserving, I'm thinking. The idea is a
comical one. *A woman old enough to keep a secret!*
Upon my word, the conception is too prodigious, too in-
comprehensible. I can't picture to myself how the creature would look," and the saucy fellow laughed until
Kitty declared that she had a great mind to lay down her
work and pull his ears for him.

"It's too bad," she said, "that we always have to have
that thrown up to us, just as if one of our sex never could,
and never had, kept her mouth shut for a moment. I'm
sure I have kept secrets for months at a time, and even
you couldn't find out a word, sir, from me, much as you
laugh now. Didn't I hear you wondering over and over
again last summer, whether Lizzie Lee was engaged to
Bob Brown or not, and didn't you appeal to me and tease
me by the half-hour together, to tell you if I knew anything about it, and didn't I put you off, and sit mute as a
mouse and demure as a nun, and unknowing as a statue,
although I knew even the exact day when the marriage
was to take place, and who the bridesmaids were to be,
and all about it ? Lizzie told me, because she said that I
could keep a secret, and I *did* keep it, sir. I think that I
could keep another if it was entrusted to me."

"Well, my little wiseacre, I'll acknowledge that you did do admirably, astonishingly well, in that instance. When I get ready to slip my head into the matrimonial noose, I shall not mind letting you know all about it. I don't think there is another woman in Christendom who would have done so well. But these Freemasons, Kit, are terrible fellows. If you should join them, and happen to let your tongue slip a little, you'd have the whole fraternity after you like a pack of wolves. You remember Morgan, don't you? Well, little sis, be warned by his sad fate," and the mischievous fellow held up his forefinger, and shook it at her with an ominous and mock gravity, which it was amusing to witness. Having delivered himself of a few equally wise oracular sentences, he took his hat and went off to a meeting of the Chapter.

But Kitty was neither intimidated or convinced. She talked with her mother until the old lady yielded the point, and the daughter of Col. Seymour, late Deputy Grand Master, was duly initiated into all the mysteries of a side-degree. The next morning, Charles came in, and walking up to her, threw an exquisite gold chain, to which was attached a medal, over her neck.

"Keep it, sis," he said, with his old mischievous air, "and wear it. May the shade of Morgan protect you from all harm! If you should ever come to share his melancholy fate, remember that I gave you timely warning. It would be very sad to have you stolen away, and carried to the Barbadoes, and fed on the gall of bitterness and the quintessence of tears; but if you should happen to tell that Masonic secret, you know there will be nothing too bad for you to expect. So be wise, little sis—wise as a serpent and harmless as a dove, as the good book has it," and as he concluded, he bent over and touched her pure and thoughtful brow with his lips.

Three weeks after this little scene which we have narrated, Kitty Seymour became an inmate of the Seminary at S——, full a hundred miles from home. Her brothers, Henry and Joseph, went on a voyage to Europe, while Charles only remained at home with his widowed mother.

The month of August came on hot and sultry. **For a** while, the heavens seemed brass, and the ground beneath, ashes, but gradually dense fogs, impregnated with fever and disease, stole up and hung over Seymour Place.

Mrs. Seymour was the first to feel the ill effect of this state of things, and soon afterwards, Charles was attacked by low and continued fever. Neither mother nor son were able to leave their couches to administer to the wants of the other. Wearisome days succeeded feverish nights, and at length it was thought best to summon Kitty away from her books, to take care of them.

" But who is to go after her," said Mrs. Seymour.

" She can come alone," said Charles.

"Impossible," rejoined her mother. "She has never traveled two miles by herself. How will she manage to come over a hundred ?"

"She will be perfectly safe," said the young man, with a positive air. "No evil will befall her, I am confident."

Mrs. Seymour was a careful mother, and the journey looked formidable in her eyes. She mused over it some-what gloomily.

"I am too sick to go after her," said Charles. "She will come all the way on the cars—hundreds of ladies an-nually make the same trip alone—there is no danger in it —nothing to be apprehended."

A letter was at length dispatched, calling the school-girl home.

Kitty Seymour was a timid creature. The journey had looked formidable to the strong and resolute eye of her mother ; to her it appeared little less than terrible. But there was a cloud of sorrow over the dear household at home. It was no time to shrink back from imaginary phantoms—no time to stand still, when the voice of duty and affection called her onward. She went directly to the Principal and laid the matter before her. Leave of absence was easily obtained. Her trunks were soon in readiness, and in a short time she was sitting solitary and sad in one corner of a densely crowded car. Not a face was familiar to her. The day was dark and the rain descended in tor-

rents. Some of the passengers slept in their seats—others
stared idly about—some tried to make their voices heard
above the rattling of the cars, while they conversed with
a neighbor. Nobody seemed, to the shrinking spirit of
the girl, so lonely and desolate as herself.

Removed two seats in front of her sat a middle-aged,
respectable looking man, whose whole appearance betokened him to be a gentleman. As he turned to look at
her, on her entrance, there was something in his physiognomy, which reminded her of her father—that kind, dear
father, who was now an inmate of the tomb. There must
have been something, too, in her face, or on her person,
that arrested his attention, for he turned twice to look at
her after she was seated. But he soon dropped his head,
and perhaps slept. He was nothing but a stranger, like
the rest. She had no claim upon his protection and
care.

Mile after mile was passed, and at length the thronged
and busy city of L—— was reached. Here they were
to change cars.

"Your checks, miss," said the conductor. "I will see
your baggage transferred. Take a seat in the saloon until
I return."

Kitty sat down amid a motley crowd. Several ruffian-
looking fellows were smoking around the stove, which was
heated to an unendurable degree, and on a settee in one
corner sat an abandoned, dowdyish looking woman in
scant, dirty garments, homespun sun-bonnet, coarse shoes,
with black, withered, repulsive features, and a long pipe
in her mouth.

One by one the respectable part of the crowd went out,
apparently for the purpose of taking seats in the cars,
which were soon to leave. Still Kitty remained quietly in
her seat, awaiting the return of the conductor. "I
think," said one of the ruffians by the stove, peeping
saucily under her bonnet, "if that 'oman don't leave pretty
considerable quick, she'll be left."

"Yes," said another, with a sort of indescribable grin,
"she will, as sure as preaching."

Kitty now felt that all of their hateful eyes were upon her. The blood mounted to her temples—her heart beat quick. She was nearly ready to cry with vexation. She drew her bonnet further over her face and sat very quietly.

"Is you traveling far?" asked one, kneeling down by the stove, seemingly to light his pipe at the grate, but really, to get a better view of her face. "Is you going up the road, or down?" Still Kitty did not reply.

"She's deaf," said one.

"And dumb," said another.

"I'll tell you, miss, the cars are on the pint of starting," said the kneeling man. "I see your carpet-bag is marked Allstreet. Do you live in Allstreet?" continued he, with the same saucy leer in her face. "If you do, I'm going there, and will look after you."

Had Kitty been older in years, or braver in spirit, she would have turned and scorched this living viper in human shape, with the fire of indignation which burned in her eye. As it was, she sprung hastily to her feet and sought the door of the saloon.

"Can I be of any service to you?" said a mild, respectful voice at her elbow.

Kitty looked, and met the eye of the man who was so like her father. In a moment she felt herself to be safe. There was that in his air and manner which instantly re-assured her.

"Thank you," she said, "I am under the care of the conductor, and he told me to stay here and await his return. But, indeed, I cannot stay in such a place as this. I will be much obliged to you, sir, if you will conduct me to the cars."

"You took the cars at L———," said the stranger. "I noticed the medal in your belt, and made inquiries about you, hoping to have it in my power to render you some trifling service. I shall be happy to protect you to the end of your journey."

Never had such a glow of gratitude before pervaded Kitty's heart. The stranger conducted her to the pleasantest car, and selected for her the best seat.

"If you will be kind enough to give me your name," he said, "I will go now and look after your baggage.".

"My name is Seymour," replied the girl, "my trunk is marked K. Seymour, Allstreet, Seymour Place."

"K. Seymour," said the stranger, in surprise, "Seymour Place. Allstreet! Surely you must be the daughter of my late brother, William. I am now on my way to visit his family. You have heard of your uncle Nathan, who went some ten years ago to California."

Kitty had heard of him from earliest childhood. Never was meeting between uncle and niece so glad and opportune.

"Ay," mused Kitty, when she was again left for a few moments to herself, "how my mother erred, when she affirmed that the only daughter of Col. Seymour could never be benefitted by Freemasonry.

THE BELLE'S VISIT TO THE COUNTRY.

"Here are cool mosses deep,
And through the moss the ivies creep,
And in the stream the long-leaved flowers weep."

CHARLOTTE BENNETT clapped her chubby little hands together and laughed a short, but merry laugh. "I am so glad," she said, "so very glad."

"Glad about what?" asked old Mr. Bennett, her father. "It strikes me that you are always finding something to be glad about. You laugh in the morning—sing at noon, and dance at night. What has occurred *now* to make you particularly merry?"

Charlotte thrust her hand into her pocket and drew forth a letter. "It is from cousin Martha Lane, the belle," she said, glancing at the old gentleman, while she unfolded it; "and she is coming up to Edenton to stay all summer. It will be such a pleasure to have her here. Her society will be a treat to me in this lonesome, far-away place; and then she is so beautiful and accomplished that she will attract crowds of visitors to the house. Harvey Green, who met with her in the city last winter, says that she is a perfect queen in appearance. She plays and sings delightfully, and always has a crowd about her. Ain't you glad, father, that she is coming out here? Won't it be delightful having such a brilliant creature at Edenton?"

"I don't know," said the old gentleman slowly and thoughtfully, at the same time extending his hand for the epistle. "I hope that you will find it so, but somehow I was never a very great admirer of brilliant women. I like to see a rosy cheek, a bright eye and an elastic step, as well as any body. I do not object to a woman who can dance and sing—but a belle, Lottie! Heaven save me from a belle! In nine cases out of ten, that is only another word for coquette."

"O father, how can you say so! That is one of your old-fashioned notions, I am sure. I wish that I was beautiful, but I shall be plain little Lottie Bennett to my grave. Heigh—hum! Well, there is no use in murmuring over one's lot. Maybe she will learn me some of her fine airs and graces, and then I shall become *interesting*, to say the least," and Lottie glided away with a step, which was half a skip, (it was so very light and airy,) to look after some household duty.

"Humph!" exclaimed the old man, mentally, as his eye followed her slight form. "She does not need a city belle's example. She is interesting, beautiful even, in my eyes, already."

The first day in June came, and with it the city belle, with boxes, bundles and packages innumerable. The little bird's-nest affair of a cottage at Edenton was full, almost to overflowing, and Lottie Bennett opened her hazel eyes with astonishment at the elegant looking being who followed all these trunks and band-boxes into the house. Martha Lane was in truth a queenly personage. She was tall and stately—her face was rosy, dimpled and charming —her hair flowed in natural ringlets to her waist, and she

had the air and manner of one accustomed to much praise
and fashionable adulation. She courtesied languidly, half
condescendingly to old uncle John Bennett and his chubby
little daughter, Lottie, and then went away to change her
apparel, and recover from the fatigue of her long and tiresome journey.

"Oh, isn't she beautiful? Oh, isn't she elegant?" exclaimed Lottie, as the door closed upon her visitor's retreating form.

Uncle John shook his head.

" *We shall see*," he said, and after uttering this laconic
sentence, he went out.

It was six o'clock when the visitor, in a beautiful evening dress, sauntered from her apartment.

She sat down in the little woodbine-covered porch, and,
with a discontented eye, gazed over the broad expanse of
beautiful woodland, which stretched away for miles in front
of John Bennett's house.

"Lor, gracious!" she said at length to her cousin, "how
dull and stupid it must be living in such a lonesome place
as this. Don't you half die of *ennui?*"

"Oh no," said Lottie. "It is not much like a city life
to be sure, but I always find enough to do. There are the
chickens to be looked after, and the garden to be attended
to, and the house to be taken care of, and company to be
entertained, and moreover, there is almost always somebody sick in the neighborhood who ought to be visited
and aided. I never find time to be dissatisfied and lonely.
Now *you* have come, I am sure life here will be pleasanter
than ever."

"Do you have much company to entertain?" said the
belle, with a slight degree of interest in her tone. "I like
to see company in the evening, when I am dressed, but
company in the morning is a perfect bore. When I am in
the city I always send word to the door that I am not at
home, if anybody happens to call before dinner."

"What! do you send word that you are not at home
when you *are* there?" said Lottie, somewhat amazed, for
she had been taught to adhere strictly at all times to the

truth. "Surely you don't deceive people in that way, Cousin Mattie?"

"Why Lor, yes, child—what's the harm? Everybody does it there, or next to everybody. All *our* circle do it. It is a very good way of getting rid of troublesome visitors, I am sure. But you don't have company here in the morning, I suppose?"

"Yes, sometimes," said Lottie, while a delicate blush stole to her cheek. "Mr. Green often rides over here, and chats with father about the crops, and brings me any new book or magazine which he may chance to have on hand. You are acquainted with him I believe. He met with you last winter in the city."

"Green—Green, did you say! Let me remember. I don't recollect any gentleman by that name, who visited in our circle. Strange that I can't recall his person!"

"He is a Freemason, and went to the city on some business connected with the lodge," said Lottie. "He met with Uncle Lane, and was invited by him to his house. He saw you there."

The belle laughed a silvery, fashionable laugh.

"Oh! I remember now," she said. "Sister Ophelia and I had so *much* fun out of that fellow. His clothes were a thousand years behind the time, but papa would have him entertained in the most hospitable manner, because he was a Mason. He even went so far as to maintain that he was an intelligent, high-minded gentleman, although I agreed perfectly with Ophelia, who said that he was Green by name, and green by nature—a most verdant animal."

Lottie's cheeks flushed deeper than ever at this remark, for the truth of the matter was, she had long before that learned to look on Harvey Green with a partial eye. He was indeed a noble fellow. Every thought, word, deed, and action had, in his case, its root in healthy, sound, moral principle. He had read, thought, and pondered much upon life—its cares, duties, responsibilities and ends. He had learned to distinguish the false from the true—the real from the seeming—the glitter from the gold—the dross from the pure ore. He was sincere and upright in his purposes. He was well fitted to be counsellor and friend, guide and protector. Lottie's weaker nature had learned to rely with implicit and unwavering confidence upon all of his professions, opinions and tastes. They had grown from childhood together. Lottie had often said, mentally, that she felt towards him as a brother; and Harvey Green thought of Lottie Bennett, as we think of blessings met with and enjoyed every day, such as the bright sunbeam— the genial friend—blessings which we never stop to esti- mate and think about, until we discover their worth by their absence.

Harvey Green was not Lottie Bennett's lover. O, no! He had never dreamed of being anything but her friend, and the friend of her father. Lottie had never dreamed of it either. She only knew that the house was very lone- some if he ceased visiting there, and she remembered how long the days had seemed while Harvey was away, the winter before, on that lodge business in the city. She was glad when he had spoken of the kind entertainment which he had received in the house of her Uncle Lane, and she had always thought of the beautiful belle, whom he had spoken of as having met with there, as the most inter- esting, amiable, and charming of creatures, because, for- sooth, she had, as he confessed, quite captured his senses. But now her eyes were suddenly opened to a new truth. While the beautiful belle had been smiling so complacently in honest, unsuspecting Harvey Green's face, she had been making fun of him behind his back. This information me- tamorphosed the belle into a monster in simple little Lottie Bennett's eyes, and the "*we shall see,*" of her honest old father now sounded in her ears something like a prophecy. Just then, there was the trampling of a horse's feet upon the green turf by the gate, and looking up, Lottie saw Harvey, mounted upon his noble horse, rapidly approach- ing the house. He was neatly, and for that section of the country, fashionably clad. He had evidently come to pay his respects to the belle. For the first time in her life, Lottie was sorry to see him. But the belle received him most graciously. No one, to have seen the air of welcome which she assumed instantly, would have supposed that she had ever objected to, or jested seriously about, his dress and manners. Again Harvey bowed before the magical power of beauty. The belle enchained him to her side by her blandishments. The country was not dull to her when he was a visitor at Uncle John's. She began in reality to love what she, nevertheless, continued through habit to ridicule in private to Lottie.

But the reign of duplicity is short. On a fortunate day for him, and an unfortunate one for beautiful Martha Lane, Harvey Green chanced to overhear the belle while she was descanting upon his awkwardness to her cousin, when the two were seated in a summer-house in the garden. He heard Lottie s warm defence of his person and character. He saw, unperceived by her, the indignation which flashed from her hazel eyes and the blood which mounted up until it crimsoned her temples. He saw the derisive sneer which curled the city girl's beautiful lips, and from that hour he hated her. He turned hastily away—noiselessly remounted his horse and rode homewards, and never again, while the belle remained a visitor at Uncle John Bennett's, did his tall and noble person darken the door.

The city belle wondered much over this sudden estrangement. It has been said that "blessings brighten as they take their flight." This was true in her case. Never had the love of Harvey Green's noble and honest heart seemed to be of such inestimable value to the proud girl as now, whe she saw plainly, that from some cause or other, it was forever lost to her. She went back to her city home in a melancholy mood. The brainless set of admirers upon whom she had, in former days, been wont to smile, now seemed to her unworthy of a passing notice. She discarded every one of them, and, in the solitude of her chamber, nursed the remembrance of the only man who had succeeded in leaving an indelible impression upon her heart. Thus sped the time, in vain regrets, in false hopes and useless desires, until one day she chanced to pick up a public print, and while looking over the hymenial list, she discovered the following:

5

"MARRIED.—In Edenton, by the Rev. Henry Storrs, Harvey Green, Esq.,⁂to Miss Charlotte Bennett—all of Edenton."

It was too much. She fainted under the announcement.

*   *   *   *   *   *   *

There is now a solitary old woman occupying a dismal-looking house in a retired and gloomy street in her native city. She never goes into society. Her grizzled locks are put plainly back from her discontented brow. Her stooping form and wrinkled visage speak of the ravages of disappointment and sorrow, as well as those of years. Little children—those lovely beings, "fresh from God," who brighten this sin-stained earth with their simple, earnest, loving natures—avoid her as they would the pestilence, and go, even at shadowy night-fall, far out of their way, rather than pass her residence. People point at the decrepit old creature, and say, "That woman was once the belle of B——. There was a time when she was much sought after and admired." This information is followed by a stare of wonder from the young and gay, and then the crowd sweeps on, and old Mat Lane is forgotten. Few know of the secret disappointment and chagrin, which preyed like a worm upon her heart's core, after the young Mason deserted her, while on a visit to the country.

———⊷◇⊶———

THERE are four good habits—punctuality, accuracy, steadiness, and dispatch. Without the first of these, time is wasted; without the second, mistakes the most hurtful to our own credit and interest, and those of others, may be committed; without the third, nothing can be well done; and without the fourth, opportunities of great advantages are lost, which it is impossible to recal, and which no amount of regret or pains-taking can in any wise restore to us.

FREEMASONRY IN ITALY.

There is many a pang to pursue me,
They may crush, but they shall not contemn—
They may torture, but shall not subdue me—
'Tis of thee that I think—not of them.—*Byron.*

A FAIRER flower than the beautiful Countess Ida Bianca
had never been reared beneath the soft skies and among
the pleasant airs of Italy. On the morning upon which
we introduce her to our readers, she sat in her palace, surrounded by menials, and in the enjoyment of all of the
luxuries of life. One beautiful hand supported her small
and classically-shaped head, around which braids of raven
hair were tastefully yet plainly twined—the other, with
circlets of gold upon the delicate fingers, hung idly over
the arm of the richly carved oaken chair in which she
was seated. A robe of sky-blue velvet, clasped at the
throat by a single emerald, and opening from the belt
downward over an under dress of white satin, enveloped
her form. Her small, fairy-like foot, encased in a purple
slipper, rested upon a low stool, and there was a dreamy
light in the dark black eyes, now half veiled by the drooping eye-lashes, revealing that her thoughts were far, far
away. A book bound in velvet and gilt, with a clasp of
gold, had fallen half open on the carpet at her side. A
nearer glance showed it to be a volume of Tasso. A vir-
ginal, with its string broken, stood on one side of the apartment, and a lute and a guitar, lying upon a rosewood
table near by, told that the occupant of this apartment
was not unlike her Italian sisterhood, whose every breath,
travellers assure us, comes fraught with music. Beneath
the windows the silvery waters of the Arno glistened in
the sunlight, darkened only where the walls of some tall
castle, standing upon its banks, or the massive foliage of
some tree, casts its shadows far out upon the surface

of the stream. Barges and gondolas were shooting along, one moment in sunshine, the next in shade, while the songs of the boatmen rung wildly and sweetly out, starting the bird upon the tree, and cheering the heart of every listener upon the bank. Guicolla, the maid of the countess, leaned half out of the open window, and laughed aloud at the sallies of wit that reached her ears from these barges, and exulted, in the pride of her young heart, over the attention which she saw her slight girlish form and attractive face excited among her susceptible countrymen. The other servants had one by one stolen out of the apartment, and the countess, in her deep abstraction, paid but little attention to Guicolla's movements and coquettish airs, but she started when she heard a footstep upon the stairs, and thrusting a letter, which had stolen out from a pocket in her robe, nervously back into its place, she resumed the volume at her feet, and sitting upright, seemed buried in its contents.

The door opened, and her uncle, the doge, a Venetian nobleman, stood before her. Guicolla hushed instantly her laughter, dropped her coquettish airs, and drew back respectfully to find a seat for the visitor.

The countess glanced up over the tall form, and into the stern, care-marked face of the nobleman. She nodded slightly toward him, but the motion was a constrained one, showing that there was no gladness in her heart at his approach, and that the bow was only the token of a consciousness of his presence.

The doge bent his gray head very low, and a smile, evidently an assumed one, stole over his wrinkled features. The countess motioned him to a chair, which Guicolla had placed beside her, without speaking or even rising at his approach. The doge received the civilities as they were tendered, and sat down in the chair. For full five minutes neither spoke a syllable. ·

"Sullen woman!" at length muttered the stern old nobleman, as he bent forward and scanned the beautiful face before him, "I have sought you in a complacent mood, but your manners are rude enough to wake up my stormiest ire. What do you mean by it, Ida Bianca? Do you mean to tell me by your actions, even before I have had an opportunity of questioning you in words, that you will not yield to my will—that you defy my authority—that you care not for my wrath—that you still persist in an adherence to this wild, romantic scheme of yours, of marrying a beggar—one who, if I have been rightly informed, is a Neapolitan, ranking hardly above the lazzaroni in Naples!"

The dark eye of the countess flashed—her slight form seemed to dilate, but she still sat silently, almost moodily, in her chair.

"In addition to his poverty," continued the doge, "is added a still darker stain—a stain which never has, never shall rest upon our noble house. *He is a heretic.* The anathema of the Church of Rome is upon him, and you, Countess Bianca, would take this viper—this half-starved, half-frozen viper to your bosom, and by your smiles, your wealth, and your titles, warm him into life. What madness! what idiocy! The count, your late husband, could he look from his tomb, would tremble with rage at the idea of such a successor in your affections."

The expression of scorn which had been slowly gathering over the lip of the countess vanished in a moment. A tear sprung to her eye, and dropping from its fringe, rolled slowly down her cheek and lay like a pearl upon the silky surface of her robe.

"Do not name him, uncle," she said, in a low pleading tone; "revile, if you must, the living, but do not stir up memories of the dead. The count has been for months in his grave, and why must you speak of him now, and in connection with this subject. It is cruel in you to do so; you who know so well the history of the past."

"Yes, he is in his grave," muttered the old man, "and for anything that I know to the contrary, your neglect and infidelity sent him there, for you never loved him."

Again the eye of the countess flashed fire, and she stamped her slight foot upon the carpet, as if crushing something beneath it. At length she sprung from her chair and stood erect before him.

"Retract those words!" she said, "for they are false—falser than the father of lies, and you know it. Doge of Venice, I dare you to repeat them! A bolt from high Heaven will blast you while the impious words dwell upon your lips. I married the Count Bianca, you well know, against my will. I was almost forced into the union by yourself and others, in order to retrieve the failing fortunes of my house. The marriage was a most unnatural one. He was old and decrepit, gray headed and fretful—I was young, gay, and, the world said, beautiful. For five years he was to me what the frost is to the flower, a destroyer and blighter. True, when I married him, I entered a marble palace, and put on velvet robes—the city bells rang merry peals, and the idle crowd gaped after me, as if no heart that beat beneath a velvet robe *could* be unhappy, and no brow wearing a coronet could feel a throb of pain. How in my inner heart I loathed the trappings that I had purchased so dearly; but you smiled—my relatives were all gratified—my rich old husband was proud of the child-bride he had wooed and won, and I strove to freeze up my heart, and wear that mask so hard to assume—*a happy face.* In vain the effort. I felt that the spring was crushed out of my life—that nothing remained for me but a frigid winter of disappointment and gloom. But I schooled my heart wonderfully—bravely. I looked upon my once fallen family, now reinstated among the nobility of the land, and remembered, that in sacrificing myself, I had heaped honors upon them. But it is hard work—Oh! you do not know *how hard!*—to gather up the priceless affections of a human heart, and sacrifice them upon a golden altar. High Heaven never demands, even as a tribute to filial love, so great an immolation. One of our native poets called me, at that time, ' *The Transplanted Flower.*' Yes, I *was* transplanted from the glad sunshine, and beauty, and joy, and hope of my early existence, among the snows and blighting frosts of a' dreary winter. But I was a faithful wife. Never until your lips breathed of infidelity, was that word connected with my name. I staid shut up day after day with my sick, suffering, peevish husband.

I waited upon him like a slave. I anticipated his slightest
wants. I strove to think my bondage light—to worship
the golden fetters that bound me. I had read, and strove
to believe with Childe Harold, that

'Few—none—find what they love, or could have loved,
Though accident, blind contact, and the strong
Necessity of loving have removed
Antipathies.'

But it would not do. Something whispered me that the
sentiment was false. I believed in my inner heart that a
twin-soul somewhere existed for me. One that would
smile with me when it felt the sunshine, and weep when
it shared my sorrows and my fears. At length my lord
—perhaps I should call him husband, but the term would
be falsely applied—died. I did not weep. I looked
calmly on his rigid features, and rejoiced that I had never
neglected him. He left me a handsome estate. I gathered
my goods and came to Florence. Here I have lived for
two years almost alone. Save your occasional visits from
Venice, I have received but few friends. I never thought
to marry. I threw off the weeds of widowhood it is true,
but it was because I felt that to wear them was little better
than mockery. My heart was not bereaved—I was a widow only in name, but I supposed that it was frozen—entirely congealed in my bosom, and I never dreamed that
anything would thaw the fountain of my affections, bidding
it flow forth to sunlight, music and gladness. But I was
mistaken. I was returning one night from a long walk,
when a horseman was thrown across my path with dislo-
cated joints and a fractured limb. My sympathies were
enlisted. I perceived by his speech that he was a Neapolitan. My mother was a Neapolitan, and I love the name.
I ordered my menials to bring him here. For weeks I
ministered like a kind benefactress to his wants, and he
paid me with *gratitude*, for he had neither silver nor gold.
I learned that his family had once been among the proudest in Naples, but there is many a titled head there now
that is hardly a grade removed from beggary. This I

learned was true of him. An old priest had educated him
most thoroughly. He understands the lore of many lands
—he can unlock, as none other can, the affections of my
heart—the sympathies of my nature. For the first time I
have found what I can love, what I admire and reverence.
I know that the ban of the Mother Church rests upon him.
It is less because he has abjured the doctrines of the Catholic religion, than because he has joined the fraternity
of the Masons. The church, desiring to have a full and
frank confession from all of its members, tolerates no *secret
societies*. It is because the Marquis Deoli has dared to
have a *secret*, unknown and unrevealed at the confessional,
that the wrath of the church is incurred."

The countess paused. The doge moved uneasily in his
chair. His brow had grown sterner than ever while listening to her words. At length he said :

"Do you still keep to your resolution of marrying him ?"

"I do," said the countess firmly, "I am now my own
mistress. No one shall attempt to dictate to me in an affair of the heart. I have once married to please you. I
now marry to please myself."

The doge's face became suffused—his lips trembled with
passion. But the flush and the tremor passed away, and
were succeeded by a sneering, mocking smile.

"Your late husband or *lord*, as you prefer calling him,
when on his dying bed, dictated, signed, sealed and delivered into my hands a little instrument of writing, which
perhaps you may possibly feel a slight interest in seeing,
although it will doubtless be useless to show it to a lady
so proud and independent as yourself." So saying he
drew from his pocket a roll of parchment, and spread it
out before her.

The countess glanced hastily over it, and at the well-
remembered signature at the end. Her cheek became
whiter than Parian marble, and for a moment she came
near fainting in her chair. It was a will, giving to a distant
branch of the house of Bianca the whole of the late count's
vast estate, in case the countess married against the wishes
of her uncle, the Doge of Venice.

"You have married once you say to please me," said the old man tauntingly, and rolling the parchment tightly between his fingers, but you may not think that it is worth your while to do so again. The count, your late husband, thought so too, and so had this little instrument drawn up, and placed in my hands at his death. As a matter of course, you will marry *whom you please*, but I thought that I would show you this."

"Wretch!" muttered the countess, " my husband never, of his own free will, dictated and signed so base a thing. He was a weak old man, and you, while he lay in his death-struggles, made him the tool of your will—the instrument of your base designs. But what I have said once I say again. Even now you shall not rule. The heart is too sacred a thing to be sold for paltry gold. Take the old man's riches. Do with them what you are empowered to do. I marry the Marquis Deoli in less than a month."

The taunting smile left the lips of the doge. He looked up in amazement at the proud, self-dependent woman before him, and rubbed his eyes, as if doubting his senses.

"Ida Bianca," he said, " are you crazy, or do you jest? You will not, for this Neapolitan beggar, sacrifice the estates of Bianca!"

"I have *said* what I should do," said the countess firmly.

The old man crushed the parchment back into his pocket and then left the palace, without uttering another word.

CHAPTER II

"I have a secret : will ye hear it told?"

NIGHT came over the waters of the Arno. Star after star glittered over the city of Florence—over its deserted streets and marble palaces. The Countess Ida, through the endless hours of that day, had hardly moved once from her chair. She still sat, as in the morning, when the doge had entered, with her head supported by her hand, and Guicolla moving around her apartment as softly as if on tiptoe. A small lamp, suspended from the ceiling by silver chains, cast a soft radiance through the luxuriant room, and in the hush of the hour, the lapping flow of the river over the rocks below came up distinctly to where she was sitting.

Her position was the same as in the morning, but a change had passed over her face.

"This then," she said mentally, "is the end of my dream —my brief, brief dream of love and happiness. Alas! Earth holds no Edens. When we think that we are about to enter a Paradise, some evil angel meets us at the gate with a flaming sword, and turns us back again into the dreary wastes of the wilderness. The Mohammedan declares that God has promised to his followers but one Heaven. Mine does not, it seems, exist upon the earth; shall I not be entitled to it in another state of existence? The walls of amethyst and gold and the pearly gates may gleam and open for me some day, but it cannot be upon the earth. Therefore be strong, O human heart! and gird thyself up to do and suffer well! I have sold myself once for gold, I will never do it again. The possession did not yield me happiness. I have pledged my love to the Marquis Deoli. I will marry him. They may take away my possessions, I can be happy in a cottage with him."

At this juncture in her meditations, the soft notes of a flute were heard beneath the window. Guicolla started to her feet at the sound, and leaned out of the casement as she had done in the morning. But the coquettish smile had long before left her lips. There was a deep shade of thought now upon the face of the Italian girl. She stole softly away from the window, and going out upon the balcony, glided down a flight of steps, and finally stood beside her lover in the moonlight below.

"Hush your music, Adrian," she said. "My mistress is sad to-night, and you disturb her. Poor thing! she is utterly miserable. I wish that we could do something to comfort her, but that is out of the question. The Doge of Venice, that proud old man whom I hate, always works mischief when he comes. I wish that he was compelled to stay forever at home. He has no business here. If I were in the countess's place, I would shut the door in his face. I believe that he will yet drive my noble lady and the Marquis Deoli mad."

"The Marquis Deoli! What of him?" asked the young fisherman, now for the first time evincing an interest in what he was listening to. "What is this doge doing to the marquis? He is a member of our lodge, and I feel an interest in his welfare. Moreover, he has been very kind to me in various ways. Here's a brave heart and a strong hand to serve him, if service can be rendered, my sweet Guicolla. So tell me what is happening above there? for judging from your manners and face, it must be something rueful."

"You talk like a child, Adrian," said the Italian girl, reprovingly. "What can you or I do, against the will of so great and powerful a man as this proud Doge of Venice? The marquis might belong *to a hundred lodges with you* for ought I can see, without being benefitted by it in such a case as this. You Masons are great friends to one another I know, but your friendship is in vain when, as is the case here in Italy, the Catholic Church is arrayed against you."

A flush of pride passed over the honest and handsome face of the young fisherman, visible to the eye of Guicolla even in the dim moonlight. He pushed back the dark locks clustering over his brow with the end of his flute, and answered in a proud tone:

"*You women know nothing about it.* The church, I know, has no fellowship for us, therefore it behoves us to work the harder, one for another; and moreover, we have sworn to see justice triumph, if possible, no matter though the oppressor be doge or peasant. If *I* cannot aid our good Marquis Deoli, some more powerful member in our fraternity may. So tell me if you know aught of evil hanging over him."

"I only know," said the girl, looking down and rolling a pebble beneath her slipper, "that if he marries my noble lady, the countess, that the Doge of Venice will ruin them both. The Countess Ida's estates will be wrested from her. The will says that they are to be given to a distant branch of the Bianca house, but they will be confiscated by the church. There is no branch of my late master's house to receive these. I knew when the doge was saying that, that it was false, for I was born in the house of Bianca, and know all of its branches. My mother used to tell me tales about the family in my childhood. She knew the whole ancestry, and kept trace of all the descendants. It is a base fabrication on somebody's part, who mean to rob my mistress thus. But she does not know it. She will marry the marquis, for I heard her declaring to the doge that she would, even though compelled to live on macaroni alone all the days of her life. When my mistress decides, she is as firm as a rock."

"There's where she's right to my thinking," said the fisherman, thoughtfully; "but what is it about this will of old Bianca's? I don't quite understand it."

"Why, when my master was dying, he made a will, forbidding my lady to marry, or, what is nearly the same thing, forbidding her to marry against the wishes of the doge. In case she does, not a remnant of the Bianca property is hers. My lady will marry the marquis, you see, and hence all this trouble. The marquis is a gentleman, although the doge calls him a beggar. He is a titled gentleman, but he is poor, like many of the noblemen of Italy. The doge, who is a zealous Catholic, hates him, moreover, for being a Mason."

"Aha!" said the fisherman, after a moment's thought, as if struck by a sudden light, "I understand this game—I can throw light upon it. Can I be admitted to-night into your lady's presence? I have something important to tell her."

Guicolla hesitated. "She is alone," she said, "and evidently does not wish to be disturbed. I am afraid to admit you."

"But I have something important to tell her, and must see her," said the young fisherman, impatiently; "lead the the way, and I will follow at the risk of her displeasure."

Guicolla turned and glided up the heavy stone staircase. She pushed open the door of her mistress's apartment with one hand, while with the other she motioned for the young man to pass before her into the presence of the countess.

The latter started when she looked up and saw a man entering at that late hour unannounced into her chamber. But a second glance reassured her, for she saw that he was followed by Guicolla, who had admitted him, and she knew that nothing but an important errand could have secured him admission. She therefore reclined back, as if waiting for any disclosure that was to be made.

The young fisherman came forward, and stood with a respectful air before her. At last he knelt upon the rich carpet at her feet.

"I have something important to say to you, noble lady, or else I should not have thrust myself into your presence unbidden," he said, gravely. "I wish to be assured, before I proceed, that I have not too deeply offended you by my abruptness."

"If your message is an important one, proceed," said the lady, impatiently. "Speak, and I will judge of the propriety of this interview afterwards. What have you to say to me?"

"I have reason to think, indeed I know, that the will which was presented to you this morning was a forgery. Your husband never dictated it, never signed it."

"How do you know this?" gasped the Countess Ida in excitement. "What reason have you to believe it to be a forgery? Prove it to be such, and I shall be the happiest of mortals."

"I was passing the other day," said the fisherman, "through the market-place. It was a dark, drizzling day. Scarcely a soul was moving among the stalls. I had in my possession a masonic apron, which I was anxious to secure against the dampness of the atmosphere. I stopped and rested the box upon my knee, while my foot rested against a rude bench. I opened the folds and smoothed the ribbons. Just then two noblemen passed under the shelter. One I know was this Venetian doge. The flutter of my ribbons and the strangeness of my occupation seemed to arrest their attention. They said something about our fraternity, I could not understand exactly what. By this time I had recovered my box, and went out; but as I was leaving, I heard the Marquis Deoli's name mentioned. Curiosity compelled me to stop and listen where I was unobserved. I heard them talking about forging that will. I saw them doing it. I could not understand what the Marquis Deoli had to do with the Bianca estate, and so I did not trouble my head much about it. But I understand the whole of it perfectly now."

"And I, too, may it please your ladyship," said Guicolla, dropping a low curtesy to her mistress, "know it to be a forgery, for there is *no* branch of the•Bianca house such as is mentioned in that will. I know all the connections, although it can't be supposed that you, my noble lady, should, for I have lived among them always, and you only for a few years."

The countess became much agitated. "This is probably true," she said, "but how am I, a powerless woman in the grasp of a powerful nobility, and in the face of the holy Catholic Church, to prove this? The attempt is idle. No one will undertake for me; the chances against me are too great," and she bowed her head mournfully upon her hand as before.

"If it will please my noble lady," said Adrian, "I think I know of those who can and will aid her in this business. There is in our lodge a young American lawyer, a great friend of the marquis, who has come to Florence to learn how to paint pictures, because he has a taste for that sort of business. He is a keen, shrewd fellow. I often go into his studio and help him mix his paints, and hold his brushes for him, and listen to his jokes, when I have nothing better to do. He will, I think, for the love he bears the marquis, look into this business; and those Yankees are hard to overreach. They are unawed by a titled nobility, and unshackled by the Romish Church."

The Countess Ida mused long. At length she said, "will you bring this American to me to-morrow? If he can, he must aid me."

The Italian fisherman bowed and withdrew.

CHAPTER III

"All's well that ends well."

It was near nine o'clock the next morning when Hiram Copley, a young American artist at Florence, stood in the midst of his studio, brush in hand, and contemplating upon his easel a figure, life-like and beautiful.

"This figure grows like magic beneath my touch," he said to himself, half-musingly. "I wish that the marquis was here to admire it. I wonder if the original of this miniature, from which I paint, really exists! I suspect that the Marquis Deoli is wiser upon this subject than he pretends to be. But here is a name, in the case of the miniature. Strange that I should never have seen it before. Ha! I have it. The Countess Bianca. I have heard of her. She is a relative of the proud old Doge of Venice. Well, I must go to work. I wish Adrian, the fisherman, would happen in, as he does sometimes, to help me about this paint."

The words had hardly escaped his lips, when he heard a footstep behind him, and turning, saw the fisherman wending his way towards him, among the piles of ancient paintings and modern engravings which lay scattered in every direction.

"Good morning," he cried, when he had caught sight of the honest face before him. "The devil is always near when you are thinking about him, it is said. I was just wishing that you would come."

Adrian touched his cap, and smiled good humoredly. "I am glad to know that I am a welcome visitor."

"Yes, most welcome, my good Adrian. First tell me if the face yonder on my easel is not a pretty one, and next, help me about my paints."

Adrian glanced up, and saw before him apparently the very face before which he had knelt the night before. There was the delicate cheek, the dark eloquent eye, the finely pencilled eyebrow. He started with surprise. "This is strange," he said; "I did not know that you knew the

Countess Ida Bianca. Pray where did you meet with her ?"

"I never have met with her, and never expect to. I am painting the picture for the marquis. I'd give my head, however, for a peep at the original. She must be beautiful, by Jove!"

"You can not only see the original, but you can benefit her if you will," said the fisherman. "My errand now is to send you to her."

The American glanced incredulously into the fisherman's face. "How can I, who have scarcely been a twelvemonth in Italy, aid so fair and noble a lady ?"

The fisherman, in a few brief words, explained to him how matters stood. "You are a lawyer as well as an artist," he said, in conclusion, "and can help my lady if you will."

"What do I know of the laws and of their administration in Italy ?" said the American impatiently. "The most that I have hoped from my knowledge of them is to keep my head out of the halter. I came here to paint, not to study law—not to dabble with the laws. I cannot aid the countess."

"But you can go and see her," said Adrian. "Perhaps you can aid her."

Copley leaned his head on the end of his brush and mused. "I will go," at length he said, "but I am sure I can do but little to aid her."

The young American was true to his promise. Half an hour afterwards found him in the presence of the countess. He was young, ardent and romantic, but he was also prudent and shrewd. He saw how the beautiful woman before him was about to become the victim of fraud and bigotry. He grew interested in her case. The marquis, his friend, was absent at Naples, and he saw that there was no one to counsel the countess—no one to aid her if he refused. The thought drove him on to action. He left his studies, and toiled day and night in the service of the countess. For months he gave his whole attention to this case, without intermission. At last success crowned his efforts. The will in the doge's hands was proved, clearly proved, to be a false instrument. All claims to control the estates of Bianca were relinquished by the old nobleman, and the countess was left free to bestow her hand where her heart had already been given.

* * * * * * * *

The traveller in Florence will notice among the works of modern art, with which the city is filled, a picture representing the figure of a young and graceful woman, richly clad, and surrounded by all the appendages of wealth. At the back of her chair, leaning almost upon her shoulder, is the form of a marquis. There is a smile of triumph in both faces, for at the feet of the lady there kneels the form of a proud old man, with one hand extended, bearing a scroll, marked "The Forged Will." It is a representation of the Marquis Deoli, his bride, and the humbled Doge of Venice. If he asks the name of the artist, he will simply find "Copley" traced at the bottom. The young American with his brush recorded the triumph of his eloquence. Not far distant is another picture. It is a homely scene. A young fisherman sitting at the close of day, with his bride; but the initiated will instantly recognise in it the honest countenance of Adrian and the coquettish smile of Guicolla.

The countess lived long in the enjoyment of her wealth and in the love of her husband. The name that had been bestowed upon her by the poet was always applied to her, and in Florence she is still spoken of as "The Transplanted Flower."

FRIENDS that are worth having are not made but grow, like plants. An old man gave this advice to his sons on his death-bed: "Never try to make a friend." Enemies come fast enough without cultivating the crop; and friends who are brought forward by hot-house expedients are apt to wilt long before they are fairly ripened.

THE COUSINS.

She was a fair, sweet girl,
  Gentle, yet gay,
And her blue eyes outshone
  The skies of May.

*   *   *   *   *   *

She is a matron now,
  Loving and loved.
The beauty of her soul
  Has long been proved.—*Mrs. Mayo.*

It was a bright September day when Frank Grey stepped on the threshold of his paternal mansion, after a seven years absence in California. He went away a mere stripling—he was returning a handsome youth. He went away ignorant and raw—he was returning worldly wise, but guileless still. He went away poor—*he was returning poor*, for he had been sick and unfortunate in the land of gold.

He stopped a moment upon the door-step to survey the scene around him. There, within a stone's throw of him, stood the gnarled old oak upon which he had swung in boyhood; beyond, babbled the stream·in which he had angled—far away over the hill, the smoke still curled up from widow Norton's cottage, and down in the valley, Ned Springler's mill kept up its ceaseless clatter.

The young man lifted his hat from his brow and stroked back the moist locks which lay in raven clusters upon his forehead. He had recalled this scene in the feverish dreams which had visited his pillow when sick and pining in a foreign land. He had longed to slake his thirst in the gurgling rivulet, and rest his wasted limbs where the old oak cast its cool shadows upon the green sward ; but, alas! there had been, then, but little likelihood of his ever doing so. He had survived the attack, however, and now stood on the threshold of home once more.

The dog, which he had played with in boyhood, failed now to recognize or welcome him by his joyous bark. Old Lion lay under the trees asleep, and did not even snap at the dragon fly that buzzed about his head, as he had been wont to do in days gone by.

There seemed to be but little life astir about the establishment. The servants were all busy in the back part of the house. He knew (for a letter had told him so, only a few weeks before) that his little sister Nelly was married to his old friend, Hal Morton, (the widow's only son,) and had gone West; and his mother—ah! his sweet-faced mother! she had been, for months, under the coffin lid, and the aster flowers and golden rods, which September always brings in its train, were now lifting their heads bravely, and nodding to each other over her unconscious dust, in the old grave yard back of the meeting-house, whose spire rose faintly in the distance, away over the hills. Frank remembered this with a heart-quiver and a groan, and he turned and knocked loudly at the door, almost as he would have done at the house of a stranger. It was opened, at last, by old Percy, the waiting man, but his dim eyes failed to recognize his young master. He surveyed him, at first curiously, and then said:

"Master Grey is not at home, sir. He has gone off with a parcel of gentlemen to survey the ten-acre lot, and won't be at home until five o'clock this afternoon. You will be obliged to call again, sir, if it's him ye want to see."

"Good heavens, Percy! don't you know me?" said Frank, grasping the old servant's hand and shaking it warmly. "Don't you know your young master—Frank Grey—who has been, for the last seven years, in California?"

It would have done your heart good to have seen old Percy at that moment. His sable face was lighted up instantly—tears started in his eyes, he trembled violently—then he forgot color and station, and caught Frank about the waist, exclaiming—

"Heaven help me! is this young master Frank? Heaven forgive me for not knowing you at first sight!"

Old Percy's extravagance of joy attracted a bevy of black boys and women from the kitchen and outhouses, and our hero soon found himself in danger of being carried off his feet. Aunt Agatha was there, who had nursed him when he was a babe—brawny armed Joe, with whom he had wrestled many a time in boyhood, and Sue, and John, and Tomkins, all of whom had grown quite out of his knowledge. But in spite of this noisy welcome, the rooms had, in his eyes, a deserted appearance. The place where Nelly's piano stood was now empty—the corner where his mother's rocking-chair formerly sat was filled with a new wood box—the clock upon the mantelpiece ticked with a mournful sound, and the rose bush which used to grow and clamber about the window, had withered and died, it seemed at the root.

Old Agatha noticed the sadness of her young master's gaze. She instantly put the corner of her apron to her eyes, and began to sob hysterically.

"Things has changed wonderfully, young master, since you went away," she said. "Old mistress, she's gone, and young mistress, she's married, and Miss Charlotte she's been sent away to school, and now old master, he's about to—about to—hem! I can't go on."

"My father is about to be what?" exclaimed Frank, in an alarmed voice. "What about him? No harm, or change, I hope will come over almost the only remaining member of my family. Has he grown old, Agatha? Does his step halt and falter, and have his locks whitened since I went away? My mother's death, that must have been a sore stroke to him!"

"Why, no, young master, I don't think he has failed at all—if anything, he is *activer* than he was when you went away. Before your mother died, he *was* getting grey, but he has dyed his hair and whiskers, and now they are blacker than a crow, and he steps about as light as he did twenty years, or more, ago. It's wonderful to see him. It seems to me he's growing younger all the time."

"Ah! Agatha. This is unexpected news. I did not think to hear it. Surely he felt my mother's death very much. He must have done so. She was so beautiful and amiable, and they were so tenderly attached to each other."

"Yes, master seemed to feel Miss Eliza's death very much at first. He walked the parlor floor the night she died, and groaned and mourned as if his heart was breaking; and it was for weeks afterwards, that he scarcely lifted up his head, or smiled. Then Miss Nelly, she took into her head to marry, and that was another sore stroke to him, for it left him here with nobody but your little cousin Charlotte for company; and he said immediately that she must not stay here, but must be sent away to school. So you see the house was left quite alone, and it has remained so ever since; but now there is to be a change here. Heaven bless old Agatha! Wo to her that she has lived to see the day. A new mistress is coming in here next week. Old Master is going to be married again."

"*Married again!* My father going to be married!" exclaimed Frank. "Impossible! Who to?"

"Why, to the widow Morton—Hal's mother. It was only last week that he called my old man Percy in, and announced the fact."

"'Percy,' he said, 'since your old mistress died, it has looked very dark and dreary here, and I have determined to change my mode of life and get married again. You must see that the house is made as neat as a new pin, from top to bottom, and must attend to all the outdoor affairs, and not let anything suffer anywhere, or go wrong. You know the widow Morton is a nice and particular woman, and will like to find things all in trim about her new home. Aunt Agatha and Sue, the cook, must manage to get up some nice cake, and some I shall order from the city. We are not going to have a large wedding. I have sent for Miss Charlotte; she will be at home in a day or two, and will oversee you all, and help to put things in order for her new aunt. Nelly cannot be here, and as to Frank, I very much doubt whether we shall ever see him again, for he is away in California, and seems determined to stay there.'"

There was nothing very wonderful in all this information, but somehow Frank Grey was astounded by it. He had never dreamed of his father's marrying again, but now that the subject was forced upon his thoughts, reason whispered " why not?" He remembered his parent as a vigorous and hale man, in the prime of manhood—according to Agatha's account he was not much changed. Was it not natural and right for him to desire companionship during the rest of his pilgrimage on earth? The house seemed lonely to Frank—to his father it probably did not seem less so. He remembered the mother of his friend Hal, as an amiable, temperate, but homely woman. He wondered how his father came to fancy her. But, just at this point, he was interrupted by a light foot-fall in the passage, and a sweet voice giving directions to a drayman respecting a trunk which he was then delivering. Just then the door swung back, and Charlotte Mobray entered.

Seven years before, Frank had left her a little blue-eyed school girl. He had thought to find her such still, but she stood blushing before him now, clothed with the beauty and grace of perfect womanhood. It was several minutes before the cousins recognized each other.

"Is it possible?" said the young man, stepping forward and extending his hand, "that my little cousin has become the lovely woman I see before me? Time is, indeed, a magician with a transforming wand. I do not believe you know me? Surely you have not forgotten your cousin Frank?".

"No, no," said the girl, a bright blush, at the same time, mantling her cheek; "I remember him, perfectly; but I should never recognize him, I am sure. Welcome home again! But," and her eye glanced mournfully about the room, "but there has been a change here—yea, change upon change—since you went away; and, now, there is to come the saddest change of all."

The eyes of both filled with tears. They held each other by the hand, and memories of the past swept through their minds. Half an hour before, Frank had felt almost like one without kindred or friends; now, a new interest was born in his heart—she, at least, sympathized with him in his loneliness and grief. There was a sofa standing in its old place by the window. He drew his cousin to it, and they sat down side by side, and then she told him how his mother had sickened and grown worse, and, finally, died—how, with her last breath, she had called *his* name, and longed to see him once more—how her uncle had, as Agatha said, walked the parlor and sighed and wept, and how Nelly—his gentle little sister Nelly—stole in, at night, to where her mother was lying in her coffin all ready for burial, and kneeling down, had refused, like Rachel of old, "to be comforted." Then followed the burial—the long train of mourners—the return to the deserted house—the months which succeeded—Nelly's bridal—how beautiful she looked in her white robes, and how sad and tearful the home loneliness was that followed. All this Charlotte told with her soft, white hand resting in Frank's, and a heart-quiver in her voice, which it was touching to hear.

A common grief knits the souls of one household very closely together, and, in that hour, Frank and the little cousin whom his mother had, years before, adopted, in her orphanage, grew very closely into each other's hearts.

It was full five o'clock, as Percy had declared it *would* be, before old Mr. Grey came in.

He started at sight of Frank, as though there had gleamed upon his vision a sight from the tombs—then he grasped him cordially by the hand—called him his boy—wondered at his astonishing growth and manhood, and, while doing this, a few natural and heartfelt tears rolled down his cheeks. His welcome to Charlotte was scarcely less cordial and sincere, and both felt that come what change there might in the household, *he* was the same kind parent and benignant guardian still.

But the days that followed were busy ones to all the household. Under Charlotte's management and oversight, the house was made beautifully clean, from top to bottom—the furniture was tastefully arranged, and Frank helped her to trim up the shrubbery in the yard, and adorn the mantle-pieces with vases of fresh and fragrant flowers.— The more he watched her, the more he was impressed by

her good sense, gentleness and beauty. She was like, and
still unlike, the little girl he had left seven years before.
Since that time, he had seen dark-eyed, beautiful Spanish
senoras, the curious Chinese with her little feet, the ruddy
cheeked daughter of Erin, the elegant Parisian, and the
blue-eyed cottage girl of England. Ladies of every clime
had crossed his path in the land of gold, but he had never
seen one like Charlotte.

It was a pleasant amusement for him, in those days, to
steal away to the rivulet, and lying down in the shadows
of the trees, gaze up at the fleecy specks of clouds sailing
overhead, and dream those visions which an ardent imagination can so vividly tint. The sunshine then grew as
golden as it had looked to him in boyhood. The little
bird which sat upon the azalia bough, sang the song of
long ago—the minnows in the stream darted about as
joyously as of old; he forgot the city, with its overpower-
ing heat, its crowded pavements and red glaring walls—
its ceaseless din and clatter—its ragged penury and
princely wealth. He dreamed of a cottage, neat and
white, in which there were music, and song, and laughter,
mingled with the gush of the stream at his feet, and the
song of the bird on the broken twig at his head. The
windows of that cottage were very bright; and moving to
and fro before them, there was a figure neatly rounded,
and a face serene and beautiful. He was startled at his
own reverie, for that face and form belonged to his cousin
Charlotte, and what right had he to be dreaming of *her?*
What right, indeed?

The right of relationship, to be sure, and he laid his
head down again upon the moss-covered roots, and determined to muse and dream as long and as deeply as his
fancy dictated.

But American life, in this nineteenth century, is not
exactly the time and place for *dreams.* Energetic, vigorous action is the watchword of the age, and he who
would not be left behind, must be up and at work "in the
bivouac of life."

Up and at work, Frank determined to go, and to earn

a right and the power of protecting the fair and graceful flower, almost the only one left blooming on his ancestral tree.

But before he went he sought the side of his cousin. She was in the arbor arranging a bouquet for the centre-table.

"Cousin Lottie," he said, hurriedly, "I have come to bid you good bye."

"Good bye, Frank? You jest, surely," said the girl, and a shade of gloom gathered over her finely penciled brow. "You are not going to leave us until after—after —after the marriage," she said in a choking voice.

"Yes," he answered, "I do not believe that I have the heart to witness that ceremony. I do not blame my father for marrying again, but, somehow, I feel that the woman who is coming in here will crowd old residents out, and I had rather make way for her before she plants foot upon the threshold. Do you think that *you* will feel at home here, after that?"

"I have no other home," said the girl sorrowfully. "What lies before me in the future, I cannot tell; but Heaven is merciful, I will trust it;" and she tore a withered leaf from its stalk and cast it upon the floor.

"Lottie," said the young man, sitting down beside her, and throwing his arm over the back of her chair, "Lottie, I am going out into the world to make, for myself, a *new home*, for the old is closing its doors upon us. Will you share that home with me? Will you be its mistress—its presiding genius--its star and sunshine? Say yes, quickly, Lottie, for my ear is eager to catch that tiny mono-syllable."

What Lottie said, gentle reader, I cannot tell; I only know that Frank Grey's dream of a home has been re-alized.

Beside a noble river in the West, there is an elegant, picturesque Anglo-Dutch cottage, as lovely as that of our distinguished American author, Washington Irving, be-side the "Tappan Zee." Tall sycamores throw their shadows in the yard—fleecy clouds sail through the clear

7

ether overhead—flocks and herds graze on the emerald
hills beyond—the azalia's boughs whiten with snowy blossoms when summer begins her golden reign; and, from
steamboats on the river, curls gracefully up, the wreath
of commerce and thrifty labor.

Through that home moves Charlotte, and there are tiny
feet *now*, which patter up and down the front steps, and
away over the green sward, crushing the life out of violets
and snow drops as they go. There are short, golden
curls drooping over the brow of childhood—curls which
grow moist with exercise, and are tossed back with shouts
and laughter, by dimpled fingers, while the hoop is chased
and the ball is bounded. In the eyes of Frank Grey,
every curl is more precious than all the mines of California, and he goes out and tosses away with his children on
the lawn, and lets their restless feet clamber over his
breast, and their little chubby hands wander at will amid
his hair.

Charlotte laughs at all this. She says she has but one
trouble in all the world. What do you think it is, gentle
reader? Why, Frank is a *Freemason*, and *will stay too
long at the Lodge!*

THE highest charity is to pay liberally for all things had
or done for you; because to underpay workmen, and then
be bountiful, is not charity. On the other hand, to give,
when by so doing you support idleness, is most pernicious.
Yet you cannot refuse to give street alms, if your charity
has no other channel—you would feel that refusal in such
a case is a mere pretext to save your money. But if your
wealth is wisely and systematically given, then the refusal
of idle appeals does no harm to the heart, but on the contrary, prepares you to aid with cheerfulness the wants of
the truly needy.

THE CARDINAL VIRTUES.

I. — BROTHERLY LOVE.

" By the exercise of Brotherly Love we are taught to regard the whole human species as one family."—*Stewart's Freemasons' Manual.*

" I HEAR," said Grace Lamar, as she laid her jewelled fingers upon the shoulder of her companion, Rosa Coles, " that this party of Mrs. Lord's is to be the most brilliant affair of the season, entirely surpassing Mrs. Maribeaux's *soiree*, although she *did* hire French and Italian cooks expressly for the occasion. Lizzie Spencer was in here this evening, and she told me that the table is magnificent— the prettiest thing she ever saw in her life; and you know Liz is a judge in such matters—every body sends to consult her taste; and then the Johnsons, who are just back from Europe, are expected, and the Lawtons, and the Jessups, and the Goldarchs, and the Silverflowers. It will be splendid, and we, Rosa, must do our best dressing to-night. How do you think this tarletan, worn over white satin, will look?"

As Grace spoke, she lifted a thin gossamer dress from the back of a chair, and held it for a moment suspended between her thumb and fingers.

"It is beautiful," said Rosa, lifting her head from beneath the hands of her dressing maid, who had just tied a knot of ribbon destined to confine a wreath of white roses and silver leaves over her curls; " beautiful, Grace, and I prophesy you will be the admired of all admirers, but that will be no *new* thing for my darling Grace. Make haste, however, or you will be late. See, Beathie has my toilet half completed already." And the young girl tossed the curls from her cheek, and rose to survey herself in a mirror opposite. The mirror showed two faces—the half-decorated person of Rosa, and the beautiful countenance, bright eyes and pleasing contour of Grace Lamar, looking over her shoulder, or rather leaning carelessly upon her neck. Both were beautiful in different ways. Grace was queen-like, almost haughty, in her bearing; Rosa was *petite*, graceful, and winning. And what they there seemed, they were. The former's only fault was pride—pride of person, pride of station, pride of family. An only and idolized daughter, she had been petted and caressed from her birth. Her father was a rich banker, and the best society had from the first courted her presence. No wonder that Grace Lamar was aristocratic in her notions.

That night, when the hours had grown "fashionably late," the two girls descended from the carriage, and swept into the brilliantly lighted apartments of Mrs. Lord. The scene before them was indeed almost like enchantment. Beautiful chandeliers were suspended by small silver chains from the ceiling overhead, and poured forth a flood of light over carpet and flower-vase, mirrors, costly furniture, and gay crowds. Every face was radiant with animation, every lip was wreathed with smiles. Grace entered, leaning upon the arm of her brother Edward; and as she moved towards the head of the room, to pay salutation to Mrs. Lord, a murmur of admiration ran round the room. Grace and Edward Lamar were the most majestic couple in the apartment.

"I wonder who that stranger is yonder," said the proud beauty to her companion Rosa, half an hour afterwards, as she leaned against a pillar in the hall, and glanced toward a young man of noble features, but of plain dress and diffident manners, who stood apart from the crowd, apparently unknowing and unknown. I wonder how he came here. He is dressed quite like a plebeian; I shouldn't at all wonder if he was a mechanic of some sort, but see them! Edward has gone up to him, and addressed him as he would speak to an intimate friend and an equal. Who can he be?"

"I like his face," said Rosa. "What a broad forehead he has; and now that he is interested, see how his eyes flash with intelligence! His dress, to be sure, is excep-

tionable, but his face will bear analyzation, and such faces
I like. See, Richard Barton and George Lord have joined
them now. I wonder who he is!"

"I don't see how, with that dress, and the grave, shy,
diffident manners that he wore when we first observed
him, he ever got into these rooms; he cannot belong to
the *elite*. Perhaps he is some poor country cousin, come
to the city to see the wonders, and Mrs. Lord could not
help inviting him." But see! Edward is bringing him this
way. What can the fellow mean by giving him an introduction?"

"Mr. Evans, my sister," said Edward. Grace bowed
her queenly head stiffly; but Rosa, after he had been
through a formal presentation to her, chatted with him or
rather to him like a blackbird. Both seemed pleased with
the acquaintance they were forming. Mr. Evans took a
chair by her side, and hardly left her the remainder of the
evening. Grace Lamar was truly glad when George Lord
came to offer her his arm for a promenade, for she had
sunk into a chair beside Rosa, after the presentation was
over, and sat silent, almost moody, in her unbending pride.
She now arose, and swept off in the trail of a crowd who
were walking arm in arm through the different rooms.
She dared not ridicule the stranger to her companions,
much as she wanted to, for he was the host's invited
guest, and for aught she knew, her relative, but she puzzled her head continually to find out who and what he
was. But no one seemed to know anything about him.
The evening glided away, and she had gained no information respecting the uncouth guest.

"Who is he?" she asked again of Rosa, when they met
in the cloak-room. "I am sure you must be tired, bored
to death."

"Far from it," said Rosa; "I pronounce him the most
agreeable man I have met this season, but I do not know
whether he lives in the city or not."

"Evans! no family by that name visit in *our* circle, I
am sure," said Grace; "there are some Evans' in the lower
part of the city, but they are all poor sticks."

"Edward," cried Grace, the next morning across the breakfast table, "pray who was that Mr. Evans that you paraded through the rooms arm in arm with, as if he were a brother, and to whom I really believe Rosa Coles gave her heart unasked. He must be a very fascinating fellow, although I saw little to prepossess one in his favor."

"He is my brother," said Edward, with a smile.

"And mine, too, I suppose," said the beauty, with a disdainful toss of the head. "If I am to sustain that relationship to him, I shall send him forthwith to get measured for a suit of clothes. Pray, *how* is he your brother?"

"He is a bright and noble Mason," said Edward; "he needed no other introduction to my notice. Much as you scorn his appearance now, my sister, there may come a time when he will act the part of a brother to even my queenly Grace. Please pass my cup."

"And *that* is his only recommendation," said Grace, with a bitter smile. "Brother, I am getting actually ashamed of you. Since you joined that miserable fraternity, the dirtiest mechanic, the most common people, you stop in the street to shake hands with, and talk to; you even hunt them up, and now I hear you claiming relationship with nobody knows who, simply on the ground of his being a Mason. You go further—you presume to introduce these common people to me as your friends. I do not thank you for the compliment."

"But you may some day thank me, Grace, for doing it. Masonry is not an idle thing. There may come a time when you will need the protection which, as the sister of a Mason, will be freely thrown around you; do not speak so bitterly of the institution now. Mr. Evans is a young man from one of the Western States. He has invented a useful machine for tanning leather, I am told, and has come to the city for the purpose of getting it patented. George Lord first met with him in the lodge. He was highly pleased with him, and deems him a man of no ordinary genius. They have become intimate in the course of a few weeks, and that accounts for his presence there last night. I noticed Rosa Coles seemed to enjoy his society, and he was also pleased. He told me at parting, that he had spent a most delightful time. Could he have said as much, had no one volunteered to entertain him beside my sister Grace?"

"Humph!" said Grace, "I generally know who I am talking to, before I talk, and I must confess that I am astonished at Rosa's behaviour."

That afternoon came on dark and cloudy, but Grace had promised some friends at the upper end of the city that she would spend an hour or two with them; she did not like to disappoint them, and so she tied on her bonnet, and issued into the crowded streets. Carts, omnibusses and drays were passing in every direction, but she hurried past them, and was soon in the broader, pleasanter streets of the upper city. Here she met the friends on whom she had promised to call, and in their pleasant society she forgot to note the flight of time. When she stepped into the street again, to pursue her journey home, she was surprised and frightened to see how near nightfall it was. Heavy dense clouds hung in the air, and a few drops of rain had already fallen upon the pavement. She had full two miles to walk, and her way lay through some of the most desolate streets in the city. She hurried on with rapid and unequal steps, until she had gained some distance in her way, but the clouds grew dense overhead—the rain fell faster—the streets grew narrower and more forbidding in their aspects. She had supposed, at the commencement of her journey, that she knew perfectly well every yard of ground intervening between herself and her home, but in her consternation, and in the gathering gloom, she now found that she had mistaken her way; she was, she feared in the immediate vicinity of the most disreputable part of the city. She stopped, trembling with fear and apprehension. The signs on the stores and shops were filled with unfamiliar names; ragged, dirty, disgusting specimens of humanity reeled by her, or stopped to scrutinize her person and dress. She was afraid to go on, for fear that every step would carry her further into danger; she feared to attract attention by standing alone and irresolute at that hour in so vile a place.

What was she to do? She knew that Edward was probably in search of her, but she had missed her way, and he would not know where to look for her. He probably would go to the upper end of the city, thinking to meet her, but she was—she hardly dared think where.

While she was musing thus, a rough voice accosted her. She turned in consternation, and beheld a middle-aged man leaning against a lamp-post, and with a most insolent eye regarding her. His whole appearance proclaimed him to be a rowdy of the most desperate character—his eyes were red, his face and body were bloated, blotched and purple. Grace uttered a slight shriek, and sprang forward. "I will get out of his way, she thought, let me go where I may." She flew like a frightened bird through lanes and by-ways, sometimes stumbling in the darkness, and then issuing into better-lighted streets. At length she paused, half terrified to death, to ascertain if possible where she was. The place was as unfamiliar to her as before—the aspect of things around her quite as forbidding.

"My pretty lass stays out late, and it mought be don't know how to get home," said the same insolent voice that had before addressed her. She turned and saw that she was pursued, and that the man whom she had seen beside the lamp-post was close behind her.

Again she shrieked, and again she sprang forward; one terror now filled her mind—the dread of being overtaken and insulted by this fiend in human garb.

"Good heavens! Miss Lamar, is this you?" said a voice which she remembered to have heard before. She glanced up, and saw the uncouth guest of the party, standing directly in her path. "You are alone, and in distress," he said, in a commiserating tone; "is there any way in which I can be of service to you? If so, command me freely."

"I am indeed in distress," cried Grace, "for I lost my way at night-fall, and cannot recover it. I wish to go to No. 99 —— Street. Will you be kind enough, sir, to direct me?"

"I will go with and protect you, if you will accept of my escort; this is an unsafe part of the city for a young lady to traverse alone at this hour. Will you take my

arm." Grace thankfully clung to her protector. How
differently she felt towards him now from what she had
felt in Mrs. Lord's brilliant rooms the night before.

As they passed under the lamps, she glanced up at him,
and thought that he had grown to be a different being in
the short space of twenty-four hours. He now looked noble, manly, attractive.

He referred to their meeting the night before, and con-
gratulated himself upon having met and having been introduced to her, as it now justified him in offering her
protection, which otherwise might have appeared insolent
and improper. He spoke of her friend Rosa Coles, and
chatted so pleasantly, that Grace was half surprised to find
herself standing so soon before the marble steps leading
up to her father's elegant mansion.

"You will go in," she said, "and receive the thanks of
my family, as well as my own, for guiding me home. I
am very grateful to you."

"I deem myself happy in having met with you, Miss
Lamar, and deserve no thanks—no gratitude. I shall leave
the city to-morrow, otherwise I would give myself the
pleasure of calling in the course of a few days, and ascer-
taining whether you have thoroughly recovered from your
fright. Please remember me to your brother. I have an
engagement which prevents me from entering to-night;
say to him that I am happy to have had it in my power
to aid the sister of a Mason. Good evening, Miss Lamar!"
and before Grace could reply, the young man had bowed
himself from the steps.

"I owe this protection—the most opportune that ever
came to mortal, to *Masonry* then—to the *brotherly love*
of the craft—the very virtue which I ridiculed and despised
this morning. How little did I dream then, that the poor
leather tanner would ever have it in his power to "act" as
Edward said "a brother's part" to me—to *me* the haughty,
self-depending, and, I fear, too proud belle of an aristocratic circle. Thus mused Grace as she turned the door
knob—divested herself of her walking dress, and then
wended her way to the drawing room.

She found great consternation prevailing in the household, owing to her late return, and that Edward had been running all over the city in fruitless endeavors to find her. All welcomed her back with unfeigned joy, and all were loud in expressing gratitude to the young stranger who had secured her from such immediate and impending danger.

"I never will ridicule the brotherly love you, Masons harp so much upon, Edward," said she, " for I have been blessed by it. I shall not quarrel with you for associating henceforth with beggars, if you please, and introducing them to me." She said this with a wicked smile, but there was sincerity in her words nevertheless.

"I do not wish to introduce my sister to *beggars*," said Edward; "I do not associate with them as equals myself, but I *do* look upon every bright and accepted Mason as my brother, whether his hand is soft, or hardened by labor —whether he is mechanic, scholar, priest, teacher, or architect—whether he is high or low, rich or poor. Masonry renders all who conform to its precepts, *honorable.* The greatest and the best of men have never deemed it derogatory to their dignity to level themselves with the whole fraternity. Masonry unites men of every country, creed, and honorable occupation."

A few months after Mrs. Lord's party, Grace's heart was made very sad by the removal of her sweet friend Rosa to the West. Mr. Coles had purchased land of the government, and deemed it best to remove to it with his family. From their earliest infancy, these girls had been much together ; every thought, feeling, and enjoyment had been shared in common, and the separation was not without bitter pangs to both. They promised to maintain a punctual correspondence, and never forget each other. We hear much of the romantic attachment of school girls. Their friendships are so ephemeral in their nature, that they have become the subject of jests and ridicule, and we must asknowledge that the term *friendship* is with them more common than reality. Still, there *are* instances in which the most opposite natures unite in bonds so strong, that nothing but death can dissever them. Such was the case with Grace and Rosa.

Rosa's first letter was filled with animated descriptions of her journey and of her new home. At the bottom of her sheet was traced, in pencil marks, the following sentence:

"You will be surprised, my dear Grace, to know that Mr. Evans, who was in the city a few months ago, and with whom we met, as you will remember, at Mrs. Lord's party, is here—our near neighbor and constant visitor. He has secured his patent, and bids fair to be as rich as your friend Rosa has ever deemed him agreeable."

"And so romance, marriage, and nobody knows what, is to come out of this *brotherly love*, it seems," said Grace to herself, as she folded the sheet and placed it in her portfolio. "Well, I little dreamed of such things when I first directed Rosa's attention to him at Mrs. Lord's party; but nobody can tell what is going to happen. There comes George Lord up the steps. I'll go down and tell him how his masonic guest is winning gold, and, I shrewdly suspect, love also, ' way out west,' " and Grace bounded down to meet the man to whom (gentle reader, we are telling you a secret,) she was already betrothed.

Grace's prescient wit was not at fault. The mutual liking which had sprung up between Henry Evans and Rosa Coles at their first meeting ended, as Grace had foretold it would, in marriage before two years had passed over the latter, after her removal to the West. Grace also wedded, and among household cares, thoughts, loves, and duties, the friendship of her early girlhood was half forgotten. When she thought of her friend at all, it was as the wife of an obscure man, in the unsettled wilds of the west, and although she remembered that she owed a debt of gratitude to this same individual, she could not repress the sighs that rose to her lips, when she reflected what a sad pity it was that such beauty, grace, and accomplishments as her sweet friend possessed, should be, as she deemed them, entirely lost.

Grace had been married five years, when George, her

husband, was called on urgent business to the capitol. She determined to accompany him. As she was crowding her way to a seat in the House of Representatives one day, the voice of a member who was speaking below struck her as being strangely familiar. She enquired of a lady near her, who he was, and was told that he was the new western member upon whom so much praise had recently been lavished. She glanced down and saw—could she believe her eyes—the "guest" whom she had once ridiculed—the Mason who had afterwards befriended and protected her—the man whose good fortune she had half envied in winning the affections and hand of sweet Rosa. Yes, it was Henry Evans the tanner—the Mason who had risen, by the dint of his genius and untiring industry, to a post of honor and affluence, reached but by a favored few. He stood undaunted, graceful, winning, and self-possessed before the greatest statesman in the land, and in a clear voice urged conviction home to every heart. Every eye in the vast throng was fixed upon him, for he held them spell-bound by his eloquence. His person was now fashionably clad—his broad white forehead seemed to swell with thought, and his eye flashed with the fires of his genius.

Old men leaned forward to catch his words—white hands clapped and cheered him. Amid the stamping of feet and cheering upon every side, he sat down. It was evident that his eloquence had gained the point for which he contended. Grace glanced up, and nearly opposite her she saw the flushed, excited, proud, animated Rosa. Her eyes were fixed with unutterable pride upon the spot where her husband was surrounded by the members who had crowded around him. It was a moment of proud triumph. How little had the scornful beauty at Mrs. Lord's party imagined that the "uncouth guest" was destined to win such laurels as these.

"It is our old friend Evans," said George, who now came with sparkling eyes to the side of his wife. I knew when I first met him in the lodge, and afterwards introduced him to my mother, that he was no ordinary character. I told your brother Edward so, and he fully agreed with me. See how flushed and happy his wife Rosa looks. I must just step across and tell her that she owes this day's satisfaction in part to me—to the BROTHERLY LOVE that exists among Masons. Had she not been introduced to him at our house, who can tell whether any of these subsequent events would have happened?

II.—RELIEF.

All things unto me show their dark sides ; somewhere there must be light.—*Festus.*

How cold, how dreary the day was! The wind sounded hoarsely as it moaned among the bare branches of the trees, and died away in distant murmurs. A white frost had fallen the night before, and nipped leaf and floweret. The sky looked like lead, and now and then a cloud, fleecy and white as if laden with snows, drifted in mid air. Blue-lipped, shivering little children, with satchels and books, hurried by to school, or stopped for a few moments at the street corners.

I had taken my drawing pencils and portfolio, and seated myself before the blazing fire. When the wind rattled the casement, I drew my vizette closer about me, and thanked God for a comfortable shelter from the inclemency of the northern blast. A piece of Bristol-board was beneath my pencil. Scene after scene grew beneath its touches. But all was dreary. A frozen mill, an ice-bound tree, a snow storm, a man striving to hold his cloak on in the blast—these were the prominent features in my pencil sketches. I could not be cheerful, do what I might. I could not forget the drear aspect of nature without.

I threw aside the pencil, and wheeled my chair nearer the fire. The coals glowed almost fiercely in the grate, and I began tracing pictures and images among them.

The door opened, and a strong blast swept through. I looked up and saw a cloaked figure—a tall, noble, and

commanding person. He threw aside his traveling-cap—
unclasped the steel buckles confining his mantle in front,
and uncle Roger sat down beside me, to thaw out before
the genial blaze his stiffened fingers.

As he sat there, his deep olive complexion became almost scarlet in hue. His keen black eye rested musingly
upon the coals. Was he too tracing imagery among
them? It might be, but it was not probable. My uncle
had little imagination, and was never, to my knowledge,
fanciful. It was more probable that he was weighing in
his mind some East India speculation, for all his latter life
had been spent there. It was to its torrid climate that he
owed his olive complexion, quick flashing eye, and suscep-
tibility to cold. The fire was peculiarly agreeable to him.
When he went into the frigid atmosphere without, his
broad stout person shook like an aspen, and he clasped
and drew his cloak closer and still closer about him. He
was a bachelor, one nearly fifty years old. His hair was
sprinkled with grey, but it looked handsome nevertheless;
indeed, all who looked upon my uncle, called him, even at
that age, a fine-looking man. I had oftentimes puzzled my
brain to discover why he had all his life remained matchless; why one, with his love of social life, affectionate disposition, and domestic tastes, had lived without enjoying
life's great charm—a home.

But mysteries are curious things, and this fact remained
a mystery in spite of all my speculations. I could not fa-
thom it; but now a stronger desire than ever before
I had seized me to know why he had never married. As
he sat in the light of the grate, he looked so stately, genial
and handsome, that the mystery grew greater to my mind
than ever, and I determined, by direct questioning, to find
out the secret.

" A cold day, uncle," I said, by way of introduction; " a
cold day, and I imagine you feel it sensibly; it is not much
like the East India climate."

" No," said he abruptly, and relapsed back into the
dreamy state he had sat in before.

" You do not like this climate, I imagine," I continued.

"Not much," was the laconic answer wrung from him.

"But you did at one time like to live in your native land," I said; "why did you go in the first place to the East Indies, uncle?"

"To trade," said he; "to buy and sell, and get again. That is what all the world lives for. Gold is the lever that moves the world."

"True," I said; "but you have won gold; you are what the world calls rich; are you happy?"

"His brow contracted. "Happier than I should have been without wealth, I presume," said he. "But perfect happiness is not the lot of man."

"You never had a family, uncle," I continued; "you have lived alone all your life. Why did you never marry? Did you never love?"

A deeper shadow stole to his cheek; I saw that I had touched upon a tender point. He did not reply immediately, but sat, I imagined, half moodily before the fire, as still as a statue.

At length he turned abruptly towards me. "Yes, I have loved," he said, "but it was long years ago. The romance of life is over with me now. The flame has gone out that passion kindled; there can scarcely be found one smouldering ember that has survived the wrecks of time and its accompanying sorrows."

"Tell me all about it, uncle," I said anxiously; "when was it that you found your *beau-ideal*—where did you meet with her? In America, or in the East Indies?"

"It was long years ago," he said, "long before I went to the East Indies, that I first met with Adelaide Sullivan."

"Was she *very* beautiful, uncle?" I queried. "Had she blue eyes, a Grecian nose, and delicate features? Was she very lovely?"

"To me," he replied, "she was as beautiful as an angel, although you perhaps might not at first sight have termed her very fair. She had eyes as blue as the violets which opened in the spring woods—lips and cheeks that might have stolen color from the rosebud, and a forehead white as snow. But beautiful as she was in person, she was more attractive in mind. She had wit, sprightliness, intelligence. She was gentle and refined. To me she appeared, in those days, of all her sex the paragon."

"And still you did not marry her," I said; "why was this?"

"Mercenary parents stood in the way—parents who said that something more than love was wanted to commence housekeeping upon—parents who frowned upon my schemes, until, in a fit of passion, I vowed to amass gold until their cupidity was satisfied; and with this vow upon my lips, I bade adieu to Adelaide, and sailed for the Indies. For long years I toiled unsuccessfully. My head grew grey with time, and thought, and care. At length the news reached me of Adelaide's marriage. From that hour I relinquished all ideas of ever possessing a home of my own—of forming the centre of a domestic circle. I amassed gold, for acquisition had grown into a passion—a habit with me, and it is a passion with me still. Just now I was planning the sale of some ten-acre lots on my plantation. There was not much romance about that operation, you will admit."

"No," I said, thoughtfully. "But what of Adelaide? do you know nothing of her now? Have you never sought her out since your return to your native land?"

"No, not I. Why should I? She is the wife of another, and has forgotten me. At any rate, she has no business remembering me; a pretty chap I should consider myself, looking up married women, and reviving old flames. No, no!" and my uncle shook his head decidedly.

Just then a rougher blast shook the casements; the day was in truth a most inclement one. The wind not only shook the casements, but forced open the door. My uncle jumped to his feet, and sprung to close it immediately; but he did not accomplish his design. A weak voice arrested his hand. The figure of a pale and half-frozen child stood upon the door-steps, as if hesitating whether a welcome waited for him inside or not.

"Come in, boy, come in!" said my uncle hastily; "a dog should not be abroad in such weather, much less a delicate child. Come in, and thaw out your stiffened fingers, dear."

The boy mounted the threshold, and tottered towards the fire. He was very weak, it might be through hunger, it might be through cold, perhaps from both combined.

I rose and offered him a low chair by the grate. He sank into it; and as he felt the genial heat of the room stealing into his benumbed frame, a few tear drops rolled down his wan cheeks.

My uncle was a benevolent-hearted man. He regarded the lad for a few moments with an expression which showed that much contact with a rough world had not entirely dried up the fountains of sympathy in his heart.

"Why are you abroad in such rough weather?" he asked. "Your parents certainly cannot have sent you?"

The child's under-lip trembled with emotion, and tears sprang into his eyes. "My father is dead," he said, "and my mother is very ill and destitute of bread."

"Poor child!" said my uncle compassionately, "and this is the reason why you are out ; you are too fine a little fellow to be sent on begging expeditions."

The boy's cheek flushed, but it was with mortified pride and anger.

"I am *not a beggar*," he said disdainfully. "I never took a copper in my life, and never mean to, without giving something in return. My mother sent me out this morning to sell this, and not to beg." As he spoke, he drew from his pocket a small roll. I watched and admired the little fellow as he untied the string and unrolled the brown paper that enclosed his treasure.

I was surprised when I saw it at last held up for exhibition. It was a white satin apron, beautifully painted and trimmed—one which must at some time have belonged to the most honorable of the fraternity.

My uncle was a bright Mason. I saw his eye kindle and his cheek flush at the sight of the satin texture now offered in exchange for bread—for the common wants of life.

"To whom did this belong, my boy?" said my uncle in a mild voice; "was this your father's?"

"Yes," said the child; "my father used often to wear it, and a pretty sight it was, sir, to see him dressed out in his beautiful regalia. My mother hates to part with it, sir; indeed, she has parted with everything else before she would part with this, but she is sick and in great distress. This morning she said I must offer this for sale, for she cannot bear to see me beg, and we have nothing else to sell. A man up town to whom I offered it told me that he was not a Mason, and had no use for such regalia, but that if I would come here perhaps I could sell it. I accordingly came, and now how would you like to buy it, sir?"

"Buy it?" cried my uncle; "no, I would not buy it for the world; but your mother, if she is the widow of the man who wore this, shall never again send you forth on such an errand. I pledge the word of a gentleman and Mason. Take your hat, boy, and show me the way to your residence."

My uncle had taken his cloak, and was already clasping it around him.

"You will not surely go forth, uncle, in such an hour, and with your East India constitution, to brave this inclement storm," I said, rising and standing before him. "You can send money and relief to this unfortunate lady, without exposing yourself."

"I *cannot* send," he said implicitly. "If the widow and child of a Mason can brave the rigors of the storm, I certainly am not too weak—too effeminate for the task. Give me my cane and hat."

I handed them to him, and, taking the child by the hand, he went forth into the wind and sleet, for the latter had commenced falling. I went to the window, and watched them both until they were out of sight. I felt, as I saw my uncle's stalwart frame braving the inclemency without, and yielding support to the delicate, fragile boy, that he was indeed one of 'God's noblemen, and I mused over that mysterious organization of men to which he belonged, and the benevolence of whose creed had led him forth to peril the safety of a constitution rendered peculiarly sensitive to cold, from a long residence in a foreign clime.

*   *   *   *   *   *   *

It was quite dark before my uncle returned. He came in, and to my surprise exhibited no great symptoms of cold. He leisurely unclasped his cloak, and sat down to the supper table, which was already spread, without a remark.

I looked into his face as I sat down to pour the coffee into the cups, but it was as unreadable as a scratched and torn page. I could not unravel his thoughts. He was serious, without being sad, and gave brief answers to all my questions.

"Did you find that poor woman in great distress?" I queried.

"Yes," said he.

"She was suffering for the want of the necessaries of life, I suppose?"

"Yes."

"Did you do anything for her?"

"To be sure I did; that was what I went for."

"True, true," I said, "but I thought you would only look into her condition, and then perhaps lay her case before the lodge."

"Lay her case before the fiddlesticks," said he abruptly. "Adelaide Sullivan's case is already attended to. She will never seek relief from a masonic lodge while there is strength in this right arm to provide for her and her boy."

"Adelaide Sullivan!" I exclaimed in surprise.. "It is not possible that your old flame, Adelaide Sullivan, has been reduced to widowhood, penury and want, and that you have just found her?"

"It *is* true," said he. "Her husband has been dead two years, and wretchedly poor he must have left her; but thank fortune, I have enough for both."

"And mean to share it with her, one would infer," I said, mischievously. "But I forgot, the romance of life is over with you, uncle. The fires of passion are extinguished—

not a smouldering ember exists. So it is not probable that you will marry her."

"It is probable," said my uncle in his straightforward way, "probable and certain. The romance of life may be over, but I have a feeling of love for this woman nevertheless—a feeling that can be smothered, but never extinguished."

And so, kind reader, it proved in the end. My uncle married her, and a sweeter, kinder woman never gladdened a domestic scene.

All things to her had shown their dark side, but at last there came through Masonry "light."

III.—TRUTH.

On all things created, remaineth the half-effaced signature of God ;
Somewhat of fair and good, tho' blotted by the finger of corruption.
—*Tupper.*

"What is truth?" asked Pilate of the Saviour. Again and again has man, while groping his way through thick mists of error, paused and reiterated the question, "What is truth?" The student who strives to penetrate the arcana of Nature, assures us that he is seeking Truth in her most beautiful habiliments. The pale-browed theologian pores over the sacred page, unravelling strange doctrines, and fancying that none so adroitly as he have succeeded in drawing Truth from her secret recesses: in his midnight musings she comes to his side, with a face as beautiful as an angel's, and a voice sweeter than the syren's spell. Every association of men claim Truth for a handmaid and a companion. She assumes in their hands characters the most diverse, and utters the most opposite teachings. But after all, Truth is a unity, beautiful and symmetrical. She dwells in no one place, or rather, she is an all-pervading spirit.

"Verily there is nothing so false, that a sparkle of truth is not in it."

But it is time to commence my story.

It was a beautiful moonlit night in the south of England. In a little cottage which stood almost upon the beach, a beautiful young girl sat, or rather leaned carelessly out of the half-open casement, and watched the waves, which came rolling in huge silver bands to the shore, and there broke into a thousand glittering fragments on the rocks. Their hoarse, steady murmer seemed to have a charm in it—the cool breeze which came inland was soothing and sweet in its influence. She tossed back the long curls which were floating carelessly over her shoulders, in order to feel the invigorating breath of the night in all its balminess. A honeysuckle had clambered almost to the top of the casement, and its sweet flowers waved to and fro, scattering their fragrance like so many censors. The little grass-plat in front was hedged about with primroses—those beautiful floral appendages which cast so sweet a charm around most English cottages; and pansies, sweetwilliams, daisies, and blue anemones peeped modestly up from their lowly nestling-places. It was such a home as England's sweetest poetess must have had in her mind's eye, when she sung,

> "Seest thou my home ?—'tis where yon woods are waving
>   In their dark richness, to the summer air—
> Where yon blue stream, a thousand flower banks laving,
>   Leads down the hills a vein of light—'tis there !
> Midst those green wilds how many a fount lies gleaming,
>   Fringed with the violet, colored with the skies ;
> My childhood's haunt, thro' days of summer dreaming
>   Under young leaves that shook with melodies."

England has many such haunts as these—flower-wreathed cottages, where glad young hearts spend their springtime, and to which they look back with restless yearnings when far away; and among the fairest, sweetest, best of these homes, stood the cottage about which I write.

"Eva Snow ! Miss Eva Snow ! I say, it wants only a quarter to ten, and why do you stay looking out at the sea, and catching your death of cold, as you very well know, here in the damp night air, without so much as a handkerchief thrown over your head ? Why don't you shut the casement and prepare for bed; all in the house have been in their rooms this half hour, and I want to shut up the windows and doors."

Eva turned her head and saw Bridget, the housekeeper, standing with a candle in one hand and a huge bunch of keys in the other. There was a frown upon her wrinkled brow, and a glance of disapproval in her eye.

"I did not know it was so late," said the young girl, rising and motioning as if to close the casement, but just then her eye fell upon a dark figure flitting across the green-sward in front of the house. A crimson flush mounted to her cheek—her hand trembled—her heart fluttered, and turning with a commanding air to the servant, she said, "leave me Bridget to close the windows; I have not yet done admiring the sea. It is not often that one sees so sweet a night as this, even in the south of England."

The servant turned away, muttering something about the romantic taste of a young girl, who kept the house eternally in commotion, and wondering what there could be in the water, which her young mistress saw every day and every night, so mighty wonderful—so very enchanting on this night in particular. But the rays of her candle flickered off in the distance—the door slammed after her, and Eva Snow was alone again.

Was she alone? No, a clump of shrubbery rustled by the side of the window, throwing a thousand sparkling dew-drops to the ground, and a tall form stepped full into the moonlight.

"Why have you come, Captain Montgomery?" said the young girl, stretching forth her snowy white hand, which was eagerly grasped; why have you come at this unseasonable hour to seek an interview in this clandestine way? Should my sire, with his strict English notions of propriety, chance to overhear us, we should never be forgiven."

"I know it, Eva dear, I know I peril your happiness as well as my own by thus coming, but I could not depart, dearest girl, without once more seeking your dear presence, without once more hearing the tones of your voice, and looking into the depths of your blue eyes. It is a cruel fate, Eva, that thus sends me from you."

"And are you indeed going?" said Eva, her lips and cheeks blanching colorless; "are you indeed going to leave England and—"

She stopped suddenly. "Me," she would have added, but the word died upon her lip.

"I shall leave England," he said musingly; "my ship is even now ready for an instant departure. I must leave you too, unless like a wise girl you decide to accompany me."

"But my father!" exclaimed the girl, "my father, you know, has a dread of the sea; nearly all his family once perished in it, after weeks of starvation and suffering—my father, I fear, will never consent to my uniting my destiny with one,

> " Whose path is o'er the mountainous wave,
>   Whose home is on the deep."

"Oh, Captain Montgomery! for my sake, give up your perilous wanderings on the sea; for my sake, buy an English cottage, and I will dwell ever by your side."

"God bless you for the words, Eva! God bless you! but *this* voyage must be performed. This voyage once accomplished, I promise to yield to your wishes—to give up my occupation on the sea. But must I now depart without you, Eva? Can no eloquence of mine persuade you to accompany me on this my last trip? Oh, Eva! for you, and with you, I would go to the ends of the earth."

"There is but one way of accomplishing this, and that is, to be married clandestinely—and that, Captain Montgomery, my sense of filial duty will never permit me to do. Prayers, entreaties, and supplications have heretofore proved unavailing with my father, and what can we hope to effect by petitioning him further?"

The young man mused. The wind played through the honeysuckle vine, lifting the blossoms as playfully as if two anxious hearts had not beat beneath them.

"You will not go, Eva, without the old man's consent?"
said the young man at last, lifting his thoughtful face to
the maiden's; "you will not go unless you can leave home,
escorted even to the sea shore by your sire, Bridget, and
all—unless they send heart blessings after you. Well,
I do not esteem you the less for this, but for you, and you
alone, will I sue again. I have been repulsed once, twice,
thrice already by your father, and my pride is wounded.
But love is, in this instance, stronger than pride. I will
ask for you again. If the old man consents, we will be
married, and away together—if not, long weary years of
separation must ensue. But it is best to bear in our
bosoms, hearts for any fate. Good night, Eva! I will see
the old man to-morrow, and try on him once more the
eloquence of affection."

The young man stooped to kiss the hand which he had
not yet relinquished, and then turned away, with long
strides across the grass-plat. Eva closed the window softly, and stole noiselessly to her pillow. Hope was whispering an improbable tale in her ear, but when did love
exist without hope?

Affection and tears are not without their power, even
upon aged and determined hearts. Col. Snow gave his
only, his darling Eva, at last into the guardianship of a
sea captain—an occupation of which he entertained the
most dreadful ideas, and saw her, five days after the interview recorded above, stowed away in the rich and beautiful cabins of the *Neptune*. Bridget followed with a dark
frown and a more ominous shake of the head than ever
her mistress to the ship, and hoped that Miss Eva would
have at least enough of the sea. She always had been
keeping every body in the house up at night to look at it;
and now she could *live* on it, she was sure that she ought
to be satisfied. But in spite of her cross way, she was not
without a great deal of affection for the child, whose way-
wardness she had tried from her infancy to control; and
so she parted from her with a gush of natural and bitter
tears.

There was indeed a great deal of romance in the young

bride's nature, and for awhile it was fully gratified. It was a pleasant thing to find herself the idol of the commander's heart—a pleasant thing to sail for days upon a glittering expanse of water, bounded only by the horizon —to watch the sea fowls that alighted panting among the rigging, after having breasted the waves and sported with the foam for miles. It was pleasant, touching upon the islands, and going on shore to pluck strange fruit, and to find herself surrounded by the natives; all this was romantic, and the heart of the English girl revelled in it. But there came, as her father foresaw, a fearful hour of trial. Huge black clouds spread themselves like a funeral pall over the sky, and the sea boiled like a red hot caldron. The *Neptune* at first, under the skilful management of her commander and crew, rode the waves like a thing of life, but not long. The sea grew wilder—the timbers groaned and labored through the surging brine— sails were riven in the blast—the masts were broken, and despair came into every heart and sat on every face.

In this fearful hour, Eva Montgomery came forth, determined to show the crew that she had courage worthy the wife of their faithful commander. Her step at first was steady, and her brow unblanched, but a sudden rolling sea coming up at that moment, she must have fallen into the ocean, had not the arm of her husband caught her as she fell.

"My poor, poor wife!" he said mournfully, "it is for me that you have encountered this. Alas! that my heart has been so wilful in its idolatry! I could perish bravely, but not by your side. O! would that we had heeded the advice of your father, and delayed our union! *You* then might have been spared. But now your fate, as well as mine, is inevitable. Cling closely to me, my love, and let us perish together. We are near some dangerous coast. I cannot make it out. I think, however, that it is Arabia. Our ship, already unmanageable, is drifting towards the rocks. When she strikes, all on board must perish."

That was a fearful hour of gloom and suspense which preceded the grounding of the *Neptune*. Eva clung

9

closely to her husband, but instead of sinking when the
vessel was indeed stranded, as he had foretold, a heavy
wave drifted them to the shore.   There they stood at last,
beneath high shelving rocks, with the sea raging like some
infuriated animal at their feet, while wild shrieks rose even
above the roaring of the waves from the drowning crew.
Now and then a pale form darted out for a moment, like
some spectre from the sea, and then sunk to be seen no
more forever.   Fearful, fearful are the perils of the sea!
Brave must be the hearts of those "who go down in
ships" upon the face of the treacherous deep!

At last, not a groan was heard; the black waters curled
and closed over every vestige of life two hours before belonging to the *Neptune*, save the two desolate beings, who
stood still, side by side, hand locked in hand, gazing with
strained eyes over the angry waters.

One feeling only animated their bosoms—gratitude, intense gratitude to God, for life—life, that most precious
boon in the gift of the Creator.   They knelt down upon
the sea-washed, foam-covered beach, and poured forth
from full hearts, thanksgiving and praise.

But their condition was a most desolate one.   Wet,
worn and hungry, they were cast empty handed upon a
foreign shore.   Huge craggy rocks loomed over their
heads, and it was uncertain whether a path would be
found, leading to their summits.   They however set themselves hopefully to work to discover some place accessible
to human feet, and after a long search, succeeded.   They
found, when they reached the main land above them however, that they were on a wide sandy plane, with no
appearance of vegetation—no sign of animal life or human
habitation around them.   They knew at once that they
were among the trackless deserts of Arabia, where the
heavens glow like fire—where the fierce Bedouin roams
lawless, and the dreadful simoon sweeps like the breath
of a furnace, withering every thing it touches; where the
gurgling of no silvery stream is ever heard, no palm tree
waves in dark luxuriance—not even the shadow of a great
rock " was to be found in this weary land."

What a place for Eva Montgomery. the petted darling
of an English family, the idol of many a heart, the delicate
floweret who had heretofore been visited only by soft
winds and gentle showers!

The heart of the strong and heretofore self-relying sea
captain now wept blood; for his own sake he was not
troubled, but how could he see the beautiful young creature, whom he had induced to leave England, withering
like some tender violet in the blast of a red-hot oven?
He knelt with clasped hands and prayed, as he had never
prayed before, that the God of Hagar would visit them in
this dreadful hour of need; and when the sun went down,
he took Eva to his heart, and laying down and heaping
the sand upon her for a covering, they slept.

For two days they roamed, without knowing whither
they went, through the dreary desert. The sun beat
upon their defenseless heads—the sand blistered their tender feet—thirst parched their lips, and hunger gnawed
like a vulture at their vitals.

The third night, they laid down, as both now earnestly
prayed, *to die.* They had not seen a human being since
they landed, and they knew that when human beings were
met with, they would be the Bedouins—those fierce wandering children of Ishmael, "whose hands," to quote the
truthful language of scripture, "are against every man,
and every man's hand against them." But they were
overtaken that night by a party of Arabs, who on their
fleet horses were ranging the sea coast in the hope of finding plunder of one kind or another. They were overtaken
and immediately secured as captives. What a dreary fate
now stretched out before them! They had no doubt but
that they should soon be sold into bondage, and separated
far from one another. This was the greatest trial of all. Eva
clung to her husband with shrieks of despair, and he sat
disconsolately among the ferocious band—who were disputing among themselves with wild gesticulations in regard to the possession of the captives—tearless, but wildly
clasping her to his heart.

It was at this juncture that the idea occurred to him

that he had somewhere seen an account of the existence of masonic fraternities among the Arabs. The thought came to him like a glance of light from Heaven. If one of the mystic brotherhood could be found now, he was safe; Eva was safe in the hands even of barbarians. He caught at this moment the eye of the chief, and gave a mystic sign. With what a thrill of wild delight did he receive an answering recognition! The Arab thus unexpectedly met with was an aged man, with a commanding brow. He waved his hand to his followers, in token of silence. The fierce combatants paused, and looked up at him, while with oriental dignity he spoke a few hurried words to them in Arabic, the import of which Captain Montgomery could not well make out. The effect produced, he soon saw, however, was a happy one. The clamor ceased entirely; they kindled a fire and set themselves busily to cooking some small pieces of meat—probably the flesh of some slaughtered camel. These they offered to their prisoners, and unpalatable as the repast may seem, it was partaken of with extreme relish by the sufferers. They gave them from goat skins, brackish water to drink, and then striking a tent, and spreading a blanket, the chief motioned to Captain Montgomery and Eva that they could go to repose.

With thankful and deeply grateful hearts they again laid themselves down.

They had not, however, rested long, before a tall figure darkened the door of their tent, and looking up, they saw by the flickering light of the fire which was not yet extinguished without, the noble and venerable form of the chief.

"White brother," he said in a subdued voice, and in broken English, "the children of the desert sleep, but they will not long. They have promised me that you shall not be carried into bondage—that you shall be given up to your consul and redeemed, but it will not do to trust the Bedouins. They promise sweet things, but the poison of falsehood dwels under their tongues. You are my brother, and TRUTH is now required of me. I will be *true to you,* though all my countrymen are false. Take the sister by the hand, arise and follow me."

Captain Montgomery sprang to his feet, and took Eva, like some wearied child, in his arms. With still, cautious steps, they passed the two rows of sleeping Arabs, who lay each on his blanket before the dying fire; at lenth they reached the spot where the party had tied their horses.

"Give the sister to me," said the chief. "My arm is strong—my horse is fleet. Give her to me—mount yonder animal, and follow."

While he spoke, he took Eva from the reluctant arm of Captain Montgomery, and sprang into the saddle. Before a word of remonstrance could be uttered, he was far away on the plain, flying as if on the wings of the wind, and all Captain Montgomery could do was to follow in his track.

This proved to have been his wisest course, for, true to his promise, the Arab chief led him, after a tiresome and perilous journey across the desert, to safety.

He delivered "the white brother and sister" to the English consul, who sent them back, after a few months spent in recruiting their exhausted physical powers, to England.

Thus triumphed TRUTH, even among the most treacherous people on the face of the globe—Truth taught by MASONRY to the ever fickle and proverbially treacherous Bedouin.

IV.—TEMPERANCE.

"I know no blessing but thy smile."

"IT's only a rosebud," said Kate Rice, as she turned with a bright blush from her mother's questioning glance; "it's only a rosebud that I am drying and pressing."

"I noticed the same flower, if I mistake not, in your hair, when it was fresh ; I afterwards saw that it had been transferred to your bosom, and now it is carefully pressed.

It is not usual for you to treasure trifles thus. Where did you obtain it ?"

"It was not bestowed upon me mamma—it was given, together with a beautiful bouquet, to sister Julia, when she was out yesterday. The bud attracted my attention, and so I culled and wore it. She had thrown the whole carelessly away; surely I can't be blamed for saving one tiny bud from her bouquet."

Mrs. Rice knew something of heart histories. She knew that it was not Kate's nature to treasure trifles with such care, and she felt convinced, from her youngest darling's blush and half-averted glance, that there was more connected with the little flower than she was willing to confess. She dropped her eyes however to her work, and forbore to question her daughter further, for she saw that her confusion had become even painful. But she determined to watch with jealous care the pale, black-eyed and beautiful girl before her, and unravel what now to her was a mystery, viz: who, and why she loved.

Kate finished tying a piece of pale-blue ribbon around the stem of the suspicious tea rosebud, and then hastily clasping the leaves of a souvenir, where she had deposited it, turned and left the room.

Mrs. Rice sewed on for an hour in silence. The clock upon the sitting room mantle ticked loudly—the canary in the porch stretched its wings in the sunshine, and sung merrily. But although Nature was bright and joyous without, there was a cloud of gloom upon the thoughtful brow of the mother. The neglected bouquet to which Kate had referred, laid upon the work-table near her, sending out a sickening perfume, such as clings to dying flowers. Mrs. Rice stretched out her hand, and touched the withering green leaves as cautiously as she would have done had she known that poison lay folded in each faded cup. "Poor, poor Kate," she cried. "The first bright, troubled, anxious dream of maidenhood I fear is upon you! Our kind Heavenly Father grant that if you love, it may be wisely, for woman, when she finds that she has made shipwreck of happiness *for life*, discovers a fearful truth. Happily wedded, my daughter will be a crown of glory to her husband. She will gladden his fireside with her cheerful spirit—she will call into exercise his admiration and love, by the guileless simplicity of her heart and the tenderness of her affections. The child who is so gentle and good, will be the ardent and devoted wife, if she meets with love and gentleness in return; but if she is wounded when she should be soothed, taunted when she should be caressed, trampled on when she should be sheltered, one of two things will be the result. She will either gather supernatural strength in the hour of trial, and rise firmly above adversity, or, grieved and heart broken, she will wither and die. Poor Kate! God grant that you love wisely, if love you must."

A half hour afterwards, a bright animated face looked in at the sitting-room door, and then entered. It belonged to a young lady, aged perhaps twenty years, but the levity of her manner, and the wild frolicsome light in her eyes, might have belonged to a girl of seventeen. She held a white dimity sun-bonnet heedlessly by one string, and walking carelessly across the floor, she threw herself into a seat by her mother's work-table.

"Julia, my love, how careless you are!" exclaimed Mrs. Rice in an annoyed tone. "You will crush your bonnet, and soil my work. One would really suppose you to be the youngest child in the house, to watch your school-girl ways. You should be dignified, like a true and genteel young lady. Even Kate is the soberest of the two, and she, at times, is wild enough in all conscience. These flowers bear evidence of what I am saying. You have thrown the bouquet, beautiful as it is, away without a thought, while Kate, I dare say, would have preserved it."

"I dare say she would! I dare say she would!" cried Julia, in a tone full of glee, "but I do not prize them much." As she spoke she reached out her hand, and lifted the withered bunch from the table.

"Where did you obtain them that you value them so lightly?" said Mrs. Rice, in an assumed tone, as careless as her child's; "who gave you the flowers?"

"Frank Hall. He plucked them for me with his own hand from Mrs. Hall's garden. One beautiful tea rose-bud was among them, but I do not see it now," she continued, thoughtfully scanning the cluster, "where can it be? Have you seen it, mamma?"

"As you place so light an estimate upon the flowers, I should not think that you would mourn the absence of one tiny bud. Why did you notice it so particularly?"

"Because," said Julia in the same thoughtful tone, "I marvelled much that Frank Hall should have given so significant a thing to *me*. Had he sent it to Kate, I should not have wondered. But he is not partial to me. If he seeks my side, it is, I fancy, in order to learn something of her. The bud should have been sent *by* me, not given *to* me;" so saying she tossed the flowers away.

Mrs. Rice did not reply, and the conversation was dropped. But enough had been said, enough discovered, to make the mother anxious for the happiness of her child. Frank Hall was the son of wealthy parents; not an ungratified want had ever shaded his brow. He had a fine person, a good heart, and fascinating manners, but there was a stain upon his character. *He loved the wine-cup.*

It is a fearful thing for a young man to permit himself to be gradually yet completely manacled by that fiend, *Intemperance.* How entirely does he destroy his victim! He roots out the best affections from the heart, dethrones reason, and enervates the physical powers; he defaces what was originally created in the image of God, until few traces of the Divinity are left. Parent! you whose eye is carelessly scanning the printed page, teach your child to shun, as he would the bright colors of the basilisk, "the wine when it is red—when it giveth its color in the cup," for in its depths swims "the never dying worm." Mother! shield your daughter from the approach of the young man, however high his station in life, however bright and brilliant the talents with which God has endowed him, however amiable his character *seems*, whose habits are convivial, who stays long in the bar-room, and seeks the assembly flushed with wine—ready to sing the song sparkling with wit—to laugh and jest at things sacred and divine. Shield your daughter from his approach, for if he fascinates, it will only be to destroy—if he wins her heart, and gains her hand, it will be to trample perchance upon the most sacred of vows, and crush hope and happiness from her young life. A drunkard's wife! What a picture those three words bring up to mind! The tear-dimmed eye—the cheek withering before old age begins—the glance soliciting pity—the languid step—the dreary cabin—the cheerless hearth—and infancy, pale, wan, and starving—starving for food, starving for that which is even sweeter than bread to the heart of an affectionate child: the love of a tender and noble father!

Mrs. Rice realized all this, and she mentally resolved that her bright-eyed Kate should never be the victim of the inebriate. But the affections once entangled, are not so easily under the control of parents and guardians as they may first imagine.

Frank Hall devised numerous ways and means to enjoy the society of Kate Rice, and that too, even under the vigilant eye of her mother. No moonlit walks were taken, during which lovers so often exchange their vows, but he came in often and sat of an evening; he met Kate at the social party, and even exchanged a glance with her at the church door, as she passed in and glided up the aisle to her seat.

It was nearly two years after the rosebud had been so carefully pressed and preserved, when Mrs. Rice was aroused by a well-known step on the threshold, and looking up, she saw Frank Hall entering the parlor. She arose to receive him coldly but civily. He approached her cordially, and extended his hand—his eye was sparkling with hope—his cheek was flushed with excitement.

"I am glad, Mrs. Rice, to find you alone," he said, dropping into a chair that had been placed for him. "I wish for a half-hour's private conversation with you. I love your daughter Kate, and now solicit from you her hand in marriage. With my family you are acquainted; of my hopes and prospects you are not ignorant. May I hope to be accepted as the suitor and the husband of your daughter?"

Mrs. Rice glanced up into the beautiful, animated, soul-lit, hopeful face above her, and the cold, repelling sentence that she had been forming in her mind, by means of which to convey to him the truth that there was in this instance no ground to hope for her approval, died upon her lips. "How fair he is!" she thought, "how noble he seems! No wonder that the heart of my child is enthralled. The words that I speak now will make him my friend or for-ever my enemy. I may wound his pride, crush his hopes, —for Kate I know could never be persuaded to wed him without my consent—and send him from me into deeper inebriety than he has yet plunged. Perhaps it is in my power to save him from the gulf that yawns beneath his feet, and this may be the hour—the moment! O! that I were well enlightened as to the ways and means of accom-plishing this. If I direct him to the Sons of Temperance, and intimate that he must join this Order before my daugh-ter can be his, his pride will take the alarm; self-love once wounded, often leads to deeper self-abasement. I will try another expedient; a new plan has occurred to me, by which this stain on Frank's character may be removed."

"Kate is young for a bride," said the matron, evasively, "and I have heard her express no very decided preference for any of her acquaintance. However, you doubtless have received sufficient encouragement from her to justify you in this step. I shall not forbid your suit. Your family I know to be honorable—your position in society respect-able; but I am a jealous mother, and ask the highest mea-sure of earthly happiness for my children. I ask a boon of you. Will you join the Masons, and live up to all of the cardinal virtues? The man who exhibits Brotherly Love, Relief, Truth, Temperance, Fortitude, Prudence, and Justice in his daily life, will be worthy of the hand of my child. Will you join the Masons, and give me a year to decide the question you have asked?"

The countenance of the young man fell. "The test is too severe a one," he said, "the time is too long."

"Not if you love my child as she is worthy of being loved," said Mrs. Rice firmly. "Upon no other conditions can my consent be obtained."

"Very well, madam, your request shall be complied with. I should look upon greater sacrifices than any that this step can involve, as light for the sake of your child; I will join the lodge to-night, or at least take a step towards doing so, and I challenge, from this hour, the most vigilant scrutiny of my conduct. I will be good, kind, true —no intoxicating potion shall pass my lips or sparkle in my hand. I will be brave, prudent, just. I will be an ornament to my race—a son for whose virtues you need never blush. I said just now that the time is too long. I take back the words; try me seven years if you will. I would serve for Kate as Jacob served for Rachel, for I love her with a passion no less strong and true."

Tears sprang into Mrs. Rice's eyes as she gave him her hand. "Heaven prosper you, my friend. I would not impose an unmerciful test on your character. I only ask a probable life of enjoyment for Kate. Adieu. Let us see a good deal of you, and remember that I feel the interest of a mother."

Frank pressed the extended hand, and hastened away. His hopes were not as buoyant as when he first entered, but they were far from being annihilated. In the ardor of his affection he rejoiced that a way had been opened, by means of which he could prove to Kate the sincerity and depth of his affection for her; and before the expiration of the day, he held in his hand a petition for admission into the ancient and honorable fraternity of Masonry.

He was admitted. The brotherhood, some of whom understood the singular circumstances leading to his joining them, clustered around him with encouraging smiles, and above all, they guarded him most vigilantly from every temptation to INTEMPERANCE. Mrs. Rice and Kate both smiled approval, from week to week, upon his course, and although an alcoholic appetite is not eradicated in a day, still it can in time be uprooted. Frank Hall came out *victorious over his besetting sin*, and led his blushing bride to the altar.

To the close of a long life, he exhibited the cardinal virtues of Masonry, and brightest among them stood, in his estimation, TEMPERANCE.

"I trembled," said he in after years to Mrs. Rice, when referring to this subject, "upon the brink of an awful precipice, but love and Masonry saved me. Had you frowned —had Kate turned away from me—had no fraternity of encouragers clustered around, and aided me until habits of sobriety became fixed in my character, I must have fallen."

Mrs. Rice turned away with a bright tear-drop glistening in her eye, and murmured, "He who winneth souls is wise!" Yea, he who saves his fellow-man through any means from the gloomy life of the inebriate, may well be written "wise" and philanthropic above all others.

V.—FORTITUDE.

"Brave spirits are a balsam to themselves;
There is a nobleness of mind, that heals
Wounds beyond salves."—*Cartwright.*

THERE was not a prettier house on King street than the one belonging to the Iversons. Heavy carpets covered all the floors; brilliant mirrors flashed in the sunlight and lamplight; richly embroidered curtains swayed to and fro, as the breeze stole in through the half-open casements of a summer evening. Every body said that the Iversons were rich—"rich as Jews." Young men as they paced over the pavement in front of the dwelling, glanced up at the richly carved door with its silver plate and knob, and wondered if they ever should be as wealthy as Iverson the broker. Some belonging to the higher class, who had been admitted within, remembered the ease and luxury that pervaded the whole household, and sighed to think that long years might elapse before they should be equally rich. They remembered that Mr. Iverson had but one child—the beautiful and proud Irene, and they wondered who would be fortunate enough to win her hand in marriage, for she had had many suitors, and rejected them all. Irene Iverson *was* beautiful, but they wronged her when they called her proud. True, she had discarded many lovers, but it was not because they lacked piles of gold as high as her father's. Like all heiresses, she was obliged to see that many of them prized her wealth more than they did her person, her mind and her virtues, and she had firmly determined to accept of no gold-bought love; she wanted the homage of an honest heart, or none at all. It was this fear and this determination that caused her so often to wear, in the presence of those who offered her adulation, the slightly curled lip, the highly arched neck, and the haughty bearing of one formed to rule. Men called her proud. They could not see the inner depths of a heart that glowed with generous and noble influences—a heart that was capable of loving intensely passionately, or of suffering keenly.

Mrs. Iverson was an invalid, and had been such for weary years. She stayed for the most part of her time shut up in her bedroom, surrounded by the drugs and vials usually to be found in the sick chamber. Her voice was weak and plaintive. For her husband and daughter, she entertained a sincere affection, but she saw no necessity of ever arousing herself from the stupor into which wealth and disease had combined to throw her, for the purpose of either ministering to or sharing in their enjoyments.

It was a dreary autumn day. The wind howled in sudden gusts through the old elms in the garden, and shook the high stained windows of the rich broker's parlor. Irene had been in her mother's room, but seing at last that she had fallen into a gentle slumber, and that the nurse was attentively watching her wants, she stole with a light step into the parlor, and taking a book into her hands, she threw herself down carelessly upon the sofa, and began listlessly to turn the pages.

"How high the wind is!" she said at length to Feme, the servant, who was dusting the parlor furniture, and kindling a fire in the grate. She closed her book and sat upright. A long, deep blast swept the pavement below them, and died mournfully away among the trees. "Feme, has father come in?" she continued, while an expression of concern came over her features, "it is nearly dinner time, is it not?"

"No, Miss Irene, he has'nt come in. Massa John Crayton said that he saw him going down towards the wharf two hours ago, with his fishing tackle. Dinner has been ready this half-hour, and that's the reason Dinah, the cook, asked Massa John about it. Massa Iverson hate cold dinner, you know, and Dinah says she *does* wish he would'nt stay out so late."

"I heard something about a new fishing boat that he is having rigged," said Irene, throwing herself back; "the *Neptune*, I think, is the name of it, but surely he has not ventured out in her on such a wild day as this. I can hear the dashing of the waves on the beach even here. Tell Dinah to take good care to keep the dinner warm, for it surely will not be long before he comes. He has not gone out on the ocean, I am certain of that. Fetch me my shawl—leave the grate open, so that the fire may look more cheerful, and if any one calls, do not admit them without first arousing me. I will read awhile."

The servant obeyed the commands of her mistress, and then softly closing the parlor door, glided into the kitchen, to give her orders to the expectant and impatient cook.

"Miss Irene says that Massa Iverson has not gone on to the water, if Massa Crayton *did* see him, and that you must keep the dinner as hot as you can until he comes."

"It is'nt in my power to keep it hot without drying and burning it into a crisp," said the negro. "I do wonder massa don't come, but it is'nt often he makes one wait."

"No, no, Dinah, and dats the reason why I think you ought to take dis time more patiently. True, massa scold if the dinner is'nt good, but he generally is here in good time to eat it. I think I hear the front-door opening now."

Feme ran to see if her ears had deceived her. They

doubtless had, for there was the tightly closed door, and no sign of life about the house, save the clerks, who with hasty feet were returning through the wind, cold and dusty, from dinner to their respective stations; and the ringing sound of their heels upon the pavement arose and then died away in the distance down the street.

Meanwhile, Irene fastened her eyes upon the volume before her, but the page was not interesting enough to enchain her thoughts. Between the sudden gusts of wind, nothing was to be heard in the parlor but the ticking of a small clock on the mantle-piece, and the falling of the coal through the grate. She turned over, closed her eyes, and fell into a dreamy disturbed slumber. She thought she stood upon the brink of a fearful precipice. Beneath her feet the water leaped madly from crag to crag; and every now and then, rising from the boiling eddies, the shadow of her father seemed to stretch towards her an imploring hand. She struggled downward, hoping to rescue him, until she found herself to be sinking and going down, down its unfathomable depths. Then the scene changed. She fancied herself the centre figure in a brilliantly lighted ball-room. Around her came obsequious admirers, but the same wan face that had looked up so entreating to her from the boiling flood, now glided like a spectre between her and them, and with shadowy finger seemed beckoning her away. The crowd saw the image of her father, too, and shrank back in alarm at the apparition. One only lingered by her side, confronting the shadow. It was Walter Wortley—the least wealthy, the least presuming, and yet the most dearly beloved of all her suitors. She turned to thank him for not deserting her, when the silvery chiming of the time-piece awoke her. She had slept three hours, and the hands of the clock pointed to six. She arose hastily. The fire had burned down in the grate, and in spite of the shawl, she felt chilly and uncomfortable. The wind was moaning as hoarsely as ever—the sky was lowering, and a cold drizzling rain had begun to drop upon the pavement. She rang the bell hastily, and Feme answered it.

"Has your master been in?" she inquired impatiently, "has he been to dinner?"

"No, massa not been here, and the dinner clean spoiled now. None of it fit to offer to anybody."

"Why have you not awakened me before?" said Irene.

"You told me not to disturb you unless sombody called, and nobody been here, although I thought once that I heard Massa Iverson at the door. What will you have now, Miss Irene? Will you try the dinner?"

"No, no," said the broker's daughter impatiently. "Go and tell your mistress that it is six o'clock, and your master has not been at home for dinner. Such a thing has never occurred before, since my recollection, for my father is punctual to a minute, and never dines out. No; stop Feme, I'm afraid that you will alarm her needlessly, I'll go myself."

Irene entered the sick room where her mother sat propped up by pillows, with an attendant beside her mixing something in a phial. "Mamma, it is quite six," she began, "and papa has not been home for dinner. It is singular; he never stays out, you know."

Mrs. Iverson cast a startled look into her daughter's face. "Have you not heard anything from him during the day, Irene?" she inquired.

"Nothing; only young Mr. Crayton told one of the servants that he saw him going towards the wharf, prepared for a fishing expedition. But he certainly has not ventured on the water in such a wild wind as this."

"No, no," said the invalid, dropping her spoon and looking through the window at the murky sky. "Mr. Iverson surely has not been rash enough to try his new boat to-day. Feme, send Ned to me; perhaps he knows something of his master."

The negro summoned declared his entire ignorance of the broker's movements. He was dispatched in search of him, but when daylight had deepened into darkness, he came home, saying that he could hear no tidings of Mr. Iverson, only that he had been seen that morning going, as young Crayton had stated, followed by Bob, his mulatto waiting-boy, towards the sea-shore. The anxiety of his family was only increased by such news as this, and when day followed day, and every search for the broker had proved fruitless, both on the sea and on the land, uncertainty and dread deepened into despair. The new boat *Neptune* was missing, and it was supposed by all that he had ventured out in it, and been swallowed up in the sea. Irene was almost wild with grief. She had been an only and idolized child, and this was the first cloud of sorrow that had ever darkened the horizon of her life. Dense, heavy, and portentous it indeed was, and no wonder the bereaved girl bowed her head and wept in an uncontrolable fit of agony.

There are times in the life of every man of business, when sagacity, patience, prudence, and the personal supervision of the master are needed, in order to avert heavy losses, and prevent entanglements and perhaps ruin. It was at such a crisis in his affairs, that Mr. Iverson, the man reputed to be worth his "tens of thousands," was taken from his family. He had but recently entered into some speculations, heavy and unfortunate, but had he been spared, he doubtless, with his keen, shrewd, money-making faculties, would have worked his way onward, and emerged at last again into the sunshine of prosperity, without his family or friends once suspecting that the shadow of a cloud had lowered upon him. But he was, as we have before said, torn suddenly from the scene of his daily toils, just at this exigency, and men less shrewd, less careful, less interested, sat down at his desk to reckon his losses and gains, and settle up his estate. The result was, that it was pronounced insolvent. Little or nothing, it was said, could be saved from the wreck of his affairs.

Irene sat despondingly among the rich furniture, that she felt and knew was no longer theirs. It seemed to her that every piece was endeared to her by some old association. The clock had counted off the merry hours of her childhood—the piano had been touched by her small taper fingers, when she sat alone at twilight, or for the amuse-

10

ment of her father when he had returned weary from his business, or at the request of—of—*one* who had stood beside her and turned the music, and now and then blended his manly tones with her silvery voice. Others, prouder, richer, had stood there too, and sung, but in that hour she remembered only him, and she wondered if, now that many others were deserting her, he would go away too. Oh, she felt that she could leave that proud mansion without a sigh, with its costly furniture—that she could move into an humble cottage with her invalid mother, and still be happy, cheerful, contented, if but assured of his remembrance, his love. The scene of her dream came back to her, and the thought struck her pleasantly, that although in that all others had deserted her, Walter Wortly had stood by her side, and comforted what to her seemed more grim and dread than poverty. She wondered if it would indeed prove true, that he would still remain. She was thinking of this when she heard a footstep behind her. She started, expecting to see a servant, or some hungry creditor, perhaps, for the purpose of inspecting the furniture, so soon to be sold, but she sunk down again when she saw that Walter Wortley had entered the room.

"I learned from the servants below, that you were here, Miss Iverson," he said, coming forward, "and ventured to come up unannounced; I heard that you denied yourself to most persons who sought your society, and I feared that such might be my fate, and in my present frame of mind I could not well brook an expulsion from your presence. You will forgive the intrusion, I hope."

Irene bowed her head and motioned him to be seated; she dared not trust her voice to reply.

"You should not so sedulously exclude yourself from the presence of those who seek you," he continued in a tone of expostulation. "Because a great and overwhelming calamity has overtaken you, you should not hide yourself, and nurse your grief in solitude."

"Few care for my society *now*," said Irene, choking down a sob; "the bird of paradise ceases to be an object of admiration when it is stripped of its plumage."

"True, true," said Wortley mournfully, taking her hand, "and yet to one heart, Irene Iverson in affliction is dearer than Irene Iverson in prosperity. I have not worshipped the bird for her plumage. She will sing sweeter for me than before, now that the hot needle has been through her eyes. Irene Iverson, the heiress, I dare not with my humble fortune woo—Irene Iverson, in affliction, may not spurn me from her feet, when I tell her that I love her, and would aid her in her distress."

The girl did not move. She durst not, lest she might dispel the sweet illusion into which she almost feared she had fallen.

*　　*　　*　　*　　*　　*　　*　　*

Two years had nearly passed away since the strange disappearance of Mr. Iverson, and no note of tidings had reached his family in regard to what had become of him. His beautiful mansion had passed into other hands—his costly furniture had gone to deck other mansions, and his invalid wife and beautiful daughter toiled in an humble yet pretty rural cottage, which Wortley had hired not far from the city. Irene's cheek was healthier now than in the days of her proudest prosperity—her eye was brighter, and her laugh was as musical as the song of a bird. True, she labored, but it was with and for those she loved; and they are wrong who suppose that in idleness there is bliss. She was a happy wife, and a proud mother, and Wortley as he sat and looked upon her girlish form as it glided about the cottage or caressed his son, almost blessed the reverse of fortune which emboldened him to ask for a hand to which he otherwise never would have aspired. Mrs. Iverson's health, moreover, seemed growing firmer—the exercise and air of the country agreed with her, and instead of staying cooped up in her room from morning till night, as formerly, she now came out to enjoy the society of her children, and rejoice at the graces of her first grandchild.

Such was the condition of the little family, when one night they were aroused by the noise of wheels on the gravelled path leading to their residence. Supposing that some friends were probably passing that way for the purpose of giving them a call, they went out into the little yard in front of the house to receive them and usher them into the mansion. The carriage proved to be a covered vehicle containing two men. In the dim, uncertain light which the moon was casting on the earth, it could not be easily ascertained who their guests might be. The carriage stopped at the gate, and as its last occupant was alighting, Mrs. Iverson gave a short scream and swooned. Irene gazed with eager eyes. Could she believe it? Was it not a fantasy of the imagination, or had the long mourned, long absent parent arrived at home once more? The last suggestion proved correct. The broker, Iverson, stepped through the gate, and clasped his wife and daughter to his heart.

It was, as will be readily supposed, a long time before our group of friends were sufficiently composed to listen to explanations, and ask questions of one another. But in after time, the broker gave the following account of his adventures :

"The morning on which I left King street, two years ago," said he, " was, as you will remember, dark and gusty; but I had promised myself to make a trial with my new boat, and you know it is my nature to be daring and adventurous when only myself is concerned. I told Bob to arrange my fishing tackle and follow me to the sea-side. He did so, as you have learned. The sea was rolling in heavy swells, but the *Neptune* was new and strongly built, and I imagined would ride them like a bird. At any rate, I thought we would unloose her and try it. We did so, myself and Bob embarking. But I soon found I was playing a desperate game. The wind grew higher, the sweep of the waves more fearful; their sullen roar, as I battled my way through foam and dashing spray, seemed like the groaning of the dead in its terrific depths. We tried in vain to come again to land ; each moment carried us further into the ocean, and soon I saw that our fate was inevitable ; we must either perish or be picked up by some vessel.

The third day, when hunger had gnawed like a vulture on our vitals, when our lips were parched for want of water, and our brains were dizzy from the effect of the sun's rays upon our unprotected heads, a vessel bound to China espied and picked us up. My thankfulness at this rescue is only known to God. Poor Bob! he was nearly crazy and famished, and in two days after entering the Chinaman, died of a fever. But imagine, if you can, my distress when I thought of my family at home; when I remembered my dear wife and my darling daughter. I knew that the impression would go forth that I was dead, and I feared that strangers in settling my estate at that crisis in my business, would wreck all, and leave you both penniless. Long, weary months I knew must pass before I could be restored to you. I could neither eat nor sleep. At this juncture in my affairs, it became known on ship-board that I was a Mason. The news spread from stem to stern, and brave, manly hearts came up to listen to my woes, and aid me in devising ways and means of returning to you. They spoke manly words of comfort, such words as cheer us when they are poured forth from brave hearts, and exhorted me to the practice of one of the greatest of our Masonic virtues, viz: "*Fortitude.*" They said that the wife and daughter of a Mason would not be left to want for the necessaries of life, and that Masons would expedite my return to you to the extent of their power. This was true. Everywhere the heart of the Mason beats with love and good-will towards his brother; it matters not on what soil you may be cast.— The heart of the Chinese glows as ardently as any other for the welfare of his brother of the mystic tie; and when at last I stood on that far distant shore, I found that moneyless, raimentless, unknown as I was, I was not uncared for. I was hungry, and they fed me; I was thirsty, and they gave me drink; I was naked, and they clothed me; I was in distress and anguish of spirit, and they taught me Fortitude. They procured for me at last a passage on board a ship bound for America, and here I stand again, preserved through Masonry, in the midst of my precious family."

The joy of all at this unexpected restoration of Mr. Iverson cannot be told. Is there nothing akin to the blessed doctrines of the Divine Redeemer, in the practice of masonic brethren, who thus "bind up with Samaritan kindness each other's wounds, pouring in oil and wine?"

VI.—PRUDENCE.

Prudence protects and guides us ; wit betrays ;
A splendid source of ills, ten thousand ways.—*Young.*

MAT BROOKS was as wild a school girl as ever was born. One day in summer she came dancing into my room, with her hair half down, and her blue eyes sparkling in glee.

"I'm going to do it," she cried, sinking breathlessly down by my table. "I'm *bound* to do it, and such fun as I will have."

"What new mischief, Mat?" I said, composedly taking up my pen-knife and sharpening my pen, "what is brewing now? Have you stuck the president's chair full of burrs, or put a mouse into Miss Larabee's desk, or 'raised Cain' generally up at the school-room, overturning desks and tables, and filling the water-bucket full of sand? Some wild exploit, I'll warrant. Be explicit, and explain matters quickly, for I'm in a hurry."

"No, I haven't done a thing yet," she said, "but I'm going to. Yet the Faculty needn't be apprehensive; I've tormented them enough lately. I'm on a new track altogether; I am bound to do something this time that will make my name

'One of the few—the immortal ones
Not born to die.'

I've been studying it for a week."

"A very long time," I said, "for you to study about *anything*, but a very brief period in which to concoct a plan for immortality. Doubtless many aspirants after fame and glory, who entertain the vulgar idea that years of thought are requisite for the accomplishment of master-pieces worthy of any renown, will be gratified to hear of this cross-cut to immortality. Please proceed."

"Oh fy!" she cried, starting up, as if already tired of her posture, "can't you guess what I'm going to do? It seems to me that any body with any wit could guess."

"I must acknowledge then that I haven't any wit."

"Well," she continued, "you know Joe Denham—he boards at aunt Louisa's." I nodded, for I had an indistinct recollection of a young man to whom I had been intro-duced in Mrs. Griffin's parlors a few evenings before, as Mr. Denham. He was a tall, dark, pleasant-looking youth, with a mass of curly hair hanging over by no means an unintellectual brow. I had heard that he was a very stu-dious young lawyer. Mat Brooks had moreover chatted to me a thousand times, I verily believe, about Joe Denham. Many a joke had she played off upon him—jokes for which she acknowledged she always sooner or later got richly paid.

"Well, Joe and I have been sworn enemies, you know, ever since Christmas," she continued.

"I don't know any such thing," I said. "Pray how has that happened?"

"Well, I can't stop to tell you," she said, "but it was a real blow up, and all about a philopena. But we've made up and *shuck* hands, as aunt Molly says, over the diffi-culty."

"To be sure," I said, "it is not supposable that two such warm friends would remain enemies for life."

Mat looked at me quizzically for a moment, and then dropped her blue eye. The corners of her mouth were drawn back, until it seemed to me that the dimples went through both cheeks, and met, maybe, in the mouth, and a crimson flush stole to the roots of her hair. She stood for an instant, and curled the corners of her handkerchief between the thumb and fore-finger of her left hand.

"We've made up at last," she continued, without ap-pearing to heed my last remark, "and Joe's going to join, through my influence, the FREEMASONS."

"The *Freemasons!*" I repeated in astonishment. "Pray what do *you* care whether he joins the Freemasons or not? I see no fun in that."

"Don't you?" she cried, her blue eyes twinkling with merriment. "Don't you see what I'm after? I mean to do that which women can't do, or at any rate never have done—*find out the secret*, and Joe's got to tell it to me."

"If he will," I added.

"O! I know that I can wheedle him out of it in some way," she said in a self-confident tone. "I'll coax, I'll flatter, I'll say all manner of sweet words to him, and when I find it out, I mean to proclaim it to the world—write a pamphlet, and explain the whole mystery, and by so doing, make myself famous and immortal."

"A very Delilah!" I exclaimed, "but I defy you to do it; the idea is chimerical. Why should Joe Denham tell you, what husbands will not tell their wives?"

"The women don't know how to manage the men; that's the reason they can't find it out. If I had a husband, I could contrive some way to make him tell me, I know," said Mat, and she drew herself up with the air of a queen.

I laughed. "You forget," I said, "PRUDENCE is one of the cardinal virtues of Masonry. When Joe Denham reveals to you a masonic secret, I will take a trip to the moon in an air-balloon. How do you propose to make him do it? You say you have been studying it for a week. You certainly must have some definite plan."

The dimples again sunk into her cheeks—the blush overspread her face.

"O! I know," I continued, "you expect to marry him, and make him confess afterwards."

"No," said she, "that is no plan at all. Joe Denham loves me. I know he does—cross and crabbed as he has been seeming since Christmas. He loves me, and will ask me to marry him by and by, when I'm through college. But I won't—I declare I won't, if his heart breaks square in two, until he tells me that secret. I will tell him—no secret, no wife."

"He will go and marry somebody else."

"We shall see," said she, tossing back her hair, and re-tying her black silk apron. "That secret I'm bound to have, and Joe Denham, before three years have passed away, shall tell it to me. Remember my words," and out she danced as quickly as she danced into my room.

For months after this conversation, Mat Brooks, I verily believe, was engrossed with this one idea, and perhaps ex-pectation. Whether she *really* expected to accomplish it, I cannot tell, but she always spoke as if she did. I fre-quently saw her and Mr. Denham together, and from his appearance, I judged that if he ever told the masonic secret to *anybody*, very likely it would be to her.

Autumn succeeded summer, winter came with its frosty breath, and then smiling spring returned again, with her buds and flowers.

I lay on the lounge towards sunset one day, with a book in my hand. I was musing upon the subject of indirect influences. "No mortal," I said to myself mentally, "knows the extent of these influences. Live where or how we may, we must somewhere touch threads in the web-work of humanity. Each individual is a sun, from which there radiates, in every direction, influences unknown often-times, even to themselves. It is a fearful thing to live, because we cannot live *to* or *for* ourselves. If we sink, we must drag others down with us."

I was interrupted by the entrance of some one. I looked up, and Mat Brooks stood beside me.

"It's just as I told you," she said, "months ago."

"*What* is just as you told me, Mat?"

"Why Joe Denham loves me, and has told me so."

"And you replied—no secret told, no wife!" I said laughing. "That was to be your response, I believe. Was it not?"

"I did, and it accomplished what I meant it should. He has promised to tell me the secret to-morrow, and then I promised to marry him." .

"Indeed!" said I, still laughing at the ridiculous idea of such a wise compromise; "but I suppose that he has laid

11

you under the restrictions imposed upon all secret tellers
—you are not to tell anybody. Isn't it so?"

"No, he says I may tell the world if I want to—yea
more, publish my pamphlet. Will you help me write it?"

"Perhaps so," I said, "but we will wait and see what
this mighty secret is. He will tell you to-morrow, you
say."

"Yes, we are going to walk, and while we are out, he
has promised to tell me all about it."

I acknowledge that I waited for Mat, the next evening,
with some degree of impatience. I wanted to see how
Denham would get out of his promise—satisfy her, and
still be true to Prudence and Truth. I did not wait long.
She came in before sunset, and throwing herself down in
the rocking chair, commenced with a nervous twitch un-
tying her bonnet-strings. Her face was flushed, as if by a
long and fast walk.

I untied her bonnet, and took her shawl from her hand.

"You come back wiser than you went, I suppose," said
I, coming towards her again, and sitting down on a cricket
at her feet. "What is the long-talked of secret, Mat?
Now for a revelation of it to the world!"

She laid her hand softly upon my arm, and looked with
her blue eye into my face. There was a softened expression
in it, preceded, if I mistake not, by tears. "I have found
out the secret," she said, "and Oh! what a secret it is. It
is to *do good with the left hand without letting the right
know it*. I have been to-day where I have seen the
wretched relieved—where I have found the orphan supported and educated—educated to be an honorable member of the most respectable portion of humanity. The
secret of Masonry consists in living together, as Christ and
God like to have men live—in one vast brotherhood, where
peace and love prevail; where the strong, instead of
trampling upon the weak, reach forth a supporting hand—
where *might* is not always recognized as *right*. Is not this
a glorious secret. Will you write my pamphlet, and publish it to the world?"

I promised to aid her, and the great Public must accept

of this meagre sketch, as the fulfilment in part of that promise. In spite of the locked doors, and darkened windows, and close mouths of those mystical creatures called Masons, you and I have, gentle reader, found out the secret. PRUDENCE is a great thing, but the Masons are not prudent enough to fool the world. Their good deeds *will* creep out to the light—the prying, inquisitive right hand *will find out what the left one has been about.* They had better look to this matter in their lodges.

VII.—JUSTICE.

Man is unjust, but God is just, and finally Justice triumphs
Longfellow.

IT had been raining for the last three days. The streets were flooded with water, the walls of the houses looked dark and soaked, the sky was murky, and now and then a cotton umbrella passed up and down the street, covering a snugly-clad gentleman, or shielding from the drizzling rain some poor woman who was obliged to go to market, and who picked her way thither, basket on arm, with a rueful face and uplifted skirts. The earth did not look as if a streak of sunshine had ever visited it—faces did not look as though a gleam of gladness had ever dwelt thereon.

In a small back room, at the west end of the city, an old man sat beside a table drawn up before a dull coal fire. This person was short and stout—his dress was old-fashioned in the extreme—his large head was nearly bald, and through a pair of ancient-looking spectacles he peered in among a mass of musty papers, with which the table was loaded. He was evidently in search of some important document; it might be a deed to a valuable estate—perhaps it was a stolen will.

Once he got up and stirred the coal in the grate, and held his hands over it, as though trying to warm them, but evidently he was in a brown study and unconscious of his acts—his thoughts were away, away, as they were bu-

ried up among the papers on the table. He did not know
whether his hands were hot or cold—he held them there
because he was puzzled and perplexed, and did not know
what else to do with them. Finally he rested his elbows
upon his knees, and ran his hands over the spot where his
hair should have grown. What was the matter with old
Mr. Dillingham?

"I say Johnce," said he at length, arising and going towards the front room, where a mulatto-boy was idly watching the rain-drops as they streamed down the window-
panes, "bring me my surtout and umbrella, and don't forget my over-shoes either, for I am going out. If anybody
calls, which is not likely upon this wet day, say to them
that I am at Henry Davenport's law office, No. 16 Bleecker's
Row. Don't let the fire go out, and if it holds up a little,
you can take the candles around to Madam Hodgekiss, as
I directed; but don't be all day about it, for there will be
nobody to mind the shop in your absence," and so saying,
the old man gathered up his papers, tied them carefully
into a bundle, put them into his breast-pocket, drew on his
overcoat, took his hat and umbrella, and stumbled out into
the rain.

"I wonder what in the name of sense has taken massa
out to day!" said Johnce, soliloquising; "his rheumatics
will get wus as sure as he's bern, and then I shall have to
be up with him o' nights, rubbing with ninement like
sixty. It's not so mighty agreeable gitten up o' nights,
'specially on sich business—I'll be shot if it is," and so saying Johnce piled on some more coal, and proceeded to as-
sort Madam Hodgekiss's candles according to orders. But
conjecture, it seemed, was busy in his brain, and he kept
on muttering to himself, "I wonder what, in the name of
nature, Massa Dillingham's going to do with those old
papers what I stumbled on, hid away up stairs in that old
box yesterday, and which I come mighty nigh using to
kindle the fire with? He acts mighty cur'us over them
anyhow. Reading and writing, and figuring among them
all day, without once noticing what I was about—it isn't
his like to do that way, for Massa Dillingham is mighty

tentive to business for common. But seems like he don't
know *what* he is 'bout to-day, nohow. I had to ax him
twice, should I draw more molasses for Ike Baugh, Mr.
Baugh's black man, and seem like he didn't know at last
whether I said ile or lasses. Whew! something strange
turning up, that's certain. Maybe it's about that little
white gal, what lives next door with old Mr. Spriggins,
and looks so pale and thin like. It's my 'pinion that they
treats that gal wus nor any nigger slave. I've seen old
Mrs. Spriggins driving her out arter water, and making
her tote big bucketsfull on her little head, and then her
clothes are not what a white gal's should be; that's my
solemn 'pinion; and I've heard Massa Dillingham saying,
when they were abusing her so loud that we could hear
her shrieking, like she would go into spasms, that something ort to be done about it. He said something about
her daddy's being a Mason, but I don't see what building
chimneys has to do in the matter any how;" and Johnce
scratched his head over this puzzling idea, and then started
with his candles.

Old Mr. Dillingham walked with a firm and steady step
until he reached Bleecker's Row. He there paused, opened
a green door, and found himself in the small and yet well
furnished apartment of Henry Davenport, a young attor-
ney of more than ordinary promise, who had just hung
out his sign and started in the practice of his profession.

Davenport evidently had not expected a visit upon so
inclement a day. He had drawn a huge arm-chair to the
fire, and with his feet thrown up half as high as his head
and resting against the chimney, he was reading Allison's
History of Europe. He was a young man of fine personal
appearance. His forehead was expansive, betokening in-
tellect—his mouth denoted firmness and decision of character, and his dark hair was slightly inclined to curl.
There was, moreover, a frank ingenuous air about him, that
rendered him an agreeable companion for young and old,
and promised to secure him plenty of business when he
had become better known. Upon seeing the plain old
man before him, he started up, shook him cordially by the

hand, and offered him his comfortable seat in the arm-chair while he went to the extreme end of the room to secure another.

"A wet day, Mr. Dillingham," he said, coming forward and dragging the seat after him, "a drizzling day, and little going on."

"More going on than there ought to be, unless it's better business," said the old man dryly, while he took off his hat and shook the rain-drops from its brim.

Davenport looked at him in surprise. Finally, as if just comprehending the drift of the remark, he uttered a short laugh, and said, "I will acknowledge that the nature of the business has something to do with the quantity desirable to have accomplished. But I don't know to what you allude. Lawyers, you are aware, fatten on mischief, and are always glad to hear of it. Is there anything going on that can give any of us the hope of a case?"

"Causes and fees are two different things, I suppose you know," said the old man quizzically.

"I know," said Davenport, "that they are not *exactly* the same, but we expect one to follow the other as surely as effect follows cause."

"And you never undertake the one, where there is no hope of the other, I suppose."

"Rarely, unless pushed for something to do; men don't love to work without an object."

"And *money* is the only object worth looking at in the world, I suppose," continued the old man, still turning his hat in his hand. "There are wrongs in the world that *should* be righted—frauds, oppressions, acts of violence, that might be looked into by you limbs of the law, but unless you see the gold glittering before your eyes, it is in vain to ask you to do it, I suppose."

The young man thus addressed sat demurely for a moment, as if at a loss what reply to make. At length he said, "I do not comprehend you, Mr. Dillingham; you will have to explain before I can answer you, I fear, satisfactorily."

"I mean just what I say," said the old man, setting his

hat down upon the table, and fumbling about his coat-pocket for his handkerchief. "I mean that *gold* is the lever that moves you—the only wedge that can be driven successfully into your heart, and open it wide enough for your sympathies to flow forth. Is it not so?"

"Do you speak of me individually, or of lawyers as a class?" said Davenport, slightly coloring.

"I speak of all of you—you are the cleverest one of the fraternity whom I ever met."

"Well, then, frankly, Mr. Dillingham, I *do not* think that we are more avaricious, more grasping, more penurious, than the rest of mankind. Our business requires us to be shrewd; we must be paid for what we do, or we should starve, and I have no patience with those who profess to look upon the whole fraternity as a host of crafty, cunning, money-making fellows, who, because they are well versed in the law, can commit any outrage and escape punishment. We have as much heart and soul as anybody; our sympathies are as easily enlisted upon the side of right—upon the side of Truth and Justice."

"Bravo! my boy, bravo! I believe what you say, and now give you a chance to prove the truth of your assertion," said the old man, replacing his handkerchief, and drawing the papers from his pocket.

"There is a little matter here that I should like to have you look into."

Henry drew his chair closer to the table, while old Mr. Dillingham untied the tape, and spread the worm-eaten, dusty, smoked, and much abused papers before him. The old man carefully spread them one by one from the pile, and then began:

"Twelve years ago," said he, "a mechanic came into my neighborhood and set up shop on the same row. He was a young fellow, just married, and with fine industrious habits. He was up with the lark in the morning and at his business—at his work he continued as steady as a judge all day. Others went off on frolics and sprees, but young Houghton staid and looked after his shop, and the result was that his shop was *well* looked after—everybody liked

him—his furniture was better made and more highly polished than any in the city, and consequently he sold more
of it, and got rich, or at any rate, he was very well to do
in the world. He had one child, and his wife, I am told,
died at its birth. He never married again, but put his little
girl out to nurse. He was a Mason, and of course we
were very good friends. I used to see a great deal of him
in those days, and knew a good deal about his money matters, &c. At last he went into partnership with Nehemiah Spriggins, one of the most close-fisted, cold-hearted
wretches that the world ever produced. I tried at the
time to dissuade him from the step, for I knew the Spriggins family of old, but he didn't somehow take to my advice, and the upshot of the business was, as I was telling
you, they went into partnership. Nehemiah Spriggins
knows how to talk smooth and palaver as well as anybody,
and I don't wonder that poor Houghton was took in.
They went on for two years together, and to my knowledge, Houghton as good as owned the whole establishment. But when the cholera came in 1839, the poor fellow
died without a day's warning, and as there was no one to
look into matters, the Spригginses made a clear sweep of
the whole, and pretended to own every thing. They pretended also to be mighty charitable, and so adopted
Houghton's poor little child into their family, because,
they said, she had no property, and nowhere to go, and
O! they have abused her shamefully. Poor little thing!
how often my heart has ached when I have heard them
beating her for nothing, or seen her plodding through the
mud with her little cold, naked feet. I am not a religious
man—that is I don't understand all of the dark mystical
doctrines over which theologians dispute, when, in my
opinion, they had better be at work doing something pro-
fitable to the race, but I *do* believe in a God, and I never
see poor little Nelly Houghton without thinking of that
day when all wrongs shall be righted—that tremendous
Judgment Day about which the Good Book tells us.
Matters have been going on so for a long time, and Nelly
is now eleven, although one to look at her wouldn't take

her to be more than eight, she is so pale and wan-like, with her large black eyes and neglected hair. There is always, too, a startled look in her face, just as if she expected a beating the next minute. I have been thinking this long time that it's a sin and a shame to see the little thing so put upon, but I didn't suppose there was any chance of getting her property for her, for the Sprigginses are as wary as serpents; but yesterday, Johnce, my boy, came across these old musty papers up stairs, and by mere accident I happened to see him just as he was preparing to make a bonfire of the whole. I have been looking into them to-day, and it's my opinion that if some smart lawyer will take the business in hand, that little orphan's property can be restored. It's about this that I have come to see you. I don't know that you will ever get a cent for your trouble, but you will feel pleasant *here*, I'm thinking," said the old man, laying his hand upon his breast. "I am a Mason, and a sworn friend to Justice."

The young lawyer rummaged awhile among the papers before he made any reply. Afterwards, he looked dreamily into the fire for the space of five minutes.

"Mr. Dillingham," he at length said, "can you secure me an interview with that little girl. Her testimony may be of some value. At any rate I should like to see her."

"I don't know whether I can or not," said the old man, thoughtfully. "The Sprigginses watch her as a cat watches a mouse, and she is seldom allowed to leave home under any pretext. But if you will come over to my place, you may see her, and perhaps get an opportunity to chat with her awhile. Do you think that you can afford to undertake her case?"

"I will try and see what I can do for her," said Henry Davenport. "If her condition is as sad as you represent it, it can hardly be made worse, even if I do not succeed in bettering it. I will retain these papers and see the little girl."

Old Mr. Dillingham took Henry's hand in his, at these words, and pressed it cordially. "Your heart is made of the sort of stuff that I thought it was, young man," he said. "Be firm as a rock, and true as steel *to the right,* and you will prosper in the world. It will not be in the power of envy, or malice, or green-eyed jealousy to pull you down. I am an old man, and have kept my eyes open all my life. The virtuous, the kind, the benevolent, always make for themselves friends, and prosper in the world; merit will sooner or later get its due reward. But I must go, for Jonce, I dare say, will remain idle during my ab· sence. Come around to my shop, and I will show you the little girl, and you can judge for yourself about her condition." So saying, the kind old man picked up his hat and umbrella, and departed.

It was not long afterwards, before Henry Davenport *did* go round to the grocer's for the purpose of getting a bird's-eye view, if no more, of the little helpless orphan whose cause he had undertaken. He succeeded in seeing and speaking to her. She was indeed a pitiable object. A little child, as Mr. Dillingham had said, with startled eyes, pale, sunken cheeks, naked feet, and tangled hair— such a child as we sometimes pass in the crowded thoroughfares of a great city, and look back after, wondering if she be ghost or goblin, shadow of misery, or *bona fide* flesh and blood. Such a creature was little Nelly Houghton—the babe whose first wail had fallen on her mother's dying ear like funeral music, who had never known any save a father's love in this cold and bitter world, and had seen death's bony hand snatching even that from her, while she was yet a lingerer on the threshold of life.

"She always," said old man Dillingham to Henry, "has that dreary light in those large black eyes of hers—a light that tells of her thinking thoughts far beyond her years. Part of her nature has been prematurely developed by suffering; she thinks and reasons already like a woman. Little Nellie has a strong mind, I know, for I have watched her a good deal from my shop windows, while she has been about her drudgery; she is as patient as a lamb, too, never returning evil for evil. If she was washed and combed and dressed like other children, she would be pretty, I think. Her features are regular, though she

does have the look of another world about her. Comfort
and kindness would act like magic upon the poor thing, I
dare say, calling color and roundness to her cheeks, and
gladness to her eyes."

Henry shook his head, but did not reply aloud. 'She
can never be beautiful," he said mentally; "grace and harmony are wanting in her features. If she was a golden-
haired, blue-eyed, poetical looking girl, there would be
some romance in undertaking her case, but as it is, she is
miserable. And as I have nothing to do just now to prevent me from bettering her condition if possible, I will
try."

Gentle reader, we might follow our young lawyer
through all the tangled intricacies of a long and tedious
lawsuit, and show you how, step by step, truth was
brought to light, innocence protected, and justice defended,
but the process would be wearisome to us, and not pro-
fitable to you. Suffice it to say, that through the united
exertions of old Mr. Dillingham, Henry Davenport, and
other Masons, who instantly became interested in the
affair, when they fully understood it, Nelly Houghton was
proved to be the heir of quite an estate, and was taken
from her self-instituted guardians, who accused her of ingratitude, and heaped all manner of opprobious epithets
upon her tender head. But their rage was idle. Nelly
was washed, comfortably clad, and sent to school. No
one rejoiced more at this happy issue of matters than
Johnce.

"That gal looks like a gal what *is* a white gal now," he
said; rubbing his hands together, "and she's pretty, too.
I always knowed it—I always *said* it, even when she was
trotting about here, looking wus nor a nigger slave. Them
Sprigginses have found out who is who mighty likely by
this time. I knowed when I found them ar papers, that
there was something 'portant in 'em just by their looks,
and I hadn't any notion of burning 'em anyhow, but I was
jist a going to take 'em to old massa and ax him 'bout 'em,
when he spied me, and axed what I was burning there.
O la! jist as if I didn't know *then* that Miss Nelly's por-

tion had been rolled up and stowed away in 'em! I's the nigger what knows a thing or two; and when I seed massa so busy over them, that he didn't know lasses from ile, and when he telled me that he was a going to Massa Harry Davenport's through the rain and splash and mud, didn't I smell the rat and say *directly* what it was about?" and so saying, Johnce stuck his hands into his greasy coat pockets, and walked about with an air of importance which it was really amusing to behold.

*   *   *   *   *   *   *   *   *   *

It was a splendid evening in autumn. The radiant clouds reflected to earth the rich hues of a gorgeous sunset, and rainbow dyes had fallen upon hillside and forest with the first frosts of September. Ten years had passed away since Nelly Houghton's case had enlisted the young lawyer's attention, and the memory of the incident had almost escaped from his mind. Old Mr. Dillingham had long been gathered to his fathers. His was the fate of a good old man—he died at peace with himself, the world, and God. Light seemed to linger on his grave. Those who looked at it could repeat from Bryant,

> " I'm glad that he has lived thus long,
> And glad that he has gone to his repose."

Through a long life he had faithfully discharged those duties which man owes to himself, his God, and his fellowmen; and why should not his end have been like the rich setting of the sun, when its day is o'er—when it goes out in beauty, and twilight succeeds!

Johnce, at his death, had found a new master in Henry Davenport, who had met the reward of his honesty and untiring application, and risen to eminence in the Senate chamber of his native State.

On the evening mentioned above, Harry Davenport was in the midst of one of the gayest parties in the capital. He was still unmarried, and a great favorite in all the circles that he frequented. Many a belle as she flirted through the splendid rooms of their hostess, cast furtive glances at the honorable young member from C——, and wondered if it lay in her power to lead captive his heart. But her acts were vain—her questioning was idle. Our hero's eyes were directed towards a spot where a tall, graceful girl, with a Madonna-like head and dark brilliant eyes, sat conversing with a gentleman of the party. Her voice fell on his ear like silvery music—her words charmed him with the wisdom that they displayed, and her face somehow seemed to him connected with pleasant memories. He could not recall ever having met with her, and yet he found himself again and again studying her features and lingering near her.

When the music at length struck up, and the dance began, he turned away from the gay revellers, and wandered out into a veranda overlooking a flower garden of great beauty. He leaned thoughtfully against one of the pillars, and looked up at the moon, riding now through the heavens, clear and unclouded.

He was aroused from his revery, by feeling the pressure of a light hand upon his arm. He looked up, and saw that the beautiful unknown had followed him.

"The Hon. Henry Davenport, I believe," said she, bowing gracefully towards him; "long years ago I had the pleasure of an acquaintance, and do not need an introduction now."

The senator started. He *had* seen her then—he was not mistaken—he *had* known her, but where? That was a puzzling question.

She seemed to read his thoughts, to comprehend his uncertainty and doubt, and continued: "You have forgotten me, as I expected. You do not remember the bare-footed, tangled-haired, frightened and pallid little girl, out of whose young heart the glad sunshine of childhood was prematurely crushed by oppression and wrong—you do not recognize in *me* the little orphan over whose cause you toiled day and night without much hope of remuneration, save those calm thoughts and pleasant reflections, which visit all who study the weal of mankind. I am Nelly Houghton. The bud, frost-bitten, worm-eaten, and half destroyed as it was, has opened into a fragrant flower, because your kind hand transplanted it to a more genial soil, and let the golden sunshine stream in to warm its root. To you I owe my wealth, my education, my friends, my position in society, and my ability to benefit my race. Is it strange that I have stolen away from the gay crowd yonder to thank my benefactor?"

"You do not owe so much to me as you imagine, Nelly," he said, kindly taking her hand in his. "To old Mr. Dillingham, the grocer, you were more deeply indebted than to me, for he belonged to a fraternity, to a brotherhood, who swear to see JUSTICE reign triumphant—to guard with the eye of an argus the rights of the widow and the orphan."

"But without your instrumentality what could he have done?" said the young girl eagerly. "Hail! all hail! to that generous brotherhood, who, 'when I was sick and in prison, ministered unto me,' but you were an agent in this affair, and as such I give you thanks."

Our grave senator looked at that moment as if he was glad to receive *anything* from her, even though it was as intangible as thanks generally are, and so he continued to look, and act, until six months afterwards, when she, strange to narrate, concluded that it was best to give him her heart—her whole heart, property, hand, and all. How could she do otherwise, when he was so *very grateful* even for the smallest favors bestowed by her hand? Yes, our senator won Nelly Houghton, and thought himself *then* amply repaid for all that he had ever done.

Johnce figured largely at the wedding. He declared to his fellow-servants, while in the dining room, flourishing about, with cake-knife in hand, "that he knowed when he found those old musty papers up *stars*, jist how matters would turn out. He knowed plain enough that there was a wedding done up in 'em, as well as a fortin' for Miss Nelly Houghton." A wonderfully wise servant was Johnce, but the world holds many, who, we find to our astonishment, after an event has transpired, knew very well beforehand that it was going to happen.

THE SHADOW IN THE COTTAGE.

"It is a fearful thing to love what death may touch."
— *Mrs. Hemans.*

It was while a summer sunset
 Burned within the western sky,
And the purple clouds grew silvery,
 Edged with every glorious dye,
That there came a fearful shadow,
 Stealing o'er our cottage floor ;
It crept on, and never rested,
 Till it reached our sweet Lenore.

She was resting on her pillow,
 Paler than a drift of snow,
While her golden ringlets floated
 In the breeze's inward flow ;
She was sleeping—so we whispered,
 As we watched her gentle breath,
And we strove to check that shadow,
 For we knew that it was *Death.*

But in vain our every effort,
 Onward, onward, still it came ;
Though we wildly clasp'd our idol,
 Shrieking o'er and o'er her name,
Still that shadow dense in darkness,
 Lengthened on the cottage floor,
Till it fell with icy chillness,
 On our darling, sweet Lenore.

But our sister never shuddered,
 When she felt that fearful thing,
Tho' she knew, as well as others,
 That it fell from off Death's wing ;

Softly, sweetly, in the twilight,
    She unclos'd her weary eye,
As the languid flower at sunset
    Opes to heaven its azure dye.

"I am not afraid," she murmured,
    "Death has lost his poisonous sting;
Angels wait to waft me upward;
    All around me, now, they sing;
Christ has made Death's icy shadow
    Brighten on my brow of clay,
Changing it to burst of sunlight—
    Warm, sweet sunlight in the day."

Then she clasp'd her thin white fingers,
    With their tracery of veins,
O'er her gentle heaving bosom,
    As if stilling all her pains;
And with lips that kept a murmuring,
    "Sisters, brothers, do not weep!"
She went off amid the gloaming,
    Like an infant to soft sleep.

We smooth'd back her golden ringlets,
    We kiss'd oft her marble brow,
But we wiped away our tear-drops,
    Whispering "she's mid angels now."
In a snowy shroud they laid her,
    Where some fragrant wild flowers grow,
And the blue-birds sing in summer,
    Near a streamlet's silvery flow.

Often now I sit at twilight,
    Searching in the Book of Light,
For the faith that turns death's shadows,
    To such sunshine, soft and bright;
I shall need it when that phantom
    Steals for *me* across the floor,
Veiling me in gloom and chillness,
    As it did our lost Lenore.

VERY MUCH IN LOVE ; OR, A SLIGHT MISTAKE.

"ARE you in love? I'll prove it by fifty things. Oh, there is no use in denying it, Cot, none in the world!"

"No use in denying *what*, Ophelia? For once I am at fault in understanding you."

"Now, Cotton Mather Royalstone, that is a—a—well, if it is not a fib, it is at least an equivocation. I mean there is no use in denying that you are in love—deeply, inextricably, mortally, dreadfully in love. I've been aware of it—let me see—ever since that first party at Mrs. Swan's. Anybody with two eyes in their head ought to have made the same discovery. You are mortally in love with Rosalia Anderson;" and the chatterbox of a speaker, namely, Ophelia Stewartson, held her pretty finger up, and shook it at her cousin meaningly and saucily.

If a blush is any acknowledgment of a fact, then Cotton Mather Royalstone *was* in love, for the tell-tale blood mounted even into his fine temples, and he cast his eyes down and played with his watch-guard almost as modestly as a girl might have done. Anybody would have joined Ophelia Stewartson, and declared our hero to have been in love at that very moment.

"But, cousin Cot," pursued the girl, in that same teasing tone, "Rosa has gone away on a visit to Niagara; she won't be back these three weeks; but that's no reason why you should shoot, hang, or drown yourself—no reason in the world. Act like a sensible fellow, and for that short space of time resolve at least to forget her. There is no use in weeping one's self to death over what cannot be helped. Stay here, and we'll all do our best to entertain you. I'll sing with you, fish with you, walk with you, read to you, and, if need be, fight for you. You won't find a more self-denying friend anywhere than I'll prove myself to be, if you'll only stay here and be sensible and

12

well-behaved, as a young man ought to be during the absence of his lady-love. I'll even write to Rosa, and beg her for your sake not to stay too long. Now ain't I exceedingly obliging?" and the little madcap took her dress in both hands, and waltzed across the room and half-way across the garden before her grave cousin, with that grave and reverend name, Cotton Mather Royalstone, could reply to and stop her. At length he caught up with her and said,

"I'll stay and be sensible, Phele—stay and be entertained famously, if you'll promise me one thing—not to write to Rosa; I don't want to be the means of curtailing her enjoyment. Instead of writing to her, you may talk to me about her; that will do just as well."

"Agreed," said the girl; "and now bear it in mind, dear Cot, I shall exert myself continually to be vastly entertaining. You, on your part, are not to be love-sick in the least; you are to be grave, sober, unexacting, and most easily pleased. You are not to mention "Rosalie," or "waterfall," or any other obnoxious subject during the whole time, although I may now and then speak upon the forbidden theme myself."

"Hold, hold!" cried Cotton, "turn about is fair play. I've heard that doctrine preached from my childhood. I have no idea of pledging my word that I will not talk on any subject, while your tongue is at liberty to rattle away at will. A pretty restriction you would place me under, truly. No, no, Miss Ophelia, I demur seriously," and the young man drew a handkerchief from his pocket and wiped his face.

" But I shall talk sensibly, you know; give you good advice, etc. Indeed I expect I shall be deeply and engrossingly entertaining when I touch upon that subject; while you, on the contrary—oh! who has not heard of the ravings of a love-sick soul? Who has not, indeed?"

The young man laughed a hearty laugh. " Well, cousin Phele," he said, "you are determined, I see plainly, to have things all your own way. My best policy will be to yield as gracefully as I can; but don't be too unmerciful.

If you are, I shall, like the lord of the forest, break away
from all constraint, and afterwards prove more untamea-
ble than ever."

"Oh! I'll be very discreet, indeed, never fear me," and
the girl began her fairy-like dance again upon the green-
sward—a dance which seemed an appropriate expression
of her young and happy heart.

Ophelia Stewartson was one of those fresh, laughing,
Hebe-like creatures, whom it does one good to look upon.
Carefully nurtured from her earliest infancy, she knew little of grief or care. Life looked to her a sunny path,
strewed with flowers. She coquetted and laughed until
the dimples seemed playing bo-peep in her full rosy cheeks.
She had a word for every body and every thing—a word
which sounded marvellously like the sincere expression of
her heart, but which, strange to say, never gave offence to
any body, but always caused a laugh.

Cotton Mather Royalstone was—hem! Well, they
said they were *cousins*, and I, not being very well versed
in their genealogy, am not prepared to disprove it. May
be they were cousins—cousins somewhere in the sixteenth
degree. One thing was very apparent: there was great
affinity between the two—whether of heart or blood, it
matters not. Cotton was just from college, and for the
present was safely domiciled in the neighborhood where
Ophelia resided. He generally escorted her to parties;
and it was at one of these reunions that Ophelia professed
to make the astounding discovery that Cotton was in love
—dreadfully in love.

For days afterwards, Ophelia, true to her promise, did
her best to entertain him, but her sly raillery was unceas-
ing, and perhaps nobody but Cotton Mather Royalstone
could patiently have endured it. But endure it he did—
endure it with a very good grace; and, gentle reader,
was not this another proof-positive that he *was* distress-
ingly in love.

The weeks of Rosalia's absence had nearly glided away.
She was expected home in a few days; but, nevertheless,
Ophelia came in one day, and stood at her cousin's side,

with a very serious, condoling air upon her sober face.
"Oh, cousin Cot," she said, "I've just heard something so
dreadful! I'm sure you'll cry when I tell you about it.
Poor fellow! you have my sympathies—I give them to
to you beforehand; it is really too bad."

"What is too bad?" said the young man, wonderingly.
"I cannot imagine what has happened. Nobody's dead I
hope?"

"Oh, no; but old Mr. Anderson—the strange old mortal—he's thrown cold water over all your matrimonial
prospects for a surety."

"Why, what has he done?" asked Cotton in a tone of
surprise.

"Why he isn't going to let you marry Rosalie; he's
going to object—prove obstinate—as many an incorrigi-
ble papa has done before him. I'm afraid you'll have to
make a run-away match of it yet."

To Ophelia's surprise, the grave young man laughed a
short laugh over this piece of information, and evinced no
very great concern. But he kept on questioning her notwithstanding.

"It isn't possible that the old fellow objects to a clever
young chap like myself, is it, cousin Phele? What does
he say against me?"

"Oh, he doesn't like you at all, Cot; he never will consent to your marrying her in the world."

The young man bit his lips, and said more gravely,
while he looked into his pretty cousin's upturned face,
"he'll wait until I ask him, I suppose, before he refuses
me his daughter's hand."

"Ask him! why it was all settled that you were to ask
him as soon as he got home, you know."

"No, I didn't know it, Phele—never dreamed of it."

"Why, cousin Cot!"

The young man still looked gravely down into the upturned face, and there was a truthful expression in his eye
that surprised her.

"Why, cousin Cot," she began again, "how did you
expect to get the girl without asking for her; you haven't

intended running away with her from the first, have you?"

"No, I don't intend *now* to run away with her."

"But you'll never get her without. You are a Freemason, and old Mr. Anderson is hostile towards the whole fraternity. He declares that it is a secret organization for political purposes, and that its tendency is the destruction of our government. He would as quickly let his daughter marry a traitor as a Freemason, he says."

"Ah!" said the young man, respondingly.

"And now, cousin Cot, if you *don't* run away with her, how are you going to marry?"

"I'm sure I don't know," he said, stroking his chin thoughtfully; "I look to you to enlighten me upon that point."

"Well, you'll have to run away; I see no other chance for you."

"With who, Phele?"

"Why, how provoking! With her you have been so madly in love with all along. Won't you do it, cousin Cot?"

"Yes, to be sure I will—run with her to the ends of the earth, if need be."

"I knew it, I knew it," cried the girl, bringing her small white hands together; "I knew it, although you just now said you wasn't going to marry Rosalie under any such circumstances. A fig for circumstances when anybody is dreadfully in love."

"Dreadfully in love!" echoed Cotton.

"Well, it's all arranged—I'm to go along, too. I always thought that it would be fine fun to be in a run-away scrape."

"Certainly you are to be there, Phele; I couldn't get married if *you* were not present;" and Cotton Mather stooped over and took her hand."

"Yes, I am to be bridesmaid. But when are you going to see Rosalie about all this?"

"Never!" said the young man, emphatically.

'Never, cousin Cot! How on earth can you get married without letting Rosalie know it? I am curious to know."

"Very easily, I'm thinking. It's little matter to me whether she knows about it or not."

"Well, if she don't know about it, who must then?" said the girl, beginning for the first time to feel that she had rattled on until she had perhaps placed herself in an awkward position; "who *is* to know about your wedding, cousin Cot?"

"You—you only, cousin Phele. If you will only enter into my plans, we can have a quiet home wedding in spite of old Mr. Anderson's ill-will to the Freemasons. Perhaps, after all, he will let his daughter attend as a guest. *You* must be the bride instead of the bridesmaid, cousin Phele; that will obviate all difficulties. That is the only important change I care to suggest in your arrangements."

The rich crimson blood rushed all over the girl's face and neck, and she drew her hand from his hastily, and held it to her eyes.

"Me! me the bride," she murmured, "and you all the time so dreadfully in love!"

Cotton laughed one of his peculiar laughs, and took her hand again.

"Yes," he said, "all along dreadfully in love, but never with Rosalie Anderson. That was your own supposition, remember. Say, cousin Ophelia, shall we have a wedding in spite of old Mr. Anderson's hatred to the Freemasons?"

The blushing creature thought seriously upon the subject for awhile, and then said archly, "It never will do to let the enemies of Freemasonry break up weddings in any such a way. If you can't get Rosalie Anderson, why I suspect *I shall be obliged to marry you myself.* I had never thought of that way of getting over the difficulty. To be sure, a home wedding *will* look much more respectable than a run-away match, and moreover, grandmother says that run-aways never turn out well."

The young man drew her to him, and said: "Old Mr. Anderson may whistle his spite to the wind. We'll have a wedding of our own, Phelia dear, and leave the Andersons entirely out. It was a happy thought to get over the difficulty thus. I only ask that the wedding may be hastened, for you know I have long been dreadfully in love."

The wedding *was* hastened. Before Rosalie returned from the Falls, Ophelia was Mrs. Royalstone.

COUSIN SALLIE'S VISIT.

Mrs. Forest sat at the breakfast table. She wore a neat morning dress—an unexceptionable cap over her curls of rich brown hair, and a collar fastened with a little knot of blue ribbon in front. Opposite was her husband—a fine, grave-looking man of thirty-five or forty. The table was covered with a snowy cloth, and the coffee-urn glittered like silver. The biscuits were white and feathery in lightness—the toast was smoking hot, and the waffles were cooked in the most approved style.

Taken all in all, they were a very handsome couple—a very comfortable-looking couple, and Mrs. Forest felt this, as she took up a letter just brought to her from the post-office, and snapped the seal. She read, and while she read, a smile settled around her lips. It was a smile hard to define. But it certainly was not one expressive of great pleasure.

"My dear," said she, as she refolded the letter, and returned it to the envelope, "we are to have company. Cousin Sallie R—— will be here next week."

The gentleman let his knife and fork fall with a ringing sound into his plate, and looked up in dismay. "Sallie R——," he said. "What in thunder is *she* coming here for?"

"To see us, I suppose. I hardly know what else should bring her here; but you receive the announcement of her visit in a strange way. You might, at least, use an expression somewhat more elegant, I should think, while referring to a visit from one of *my* relatives."

"Perhaps I might, Fanny," he said, "but I don't like Sallie R——; you know I don't. She is haughty, censorious, and arrogant—a woman who is all head and no heart—one of the kind I despise more than I despise anything mortal."

Mrs. Forest bit her lip.

"I am sure I don't know what cousin Sallie R—— has ever done, that you should speak in such a harsh way of her. She has always been called very smart."

"Yes, she is too smart in her own estimation—that is the fault I find with her. I remember her as a school-girl, busy, meddlesome and self-conceited. Why Fanny, you have not forgotten, have you, that she came near breaking off our engagement, 'in the days when I went a wooing,' by her tattling and tale-bearing? I hear she has been married since. Is her husband coming with her?"

"Oh no!" said the lady, while a slight blush suffused her cheek; "she writes to me that her husband was an uncongenial spirit, incompatible in temper, &c. They have not, I judge, lived very happily together, and now are separated. I am sure I am sorry that cousin Sallie has been so unfortunate."

"Humph," said Mr. Forest.

"She will stay with us several weeks," continued the lady, "and I hope for my sake, my dear, you will treat her courteously, and let by-gones be by-gones."

"For *your* sake, Fanny, I would be gracious to most things. I am fond of your father, mother, sister Nell, and cousin Jack, and Frank Weston, your nephew—*he* is a capital fellow! He promised to come up this Fall and shoot birds on my plantation; I wish he would. But this Sallie R——: it's just as I've said. I wish she had taken it into her head to go to Patagonia, rather than to come on a visit to us. But, as poor Robinet says in the story, we must, I suppose, 'make the best of it.'"

Mr. Forest got up, took his hat and gloves, and went

out; but as he was closing the front door, his wife called after him: "Robert, if cousin Sallie comes, I shall need that new china at Allison's; I wish you would send it home this morning—and those curtains at Morton's; I shall want those too, for the parlor ones look positively shabby."

"Very well," said the gentleman, "I will attend to it."

All the morning Mrs. Forest went hither and thither, inspecting domestic affairs. She looked into numerous jars of preserves, to see if any mischievous fermenting process was going on within; she baked cake, and embossed it beautifully; she white-washed the chamber walls afresh—for several days she was the busiest of the busy. Every night her husband found her too tired to entertain him. If she spoke at all, it was about some new household arrangement.

The day before the guest was expected, she again stopped him at the front door.

"I wish," said she, "you would step up to Leslie's and send home a new carpet. Now the curtains are up, the old one looks shamefully; I didn't know it was so faded and threadbare before. I shall be ashamed for cousin Sallie to see it. You know how nice and particular she is about every thing. I'm afraid she'll make fun of it."

Mr. Forest stopped, and knocked his boot-heel impatiently upon the door-step.

"Fanny," he said, "it annoys me to see you so anxious about genteel appearances just now. I have a heavy debt to meet to-day, and not a dollar of the money in my pocket. It has all got to be raised. I cannot get a new carpet; we can do very well without it."

"We could, if it were not for cousin Sallie's visit," responded the wife. "If you haven't got the cash, why buy on credit. Thousands do the like every day. You can settle for it easily enough at Christmas."

"I don't know," said the man, musingly. "I don't like to do it." Just then, he glanced at the anxious face of his wife, and he saw that she had her heart quite fixed on the purchase. "It won't break me," he said mentally, "and it will gratify Fanny."

13

"I'll send Leslie's clerk up to take the measure of the room," he said, as he turned away. But as he went down the street, there was a cloud upon his brow and a load at his heart.

"I wish this visit was over," he murmured to himself. "There will be no peace in the household as long as her coming shadow falls across the threshold. For my part, it's precious little of my company she'll get. I intend to keep clear of the house until she is safely out of it. I wonder how Fanny can so cheerfully make preparations for her reception. But she is her third cousin I believe. Blood is said to be thicker than water. Perhaps that's why she is working now like a slave."

The carpet was brought home—the china graced the board—the hundred-dollar curtains were at the windows. Taking it all in all, the house was quite an elegant affair; and Mrs. Forest went out with a smile of welcome upon her lips, when the stage stopped at the door one cloudy afternoon, and set her cousin down upon the green-sward in front of the gate. But a glance sufficed to show that it was the cousin Sallie of other days.

She was a tall slender woman, with a purple dress, gloves and straw bonnet. She had trunks and bandboxes innumerable, and every thing was nicely arranged about her. When Mrs. Forest reached her, she was wrangling with the driver about pay. She affirmed that he charged altogether too much, while he declared that he demanded the usual fare.

After awhile, the affair was settled. The poor driver, tired, perhaps, of quarelling with a woman, let her have her own way—took the money she held out to him, and drove off. Then, for the first time, she glanced towards Mrs. Forest.

"I declare Frances," she said, "is this you? I've had my life half worried out of me by that chap. But I never give up. He may cheat other people if they'll let him, but he shan't cheat me. I'm too keen for that, I assure you!" So saying, she extended her long, slim, ringless hand for Mrs. Forest to shake.

This ceremony over, the lady conducted her guest into the house, and ordered a servant to bring in her baggage. This was no small task; but the visitor stood by the window, and watched him until the last bundle was stowed away in the upper room. Then she went to dress, and nothing more was seen of her until tea-time.

When Robert Forest met her then, he showed little of the free and easy hospitality with which he usually greeted his friends. He did not take her hand—he scarcely inclined his head at her approach. "Be seated," he said, waving her to a seat some distance from his own. "Shall I help you to a piece of this cold fowl. Perhaps, as you have been traveling, a wing, or a piece of the breast, might not be unacceptable."

The lady addressed bowed stiffly. She *would* take a wing, if he pleased. Most women would have been disconcerted by such a reception from an old acquaintance and relative, but Sallie R—— was never disconcerted in her life. No arrangement of circumstances—no accident—no introduction—no surprisal — no unlooked-for event—no exhibition of dislike, had ever for a moment caused her confusion, or muddled the current of thought in her clear brain. She now sipped her tea from the china cup before her, as coolly and calmly as though she had been sitting alone in the sweet sunshine of May.

Mrs. Forest evidently felt this to be an embarrassing state of affairs, and exerted herself to talk. She inquired about her relative's journey—the state of her mother's health, and various family matters. The visitor replied in her usual abrupt manner.

While this conversation was going on, Robert Forest had time to examine more narrowly her countenance and appearance. She had a narrow face, which, when free from cosmetics, was both clear and colorless—a high forehead, with the light brown hair combed back stiffly—eyes grey and piercing, but owing to an inflammation in the lids, they were always red—a tall and slender form, not by any means showily dressed. But the most remarkable thing about her face was the entire absence at all times

of every emotional feeling. She never exhibited any out-
burst of enthusiasm, love, delight, or sorrow—never as a
child had she been known to do it. In her school days
she tormented her teacher by informing her very coolly
one day, that there was not a girl in that school refined
enough for her to associate with. She sought doctors and
lawyers to talk with, and surprised them by the strange,
unchild-like propriety of her language and ways.

Kindness, pity, love, were plants that had never
bloomed in the sterile soil of her heart. She loved to repeat high-sounding phrases from books—she advocated a
high tone of sentiment, but the sensations of love and
sympathy were unknown to her. Among her companions
she was reserved, proud and dictatorial. Her teachers
never pleased her. She sowed thorns in their pillows with
a prodigal hand, and no sweet kindness, no stern severity,
ever won her to a better course. It is a sad thing to see
a child of this type. But such was Sallie R——, and
the promise of her childhood was fulfilled in womanhood.
The bud had been bitter—the fruit was hard and acrid.

The next morning, while seated at the breakfast-table,
a sunbeam flashed over the gilded rim of her saucer. The
whole service was so beautiful, she could not well help ob-
serving and commenting upon it, but "why," she said,
"did you buy this kind of a cup, Frances? White is
much better—anything but white is vulgar, and decidedly,
in bad taste."

Mrs. Forest bit her lip, but said nothing. The parlor,
with its beautiful curtains and carpet, was criticised in the
same way. The preserves were condemned—the cake remained untasted. Nothing about the establishment pleased
the visitor. Never a word of approval passed her thin
lips.

Mrs. Forest was a woman whose feelings took hue and
coloring from every thing around her. Her husband was
now seldom at home—he ate, and left as quickly as possi-.
ble. There was nobody but that hard, stern woman following her about all day, finding fault with every thing,.
and distilling, by her cold, suspicious half-sentences, the

poison of distrust and discontent into her soul. It was a dreary life to live. Little sunny-hearted Mrs. Forest felt it to be such. She wondered why her husband was forever away from home. She grew nervous and irritable. Who that is placed in intimate communion with such a spirit, does not? And the small sweet flower of domestic love paled and drooped by a hearth-stone where it had once flourished in fragrance and beauty.

With Robert Forest, things were, if possible, in a worse state than they were with Fanny. It is a serious thing when man is driven away by any train of exercises from the hallowed influences of *home.* There stands the altar whereon his best affections should be laid—there is the shrine where his heart's priceless jewels should be casketed —there burns the fire whose brightness should illumine every corner of his soul—there beam the eyes whose smiles should lure him far—there is the echo of steps which should be music in his ear—there grows a flower, the fragrance of which should be more delightful to him than any odors the winds waft from Araby—the small white flower of domestic peace.

Robert Forest knew all this, and, perhaps, his conscience was ill at ease when he turned for amusement to the crowded bar-room and the convivial scene. Sometimes he came home late at night. Once, Fanny asked him why he stayed so long, and he, without referring again to his dislike of her cousin, replied impatiently, "It is lodge night—don't be always questioning me."

His tone—his manner—his irregularity at home, all served to wound the sensitive spirit of the affectionate wife. She could not banish the remembrance of them from her thoughts, and a cloud of gloom, in spite of her efforts, settled upon her brow. The quick, sharp eye of her cousin was upon her. She seemed to read her inmost thoughts. But she forbore alluding plainly to her dejection. She chose rather to harrow the soul with inquisitorial cruelty —to torture and rack it by slow degrees. As she sat by the window, apparently busy over some knitting, and Mrs. Forest sat near, repairing dilapidated hose, she broached the subject.

"It seems to me, Frances," she said, "that Robert is away from home a good deal. Has he treated you with such neglect ever since you were married?"

"Neglect!" the word stung the sensitive little woman, to whom it was addressed, like an adder. She started, and could hardly keep the tears from forcing themselves into her eyes. "Neglect!" she said, "Robert does not *neglect* me. I am sure, a kinder, better husband never lived. I do not like to hear that word applied to him."

"But, nevertheless, he is away from home all the time. I do not believe he has spent three waking hours under this roof since I came here. I never saw a man who stayed away from his family so much in my life. If it isn't neglect, I am at a loss to know by what name to call it. It is certainly a strange way of exhibiting love and affection."

"I know he has been absent a good deal since you have been here, but it is not a usual thing for him to stay away from home so much. He is a Mason, and there have been meetings of the lodge and chapter, I learn, of late. That accounts for his absence in part."

"A Freemason!" Here a smile of ineffable contempt curled the lips of the visiting lady. "Oh yes!" she said, "a Freemason! that explains it all. Their orbits are always as eccentric as a comet's—they are here to-day, and gone to-morrow. There is no accounting for anything *they* do. I didn't know that he was a Freemason, or I should not have said a word."

"Why, cousin, don't you like the Freemasons? Some of the best men in our section of the country belong to them. I am sure there is nothing wrong about them. If there was, Robert would not have joined them. He was a member of the lodge before I married him. I have never spent an unhappy moment about it."

"You haven't? Well, I suppose

Where ignorance is bliss,
'Tis folly to be wise.'

You are, probably, much happier than you would be if you knew the exact truth. My husband thought that he could join the Masons, and I be none the wiser in consequence of his proceedings, but I showed him."

"You certainly did not disagree upon the subject of Freemasonry?" said the little woman, opening her eyes with astonishment; "you did not fall out, and go different ways in life just on account of that?"

"That was the root and branch of his offending. We got along very well, until he took it into his head to be very smart, and join those fellows. After I found out about his joining, I harrowed and tormented him continually. I told him that I knew it was a place where they went to drink and carouse, and I intimated to him pretty plainly that I didn't intend being treated in any such way. Finally, he owned that they did sometimes have *refreshments*. Refreshments, indeed! don't I, and don't every sensible woman know, what these refreshments are? Brandy-and-water, Champagne and Madeira. Every sensible woman knows, too, that their secrecy is used to veil all this. O yes, secrecy is a precious thing with them; it is needed to hide their evil deeds. Women may submit to this who choose, but I want to know what each and every member of my establishment is about." So saying, Sallie R—— gave her head an affected toss, and went on with her knitting more industriously than ever.

In spite of her better judgment; in spite of the deep affection which dwelt in the heart of Mrs. Forest for her husband—an affection which twelve years of married life had continually strengthened and deepened—she could not keep from being annoyed, fretted, and disturbed by the dark accusations and insinuations thrown out by her cousin. As we have before said, she was an impressible woman. Smiles and frowns had a powerful influence over her soul. Had Sallie R—— only referred to this subject once, and then been silent, Mrs. Forest would gradually have forgotten it, but the lady dwelt day after day upon the disagreeable theme. She held it up in every ridiculous light that she could think of. Alas! for the poor little wife. Was there no comforting spirit to whisper the exact truth in her ear, and refute all these false imputations—

these foul slanders on a craft whose mission in this world of ours, be it what it may, certainly is not an *evil* one?

Things went on thus for weeks. At length, much to Robert Forest's relief, cousin Sallie R—— concluded to take herself home. She, perhaps, thought that she had sowed sufficient discord and unhappiness in the household where she had visited, and left, hoping to find some more promising field.

Robert Forest, after her departure, went back, as of old, to enjoy the delights of domestic life, but there was no sunshine upon the altars where he had worshipped—no fire to warm, or to consume. Like some incubus that could not be shaken off, Sallie R——'s spirit lingered behind her; and in addition to all these dispiriting domestic influences, troubles gathered over his affairs without. Pay-day came. Many debts had somehow accumulated during the year, and must now be met, and he did not always have the needful to meet them with. Gloom gathered upon his brow, and the reflective spirit of his wife caught a deeper tint from its sombreness. There were the china, carpet, and a thousand other needless things yet unpaid for. They had been purchased to please the eye of a woman whose visit had done them evil and not good. Both husband and wife felt this keenly.

One dark winter afternoon, when the wind wailed among the branches of the trees, and the skies sent down steady drizzling showers of mist and rain, Forest went home and threw his hat upon the table. "Fanny," he said, "I expect every thing we have will go at sheriff's sale. There are those detestable curtains and carpet," he continued, glancing around him, "of which heaven knows I would be glad to be rid—*they* are associated in my mind with nothing but trouble and discomfort, but there are other things here, that whisper memories precious and sweet to my heart—memories of days when you and I sat with hand clasped in hand, heart beating responsive to heart, and talked and smiled together. The sunshine was golden here in those days, but somehow there is precious little of it left," and he got up and strode across the floor

with a quick step. Mrs. Forest was sewing. Tears
streamed down her pale cheeks, but she did not look up.
Just then there was a ring at the door-bell. Forest went
to see who was there. He soon returned. "Fanny," he
said, taking up his hat again, "it is lodge night, and I
must go, for Morris has called for me. Don't sit up—I
may not be at home until after midnight. You had best
go to bed, and sleep, if you can."

Sleep !   Did the husband think that sleep—a gift of God
to the weary and heavy-laden—a balm of forgetfulness
which settles like healing dew upon the wounded and sorrowing hearth—comes *easily* to the eyelids of a woman,
whose household divinities had been thrown down, or
stolen away, or ruthlessly trampled upon ? Did he think
the pillow would be soft beneath temples that throbbed
and ached with agony, and would not be eased ? Did he
not know that the coy goddess would not always come
when called for ? That she does not seem anxious to lay
her healing touch, like the Saviour of old, upon eyes made
blind and red through weeping ?

Alas for woman ! Her empire is in the affections—her
throne stands close by the hearthstone of HOME. Man
may go out, and build temples to ambition. He may buy
and sell, and get gain, and content himself with the traffic
—he may ride on to the blood-red field of the warrior, and
his pulses may wildly thrill at the trumpet-call of his
country—he may urge his way to fame, and smile over the
laurel wreath won in the midst of carnage and desolation
—but not so the true *woman.* She must quaff sweet waters
from the springs of affection—she binds to her heart the
blossom given to her as a memento of love—she asks not
for fame or wealth—she is happy if she can make

> "The humblest hearth
> Lovely but to one on earth."

Her heart, if blessed at all, must be blessed with the
words of home love—she must have kindly looks to cheer
her on—she must hear tender accents—she must have
household gods—love, home and friends, are the things to

which her soul turns in its hour of feverish need, and, when robbed of these, she is robbed of her *all*. The ashes of desolation gather thickly upon her soul. Sleep flies like an affrighted thing from her pillow—beneath her yawns the grave of her joys—over her head the clouds lower black with gloom.

Fanny Forest could not have slept that night had a bed of roses invited her to repose—had the sweetest music been sent to serenade her—had poppies breathed their somniferous influences around her. Hour by hour she sat and watched the fire paling in the grate, or started up when the clock chimed off the time. At last, the outer door opened—there was a step in the hall, and, directly afterwards, Forest came in. His face was light, almost cheerful.

"Fanny," he said, "things are not so bad as I feared. Help has sprung up in an unexpected quarter. Many to whom I am indebted are Freemasons. They will not press me harder than they can help. It is like wine to a weary man's soul to find that he is surrounded by brethren and friends."

Mrs. Forest burst into a fresh gush of tears.

"Robert," she said, "did you know that of late I have got to disliking those Freemasons very much? I wish you had never joined them."

"Never joined them, Fanny! Well, if I hadn't, I should now have been a ruined man—that's certain. What makes you opposed to the Masons?"

"Cousin Sallie prejudiced me against them. She says that they are an association of bad men convened for the worst of purposes. She used, on nights when you were absent, to make me perfectly miserable about you. Oh Robert! I would rather be deprived of every comfort in life, than know, or dream even, that you go with a multitude to do evil."

Forest brought his clenched hand down impatiently upon the table.

"Fanny," he said, "must that woman's poisonous influence be forever here, darkening my hearth-stone? I have seen many a bad woman, but I verily believe she is the greatest devil of them all. To please her, we got in debt, and after it all, found that she was not pleased. She parted from *her* husband, and then came here for the praise-worthy object, it seems, of making you part with yours. She is a parlor serpent, but, perhaps, we can manage to extract her fangs. The woman who wars with Masonry, Fanny, falls out with one of her best friends. Its *protective* influences are of untold value to her. The wife, the sister, and the daughter of a Freemason, are, in many respects, safe and happy personages. They are surrounded at all times by watchful eyes—by interested observers. They will never be seriously harmed. Were I to die to-day, you would not be without friends. Every brother in the fraternity would aid you, if he could. Masons would come in, with all the solemn insignia of office, and bear my remains to their last resting-place. Over the grave my virtues would be extolled, my weaknesses pardoned. They would form a chain around my resting-place, and while giving back ashes to ashes, earth to earth, dust to dust, they would throw over me the evergreen—fit emblem of immortality, of unending spring. The dust would be gently laid upon my coffin by many kind, helping hands. What we do in the lodge, must, it is true, ever remain a secret to the uninitiated, but rest assured, my dear wife, that nothing is done there *morally* wrong. If there was, would clergymen stay among us?—would sober, steady, upright citizens, give us year after year, age after age, generation after generation, approving smiles? Be satisfied that what I say upon this point is true. Judge us by our *public acts*, and then tell me, if a tree which bears such precious fruit, can have its root in bitterness and evil?"

Fanny Forest was convinced and comforted by the words of her husband. Happiness once more reigned in the household, and both husband and wife now ardently hope that their cousin Sallie has made them her last visit.

DOES FREEMASONRY PAY?

"HALLO, here !"

" Well, what is wanted ?"

" I want you to go with me to the lodge to-night."

" I'm not a Freemason ; you have mistaken your man now."

" Neither am I one; but if I don't get black-balled, I expect to shortly. I'm going to the hall to join, and I want you to accompany me. Will you go ?"

The young man addressed shook his head. " It won't pay," he said ; " I make a point of never doing anything unless it pays. Now I don't believe this Masonry does. You will spend time and money, and what will you get in return ? A mighty *secret*, I suppose. No, sir, believe me, Milton, the thing won't pay."

" Perhaps not," said Milton, " but I've a fancy for join-ing. I'm a social fellow, you know, and like to be one of a brotherhood. I'm a young man just starting out in life. I shall oftentimes need assistance, advice, friendship, and aid, and I am willing to pay something to secure this. I am determined to join."

Barker, the young man to whom these thoughts were addressed, shook his head again, and laughed. " ' Don't pay too dear for the whistle,' my good fellow," he said. ' All is not gold that glitters.' ' Look well before you leap.' These are all wise old sayings, Tom ; perhaps you would do well to heed them. Come in here and spend the evening. I'll order champagne and candles, and we'll have a *set-down* together. Let that tomfoolery alone ; it won't pay."

" No, no !" said Milton, " I know what I'm about. I'm bound to be a Freemason. So good evening, if you will not go with me." And Thomas Milton kept on his way to the hall.

Barker stood and looked after him a minute.

"It's a pity," he muttered to himself, as he turned and went into his store, "that Tom Milton hasn't got better sense. He's a fine fellow—a devilish fine fellow, and with his talents and opportunities he ought to make a fortune, but he'll never do it. He don't understand taking care of the dimes. At church collections, missionary meetings, and the like, he can't keep his hand out of his pocket. What benefit will *he* ever reap from Freemasonry ? None whatever. He'll give, and never receive. I'm sorry for Tom—downright sorry for him." And Lewis Barker ran his fingers through the brown locks which clustered thickly around his forehead, and put on a look of commisseration, such as he thought well befitted the occasion.

Thomas Milton and Lewis Barker were merchants in a small inland town in Georgia. They were both of them doing a very good business at the time we write of. Both were young men, and were surrounded by rich and influential friends.

There was, however, one striking difference between them. Milton was a social, free and easy being—one who liked to talk, and had a pleasant word for every body ; even the little child by the roadside shared his smiles. He was liberal too. Not a benevolent scheme was broached, but he had a finger in it. He felt a kindly interest in every thing by which he was surrounded.

But in Lewis Barker's character there was a vein of selfishness ; he, in common phrase, understood the art of looking sharply after the real or imaginary interests of "number one." In short, he too often forgot the golden rule, "whatsoever ye would that men should do unto you, do ye even so unto them." But notwithstanding this dissimilarity in character, the young men were fast friends, and were much together.

Time passed on, and young Milton went regularly to the lodge-room. Barker stayed at home footing up his books, or to talk with Alice Moore, a pretty girl to whom he was engaged, now living on Third-street.

Once or twice he met Milton on his way to watch a sick

brother. There was a happy expression about his face, which seemed to say ,*Freemasonry pays.* Then, in spite of himself, young Barker could not keep from wondering what those fellows were about. Going to the lodge, or off on masonic duty, seemed to be mere pastime with them. They went anywhere and everywhere with alacrity. They were mystical beings truly. Even Milton, with whom he had always been intimate, had suddenly grown enigmatical and strange. He did not fully comprehend his movements as of old.

*   *   *   *   *   *   *

There came a time of great pecuniary embarrassment, such as frequently occurs in the haunts of trade. Men behind the counters and at the street corners wore solemn faces, and worked or walked with hurried movements. Barker and Milton both shared in this monetary depression. But somehow, the latter seemed to rise above his embarrassments more easily than the former. Perhaps Freemasonry had something to do with this. If so, it certainly paid in that instance at least. It was at length agreed that our two young friends would do better in the city than in an inland village. Accordingly, they severed family ties, broke up old associations, and removed to the flourishing city of A——.

For awhile, every thing betokened for both brightening prospects. There are few things denied to well-directed industry, and both possessed this in an unusual degree.

But alas! "it is not in man who walketh to direct his steps." In 1839, the yellow-fever, that scourge of the South, visited the city. Barker and Milton were among its first victims. Both were seized at their boarding-houses, and both were thought by their attending physician to be in a critical situation.

To the bedside of one there came a crowd of masonic brethren, ready to watch, aid, comfort and console. Nothing that the tenderest affection could devise was left undone—nothing that the most untiring energy could accomplish was left unexecuted.

To the couch of the other there came *hired* watchers, who in nine cases out of ten sleep while the victim groans. The cooling draught was given grudgingly to his lips— the pillow was seldom moved beneath his aching temples —the long nights were never enlivened by one kind word of sympathy. Before him lay the grave—a tomb grudgingly given in the potter's-field, and the sexton he supposed would be the only attendant at his funeral. Such a prospect is gloomy in the extreme. At that hour Lewis Barker thought, with a groan, of the village left behind— a village still gladdened by the sweet face of Alice Moore. And thus he lingered between life and death, until his old friend Milton became convalescent, and went to his bedside to wait upon him.

"How happens it," he said, as he grasped the hand of Milton, "that you are recovering so rapidly, while I lie stretched here, with the fever still running rampant through my veins. I was told at first that the physician pronounced you the sickest of the two."

"I owe it in part, I suppose," said Milton, "to the excellent nursing which I received. Good nursing is worth more than medicine to the sick. But brighten up, man ; you will soon be well again. I expect to dance at your wedding yet. It will not do to let you die here. Alice never would forgive me."

Barker turned his head wearily upon his pillow. "After all," he thought, "Milton was right. Freemasonry pays. If I ever get well, I mean to join the lodge ; and if Alice objects, I'll tell her of this incident in our lives. How could I be so deceived in this matter ? Milton did not need my commisseration in the least. How strange! *Freemasonry pays.*"

Barker was true to his resolves. He recovered—married—and joined the lodge ; and now Freemasonry has not in all its ranks a more devoted brother.

THE FOREST HOME.

"There is no help for Brooks, I suppose."

"None in the world."

The first speaker shook his head. "It seems hard," he said, "to have a man's possessions swept from him in any such way? Why was he fool enough to put his name to those papers?"

"Because he has a kind, good heart, I suppose," responded the other, "and will at any time do almost anything to accommodate a friend."

"And this is what he gets for it. For my part, I'd rather not be quite so good-natured," and, with something like a toss of the head and a derisive laugh, Miller turned down the street and entered his office.

"Yes," mused Willis, the speaker, still standing in the street—"hatred for love—ingratitude for kindness, and slander for well-doing—this is what a man often gets in this world. But what of all that? upon us all is laid an obligation higher than any imposed by mortals. 'Be ye kindly affectioned one towards another,' is the command of Heaven, and I had rather meet with some reverses of fortune—experience a few of the ups and downs of life, than to go to the grave's verge close-fisted and suspicious ever of my kind."

As he said this, he walked on and overtook Judge Horton. "Brooks's property is all advertised to be sold at sheriff's sale, I'm told," said the portly Judge, sticking his thumbs in the arm-holes of his vest, and turning square around, with an anxious expression upon his face.

Willis bowed. "I'm sorry," continued the Judge, "sorry as though my own brother was the sufferer. What on earth is he, with his family, to do? There's Mrs. Brooks, who never did a day's hard work in her life, and Edith, his daughter, who is too sweet faced and lovely to blush unseen, and his two boys, Dick and Harry, smart intelligent lads, who ought soon to be in college. What is going to become of them all? Brooks ought not to have gone Green's security for such an amount; but it's just like him—he'd go his death for any of us whom he calls friends."

Willis did not reply, and the Judge stood mute for a moment.

"I'm going to do all I can for them," at length he said, "and the fellow will have the sympathy of all his fellow craftsmen. But when we are in distress, we sometimes need something more tangible than a look of pity, and a kind word—though these strengthen a man oftentimes, as a giant is said to be strengthened by wine. I've got a house and lot on Third-street, where he is at liberty to live, rent-free for the present, if he'll accept of it; and I'll get him a situation as clerk in our office into the bargain. His boys will have to help him scuffle for a livelihood for awhile, and Edith can give music lessons."

Willis started and blushed. He was a young man—and Edith Brooks had long held a favorable position in his eye. He had never been on any particular footing of intimacy with the family, but he had been in the habit of seeing Edith almost daily, and somehow, her image was often uppermost in his mind. The idea of her being now condemned to the drudgery of teaching was repulsive to him. He struck his walking-stick so decidedly into the sand at his feet, that some of the shining particles flew up and struck his hand. But he was still silent, and the two passed on up Broad-street together.

Everywhere, before the stores, and at the corners, little knots of men were talking over Brooks's misfortunes. Many of these were Freemasons, and all expressed regret and sympathy. But where had Peter Brooks meanwhile hidden himself?

He sat in the parlor at home, with his elbow resting on the table, and his hand supporting his head. His face was grave to sternness—his cheeks were sunken and pallid--his hair was dishevelled, and on his forehead there were furrows which seemed to be the imprint of years, but they had in reality been planted there by the relentless fingers of care.

"Alice!" at length he said in a hoarse voice.

His wife, a sweet faced woman, some thirty-five years of age, arose hastily and stood beside him.

"My head aches very badly," he said, looking up with faded eyes into her face, "I believe this security affair will kill me. It is too bad! too bad! all that we have embellished and loved—depended upon and worked for, must go now. Our children will be portionless—we, ourselves, in our old age, little better than beggars."

Mrs. Brooks's face, to his great surprise, was very calm—almost serene. She passed around to the back of his chair, laid her soft white hand upon his throbbing temples, and drew his head to her bosom. There was balm in her gentle touch, as well as music in her soft voice.

"It is a great blow to us all," she said quietly.

"Yes, Alice, the greatest that could possibly have fallen upon us. Heaven help us to bear it."

"I do not look upon it as being quite as bad as that, Peter. I had rather, a thousand times over, lose this pleasant home, where we have all been so happy together, than to lose you, or one of the children. We are all alive, and can still love, comfort, and help one another."

"True, true, Alice. I had not thought of that. We have still something to be thankful for."

"O, yes," continued the wife, in the same hopeful tone. "Much, much, to call forth gratitude, if we will but look at the matter aright. We are all in the enjoyment of excellent health. I had rather lose my property, than to have one of us smitten by an incurable disease. There are paralysis, cancers, palsy and epilepsy, any one of which might have struck us down, and made us drag, dying, miserable bodies about during the residue of our lives. But we are all well. The children have cheeks as ruddy as apples. We are remarkably vigorous, too, for people who will soon be in the decline of life."

"Yes," said Mr. Brooks, musingly.

"And, then, Dick and Harry are such promising boys,

and Edith is so affectionate and amiable! How many boys give their parents anxiety and care, and end, perhaps, a course of dissipation by getting into the penitentiary. But our boys have never been given in the least to sowing wild oats. What a great blessing that is!"

"Yes," again responded the husband, while a glance of pride and affection shot from his kindling eyes. "Dick and Harry are fine fellows—I wanted to do a good part by them; educate them, and set them up in business, but the game is up now," and again he sighed.

"They will not mind making their own way in life, as hundreds of smart men have done before them, I dare say," continued Mrs. Brooks, still cheerfully; "and Edith bore the news of your failure so well. She doesn't seem to mind going to live in a cabin in the forest in the least. She said that it would be delightful living in the country, and raising chickens, cultivating flowers, and supplying the table with vegetables of our own raising; and she said that she would have a little school, and board at home; and I don't know what plans she has not laid out for the future."

"God bless her!" fervently ejaculated the sire. "God bless her sweet face now and forever more! But the world, Alice! I dread the sneers of the world; business men will coldly shrug their shoulders, and say that I have been short-sighted and verdant to be taken in in any such a way; but I always liked Green, and I had no idea that he would run away and leave me with his debts to pay."

"No," said Mrs. Brooks, "I know that you have a good, kind, unsuspicious heart, and we all love you the better for it. I had rather live in a cabin with you, than to dwell in a palace with such a man as Miller, for instance. When he dies, he will be rich, perhaps, in gold coin; but he can take none of it with him, while the niggardly, cross-grained dispositions and affection that he is culturing here, will go with him to the Judgment. How poor he will feel there, my dear husband! No! no! I like my husband all the better for his open hand and generous heart, and there is One above who likes him too;" and

Mrs. Brooks bent her head over, and touched his cheek with her lip.

Gradually the bankrupt's brow cleared up. He took his hat and went out into the street.

"There goes Brooks!" said Willis, touching Horton's arm. "He looks cheerful enough. I don't see how he can take his misfortunes so coolly. He don't seem at all dispirited, only a little pale perhaps. Let us pass over and speak to him." The two crossed over, and warmly grasped his hand.

"Brooks, 'pon my word, you are bearing this little clap of misfortune like a man—very little worsted by it, I see. Well, I'm glad to se it. I was just telling Willis of a little business I had with you this morning. I want you to take a clerkship in our office, and there's my house on Third street, which you are perfectly welcome to."

"Thank you, thank you, Judge; a friend in need is said to be a friend indeed. I cannot accept of your house, for I am going to move my family to the country; but I'll take the clerkship. I expect to earn my bread now by the sweat of my brow. Every morsel is to be honestly, perhaps painfully, but I trust nobly, earned. He who gives me the opportunity of labor, will confer a favor upon me and mine."

"Well, the clerkship is yours, and I will aid you in any other way that I can. I know of a hundred men who will stand by you, too, in almost any emergency. A fellow with such friends as you have need not be down-hearted;" and the Judge wiped his eyes with his coat-sleeve, and passed on.

Almost everywhere, Peter Brooks met with unexpected sympathy; his heart grew light, almost gay, over these manifestations of friendship.

Time passed on, and a little log cabin in the wilderness received the family, who had before scarcely known what it was to have an ungratified want. Every thing, almost, that they had once called their own, had gone under the hammer. Costly pictures, plate, furniture, carpets, window shades, books, all were gone. As Brooks watched the cherished mementos of other days disappearing one after another, the cheerful air of his family was hardly sufficient to dispel his gloom.

"Alice," he said again, "this is too bad! too bad! If this property were going for debts that I had contracted—for luxuries which we had purchased and enjoyed—I should not mind it so much; but it is going for what never afforded us any pleasure. Others reaped the benefit of what is now passing away from us forever."

Mrs. Brooks simply said "yes," and then went on her way as quietly and cheerfully as before.

The little log cabin was very dark, and very rough. No windows of glass admitted the golden light of Heaven. But Edith Brooks's laugh rang out there like bird music, and the boys came in with sparkling eyes, and noisy tongues, declaring simultaneously that such fish never were seen, as could be found in the stream which went foaming and dashing, and anon sleeping in quiet hollows far down in the depths of that wide old forest. The months, God's ministers sent to talk over with us the sweet and instructive lessons of Nature, sped swiftly away. June came in with her dewy feet and rose-garlanded brow. August, with his sultry breath and-dust besprinkled robe. October, like a warrior just returned from the field, with his trailing garments crimsoned with blood. And last of all, December, with his icy breath and ruddy fires.

Through all these, the Brooks' family went cheerfully on their way, and "God sent to their souls a new baptismal of *peace.*"

To the imaginative spirit of Edith, it seemed that the Divine hand had written the country all over with "living epistles" of goodness and mercy—epistles to poor, starving and blinded humanity. She listened to the wind rustling the green leaves, and watched the birds building their nests among the boughs, as she sewed by the door. Dick and Harry worked like giants, paling in the garden, clearing away under-brush, and raising vegetables and flowers for market. Never had they seemed happier in their lives. Their shouts startled the hare from its hiding place, and the thrush from her nest-building.

The low, dark walls of the cabin were white-washed with perfect neatness. The floor was scoured until it was as stainless as the pine table which stood against the wall. Roses and althea, pansies and jassmine, were taught to bloom in the yard, and the wilderness assumed a new and lovelier aspect.

Mr. Brooks pursued his vocations in the clerk's office with great diligence. As Judge Horton had foreseen, a host of friends clustered around him, ever ready to lend him a helping hand, and plenty came into the Forest Home.

One night—when September had come with its golden days and cool nights—its aster flowers in the woods, and golden rod nodding by the fences—when the fire flamed and flickered, and blazed up the ample chimney—Peter Brooks came in from his daily horseback ride to the village, threw off his overcoat, and sat down in the rocking chair which Edith had placed for him before the hearth. He looked around upon the tidy cabin and its cheerful inmates with a smiling air.

" Wife," he said, at last, " I believe we have lived in this out-of-the-way place three years or so; havn't we?"

" Yes; three years, come December."

" Things look a little more cheerful than they did when we first came; don't they?"

" Yes; somewhat more so, I will acknowledge," said Mrs. Brooks, smiling.

" Do you know, Alice," he said, " that I have often blessed God for making me a poor man?"

" No, I did not. On the contrary, I thought you took the matter rather sadly at first."

" So I did, Alice. But I am now convinced that there is one, even God, who knows what is best for us. Had I never met with reverses of fortune, I should never have known what treasures I possessed in you and the children —I should never have known what firm and reliable friends a parcel of Freemasons can become when misfortunes assail a fellow—I should never have known how deep a baptism of *quiet* rests upon an humble country life. Now, when we move back and take our old stand in society, I shall understand all these things."

"When we move back, father? Pray, are we *ever* going to move back?" cried Edith with surprise. "I didn't think we would ever get rich enough to move back."

"I have bought our old place again, to-day, and the pictures and the piano and most of the furniture has been re-purchased, daughter. Next week we will leave our forest home and try village life again. I must send Harry and Dick to college, and Mr. Willis, I think, will welcome my daughter with a hearty good-will back to Greenville."

At this remark, Edith blushed deeply.

"How have you been able to do all this, husband?" said Mrs. Brooks, with surprise. "How could you re-purchase our old lot in Greenville?"

Mr. Brooks drew from his pocket a long letter, announcing the fact that a relative in England had died, leaving him an unencumbered estate.

"Here is the secret of it all, Alice," he replied.

"I did not know that you had a relative in the Old World," said Mrs. Brooks, thoughtfully.

"Neither did I; but Horton, who heard of this heirless estate, traced it all out, and established my claims beyond a doubt. We are rich again, Alice—rich in dollars, but richer in a quiet confidence and trust in one another—a confidence born of affliction and baptized in tears."

Seven years have passed since that night. Edith Brooks is now the wife of Mr. Willis. Dick and Harry are both successful lawyers, practicing their profession in an inland town, and Mr. Brooks and his wife are quietly going down the vale of life together. Side by side they met the storm and outlived the tempest. Their feet will soon go up the purple mountains to the far heights of the "White City," whose maker and builder is God. Mingled with the anthems which will then flow from their tongues, will be a strain of thanksgiving, that while on earth they were chastened and disciplined, restrained, strengthened and guided by the unerring hand of infinite love. They will clearly see, amidst the brightness of the day that never dies, that not one drop of affliction could have been spared from the cup which they were made to drain. Oh! blessed are the lessons of adversity! By quiet, patient endurance, as well as daring action, the Great Father is glorified, and those who tread with unfaltering steps and unmurmuring lips onward, right *onward*, where the narrow path of duty leads, shall at least sit down in peace beside the Crystal Fountains, and pluck the golden fruitage of a happier life.

THE MISER'S GIFT.

" Thousand evil things there are, that hate
To look on happiness."

THERE was a gentle tap at Squire Ringgold's office door.

"Come in," he said, without rising from between the arms of an ancient chair, which he had drawn up before the table, or once raising his eyes from a ponderous law-book, whose pages he was carefully searching.

The visitor either did not hear the invitation to enter, or else hesitated about accepting it. It was several minutes before the door opened.

"Come in, I say," cried the Squire, elevating his eyes and voice at the same time.

A slight noise outside the door was now heard; a hand was upon the knob, and a girlish form soon afterwards entered. In her hand she carried a sealed letter.

"Ha! Julia, is that you!" said the Squire, with something like wonder in his tones. "Why couldn't you come in without making all that fuss? You kept me wondering for full five minutes who was on the outside."

"I was not quite sure, father, that I should find you alone and unengaged."

"Unengaged, child! When did you ever see or hear

of my being idle? But what do you want? Why do you care whether I am busy or unoccupied? Has your aunt sent you after those flower-seeds I promised to bring home with me to dinner?"

"No, father," said the girl, and her delicate cheek glowed like the crimson heart of a summer rose. "I came on a very different errand—one which made it imperatively necessary for me to find you alone. I have a letter here directed to you."

"A letter!" said the old man with a puzzled look, at the same time taking it from her hand—"a letter! Pray, who is it from, and where did you get it? You are not my clerk."

"I know it," said the girl; "this missive did not come through the post-office; it was given to me by the writer, who requested me to give it into your hands."

"The writer, Rufus Potter, the young clergyman at Morton," continued the old man, glancing over the signature at the bottom. "Ha! Julia, child, what does this mean? I know of no reason why *he* should have honored me with an epistle. I have never before reckoned him among my correspondents. Sit down here upon my knee, child, as you used to do long ago, until I have found out its contents. Don't blush so like a half-guilty thing. I suspect, from your confusion, that you know what the author wants, even before his letter is read."

The girl sank down as desired upon her sire's lap. The old man read the letter carefully from top to bottom.

"And so, Julia," he said, as he folded it, "you have a lover—one, too, as poor as a church mouse. I am sorry young people will set aside common sense, and be romantic; but they will; it's natural. When I was a young fellow like Potter, I fell into the same error—courted a girl for her beauty—afterwards loved her for her merit, and married her because I loved her; and the consequence was, that I have scratched a poor man's head ever since. Had I acted more rationally, I might have been as rich as your uncle Peter is now."

"And perhaps as miserable," added the girl, archly.

15

"Perhaps as miserable," repeated the old man; "that's a fact, girl—perhaps as miserable."

"You never regretted, sir, I am sure, marrying my mother. You wept as if your heart were breaking on the day she died."

"True, true," said the old man, while a tear sprang from its cell at the mournful recollection. "She was a good woman, Jule; a better one never trod this sin-cursed earth. But had I been richer, child, I might sometimes have made her happier."

"Would the riches without *her* have made *you* happier, father?"

"No, child, I would not have cared for riches then."

"Or would the riches without *you* have made *her* happier, father?"

"Well, child, I don't believe they would. She was an affectionate being, Julia. She clung to me in the darkest hour, and never murmured if I could only stay with her. She had a true woman's heart."

"But a kind Providence had so arranged it, that you could not possess each other and the riches too. I cannot see how you acted unwisely, father, in taking that which afforded you the greatest happiness."

"You reason like a girl in love, Jule—like a girl in love with a poor man. The world would teach you a different philosophy from that."

"But the philosophy of the world may be false," said the girl, "while mine is correct. It looks to me to be plain common-sense reasoning. Why should we take a rock, when it is bread we are hungering after, simply because the bystander says that a rock is what we ought to take? I wot not."

"But who is this young fellow—this Rev. Rufus Potter —who comes to me now, begging for my only daughter— my pet lamb—my choicest treasure? Where did he come from? do you know?"

"I know better where he is going," said the girl, glancing her beautiful hazel eyes upward, "and, father, I should like to go with him."

"Where is he going?" said the old man, not fully comprehending at first what she meant. "Has he been called away to a distant field, where there is the offer of a larger salary? Morton has not a very wealthy congregation."

"No; I do not know that he has had the offer of a better living on earth, but he is going to the city of the New Jerusalem soon. Its gates, father, are like pearls, and its foundations are of all manner of precious stones—its streets are like gold, and there is no night there—its inhabitants are for ever young and beautiful; they are clothed in white, and sighing and sorrow have fled away. There, father, is where the young clergyman at Morton is going; and can I be blamed for wanting to go with him?"

The tear that had sprang to the old man's eye now rolled slowly down his cheek, but his daughter drew from a pocket in her apron a delicate white handkerchief and wiped it away.

"Those are strange unworldly thoughts of yours, Julia, dear," he said at last; "but this is a bitter world, child, and its paths, thorny and tear-washed, have to be traveled before the New Jerusalem can be gained. The young fellow is well enough, I dare say; he is fine-looking, a good orator, and a good Christian. But, Jule, he'll let you starve, I'm afraid. I have little or nothing to give you. His salary is not large. You cannot live on love alone. Peter might make my only child happy, but he is as stingy as though he was not worth a cent."

The young girl's face grew very sad. She became pale and silent. The old man, too, was thoughtful.

"Julia," he said at last, "I have thought this matter of marriage all over. You are my only child. There is nothing I desire so ardently as I do your happiness. On the one hand, you may contract a mercenary marriage without love; on the other, you may marry for love alone. I leave you to make your own choice."

"Father," said the girl, "I would do nothing contrary to your wishes, but I love this young clergyman at Morton better than I shall ever love another. I am willing to encounter poverty with him. But uncle Peter is childless and wifeless. He has gold in abundance; he surely will give us something; I feel confident of it."

The old man sighed, and shook his head.

" Mr. Potter," he said, " is a Freemason. I remember seeing him once clad in his regalia. I think he holds some high office in that body. You know your uncle's prejudices against the Order. That alone will be sufficient to make him regard with aversion the clergyman at Morton. If you marry him, I cannot promise you any assistance from my miserly brother Peter. He is rich, and, as you remark, ought to aid my only child; but he is niggardly in disposition, and most inveterate in all his prejudices."

What the old man said about his brother was very true. He had coined his soul into gold. The sweet affections which embellish life, and make existence desirable, had been sacrificed by him upon the altar of Mammon. No wife had ever smiled upon him; no children had ever clambered upon his knees, and stroked, with their soft white hands, his rough and sun-burned cheeks, and called him by the endearing name of "father." Gold—gold— gold was his thought by day, his dream by night. Premature wrinkles were upon his forehead. His head had grown grey before its time. He lived to hoard, and well merited the name of miser.

Julia Ringgold was, next to gold, his greatest favorite. But his temper was by no means always the same. Sometimes he frowned on those, on whom an hour before he had lavished smiles. A word, a look, a deed, trivial and unimportant, was oftentimes sufficient to estrange him for months.

But the hearts of the young are sanguine in their affections. Hope whispers flattering tales, and Julia Ringgold, in a few months after this interview with her father, gave her hand and heart to the idol of her affections, trustingly and without fear.

Uncle Peter, as he was everywhere called, did not, by any means, smile approval upon this match. But Julia was economical in her habits, and the young clergyman at

Morton was a popular and approved minister. They began their married life in the little parsonage. And domestic love—that one bright flower of Eden which survived the universal wreck—gathered sweetness, when shadowed by the Cross.

A truthful writer has said that "there is nothing on earth so beautiful as the household on which love for ever smiles, and where religion walks, a counsellor and friend. No cloud can darken it, for its twin stars are centered in the soul. No storm can make it tremble; it has an earthly support—the gift of Heaven—and a heavenly anchor. But the roof beneath which it dwells, shelters a sacred spot, where the curious eye must not peer, nor the stranger's foot tread." Such a spot Julia felt her home to be; and as she looked into her husband's smiling eyes, she cared little for uncle Peter or his gold.

But time is a great destroyer of romance. Children sprang up like olive plants around their table. The clergyman began to find his salary hardly adequate to supply the wants of his numerous household. But he toiled on, and seldom suffered himself to despond. "Faithful is He that calleth you!" seemed ever to be ringing in his ears. "He who soweth in tears shall reap in joy."

It was about this time that the yellow fever visited a neighboring city, spreading devastation and death in its track. Uncle Peter had gone thither for purposes of trade, but as soon as he heard of the appearance of the scourge, hastened to Morton, hoping to escape infection.

But the fatal fever soon raged in his system. The night air of the metropolis had sowed its poisonous seeds. As soon as the nature of his disease was ascertained, the simple-hearted villagers, who knew little of its character, and had taken the idea that, like small-pox, it was contagious, fled from him affrighted. No nurse could be procured to wait by his bedside. Men who, in the days of his health, had been obsequious and cringing in his presence, now never entered his meanly-furnished chamber.

He lay down on his pallet, and prayed to die. He could obtain neither medicine nor food. He saw nothing before him but a lingering death—death from starvation, if not disease.

One day a tall manly form entered his apartment. He paused beside the bed, and uncle Peter recognized, at a glance, the pastor at Morton.

"You are ill," he said, as he stooped and took the yellow, shrivelled hand of the miser's in his. "You are ill and suffering for the want of nursing. I have come to take care of you. I have brought with me medicine and food. I hope to see you yet restored to health and happiness."

"You !" said the miser, scarcely believeing the evidence of his senses. "Have *you* come to my aid—you, whose name and character I have so often reviled, and whom I have so thoroughly hated? I am no Freemason. On the contrary, I have always been a most inveterate enemy to the Order. I cannot comprehend the motives which have brought you to me."

The clergyman's face assumed almost an angelic expression, as he replied :

"True, you are not a Freemason. True, you are not a Christian. You have in many ways shown yourself to be my enemy. But *I am both a Mason and a Christian.* As such, I am bound by the strongest of bonds, by the most benevolent of motives, by all the commands and hopes and promises of Christianity and of Masonry, which rests on the broad basis of religion itself, to aid suffering humanity whenever and wherever I may find it. Never shall it be said of me, an ambassador of Christ, that mine enemy even hungered, and I gave him no meat—thirsted, and I gave him no drink—was sick, or in prison, and I visited him not."

"It is false," said the miser, raising himself up with a degree of strength, the effect of passion and excitement, and resting his sallow, wretched face upon his hand. "It is all as false as the father of lies. Christianity and Masonry teach no such disinterested principles of benevolence. You are interested by mercenary motives in coming here. You would influence me to give to Julia, your wife, a portion of my estate, but I tell you plainly that my will is made. I shall leave my possessions to one who has never disgraced herself by marrying a beggar and a Freemason, as she has done."

The clergyman stood meekly, until the miser had completely exhausted his physical strength by the vehemence of his passion, and was compelled through weakness to sink down again upon his pillow.

"You can will your fortune to the wind, uncle," he at length said, mildly, "if you choose to do so; Julia and I are very happy without any portion of it. I did not come here after your gold. I seek not yours, but *you*. You are the one I am anxious to save. You misunderstand my motives; you misconstrue the spirit of the doctrine I profess and teach. May the Holy Spirit heal you of your infirmities and enlighten your soul. I shall not suffer myself to be driven from any post of plain and positive duty, by the vituperations and anger of him whom I would aid; so take my medicines, and make yourself easy in regard to the *motives* by which I am actuated in thus seeking you. They are such as my God will approve, and that is enough for me."

The miser was not only exhausted by the effort which he had made, but he was awed into silence by the coolness and dignity of the one thus addressing him. He swallowed the medicine soon afterwards administered to him, without uttering a word, and quietly suffered himself to be moved and treated as the clergyman saw proper.

The Mason and minister did not watch alone. A sweet pale face came at times, and looked with the pitying eye of an angel upon the wretched sufferer. A soft and gentle hand smoothed his pillow. A light footfall could be heard in the taper-lit apartment at midnight stealing around the room. And his chamber put on an appearance of tidiness and comfort, under the ministrations of the clergyman's wife, such as it had never worn before. In his heart of hearts, uncle Peter at times blessed her, but he was too ill to manifest any pleasure in her company, any gladness at her presence.

The violence of his disease at length abated. It had yielded to the skilful treatment of his self-constituted physicians and nurses. He was able to get up and go out again into the broad sunshine and the haunts of traffic and trade.

To the clergyman and his wife he was civil, and at times almost affectionate. He came occasionally to the parsonage, and still oftener, to Mr. Potter's church. He fondled Julia's children, and took them upon his knees; but he never intimated by word or deed, or sign even, that he intended to bestow upon his niece any portion of his hoarded gold.

* * * * * * * * * *

It was a bleak, blustering, winter afternoon. Mr. and Mrs. Potter had been out all day on parochial visits. As they stopped in the hall, on their return, a large round box met their eyes. It had evidently been deposited there during their absence. Julia, although her fingers were numbed with the cold, stepped towards it, wondering what kind heart had bestowed upon them, thus modestly, its donation.

"Somebody has sent us a cheese, dear," she said, as she stopped and surveyed the dimensions of the box. "I reckon it's a cheese! But here is something penciled on the lid," and stooping down, she read: "*A gift from Uncle Peter.*"

"What is that?" said her husband, pausing beside her.

"Uncle Peter has sent us a cheese, as I live," she continued, glancing archly into her husband's face, and removing at the same time the lid. "What is going to happen? Such unheard-of liberality is astonishing. Is the world coming to an end, I wonder? See, dear, what a large, golden-looking cheese! Who would have thought it?"

The clergyman smiled.

"We must have some of it for supper to-night, Julia," he said; "I think I shall relish a piece right well."

Julia returned the cover to its place, and passed out to relieve herself of her bonnet and cloak.

When the snowy cloth was spread for tea, she sent the servant girl after the box.

"Bring it into the pantry," she said; "I will cut it myself. I wish that uncle Peter was here to tea with us."

The girl soon returned.

"Please ma'am," she said, stopping in the doorway, "I can't lift that 'ar box. It's as heavy as lead."

"Can't lift it, Susan!" said Julia. "Why I could almost lift it myself, and you are twice as strong as I am. What ails you?"

"Why, ma'am, it's the heaviest cheese I ever seed or heard tell on in my life; I really believe it would weigh a thousand pounds. May I ax John to help me?"

"Yes; tell John to bring it," said Julia carelessly. "I think you both together will muster up strength sufficient to fetch it here."

The box was brought, and deposited upon the pantry table, but not without difficulty. The next operation was to remove its contents; this was at length accomplished. Julia took the knife and penetrated the golden rind. But what could the cheese be made of? She could not cut it. The edge of the knife came in contact with something as impenetrable as a rock. She drew it out, dulled and blunted.

Her curiosity was excited. She hastily sliced off a piece of the rind. To her surprise some gold coin rolled out and fell at her feet. A few more incisions told the tale and revealed the mystery. The cheese was nothing but a rind. The inside had been carefully scraped out, and the aperture filled with gold. Uncle Peter's gift was one of no mean value. It was a *golden* cheese indeed. It contained a very handsome fortune.

"Would you have thought it?" said Julia, as she looked up into her husband's eyes, who had been called in by her loud exclamations of wonder and surprise. "Who would have dreamed of this, dear."

The clergyman smiled.

"The blessing of the Lord, Julia," he said at length, "maketh rich, and He addeth no sorrow with it. Those who fearlessly do their duty at all times and under all circumstances, actuated by pure and good motives, have little to fear from poverty or disgrace, As a Mason and a Christian, I visited him in sickness, asking and expecting for myself and family only the Mason's and the Christian's reward. But lo! we are made rich by the MISER'S GIFT."

<hr/>

BROKEN SHRINES.

I MET a fair-haired child, and it was weeping. In its hands it held a broken vase, from which the flowers were scattered and the fragrance had departed. Poor thing! I said, do not weep, for earth is full of Broken Shrines, and this is one of them.

We journeyed on and met a beautiful bride. Her step was as light as the spotted fawn's, and on her cheek there was a glow such as mantles the heart of a rose. Her careless laugh rang out as wildly, sweet, and clear as bird-music; and the aged and the young, as they turned aside to let her pass, murmured, "how lovely!" Her's was the shrine of a beautiful spirit, which danced in her eyes, rang in her laughter, and beautified the whole casket containing it. I said, "Glad-hearted being, go on, and may earth hold for you no Broken Shrine."

But I saw her again. In her lap there lay a lifeless infant. Its eye of blue was half-unclosed; its little dimpled hands lay crossed; its whole figure was like a waxen toy. The mother wept, and "would not be comforted," because her darling "was not." The shrine of her choicest affections lay wrecked on her bosom. "Poor thing," said I, "another Broken Shrine!"

Once again I looked, when a few circling suns had passed. The young bride's lip was mute—her eye was lustreless; she neither laughed nor wept, and I saw that the shrine of her own beautiful spirit was broken. The weeper had become the wept for, the mourned over, the departed. Tears were rained into her coffin, and drooping heads followed her to "the narrow house appointed for all who live." How beautiful that BROKEN SHRINE!

I turned and met an old man. His white locks floated like snow over his wrinkled brow—his weak steps were tottering and slow—a friendly staff supported his frame, and his hands trembled like aspen leaves in a breeze. But I saw that tears as well as age were now dimming his eyes.

"My only, my idolized son," he said, "has become the victim of intemperance. He was the shrine of my best hopes. On him I hoped to lean in my dotage; but he has just now, with horrid oaths and imprecations, driven me from his door. I did not think, in his proud, beautiful boyhood, that it would ever come to this. I nurtured him carefully then, and thought that in my age and loneliness he would repay the debt of kindness he owed me." And the aged one "lifted up his voice and wept."

"Weep on, old man," I said; "yours is the most mournful of all earth's Broken Shrines. The crushed bud can be replaced—the dead infant lives in heaven—the sorrowing mother has regained her dead. But oh! when the God-like in man departs, HOW FEARFUL THE BROKEN SHRINE!

———◦◇◦———

THE HOUR-GLASS.—The hour-glass is an emblem of human life. We cannot, without astonishment, behold the little particles, which the machine contains, pass away almost imperceptibly, and yet, to our surprise, in the short space of an hour all are exhausted. Thus wastes human life. At the end of man's short hour, death strikes the blow, and hurries him off the stage to his long and darksome resting place, from which there is no more rising till the trumpet-sound of that morning in which all mankind will rise to a never-ending eternity of bliss, or to an everlasting contempt and shame.

THE ORPHAN'S MINIATURE.

CHAPTER I.

"How still she sleeps! The young and sinless girl!"—*Rockwell.*

EUGENIA MARION was dying; there was no disbelieving
it. The black, lustrous eyes had assumed a glassy look—
the pale, powerless lids had dropped half over them, and,
through the purple lips, the breath came strugglingly.
Her long, silken hair floated, unbound, over the snowy
pillow, and the blood was settling beneath the nails of the
attenuated fingers, which were clasped upon the counterpane. There was, moreover, a strange, deathly look about
the mouth; the nose had assumed a sharper outline, and
the cold sweat had gathered almost into beaded drops upon the forehead.

Some one has said that " Death is beautiful—not as the
end of man—not as the extinction of a noble and wonderful being—not as the final result and close of existence—
but beautiful in its time, as the momentary passage to a
fairer land; the extrication of the soul from its temporary
dwelling place; the resting of the no longer needed body;
the free ascent of the delivered spirit to its new abode."

I know not but that it is so, and yet it seemed sad and
mournful for one like *her* to die.

She was a widow and mother. It must be a bitter thing
to leave one's offspring to a lonely, unprotected orphanage
in a world like this. Was it the agony of parting forever
from her child, or was it the pang of dying, which caused
that young mother at times to start so wildly from her
pillow, and essay to move the fast stiffening lips, which
even then refused to utter sound? Her eyes, too, moved
restlessly, and at last seemed fixed upon a tiny little creature of two years old, who, upborne in her nurse's arms,
gazed with a wild, startled look into her dying mother's

face. Poor Ellen Marion! How little did the child realize what was passing away from her then, forever—she did
not know, in her infantile simplicity, that the tomb was
closing over the fondest heart that ever beat for her.

Mrs. Marion was dying in her paternal mansion, but her
mother had long before preceded her to the grave, and
no one was left then to witness her death-struggle but
her white-headed and decrepit sire, whose wrinkled face
and palsied limbs told that his pilgrimage on earth was
nearly over, and that he would soon demand a place beside her in the village church-yard. One or two servants
had come to minister to her wants, and to support her
child, and a neighbor or two had dropped in when they
heard that she was dying. It was May, and a window
stood open at the foot of her bed. A sweetbriar, which
had been planted by her own hands, looked in and nodded
its delicate blossoms in the wind, shaking perfume from
every petal, and a mocking-bird, perched upon the topmost bough of a locust-tree in the yard, filled the house
with its matchless mimicry. Old Mr. Absalom had but
two children—the fair, girlish creature, who now lay before him dying, and a son, who was married and living in
a neighboring State. Word had been sent to Edward
Absalom of the illness of his sister, and he was now hourly
expected at the Glen.

Old Mr. Absalom sat down upon one side of the bed,
and resting his crutches upon his knees, extended his
tremulous hand and clasped Eugenia's wrist, as if anxious
to see if the fluttering, uncertain pulse was not growing
stronger—if the spark of life was not rekindling. He had
not wept before for years, but now tears rolled down and
lodged in the wrinkles on his cheeks. The thin, white
hair, too, yielded to the wind, that stole in through the
sweetbriar at the window, and drifted like snow over his
venerable forehead.

It is an affecting sight to see an old man shedding tears.
The language of that weeping seemed to be,

> "My flower, my blighted flower, thou that wert made
> For the kind fostering of sweet summer airs.
> How hath the storm been with thee?"

"Dran-pa! don't cry," said the child. The old man looked up, and saw little Ellen stretching her plump arms towards him. He reached out his withered hands, and folded the sweet little cherub to his bosom. "Mamma tick!" continued the little creature, stroking with her soft palm the old man's face; "mamma tick, but mamma get well."

The words had hardly escaped from her lips before the white sheet grew still upon the upheaving breast—the breath no longer came through the lips—the clasped fingers slowly dropped apart—Eugenia Marion was dead.

The old man yielded back into the nurse's arms, the sweet burden in his bosom, and then flinging himself down upon the pillow, with his cheek pressing the face of his dead daughter, he groaned in agony of spirit. But he arose at last, and aided by two domestics, tottered from the room, yet at night, when the pale moonlight came in through the little window, and the corpse of his child had been dressed ready for the grave, he crept back upon his crutches, and kneeling by the table, clasped his withered hands, and prayed most fervently—prayed for strength to tread "the dark valley of shadows," upon which, even then, his trembling feet seemed entering—prayed for the infant, who had that day been left an orphan in a sinful and cold hearted world.

The whispered orison brought down a blessing. Peace, like a dove, folded its wings about the old man's heart, and a still, small voice whispered to his spirit, "my grace is sufficient for thee."

CHAPTER II.

"Oh, let me wipe
The tear from thy too mournful eye, and make
Thee happy, dearest father, by my love!"—*Mrs. Mayo.*

EDWARD ABSALOM and his wife arrived at the Glen the next evening. Both looked wearied and travel-soiled, for they had journeyed all night in hopes of reaching the bedside of their sister before death summoned her away. But they were too late. There was nothing left of her to wel-

come them, but the senseless body—the spirit had plumed
a wing for immortality. They stood with tears, and saw
her committed to the grave, and then, taking the old man
and child with them, they returned home.

It was hard for old Mr. Absalom to part with his dwelling—the spot where he had spent all of his married life—
where children had been born unto him, and where his
wife, and now his daughter, had died. But he could not
dwell alone, and little Ellen needed some one more trust-
worthy than colored servants to look after her personal
comfort and spiritual well-being. The old homestead was
therefore relinquished, and Mr. Absalom became, in his
old age, an inmate of his son's family.

Edward Absalom was a man without any marked char-
acteristics—in other words, he was somewhat like the
chameleon, taking shade and coloring from every object
with which he came in contact. When chance threw him
into the company of Christians, he was devout and pious;
he said his prayers as scrupulously as a Mussulman, and
wore a face of great gravity; but if thrown in an opposite
direction, with the rude and profane, he laughed at the
jests that went round, and became for the time all that
they desired him to be. His principles were the result of
events; there was no fixed stamina of character in his
composition, and yet, with all this vacillating, he had not
a bad heart. In it there was a fountain of generous sympathy, easily touched, and, thanks to his wife, his life, in
the main, was marked by kindness and amiability. Her
influence over him was of the very best nature, for she was
truly an excellent lady—meek, kind, just and generous towards all. Had he married a woman of an opposite character, he would just as readily have yielded to her influence,
and would have become, at her dictation, harsh, irascible
and severe. His whole nature reminded one of a stringed
instrument, that yielded discordant or harmonious music
according to the skill of the fingers touching it. As it
was, his family was well ordered, and his life flowed on
evenly and respectably. He had a family of three children
—two boys, Edgar and John, and one little girl, Eliza, to

whose companionship and love the little orphan, Ellen Marion, was now introduced. His home was on a large plantation, remote from neighbors, from church, and school. The house was a large white building, standing in among umbrageous oaks and fragrant locusts, and that most beautiful of all shade-trees at the South, the China-tree. In the front yard, flowers were cultivated in great abundance. Beds in the shape of diamonds and hearts, and triangles, circles and squares, were tastefully laid off, and surrounded by borderings of box-wood, while the rarest exotics blossomed within, and shed a breath of sweetness through the house. A pleasanter place for repose can hardly be imagined than the front and back piazzas, stretching upon two sides of the planter's house, afforded; and here, old Mr. Absalom sat himself down on the eve after his journey, and mentally thanked God that so quiet an asylum was afforded to his old age. His grand-children came clustering about him. John and Edgar were much amused at the sight of his crutches, for they had never seen a pair before, and during the evening borrowed them for the purpose of taking extraordinary flights from the piazza steps to the ground. Little Eliza, the youngest of the trio, clambered upon the rounds of the great arm chair, which Mrs. Absalom had kindly ordered for her venerable parent, and stroked her cousin Ellen's hair, who, frightened at the strange faces about her, clung to a seat in her grandfather's lap, and refused to meet any effort that was made by Eliza to make her acquaintance. The latter was full three years her senior—a blue-eyed, golden-headed child, with regular, if not beautiful, features. The little white dress that she wore set off to great advantage the rosy flush on her cheeks, and the clear transparency of her complexion. She was, in truth, a lovely, fairy-like creature, and formed a pleasing contrast to Ellen, whose pale face was lighted by eyes, dark, full and lustrous like her mother's—eyes in which it seemed, young as she was, lay the shadow of a great sorrow.

The gate opened, and the form of a young man was discerned coming up the path, through the dusky twilight.

"There is Mr. Brigham," shouted John, who just then had completed a flying leap; "let's run and tell him that grandfather has come, and show him the crutches," he continued; and suiting the action to the words, he dashed off down the walk, followed by Edgar, who carried the other crutch.

"Mr. Brigham!" said old Mr. Absalom. "Pray, Eliza, who is Mr. Brigham? I am sure I never heard anything about him before."

"That is our teacher, grandfather—or tutor, as papa sometimes calls him—Mr. Henry Brigham. On! he is a very fine gentleman, I assure you, and we all love him dearly. He has taught us to be very good since he came here—at least mamma says so. He goes out to walk every evening, and sometimes we go with him, but we did not go to-night, because we were expecting papa and mamma. I wonder if he has brought me the magnolia flower that he promised." So saying, the girl sprang lightly down the steps, and ran to meet the group, who had paused to examine the crutches, in the walk. This examination finished, they proceeded towards the porch, Eliza trying meanwhile to fasten the ponderous magnolia to her hair, where, owing to its weight, it refused to remain. Mr. Brigham once more stopped to assist her. The flower was at last satisfactorily arranged, and then mounting the steps, the tutor received an introduction to the old gentleman from Mrs. Absalom, who just then appeared in the door. The teacher shook the venerable man heartily by the hand, and sitting down upon a bench, inquired most kindly respecting his journey, his infirmities, and the grandchild in his lap.

Mr. Henry Brigham was a young man—scarcely eighteen years of age one would have supposed from his appearance. He was tall, slender, and prepossessing in his person. His high, broad forehead towered above a pair of dark eyes, in which there always lingered a most benign expression, and his whole countenance had an intellectual cast, always pleasing in the person of students. He had been for several months, it seemed, an inmate at the

14

planter's, and the affection with which the children regarded him, together with the high moral notions that he
had managed to instill into their minds, showed that he
was faithfully discharging his duties in that most respon-
sible of all stations—that of an educator of young, immortal beings.   Childhood!—that most imperishable leaf in
the volume of human existence—how often it is given into
the hands of those who will blot its fair pages, or trace
them over with distorted moral imagery ! Proud, exacting
father ! Fond, indulgent mother ! beware how you suffer
the training of your child to pass out from under your inspection.   See to it that your darling, while imbibing intellectual draughts, does not also drink in moral poison !

Mrs. Absalom fully appreciated the character of the man
to whom was intrusted the care of her offspring. She
often mentally thanked the Providence that had guided
Mr. Brigham to their door, and did all in her power to
make his situation a happy one in her family.

Mr. Absalom, the planter, soon joined his father and the
group upon the porch, and the whole party were engaged
in a pleasant conversation, when the supper bell sounded
from the dining-room. The boys ran to their grandfather
with the borrowed crutches. Mr. Brigham very kindly
offered to assist him, if assistance was necessary, while the
planter, taking his little daughter by the hand, and the
orphan in his arms, preceded the whole group to the supper table. Here the old man reverently lifted his tremulous hand, and asked a blessing upon the bountiful supply
of food smoking before them, while even Dinah, the colored
woman, who stood, tea-waiter in hand, behind Mrs. Absalom's chair, dropped her head, as if recognizing the Divine
Presence invoked.

CHAPTER III.

" Of her bright face, one glance will trace
A picture on the wall."—*Pinkney*.

UNDER Henry Brigham's tuition, the children at Mr.
Absalom's plantation continued for nearly six years. The

boys had commenced the study of Latin and Greek. Eliza, who had a great passion for botany, had become quite a proficient, even at her early age, in that difficult science, and little Ellen could read quite fluently. Old Mr. Absalom had got, moreover, to considering Mr. Brigham's presence as almost indispensable to his existence. The tutor was eyes, ears, and limbs for him. The dignified and amiable character of the young man, had left its impress upon every member of the family—even the servants loved to wait upon "Maus Henry" as they termed him. Mr. Edward Absalom, who was busy all day upon his plantation, concerned himself but little in regard to his children's proficiency in their studies. His wife had expressed herself well pleased with the tutor—the young folks liked him—his father praised him, although as he jestingly remarked, he shrewdly suspected that the secret of that praise lay in their both being Freemasons. He always found the young tutor cheerful, obliging, and entertaining in conversation, so he paid him annually his salary, and was contented.

But one day the postman brought to the house a letter, with a black seal. Henry instantly recognized the well-known handwriting of his mother, and opened it with trembling anxiety. It contained intelligence of the demise of his father, and begged him to give up his place as tutor in Mr. Absalom's family, and return to the paternal mansion, now so desolate and lonely.

Henry was a good son, as well as a good tutor. He carried the letter immediately into the breakfast-room, and read it aloud to the whole family. The children clustered around their teacher, and declared that he must not go. Who would teach them when he was gone? Mrs. Absalom looked very sad, but she simply said, "Mr. Brigham, it will grieve us all to part with you, but I see plainly that it is your duty to go—so we must try and give you up."

Old Mr. Absalom dropped his crutches—hemmed—coughed, and finally leaned back in his arm-chair, and shut his eyes, without saying a word, while the planter watched the face of his wife, as much as to say "Well, what are we to do now?"

Mr. Brigham, whose grief at the death of his father, was deep and sincere, retired immediately to his own room to pack his trunks, and make the preparations needful for his journey. It was decided that a servant should take him in the carriage that night to the depôt, twelve miles distant, so that he might proceed by railroad to his mother's residence without delay. He had nearly completed his task in silence and in tears—for spite of his manhood they would flow when he reflected that the hand which had guided his infancy, and the lips that had uttered admonition in his maturer years, were in the dust—when he took his Botany, and his attention was attracted to a beautiful book-mark, given to him by Eliza, and bearing upon the perforated board the inscription, " *Thy voice is ever welcome !*" He read the words again and again. It seemed to him that he had never noticed that motto before. He thought of the fair young creature, who was fast growing up into beautiful womanhood—he recalled at that moment her figure, as she had often stood before him in the schoolroom, with her hands full of floral treasures, ready for analyzation—he thought of her hair, breaking in golden ripples over her shoulders—of the faultless symmetry of her form—of the delicate hue mantling her cheek—of her bounding steps, when coming forth to meet him—and no wonder the young man closed the book nervously, as though a fresh pang had rent, just then, his heart.

LOVE! thou mysterious thing! Whence dost thou come ? making the human heart the temple of thy worship. A leaf, a flower, a book, a trifle lighter than vanity, reveals at times, thy presence.

As Henry Brigham descended the stairs, he met Ellen Marion. She had a white tea-rose in her hand. He took it from her fingers and pressed it to his lips—then, fastening it in the button-hole of his coat, he took her little hand gently in his, and led her out on to the front porch. "You must be a good child, Ellen," he said, affectionately drawing her towards him, " you must be a good little girl, and not forget your book, and see that your grandpapa has every comfort, and never forget me. But what is this, my child?" he continued, taking hold of a little blue ribbon around her neck, and drawing a small gold locket from her bosom. "How happens it that I have never seen this before?"

"It is my papa and mamma," said the child—"my papa and mamma, who are both dead. See how beautifully papa looks in his pretty silk apron, that mamma painted for him! Isn't he beautiful?" she continued, as she touched a spring, revealing the small ivory miniature of a lady and gentleman—the latter dressed in masonic regalia. "My mamma put it around my neck when she lay on her death-bed, but Winney, the servant, will not let me wear it, because, she says, that I shall soil the ribbon; but when I get to be a young lady, grandpapa will buy me a gold chain, and then I will wear it all the time."

"Keep it sacredly, Ellen," said the young man; "never lose it, for there may come a time when it shall be worth more than silver or gold to you. In this world of change," he continued, as if soliloquizing, "there is no knowing what reverses of fortune may overtake one seemingly as fortunate in life as yourself, my pet" He took the child in his arms—kissed her soft cheeks—looked into the depths of her dark, lustrous eyes, as if he would drink into his own soul a portion of the childish innocence outshining through them, and then went to bid adieu to the family where he had lived so long and so happily.

The carriage had arrived at the gate; his trunks had been brought down and strapped on, and the driver was already in his seat, snapping his whip over the heads of the restive horses, before this sad ceremony was through. All were there to bid him good-bye, and to wish him much happiness, but Eliza. She was nowhere to be seen. Henry looked everywhere for her; at length he turned reluctantly towards the carriage, and was proceeding down the walk, when the shrubbery rustled, and the girl stood beside him. Her eyes were red, as if she had been weeping.

"Good-bye, Mr. Brigham," said she, while a flush mantled her face. "We shall never have another teacher whom I shall love as I have loved you, because we shall never have another who will be as kind to us. Papa says that he shall send Edgar and John to school, and hire a governess for us girls, but I shall hate her, I know I shall."

" *Hate*, Eliza, is a very strong word," said Mr. Brigham, taking her hand in his. "I hope you will never permit yourself to hate any human being; hate their vices, as much as you please, my dear girl, but remember that they are made in God's image, and never permit yourself to hate that. There is a blessed alchemy, my dear child, that separates sin from the sinner—that enables us, while despising the one, to pity the other. If I have failed to teach you this, my tuition has been defective. Live, my dear Eliza, in such a manner as to show the world that I have *not* failed in imparting this great lesson to my best loved pupil."

He stopped, as if fearful that he had said too much—raised her soft white hand to his lips, and then jumped into the carriage, and was wheeled away.

CHAPTER IV.

" Decide between what you have been, and will be."—*Byron.*

" I HAVE engaged a governess for the girls," said the planter to his wife a few evenings after Henry left—"a Mrs. Walker, who comes with half a bushel of letters, recommendatory of her character, qualifications, &c. She is a member of the church—a widow, and has one child, which she will bring with her. John and Edgar, I have entered at Mr. Bryson's academy in Glenshow. Get them ready as soon as possible, and pack them off, for they will be late at best."

Mrs. Absalom bowed. Oh! could she at that point have lifted the veil which hides from mortal ken the future, how would her sensitive heart have been pained! But " Heaven, from all creatures, wisely hides the book of fate."

John and Edgar were delighted at the idea of going away from home to school. The thing involved novelty, and what child is not pleased with that? They were soon ready, and left the gate, after their adieus had been exchanged with the family, waving their hats, and shouting back to Ellen and Eliza, who had clambered upon the gate so as to see them as long as possible from the most commanding position.

That same evening, Mrs. Walker arrived. Ellen looked out of one of the front windows, and saw a thick-set lady, clad in black, coming up the walk, assisted by her uncle. She was apparently about thirty-six years old. As she reached the piazza steps, she swept back her long sable veil and revealed a face square in outline, florid in complexion, and coarse in feature. When she spoke, she displayed a row of false teeth, but one of them had been broken from the plate, and a small piece of metal, to which it had been attached, supplied in part its place. She was followed by her daughter, Isabella Walker, a miss apparently about twelve years old, who wore a white dimity sun-bonnet and a short calico dress. But when the sun-bonnet was laid aside, the Absaloms perceived at a glance that the girl was very handsome. Her raven hair was combed over a forehead as white as alabaster—her eyes were as brilliant as stars, and her small exquisitely shaped mouth bore no resemblance whatever to her mother's. Those eyes, starry and beautiful as they seemed, how often were they afterwards known to flash with anger, and that lovely lip to curl with scorn and contempt!

O Beauty! fearful endowment! How many, because *thou* hast crowned them, neglect the cultivation of those graces of heart and mind, " without which woman is a lighter thing than vanity!"

Mrs. Absalom came forward with the easy grace for which Southern ladies are so distinguished under all circumstances, and welcomed the new governess to her home. She directed the servant to take her baggage upstairs, and then proceeded to show the lady the way herself. Mrs. Walker, followed by Isabella, mounted the stairs.

Ellen was startled by a quick step near her. "Is *that* coarse-looking creature to take Mr. Brigham's place in the school-room, and that calico-dressed girl to be our companion?" said Eliza, whose face was flushed with excitement, and whose blue eyes sparkled as Ellen never remembered having seen them do before. "I will never love them—they shall never come near me—I despise them already—I ha——." She stopped short, with the half-pronounced word upon her lips.

"No, I must not hate them," she continued, as if to herself; "*he* said I must not permit myself to hate a human being—that I should disgrace his teaching if I did, and I will not do that—no, I will never do that. I take back all that I just now said," she continued, after a pause, "crazy-headed, wicked girl, that I am. I will be as gentle in the presence of that coarse woman as a lamb—I will heed her slightest wish—I will anticipate her wants—I will study to be *a perfect moral human being*, and all for his sake, who bade me show to the world what his teachings have been." Eliza's voice had sunk almost to a whisper—a calmer light had come to her eyes—she sank down upon a low seat, so that her white dress swept the carpet, and rested her flushed cheeks upon her two dimpled hands. Ellen gazed at her, with a wondering expression on her face. Often afterwards she remembered the beautiful enthusiasm of her cousin's manner upon that evening.

"Sagus is at the gate, and axes if old maus Absalom, or anybody here, want any bead-bags, or mocassins," said Winny, sticking her black face through the door. "He say he have some first-rate ones, if old massa want to buy."

"Who, in the name of sense, is Sagus?" said old Mr. Absalom, picking up his pocket-handkerchief, "and what does he suppose I want with bead-bags and such trinkets?"

"He's an old Ingin, maus Absalom, what live tree mile, or tree and a half mile from here. Very fine old Ingin, too, so all the black folks here dat know him say. Monstrous fine Ingin. Shall I ax him in?"

"To be sure," said the old man. "Not that I expect to buy any of his trinkets, but then I like to be civil to every body, even to an Indian. Ask him in, Winney."

The negress turned to obey the command, and it was not long before the Indian's peculiar tread was heard in the porch. Here he stopped, however, as if unwilling to enter the white man's dwelling further. The servant urged him forward—it did no good. He stood with his brawny arms folded across his red breast, and leaned against one of the posts supporting the piazza.

"He's in the porch, maus Absalom," said Winney, again re-appearing at the door. "He won't come in here, though I axed him ever so many times. You'll have to go out dare to see him."

The old man did not say anything, but picked up his crutches, and hobbled out on the porch. Winney followed with his great chair, and seated at last at his ease, he began to inspect, with spectacles on his nose, the bright bead-bags and curious over-shoes that the red man produced from beneath his blanket.

The girls, Ellen and Eliza, hearing the noise on the porch, soon came to look at the Indian's work also. Eliza had often met with Sagus before. She had seen him during her botanical excursions with Henry Brigham, and the kindness, almost deference, with which the latter treated the red child of the forest, had excited her wonder, as well as her admiration. She did not know then, as she did afterwards, that there was a mystic bond of union between them—a bond stronger than adamantine chains. She had never mistrusted that Sagus was a Freemason. Old Mr. Absalom had come out on the porch, never dreaming of purchasing anything as valueless to him as a bead-bag, but strange to tell, he bought nearly all that Sagus spread before him, and spoke in those kind tones with which old men sometimes address their children. Why was it so? No private word of explanation had passed between the two, and yet they knew and understood each other, upon one subject at least, perfectly. What mystic tie is that which binds together in one strong, loving and beautiful fraternity, the men of every nation and clime? What language is that, which passes so silently from heart to heart! What chain is that, whose links, unseen by curious

17

eyes, still bind in golden fellowship, men who were strangers but one brief hour before?

Old Mr. Absalom had dispatched Eliza with the key to
his secretary after his purse, from which to obtain money
to pay for his purchases, when Isabella Walker came down
stairs, and appeared in the door leading on to the porch.
As her eye fell upon the erect form of the red man, who
still stood in native dignity, leaning against the post, with
his blanket wrapped as proudly about him as Cæsar ever
wore imperial purple, she uttered a scream, and ran back
into the house, exclaiming, "O, the brute! the brute!—
he will kill us every one! I saw the end of his scalping
knife, I am sure, under his blanket. I did not think mamma
was coming among the Indians. The horrid wretches!
I am as afraid of them as of death!"

Eliza, whom she had met in the passage, and to whom
part of this tirade was addressed, stopped short and looked
the governess's daughter full in the face. At first, her lips
curled contemptuously, but a better spirit seemed instantly
to look through her eyes.

"The red man will not harm you, Miss Walker," she
said calmly. "He is a friendly Indian, one who often comes
to this plantation, but he seldom, indeed he never before
has visited the house. Would you not like to purchase
some of his bags? They are quite pretty, I assure you."

"The wretch! no!" said Isabella, impatiently. "I do
not want any of his gaudy trash. Is that some of it?" and
she trod with her toe upon the fringe of a shot-pouch,
which had been dropped accidentally in the passage, crushing the pretty blue glass into a thousand atoms. Eliza
snatched the wreck from beneath her feet, and hurried
out to where Sagus stood coolly surveying the whole scene.

"Ugh!" he said, as Eliza poured the bright silver into
his palm. It might have been an exclamation of satisfaction over the glittering treasure—it might have been an
expression of contempt for the pert girl, whose cruel in-
vectives—"brute! wretch!" must still have been ringing
in his ears.

As the Indian turned to go down the steps, his eye fell

upon the locket suspended from Ellen's neck.   He pointed
his tawney finger towards it. Ellen good naturedly touched
the spring, and revealed to his sight the miniature within.
A grunt of delight escaped his lips, as he saw the figure of
Judge Marion, clad in masonic regalia.

"You that man's pappoose?" said he, pointing to the
picture. Ellen smiled and bowed. The Indian smiled too,
and then passing out, was soon lost to sight.

Mrs. Walker proved to be, so far as the sciences were
concerned, a valuable teacher.   She was strict, punctual,
methodical, thorough, and competent to explain and impart all that it was necessary for her pupils to understand,
and yet both her young charges saw and felt every hour
in the day that she was not truthful, open-hearted, and
morally excellent.   *How* did they know it?   She committed no startling acts—told no glaring falsehoods. They
read it in the cold blue eye, which, when they sought to
scan the inner depths of the soul through it, turned away
from their gaze, as if it could not, and would not bear the
scrutiny which Henry Brigham's full dark orbs had never
shrunk from, but rather invited.   Children have, I have
sometimes thought, intuitive perceptions of character.

CHAPTER V.

"Cease. if you prize your beauty's reign."—*Byron.*

TIME flies rapidly.   To-morrow succeeds to-morrow, and
we are all the time unconsciously growing old.   At length
the school girl finds herself the young lady—the matron
sees that wrinkles are gathering upon her brow, and grey
hairs are silvering her locks, and the reflection is forced
upon the minds of both, "How fast time flies!"

Mrs. Walker had been nearly two years in the family of
the planter, when an event occurred which filled the house
with lamentations and tears. Mrs. Absalom died.   She
who had so long and so faithfully filled the office of daughter, wife, mother, aunt, mistress, and friend, closed her
eyes in death, and left the hearts of many sad and sorrow-

ing, and lamenting her loss. In her, all the beautiful pro-
prieties of the female character had been harmoniously
blended. She had long been the central point around
which every member of her vast household revolved, and
no wonder that her demise left them to fly off, like planets
lost from their orbits. Even Isabella Walker, fiendish as
she sometimes became in temper—harsh, exacting, mali-
cious, and spiteful towards all around—would partially
succumb beneath Mrs. Absalom's mild rebukes, and would
shrink away from her observation until her wrath was
overpast. Isabella was insolent to her mother, oftentimes
calling her to her face in the school-room, "old girl" and
"*Betse* Walker;" but to Mrs. Absalom she never dared
be otherwise than respectful and deferential. She oftentimes tried to quarrel with Eliza and Ellen, disputing
every right with them to the last, but Ellen, who had a
gentle, yielding disposition, always gave up to her in the
outset, and Eliza, firm to her resolution of becoming all
that Henry Brigham would approve in character, and
who remembered having often heard from his lips, the
christian as well as the sage remark, "it is better to suffer
wrong than to do wrong," oftentimes quietly gave up her
rights, and taking her book, retired to one corner of the
school-room, carefully avoiding, for the time, all intercourse with the tormenter. But there were days in
which Isabella carried her insolence beyond all endurance
—when Eliza Absalom felt that the point was reached,
when "forbearance ceased to be a virtue." She would
then arise—her slender and beautiful form would seem to
dilate—her blue eyes gathered a fearful brightness—her
delicate lips took a decisive, if not a contemptuous curl,
and words, strong words, rolled from her tongue. Isabella
shrank away from her then—she could not bear the light-
ning flashes of her virtuous eye; her victim had turned
in indignation upon her, and she was too cowardly to follow up the attack. This girl, however, who daily became
more and more repulsive in the eyes of all who knew her
intimately, was developing in her person almost every
charm. Her cheek took the deep carnation of the rose—

her black eyes became even more starry in their wonderful beauty—her soft hair hung in a mass of shining curls to her waist, and her form grew into perfect symmetry. Strange that so lovely a shrine should ever encase so terrible a spirit! But do we not read in the Inspired volume that the arch enemy of mankind has sometimes taken the form of " an angel of light ?"

When strangers were present, or when Isabella had any object to effect by the transformation, she became suddenly all that was amiable and benevolent in disposition. She had a shrewd, active, and discerning mind, and when she pleased, could accommodate herself to any society. She could veil herself in hypocrisy so deeply, that none but an educated eye—one accustomed to observe closely all her manœuvring—could detect the presence of the mantle that she wore. She was, moreover, coquettish. She coveted admiration more than anything else on earth, and when John and Edgar visited home, during the college vacation —for they had passed from the academy into college—she arranged her beautiful person in the most becoming attire, and put forth every fascination in her power to charm them.

It was perhaps six months after Mrs. Absalom's death, when Isabella had one day exhausted every epithet of abuse upon her mother, who had displeased her—beaten the servant that waited upon her, and quarrelled with Ellen and Eliza, that she took a novel and retired into a summer-house, overgrown with Cherokee roses, situated in the yard, and was soon deeply buried in its pages. Fiction seemed to be the only thing that exercised the evil spirit inhabiting her. She read on for half an hour, undisturbed.

" Eliza!" said a deep, manly voice behind her. She started to her feet in confusion, dropping at the same time her book, and turned to see who spoke. A young gentleman, with a faultless person and engaging address, met her eyes. He blushed and apologised when he discovered his mistake, and stated that the arbor having been a favorite resort formerly of Miss Absalom, who was at one time

his pupil, he made bold to seek her there before entering
the house. He begged to be forgiven for his intrusion,
and instantly turned away.

For once in her life Isabella was bewildered, and felt
that she had betrayed her bewilderment in awkwardness.
She was provoked with Eliza and with the stranger, but
this feeling was soon lost in wondering who he could be.
"Eliza was at one time his pupil! She said she never
had any tutor but that puritanical Henry Brigham, about
whom she and Ellen are everlastingly prating. This certainly cannot be him." But subsequent reflection convinced her that it could be none other.

"Is Henry Brigham such a looking man as that?" she
queried mentally. "If so, I do not wonder at all the talk
I have heard about him. And he too is romantic, it
seems, by his coming here to look after her. A pretty
love scrape may grow out of this tutorage business, after
all, and Miss Eliza get a genteel husband thereby. That
shall never be, though," she continued emphatically,
clenching her hand until the nails almost forced the blood
through the soft flesh in the palm; "never be, if I can
help it; and I will move hell beneath me, rather than be
thwarted in my design. I think that I could love such a
man as that myself, but that is neither here nor there;
Eliza shall not have him. I hate that girl for her cold im-
periousness. She and her mother are the only two beings
that ever made me shrink before them. I hate her eyes—
I hate the puritanical perfection of her character—I hate
her, soul and body."

This amiable soliloquy ended, she picked up her book,
and began again to read, but she could not interest herself
in the story. The charm had fled from the pages; and,
crushing the volume into her pocket, she took a path leading into the house through the back door, and up a private staircase. As she passed through the piazza, she saw
her mother standing under one of the China-trees, talking
with the planter, and she paused a moment on the stairs
to catch echoes from the parlor. Ellen and Eliza were
there, with the stranger, and the sounds were cheerful, al-

though neither loud nor boisterous. She called the servant, and arranged herself most carefully for the tea-table. White rose-buds, mingled with arbor-vitæ, were woven amid her curls; an embroidered robe of snowy whiteness and gossamer texture, neat fitting slippers and gloves, and a beautiful linen cambric pocket-handkerchief, were called into requisition to complete her toilet; and thus arrayed, she went again into the presence of Henry Brigham, at the summons of the tea bell. He bowed graciously when introduced to her. How little did he imagine that the beautiful creature before him carried a serpent's fang beneath that lovely exterior, which should yet poison his happiness to the inner core!

CHAPTER VI.

Without thee, I am all unbless'd,
And wholly bless'd with thee alone.--*Bethune.*

"*Thy voice is ever welcome!*" This assurance had haunted the tutor during his long absence from Eliza—haunted even his dreams. He had come back at last to see if it were indeed so. He wondered if the fair-browed child, whom he had left years before weeping on account of his departure, would greet with gladness his returning footsteps. He knew that she must now have grown into womanhood, and he yearned to see if the rich promise of the bud had been fulfilled in the flower.

On the night on which Isabella Walker had arrayed herself with so much care to meet him, his eyes sparkled with unusual animation, for he had not been disappointed in his expectation. Both Ellen and Eliza had grown into maidenhood; and as they moved to and fro that evening before him in the parlor, clad in robes of the most sombre black, which set off to great advantage the beautiful transparency of their complexions; as both turned so confidently towards him, and addressed him, not as a stranger, but as a brother or friend whose memory had been fondly cherished in their inner hearts for years, he was sure that he had not been wrong in the estimate which he had made

of the love of one young heart. He felt that he had two
homes in this wide dreary world, and that after a long absence, he had come back to one of them to find himself
petted and loved, jested with and looked up to as of old.
True, the woman who had been a second mother to him
in days gone by, was not there to welcome him ; he was
reminded most painfully of this by the mourning weeds
that he saw about him—by the tearful glances which the
girls now and then cast towards the portrait hanging
against the wall—by all they told him of her sudden death,
and of the funeral succeeding it—but Eliza was still there,
and he felt that where *she* dwelt, there would always be
happiness for him. Beware, young heart, where and how
you garner up your deathless affections, for the whirlwinds
of passion are abroad in the world, and may sweep your
idols away like chaff on the summer threshing-floor !

After supper was finished, the young people went back
to the parlor, accompanied by Isabella. Eliza, who knew
her character, and whose eye had been attracted to her
dress at the supper table, could not refrain from feeling
vexed and uncomfortable. How hateful the creature looked, sitting there with the soft light of the lamps streaming
over her snowy array, and with those white buds peeping
out from her raven hair. Her extreme loveliness had
never for a moment before struck Eliza as it did that night.
Did not Henry think her beautiful? Was not Henry, who
as yet had never seen the angry flash of those starry eyes,
yielding his heart captive to so much loveliness? She
glanced into the face of the young man. He was not even
looking at her, but was inspecting some sea shells, which
he had picked up from the mantlepiece. Eliza drew a
long breath of relief. "How jealous I am," thought she,
"of his love; and how silly, contemptably silly, such weakness is in my character. He has never yet, and probably
never will say, "*I love you.*"

Isabella moved to the piano, and unasked, commenced
playing. She was a splendid musician—and with Mr.
Brigham the love of music amounted to a passion. As her
fingers ran over the keys, he started from his seat, laid

aside the shells, and moved near the piano. Finally, he stood behind her, and turned the leaves of the song she had commenced.

Music, sweet language of Heaven! How have earthly, sinful creatures perverted thine excellencies, as they have perverted all God's rich gifts to man.

Neither Ellen nor Eliza moved from their places before the bright fire that had been kindled in the grate to dissipate the chills of the night air.

Isabella played on for nearly two hours. Piece after piece was executed, then thrown aside. Henry hung over her in silence; he seemed to have forgotten everything, but what was transpiring before him. When he turned again towards the fire, a shade of sadness had stolen over Eliza's face. Did he notice it? Could he divine the cause? Oh, no! but a keener eye than his saw it, and gloried secretly upon beholding it.

CHAPTER VII.

"Wast thou but a fiend, assuming
Friendship's smile and woman's art?"—*Byron.*

HENRY BRIGHAM'S visit was protracted day after day, until three weeks had elapsed. During this time, the coquette had played her part well, sometimes enchaining the young tutor for hours to her side by her blandishments—sometimes illy concealing her chagrin when her arts failed, and she saw him breaking away from her to sit by Eliza, or to aid Ellen with her lessons. Old Mr. Absalom was delighted at again beholding the tutor, and managed, in his loneliness, to monopolize a good deal of his time—time which Henry very gracefully yielded to the infirm old man, now in his dotage. How beautiful is reverence in the young and hapy! reverence for the hoary head, and kindness to the old man! "As the understanding ripens, and this sentiment is cultivated," says an American lady in some advice to her young friends, "it embraces all that is great and good among men, all that is vast and magnificent in nature and in art; shedding over the character of

its possessor an indescribable grace, softening the very
tones of the voice, and rendering it impossible for the manners to be wanting in deference and courtesy towards parents, or teachers, or the aged of any description."

Eliza and Ellen marked this delicate tribute of respect
rendered to their grandfather, and both admitted ·the amiability which cheerfully gave up a ride or a walk, or an
evening that might have been spent in gayer society, to
the old man, who, with his crutches and Bible, passed a
great deal of his time, since the death of the excellent
Mrs. Absalom, in the solitude of his own little room.

Busy as Isabela was with her scheming, during the days
of that memorable visit, there was another in the household who had also matured plans for action, and was
scarcely less busy—scarcely less hopeful in regard to results. Mrs. Walker now put on her most amiable smiles
—wore her most tastful caps—hid most adroitly the defective tooth—spoke in her blandest tones to all—especially to Mr. Edward Absalom, the planter. What object
had she to accomplish? Anybody with half an eye in
their heads might have discerned at a glance her purpose, and even the servants in the kitchen repeated to
each other her honeyed phrases, and laughed at the thin-
ness of the veil under which she hid her designs.

Eliza, who was painfully sensible to her father's yielding,
unstable disposition, remarked all of this manœuvring on
the part of her governess with extreme dissatisfaction.
She trembled in view of results. She wrote long epistles
to Edgar and John, in which she poured forth her indignation, and called upon them to devise ways and means in
which the house might be cleared of that abominable governess and her daughter. She was answered kindly ; but
was surprised that her brothers did not seem to enter
fully and heartily into all her views and feelings on the
subject of her father's marriage. John, on the contrary,
spoke of the union as one rather to be desired. than otherwise, while Edgar alluded to the subject in a trifling way,
and wound up his letter with a message to Isabella, regretting that college duties debarred him from the plea-

sure of taking those long horseback rides with her, which he had enjoyed so much during his last vacation.

Well did Lamartine say, "Beauty is an endowment having magic power—to be beautiful it is to be powerful." Had Eliza known all, she would have known that the spell of Isabella Walker's beauty was like the fascination of some poisonous serpent upon both of her young brothers, and that both longed for the annual commencement of the college to be over, so that they could fly back to the enchantress who had exerted her fascinations so skillfully, charming both during the brief vacations that they had passed at home, since her residence beneath their father's roof. They secretly hoped that something would occur to detain the beautiful Isabella at the plantation, for neither could think of going home, and finding that she had left, without a pang at the heart. So adroitly had the coquette managed her flirtations, that each of the brothers supposed himself to be the peculiar object of her regard; neither imagined that the other saw her in his dreams at night, and dreamed of her over his books during the day. This fact will account to the reader for the tone of their letters to Eliza.

The latter was just finishing the perusal of these dissatisfactory epistles, when she heard the step of Henry Brigham in the passage, coming towards the parlor where she was standing. Fearful of discovering to him her chagrin, she thrust the papers into their envelopes, and was stowing them away in her pocket, when she heard Isabella Walker's voice, in tones of measured sweetness, asking the tutor for a ride on horseback, from the staircase in the hall.

"I can show you the ruins on the hill, as I promised, this evening, Mr. Brigham," she said, "unless you are otherwise engaged. I am already dressed for the ride, you see," she continued, as she shook her riding cap in her hand, the plume of which nodded gracefully over the banister, and she leaned forward so as to display to the best advantage her elegant form, dressed in a riding habit of light green, with a pretty linen collar running around the throat. "Don't say no, now!—don't be ungallant, I beseech you, or I shall have had the trouble of dressing for nothing."

"Certainly, I am at your service," replied the tutor. Was there a slight tone of vexation in his response, or did Eliza only fancy it?

"Perhaps," he continued, "Miss Absalom and Miss Marion can be persuaded to accompany us. I will ask them."

"Certainly," said Isabella, as she turned to remount the stairs.

"There are only two idle horses on the plantation Maus Henry," said Mike, the negro man, who was questioned about it half an hour afterwards. "Miss Isabel *knew* it too," he continued to himself, "for did not she ax all about it before she saw Maus Henry in the passage? To be sure she did. Well, some folks is pert—there's no mistake about that."

Nothing remained now for the tutor to do, but to accompany Isabella on her excursion alone, as she wished. He assisted her to the saddle and was soon galloping by her side. Did his heart go with him, or did it linger with that sorrowful girl, who bowed her face over her embroidery in the parlor? Ellen was reading to her grandfather in his room, and knew nothing of the equestrians for an hour afterwards.

There is no exercise in the world so exhilerating as riding on horseback. The blood flushes the cheek—the eyes sparkle, and the whole spirit feels as buoyant as the bird upon the wing. Henry soon lost his chagrin, if indeed he had experienced any, in the fresh sunny air, and he listened to the gay tones of the beautiful creature who rode beside him—laughed at her criticisms, plucked fruit for her from the boughs of the orchard trees that they passed, and fell into raptures over the ruins of an Indian wigwam which she pointed out to him over the top of a hill.

"Shall we ride so as to get a nearer view of it, Mr. Brigham?" she said, as she turned the neck of her steed with the end of her riding whip. The two galloped away, and had nearly reached the place of their destination when, some one started up from the roadside. It was Sagus, who had thrown himself at full length, it seemed, beneath a little clump of pine-trees.

"The wretch!" screamed Isabella, without stopping to think whom she was addressing. "That dog of an Indian came near making my horse throw me. I am afraid of them," she continued, turning to her companion, who was trying to reign up his horse; "I always did hate an Indian."

An expression of disapprobation passed over Henry's face. Did he remember the gentle teachings which he had given a beloved pupil years before, when he heard that offensive word, "hate?" I know not. But without heeding her remark, he rode up to the object of her disgust, and offered him his hand. The Indian smiled, took the extended member between his palms, and said a few words in his native language. Isabella did not understand the guttural sounds. Once the red man's piercing eye rested upon her face, while an expression of contempt curled his lip. Was it possible that she was the theme of his discourse? She remembered how she had once crushed his beads beneath her foot, and in spite of herself, she felt uncomfortable.

"Mr. Brigham," she said, in a tone of light raillery, "I admire your condescension. But the sun will not wait for us, and we shall be late home." Yet the Indian did not relinquish his hand. Neither did the young man seem impatient to obey the wishes of his companion. He listened to his red brother's impassioned address—listened, as if to the admonitions of a father, or the advice of an esteemed friend; and when he turned from Sagus, the spell which Isabella Walker had hoped to weave so adroitly about his heart was broken. He saw her character—not in all its deformity, but his eyes were partially opened—he knew it was not good, genuine, excellent.

He accompanied her now in silence, looked at the beauties that she pointed out, and then turning, rode homeward.

During the remnant of his visit, he seldom left Eliza.

In vain Isabella tried this plan, and resorted to that artifice, to draw him away, and regain the influence which she imagined she had over his heart. It was all of no avail, and mentally the coquette cursed in her heart the Indian, and swore to be revenged.

It was on the night before the day on which the tutor left the plantation of Mr. Absalom, that he sought, in company with Eliza, the very arbor where he had surprised Isabella on the day of his arrival, and there he made a formal declaration of his love to his companion. She heard him with a flushed cheek, and a tremulous hand. He told her how the inscription upon the bookmark which she had given him years before, had haunted him like remembered music—how he had hidden it away, too jealous of her love to let other eyes peruse what was, he hoped, only designed for him to read, and now he begged to know if it was indeed true that his "voice *was* ever welcome." If so, would she be soothed by its tones through life? He promised that it should never speak harshly to one whom he loved so well.

Eliza seemed to herself to be in a delightful dream. Was it true that Henry Brigham was suing for her love? Was he not noble, all that her imagination could picture in its *beau-ideal?* Had she not loved him from her earliest childhood—had she not carried his teachings with her, squaring her life by them, and striving for his sake to be all that is good? Certainly, and she told him so.

The lovers sat long that evening, there in the twilight, and planned bright scenes for the future. If they had parted the rose vines and looked out, they would have seen a face, livid with passion, distorted with hatred, and fiendish in expression, glaring upon them from behind where they were sitting. But when did two happy lovers ever dream of danger lurking near them? Henry certainly never thought of being overheard, and Eliza, although on her return to the house, she fancied she caught the glimpse of a white robe flitting up the back staircase, was too happy to heed the circumstance.

CHAPTER VIII.

"My hopes of future bliss are o'er,
In Mercy veil the past."

BEFORE the college commencement, which John and Edgar were so eagerly anticipating. occurred, Mrs. Walker had Edward Absalom the planter captive at her will. They were married one morning while the family supposed they had simply gone out to ride. Mrs. Walker returned, bearing the name of "Mrs. Absalom." Would that she had borne her virtues also.

Old Mr. Absalom regretted this event quite as much as anyone. He had never liked this scheming governess since her first entrance into the house, but it was now too late to complain. She was there, its mistress and his daughter, and all that could be done now was to submit to her exactions in silence. Exacting she indeed was, and soon gave the old gentleman to understand that old people are very troublesome members of a family sometimes. But a change seemed to have passed over the spirit of Isabella. She now sought, by every means in her power, to conciliate and win the love of Eliza and Ellen. She no longer answered them pettishly; she brought her embroidery into their room, and worked for hours; she read aloud to them, and seemed determined to show them how pleasantly she could serve them. But when Eliza chanced to drop asleep, as she sometimes did upon the sofa, and Ellen became absorbed in her work, counting the stitches, and assorting her silks, what expression was that which crept over Isabella's face? What fiendish light was that which lit up her starry eyes? What meant the compression of those livid lips? Why, when she sought her own room, and the darkness of the midnight was over the face of nature, did she pace with uneven steps her chamber, and mutter threats, with hands clenched and teeth set firmly together, like a maniac's?

Oh, woman! woman! thou creature of intuitive perceptions and subtle sympathies—thou who art appointed to guard vestal fires, and fan expiring virtues into renewed life and vigor—thou who hast a small sphere for labor, and yet art daily touching upon chords which must vibrate throughout eternity—beware how unhallowed passions enter thy breast—let not fierce mental conflicts shake you like a reed in the blast—be gentler than the summer breeze—forgiving even the treachery of thy bosom friend. Be a type and an embodiment of all that is good and beautiful in life, for when once fallen, how mean, how abject a creature thou art. The slave, clanking his chain at every step, is a grade above thee. Fiends when once admitted, make a chosen and favorite haunt of thy bosom, and reason cannot exorcise them away.

Passion had made Isabella Walker its slave. She loved Henry Brigham—loved only as fiery natures like hers can love, and she swore again and again, mentally, that Eliza Absalom, come what would, should never become his wife. She sought by every means in her power to ingratiate herself into the unsuspecting girl's confidence. She intercepted letters, and wrote false ones, but nothing like an estrangement could be effected between the lovers. They had known each other too long and too intimately to distrust each other's worth. When a letter failed to reach Henry, he sought a personal interview, and thereby learned that an enemy was somewhere at work, endeavoring to undermine their mutual confidence. Even Eliza did not suspect Isabella. Her conduct of late had been so changed—she had greeted Henry so coldly when they chanced to meet, that she never mistrusted that passions, fiercer than volcanic fires, were smothered in her heart.

The day for Eliza's bridal was at length appointed. The planter, who, since his second marriage, had seen that the position of Eliza bade fair to become an uncomfortable one in his family, very gladly assented to her marriage with Brigham, whom he esteemed. Old Mr. Absalom was delighted. He decided to settle upon his grand-children his property, and in future, both himself and Ellen would, he thought, have in the home of Henry Brigham a quiet and peaceful asylum. Both Henry and Eliza entered most heartily into the old man's plan, and all were looking forward to the bridal day with bright anticipations. Isabella entered most readily and cheerfully into all the preparations going on for the marriage. She trimmed the cake with her own hands, bringing each loaf to Eliza, to secure her approbation. Upon one cake she wrought with silver leaf two united hearts, and threw around a wreath of flowers. Beneath this emblematic device she inscribed, by means of raised icing, the words " *Thy voice is ever welcome*."

Eliza started when she saw the sentence. " How," she thought, " did Isabella obtain a knowledge of those magic words ?"

" How do you like the inscription ?" said Isabella.

Eliza glanced into her face. There was no unusual expression there—nothing that betrayed a consciousness of any particular significance in the words. Could Isabella hit upon this inscription carelessly ? Eliza could not tell. She simply blushed, therefore, and said " The loaf is beautiful—very pretty, indeed."

Ellen and Eliza were seated in their little chamber that same evening, when the door opened, and Isabella again entered, bearing a box of dried figs in her hands. " See what I have brought," said she carelessly. " I am so fond of these things, and am determined to have a feast to-night. Will you have one?" she continued, taking one from the top of the box, and handing it to Eliza. " Here, Ellen," she said, " here is one for you. She then took one herself, and commenced eating.

" Bah !" she continued, " these figs are not good. There is a sickish taste in mine," and she threw the fragment into the fire. Eliza soon perceived there was a singular taste in the one she had taken. It was very acrid. She also threw hers into the grate, and instantly a strong smell of garlic pervaded the room. " The wretch !" exclaimed Isabella, " to sell me these for good figs, when every one of them is spoiled. How does yours taste, Ellen ?"

" It is very good," said Ellen, quietly. " I see nothing unusual in it."

"It must be the only eatable one in the box then," said Isabella, rising and going towards the door. "I mean to throw these all away."

A half hour went by, and Eliza became deathly sick. She never mistrusted the cause of her illness—the incident of the figs had not made any impression upon her thought, but her lips became livid, and strong convulsions shook her frame.

Ellen watched over her, and tried to administer to her some medicines, in which she hoped her cousin would find relief, but she saw that she was momentarily growing worse. She moaned in the intensity of her agony, and finally, becoming alarmed, dispatched a servant after a physician, and called her uncle into the room. Old Mr. Absalom, hearing the noise, soon followed. The physician lived a long way off, and it seemed to Ellen, during the watches of that apparently endless night, that he would never arrive. At last Mike returned, saying that the doctor was not at home, but his wife said she would send him over to the plantation to see the young lady early the next morning.

Alas! before that morning dawned brightly and beautifully over the woodland, Eliza Absalom lay amid her wedding preparations—the orange wreath and silvery robe—a stark, rigid, dark, bloated corpse.

Fearfully, awfully fall such sudden dispensations of Providence upon families and neighborhoods. The gay pause in their career, and for a moment seem alarmed at the feebleness of a mortal's grasp upon sublunary things, but the realization of this fact soon dies, and they dance on as before. The preacher and the moralist draw new lessons from every fresh event, and all seem startled, until the green sods of the churchyard have closed over the one thus suddenly bereft of life; they go back then, enter the haunts of men, and the currents of trade, noise, politics and commerce flow on as before. The Absalom family stood, as if paralyzed, around the yet unshrouded remains of her, who but yesterday had moved before them, flushed with life and hope. Even Mrs. Walker, or rather, as we must now call her, Mrs. Absalom, seemed stunned by the event. Ellen wept as if her young heart would break, while Edward Absalom, who really loved his children, groaned over her still and motionless form. How little did the weak, blind man suppose that he was at that moment nurturing in the bosom of his family the deadly serpent that had poisoned his child. Did any one there think it strange that Isabella Walker never came to look upon the face of the dead ? that she avoided the room where the dead girl lay, and shut herself in her chamber, refusing even to come down to her meals, and leaving the morsel untasted which Winney carried to her ? No, every one was too much absorbed to notice anything; even the fiendish light which visited the murderer's eyes, and the shudders that swept at times like autumn winds through her frame, passed unheeded.

Once, during the second day after Eliza's death, Isabella stole to her door, and put her ear to a crack to catch the echoes of bustle and footsteps passing through the hall. It was then that her face took a triumphant expression, and a low, diabolical laugh came through her lips. What meant it ? Henry Brigham was going in for the first time to look upon the remains of his dead bride. It was then that the fiend in her nature triumphed. But how was it with the bridegroom ? Oh what pen can picture his wretchedness, as he knelt beside the dead ? Our's is inadequate, and we shrink from the task. We will only record the fact, that when the burial service was over, Henry Brigham went out, never again to revisit a spot where he had been supremely happy, and so wretchedly miserable.

<hr>

CHAPTER IX.

" Thousand evil things there are,
  That hate to look on happiness."—*Maria Brooks.*

THREE years pass rapidly away. To the happy, they bring few marks of decay—upon the brows of the wretched, they engrave furrows of care and sorrow.

In the family of Mr. Absalom, the three years following

Eliza's death made great change. Old Mr. Absalom, unable to bear the neglect of the new mistress of the plantation, and the crushing sorrow and disappointment that accrued to him at Eliza's death, died. His last request was to be taken back, and deposited beside Eugenia at the Glen, but Mrs. Absalom objected to the useless expense, as she termed it, and the old man was buried beside Eliza, beneath a little clump of ceder trees, gracefully crowning the summit of a knoll on the plantation.

Edgar and John had returned from college, after having graduated, both secretly idolizing the beautiful basilisk that lay in the sunshine of their paternal mansion. She played her part with both adroitly and well for awhile; but John, discovering at length her hollow-heartedness and deception, deserted her in disgust, and left home for Europe. Edgar, however, who was now more ardent and impetuous in his temperament, fell subsequently in a duel, which he fought with a young neighboring planter, on her account.

How sped those years with Ellen Marion—the beautiful orphan girl—who now stood alone in her uncle's family, bereft of all whom she loved—all who had treated her kindly, and had cared for her welfare.

Bitterly the winds of adverse fortune sweep over some young and handsome heads, and Ellen Marion's was one of these. Had the soft eyes of her dying mother been permitted to scan the future position of her child in the world, how would she have shrunk back from the valley of shadows before her, and yearned and prayed to live for the sake of her darling daughter!

Her grandfather had, at his demise, left a fortune that rendered her independent, but Mrs. Absalom had one growing passion in her nature, the love of money, and she looked upon the orphan's inheritance with greedy eyes. She not only looked, but she schemed and planned for robbing her of it. She charged her exhorbitant prices for board, unknown to Ellen; continually importuned her husband, who had the management of her niece's estate; and Ellen at last was astounded by the discovery of the fact that she was not only an orphan, but penniless in the world. Penniless! yea more, she was homeless; for Mrs. Absalom told her plainly, that now that her fortune was gone, and she had nothing wherewith to pay her board, she must look for a home elsewhere.

Homeless in a world of homes! what a sad condition is that? Vestal fires may burn, but none burn for you—welcoming voices and smiles may abound, but none wait your coming— sad, desolate, and weak, you stand in the midst of a wide, wide world, without knowing where to look for succor, or turn for aid.

Gay, light-hearted lady reader, you who have taken up this book, and are turning, with white, soft and jeweled fingers, the pages, eager to know the sequel of this tale, stop a moment, and if you are in the possession of a comfortable home—if friendly voices greet you, and eyes brighten at the sound of your footsteps—thank God sincerely for his countless mercies to you. Earth holds its thousands, who, like the Saviour of mankind, have not " where to lay their heads," and among these are orphans, thrown out rudely, by adverse circumstances, upon the world.

Ellen was one of these. She knew not where to turn. She could not think of one human heart that cared for her. Her pride shrank from remaining in her uncle's family, but what could she, a delicate Southern girl, brought up to be waited upon by menials all her life, do in the world? True she had an excellent education, but she knew of no one in need of a governess; and then she instinctively shrank from the drudgery of life.

Agitated by such thoughts, she strolled out one evening, and sank down upon the mound covering the remains of her grandfather. She buried her face in her hands and wept. The wind, roaring through the cedars above her, had a melancholy sound—at her feet slept two hearts, whose love had been poured out upon her childhood freely and without measure. The world looked cold and dreary to her now, and she longed to be laid in the quiet cell beside the revered form of him she wept above.

She had occupied this position some moments, when she

was startled by a quick footstep behind her. She instantly sprang to her feet, and turning, saw Sagus in front of her. She had not seen the Indian since the first night after Isabella Walker's arrival at the plantation, but she recognized him at a glance. The red man scanned her from head to foot with his keen black eye. He saw that she had been weeping, for traces of tears were upon her cheeks. His eye dwelt especially upon her attire. At length he espied a small gold chain which Ellen wore, and to which was attached her parents' miniatures. The sight of it seemed to recall at once her person to his memory. He recognized the child who had so kindly showed him the picture, while standing, years before, in the planter's porch, after having sold old Mr. Absalom his bead-bags and mocassins.

"Ugh!" said he abruptly. He set down his rifle, folded his arms, and leaned against one of the trees. Ellen's first impulse was to fly. She was timid, and did not feel quite safe, standing face to face with an Indian in the twilight, and at such a distance from the house. But there was something friendly in the manners of the red man—something that touched her heart. Friendship was becoming with her—a rare thing. She felt like encouraging it, even in an Indian.

"Sick?" at length queried the intruder, in his abrupt tone. "Sick?"

Ellen shook her head. In spite of herself the tears began to flow afresh, and she felt choked for utterance.

"Not sick," she at last found voice to say, "only utterly miserable."

"She wolf down yonder," said the Indian, pointing towards the house, "she wolf eat up everything—hey?"

Ellen looked at the red man in amazement. She did not fully comprehend him, but his saying seemed strangely true. She did not reply.

"Sagus sorry all the time—sorry when Mike told him that Mr. Absalom married she wolf. Her young one showed its teeth in the beginning. Sagus didn't think then, that the Mason's child would suffer, but when he see the heap out yonder—pointing to Mr. Absalom's grave—

and these here—when Mike told him she wolf married, then Sagus found it might come to this. What has she been doing?"

"I have no home," said Ellen. "That is why I weep. I have none to love me—none to care for me."

"Ugh!" said the Indian, leaning his chin upon his brawny red hand, as if in meditation. He stood motionless in this attitude for a long time. At last Ellen moved. The gloom of night was thickening, and she feared to remain longer.

The Indian raised his head. "Come here to-morrow night," he said. "Sagus help you;" and picking up his rifle, he plunged off over the hill, in the direction of a forest.

Once he turned. "Be sure and come," he said, and then continued on his way.

"What does the creature mean?" thought Ellen. "How can he help me—he, the last lingerer of his tribe—a tribe withering and fading away before the usurper. He has no home now upon this soil. How can he furnish me one? The thing is impossible," and thus musing, she entered the house.

CHAPTER X.

"Do I see
A human face look down on me?
And doth a roof above me close?"—*Mazeppa*.

THE next evening the orphan could not resist the impulse of straying out, as she had been directed to do, in the direction of the graves. She again sank down upon the mound, and again buried her face.

"Ellen Marion!" said a voice close by her. She looked up, and the Indian, accompanied by Henry Brigham, was near her. She had not seen the tutor since the death of Eliza—she was now struck with his altered appearance, and with the pensive melancholy that had supplanted the heart-rending grief once pictured in his face.

"You have not forgotten me, surely," said he, coming

forward with a smile, and taking her hand. " I have not
seen you for a long time, but I trust I am not quite forgotten."

The orphan was so overcome by these tones of kindness,
that she could not control her emotions, but wept freely.
That voice was associated with all that she had known of
peace and happiness in this life. Since she gave him the
white tea rose-bud upon the stairs, what a blighting and
blasting had come over her prospects. There are moments in which the most trivial acts of our childhood come
back to memory with great distinctness. At that period,
Ellen remembered the words that her tutor had uttered
over the minature suspended to her neck, and they seemed to her then, to have partaken of the spirit of prophecy.

Her interview with the tutor was long and earnest.
They went together over the past, in which they were fel-
low-sufferers, and discussed the future. Brigham had
studied, and was then practising law. A glance at the orphan's case showed him the chicanery and fraud that had
been practised in wresting from her her estate, and he
mentally determined to regain it for her, if possible.

" Go back, Ellen," he said, speaking to her in a mild
tone of authority, that had guided her in her school days,
" go back, and claim a home beneath your uncle's roof.
That home is justly yours. Do not suffer yourself to be
driven from it by frowns and bitter words. You have
rights, and show Mrs. Absalom that you will maintain
them, mildly, but firmly. I will aid you to the utmost.
Your property must be regained for you."

To make a long story short—for we have already exceed-
ed in our narration the bounds that we originally assigned
ourself—after a long and tedious legal process, during
which the orphan suffered much abuse from Mrs. Absalom, her rights were vindicated, and she was again placed
in possession of her inheritance. Henry Brigham was,
from the hour in which he found her sobbing by her grandfather's grave, her most zealous friend and protector—and
when time had assuaged the griefs, and righted the wrongs
of both, they who had been cemented in affection by com-

mon suffering and mutual esteem, united their hands, plighted their troth, and went out together to tread the rough paths of the world, side by side.

Years sped over them—a household grew up all around them, and, in the happiness of the present, they forgot the sorrows of the past.

It was at the close of a frosty winter, that a vagrant crept one day to the marble steps of the Hon. Henry Brigham's house—for the tutor had gained that distinction in the world that his talents and virtues merited—in the city of B——, and sat down. Every now and then she glanced up to the warm crimson shaded windows, and listened to the laughter of a group of children who were romping through the hall.

Beggars upon the steps are no novel sight to city dwellers—the gay and happy sweep past them, into their comfortable houses, without asking whence they came or whither they are bound.

Ellen Brigham, the rich senator's wife, as she lifted the curtain and looked out, never thought of recognising in the wretched being at her door, the once proud and beautiful girl who had embittered her early life—Isabella Walker.

"Heaven is just," at last murmured the vagrant, as she caught a glimpse of Ellen. "I came here, thinking that I would go in and confess my crimes, but I cannot do it. I cannot tell the master and mistress of this princely mansion how, long years ago, I poisoned his bride and *her* cousin. I cannot tell how, step by step, I have gone downward—how I have been dragged to ruin by my fierce ungovernable passion. They are happy now—happy in their ignorance."

The next night a corpse was found by the watchman in his round—it was the corpse of a loathsome beggar. The coroner who held an inquest over the body said—*died of starvation and disease.*

The hearse that bore the beggar's rough coffin to the potter's field passed a carriage containing the smiling wife of Senator Brigham and her children. How little did
19

Ellen think, in her happiness, that near lay the wreck of the beautiful but fiendish Isabella Walker. She subsequently heard, however, that her uncle was dead, having suffered much from the neglect and unkindness of his wife—that his property had been squandered by Isabella and her mother, and that both had gone, no one knew whither. It was not until long after these events happened, that Mrs. Brigham heard from Sagus, who kept an eagle-eye upon the she-wolf, as he persisted in calling her, the story of her death and of the death of Isabella.

A cold shudder ran through her frame, as she listened. "Had it not been for *these* little miniatures," she said, taking the locket from her belt, "I might not have Sagus for a friend—without Sagus' aid, Henry would never have heard of my distress—without Henry's assistance and love, I should have been, Heaven only knows where." How many pleasing associations were there at that moment clustering about the Orphan's Miniature!

<hr/>

My daughter, go and pray. See, the night is come. Yonder, one golden planet glimmers through the clouds. The wavy, trembling mist is gathering around the hills. Now and then some lonely wagon glides through the distant shadows. All is silence and repose, and the trees along the road shake off to the vesper-breeze the dust of the day. The twilight hath heralded the queenly Night, with her crown of stars, and one by one they burst upon the sight in glowing sparkles. The crimson fringe in the west is fading out. The surface of the waters in the shade grows silvery in the starlight. The furrows, paths, and thickets all mingle and blend together, and lose themselves in the shadows, so that the passing wanderer is doubtful of his way.

THE MOONLIGHT ON THE MOUND.

The moonlight now is falling on a mound.
  White with thick snows, beneath a distant sky,
You scarce would know the head-stone from the ground,
  Both gleam so white, if you were passing by.

My thoughts have lingered all the day,
  Around that grave so narrow, chill, and drear—
I scarce can believe it is so far away—
  I may not see it yet, in many a year.

Ten years ago, and she who slumbers there,
  Tarried one fleeting moment in my view,
The lamp-light fell upon her soft brown hair,
  And lit her eyes—deep, dark, serenely blue.

One fleeting moment, on a festal night,
  Was all I saw of her, just made a bride,
But she was smiling, as she passed from sight,
  On him who moved all proudly byher side.

I knew that she was happy—gentle—good as fair;
  My heart invoked a blessing as she passed—
I hoped her snowy brow would never wear,
  A line of grief—a shadow—to the last.

But ah! a wrung, a wounded heart was laid
  Beneath the sod upon her burial day;
You never would have dreamed, the same fair maid
  I saw, was being thrust from light away.

Death bruised her heart—DEATH wrought her wo,
  He stole sweet cherubs from her household bower;
There are two little head-stones, hid by snow—
  You could not find them in this wintry hour.

But April will come on with soft warm days,
  The frost will melt, and violets deck the sod;
It will be easy then to find the ways—
  "The gate of flowers," through which they passed to God.

And May will bring a greater gush of flowers,
  And June will stir the air with life and song,
But *they* will sleep, as in these moonlit hours,
  As still and pale—as cold, and deep, and long.

Heaven help the mourner!—he whose bitter tears
  Lie frozen thick, like pearls on those three graves;
Heaven light the gloom, which shrouds his coming years,
  And hush grief's tempest—still the raging waves!

Heaven help the mourner!—it is for *him* I weep,
  And not for those gone hence—I know not where—
A gracious God will surely fold and keep
  Them safe from harm, within a balmier air.

But he who wears with his slow feet a path,
  Hard—trod and narrow—through the feathery snow,
Close by those head-stones, heedless of the wrath
  Of wintry winds—Heaven ease his load of wo.

Be with him, Father!—in the glad spring time,
  When birds go up from orange bowers
To build their nests, and bees are mid the thyme,
  And that worn path is fringed by flowers.

May a calm joy within his soul be born!
  May he look upward to a brighter sphere,
And bless the hand which smote, and made forlorn
  His household at the closing of a year.

THESE SECRET SOCIETIES.

CHAPTER I

" If I tell it to one, she will tell it to two,
  And the next cup of tea, they will plot what they'll do.
    So I'll tell nobody,
    I'll tell nobody,
  I'll tell nobody, no—not I!"

IT was a rainy morning in winter. Four ladies sat in a snug little parlor at Rayville, and busily plied their needles, and gossipped while they worked, without fear of interruption. They talked about the weather, the roads, the fashions, the church, and lastly, about the Freemasons.

"I hear," said Mrs. Howard, with a good degree of asperity in her tone, "that the Masons are on the increase in Rayville; no less than sixteen have taken degrees within six months. Well, of one thing I am certain, Mr. Howard is not among these. He knows my opinion of these secret societies, and would not, I am sure, provoke my displeasure by joining any of them. I have no good opinion of the Masons—I never had. I do not believe in a clique of men getting together and having *secrets* which even their wives are not permitted to hear and understand. Mr. Howard will never join the Masons while I live."

Mrs. Stewart, a mild-looking lady who sat near the speaker, smiled, but went on with her work, without saying a word. Her husband was a Mason, and the fact was universally known.

Mrs. Wells looked up at the leaden sky without, and at the raindrops which were slowly trickling down the window-panes. At length she said, "It seems to me, Mrs. Howard, that you have allowed yourself to be too much prejudiced against a class of men including some of our best members of society. My husband is not a Mason, but my brother is, and in his integrity I have as much confidence as in my own. He would not voluntarily hold fellowship with any who meet to devise evil. Of that I am confident."

" For what do they meet then ?" chimed in Mrs. Howard; "pray, for what purposes do they meet in secret conclave, once a month, with locked doors and barred windows? I, for one, should like to know. They must have a vast amount of business of some kind, it would seem, from their meeting so often ; and if i'ts of a reputable character, why not be open as the noonday about it? People who do philanthropic acts are not often chary of letting the world know about them, and in many instances, trumpeters are hired to herald forth deeds of benevolence—donations to colleges—*secret* missions of good, etc., and so on. No, it is human nature to love praise, and whatever is great and noble will win it. Therefore, if Masons did great and noble deeds, the world would find it out. There would not be such profound secrecy maintained, I assure you."

Mrs. Green, an old lady who sat by the fire, with a bright pair of gold-bowed spectacles mounted upon her nose, and a nicely plaited muslin cap shading her partially silvered locks, now took up the subject.

" Agnes," she said—referring to Mrs. Howard—" has always been bitter against the Freemasons. I believe that she would refuse aid from them were she in distress, and no other relief was offered."

" I do not imagine that it would be proffered," said Mrs. Howard, with a light, derisive laugh. " I do not believe it often *is* offered. We hear a great deal about the good done by the Masons—but it must be a latent species of goodness ; no individual instance of it ever came to my knowledge. I know that there is a great deal of fuss made of late about the establishment of masonic schools and colleges, but I take it, that the children of wealthy Masons are the ones to be benefitted. I do not believe that many orphans, who have not the wherewithal to defray expenses, will be made much wiser by these schools. As to taking care of the sick, why anybody with one grain of compassion about them, will do that. Few, in these civilized times, will stand by and see a fellow-being suffer for want of a few necessaries of life. No, no! you cannot convince me that these Masons are such benevolent beings as you all try to make out they are," and Mrs. Howard laid down her work, and went to the piano to play a song. The other ladies worked on in silence, and the subject of Freemasonry was forgotten.

It was perhaps a month after the conversation above, when Mr. Howard came in earlier than usual from his counting-house. He had a paper in his hand, and seemed somewhat in a hurry. "Agnes," he said to his wife, whom he met in the passage, "I wish that you would order supper a little earlier than usual to-night. I have business to transact after tea. Tell Hannah, please to have supper as early as half-past six."

Mrs. Howard nodded a good-natured assent; but secretly, she wondered what business could call Mr. Howard out after nightfall. He seldom went out, but spent his evenings either in the parlor with his family, or in the library among his books. She had long thought and declared him to be a model husband. But tea came in on that night as he desired, and immediately afterwards he went out. He did not return until midnight. Mrs. Howard was waiting for him by the parlor fire. The children had been in bed full three hours.

"What! up yet Agnes," he said, as he came in and set his hat down on the centre-table, and deliberately pulled his kid gloves from his fingers. "I expected to find you in bed. Why did you wait for me?"

"Because I have been expecting you home every moment for the last three hours. Pray, where have you been, and what kept you so long?"

"I have been to meet the lodge," said he, in the same calm tone, stepping towards the hearth. "I have joined the Masons."

Mrs. Howard was thunderstruck. Her face became a picture of astonishment. She hardly believed her own ears. It was the first time that her husband had ever gone deliberately in opposition to her wishes. And then there was a calm unconsciousness of wrong expressed by the tones of his voice, and by his whole demeanor, that she was at a loss to understand. They had many times talked the subject of Freemasonry over, and she had always shown herself to be particularly bitter towards the whole fraternity. Her first impulse was to reproach him, but she did that which was more natural for her to do, —for although deeply and easily prejudiced, she was not a shrew—*she burst into tears*.

It was now Mr. Howard's turn to look astonished. He surveyed her for a few moments in wonder, and then said, "Agnes, this is silly, idle, foolish. I thought that you were a sensible woman."

"I imagine that I am such," she replied.

"You are far from showing it in this instance," he said. "You have arrayed yourself in deadly hostility against you know not what. Why should you be so bitter against an order of men, of whose proceedings you know so little."

"It is because I *do* know, and *can* know so little, that I despise them," said Mrs. H. Good deeds do not shun the light—good organizations of men invite an investigation of their proceedings and principles—it is only owls, bats and beasts of prey that shun the light, and hide in secret places. I never thought, Edward, that you would do this. I am grieved that you have done it."

Mr. Howard looked steadily into the fire for a few moments without replying. At last he said, "What is done, *is* done. I am a Mason now. Your tears or reproaches cannot alter the matter. You ought to have enough confidence in me to believe that I would not engage in anything wrong. You have lived with me thirteen years. Surely you have had time enough to test my character. Words will do no good in this instance. I could not convince you by means of them, that I am in the right and you are in the wrong. So we may as well now drop the subject, and never again refer to it for the sake of domestic peace. I do not regret the step that I have taken, however; I only regret that you are weak enough to be troubled by it. Remember, that in condemning the Freemasons, you condemn some of the wisest and best men of every age and country." So saying, this obdurate, hard-hearted, philosophical, secret-loving Freemason, although only a few hours old, stepped towards the door, and left his wife to finish her crying fit, and follow when she felt disposed to do so.

"What," thought the latter, as the door closed upon her husband's retreating footsteps, "what will my neighbors, Mrs. Wells, and Stewart, and Green, think of my boastful conduct the other morning in regard to my husband joining the Masons? Fool that I was! I over-estimated my influence with Edward, over-estimated it entirely. I will never voluntarily refer to the subject again. Edward may go to the lodge until he is too blind to go. I never will ask him a question, or say why do you do so? Not I. If he wants to have *secrets*, he may keep them—that's all. I'll never try to find them out. I'll treat the matter henceforth with perfect indifference." And Mrs. Howard kept, for a long time, this resolution. Her husband went regularly out on lodge nights. She never sat up for his return. Masonic books and papers came silently into the house, and were as silently read and placed in the bookcases. Regalia were bought and worn. Mrs. Howard never expressed admiration or disapprobation.

CHAPTER II.—JOHN ADAMS.

· ONE day, while seated at the dinner-table, the Mason's wife was not a little surprised to see her husband enter the dining-room accompanied by a stranger, whom he did not introduce to a member of his family. The new comer had on a calico shirt, somewhat soiled, and a dusty, threadbare coat. His physiognomy was far from being pleasing —so Mrs. Howard thought—but her husband treated him with attention, helping him bountifully to everything upon the table. She could not help wondering who he was, and why Mr. Howard brought an unintroduced guest to the table; but glancing at him again, she saw that he had a masonic pin stuck into the bosom of his soiled shirt. Mrs. Howard closed her lips tightly. She suffered the two to finish their dinner in silence, and although she met her husband two or three times in the course of the evening, she never asked aught about the stranger guest.

"It's one of his precious masonic friends and brethren, without doubt," she said to herself. "I will not trouble myself to ask anything about him; not even his name. If he chooses to have secrets, he can keep as many as he pleases, for me. I shall not vex myself about it; but I wish that he would bring decent looking people home with him, if he brings any. If all his masonic brethren look like that, they must be a precious set."

A few months after thus soliloquizing, Mrs. H. was alone one evening, and feeling lonely, she opened the piano to play. A paper had in some way got wedged down beneath the lid. She glanced her eyes over the top of it, and saw that it was a masonic paper. She was hastily closing it, when her eye fell upon her husband's name, "EDWARD HOWARD," signed to what seemed a letter. "Ah! ha!" she thought, "has it come to this? Is Edward writing for their journals? I must see what it is, at any rate." And she began at the beginning, and read the piece deliberately through. It was headed "An Impostor." It stated that a person, calling himself "John Adams" had received from the Rayville Lodge quite an amount of money under plea of distress—that said money had never been refunded, and that John Adams was unworthy of masonic love or confidence.

Mrs. Howard could not help smiling complacently over this information. "I thought they were all *perfect*," said she to herself. "What was it that Edward said to me on the night that he joined? That the lodges were made up of the wisest and best men of every age and country! Astonishing! This John Adams is doubtless one of them."

She came near asking her husband the next day if John Adams was not a specimen of Masonry, of whom he was proud; but she did not—she closed her lips, and did not suffer the thought to escape. Were all equally wise, many a domestic broil would be avoided. The tongue is a little member, but it has stirred up great strife, and causes as trivial as this would have ended in mutual estrangement and separation for life. Mrs. Howard did not like the Masons, but she was a discreet wife, and kept her antipathy a good deal to herself.

CHAPTER III.

"Death! Strange that there is such a thing in the world, and men ever suffer it to be forgotten." First to Edward Howard, came the darkened chamber—the muffled tread of watchers around the bed—the hollow cough —the accelerated pulse—the fever—and then came the white shroud—the long coffin—the tears of mourners— the dirge over the grave—and—the drama, that we call Life, had ended. Where was the busy being of yesterday? The man of high hopes, warm affections, and noble purposes? Echo answers, " *Where ?* " Time, as he whets his scythe and shakes the sands rapidly from his hour-glass, whispers " *Where you, O mortal, will soon be !*" But mortality looks with streaming eyes into the hollow abyss and asks, " *Where is that ?* If a man die, shall he live again ?" Momentous question, where all are so frail !

Around the grave of Edward Howard there moved a solemn procession in strange array, each one of whom cast into the earth, upon the breast of the unconscious sleeper, a little sprig of evergreen, thereby proclaiming *their* belief in man's immortality. They said, by this mute sign, "Sleeper, thou shalt awake! Over this grassy bed, that we have hollowed out for thee, shall yet stream the golden light of a resurrection morning. Sleep on, but not for aye! Death may pluck thee away, but like the evergreen, thou shalt live in unfading beauty. Thy home is beyond the stars. Rest in hope, O sleeper! Earth shall not hold thee long in its cold embrace."

Beautiful emblem! If I fall asleep with the Christian's hope animating my bosom—unless cold scepticism seizes my heart, and the gloom of an atheist settles over my

dying pillow—unless I proclaim with purple lips and gasping
breath my disbelief in God—in the Bible as a revelation
from His hand—in man's immortality, and Heaven's eternity—cast ye the evergreen upon my coffin! Let it lie
there, saying to all who approach and gaze, " *She shall
live again! So she said, and so we believe.*"

Agnes Howard did not object to this masonic burial.
She was too deeply afflicted to harbor aught of enmity
against any body of men, with whom her husband had in
days gone by co-operated. She looked on the array as
one who dreamed. She could not realize that she was a
widow, and her children were fatherless. Great mournful
truths come slowly home to the heart. It is difficult to
feel them at first. But when day glides by after day, and
still the beloved comes not back—when the chair at the
fireside is long empty, and the tones of the voice die even
upon the memory, then we know and feel that death has
been among our household idols.

Agnes Howard, after the settlement of her husband's
estate, found herself poor—hardly able to live. To her
surprise, every path was made smooth to her feet. She
and her children were looked after and aided in every
emergency by—whom—the *Freemasons.* She had laughed
many times at the imaginary good ascribed to them. She
now found that she had been mistaken in her estimate of
them—that theirs is indeed an active benevolence—one
that neither slumbers nor sleeps.

One morning she met the three ladies with whom she
sat, in the introduction of this tale. The subject under
discussion was again *Freemasonry.* Agnes Howard wept
as she remembered the past. " My friends," said she, " I
have been in error; there may be no divinity in man's un-
regenerated nature, but there *is* such a thing as men com-
bining together for good and God-like deeds. I am no
longer an enemy to all of THESE SECRET SOCIETIES."

THE GENIUS OF MASONRY;

OR,

A LESSON BY THE WAYSIDE.

He that loveth not his brother, whom he hath seen,
How can he love GOD whom he hath not seen ?—*St. John.*

THERE was a neatly whitewashed cottage standing under a gracefully dropping elm-tree, at the bend of a winding cottage road.   Honeysuckles grew and twined into fantastic shapes over the low portico; white rose-bushes nodded over the humble little fence that surrounded the enclosure; trim rows of box grew upon each side of the nicely-gravelled paths; a heavy mass of ivy clambered to the top of the old chimney, and trailed down upon the roof in dark, rich festoons of Nature's own weaving.

It was a pretty rural scene, and Charlie Woodson, who was returning from a long afternoon's ramble, stopped and leaned over the little gate to contemplate it.   There was an air of peaceful beauty over every thing which he saw, that quite charmed him.   A mocking-bird, perched upon the topmost spray of the elm, was swinging to and fro as if stirred by its own outgushing melody; fat, sleek-looking cows were slowly winding along the road, follow-ed by a flaxen-headed, sun-burned little urchin, who hopped first upon one bare foot and then upon the other, and drove before him a hoop of goodly dimensions.   Crickets were waking up in the tall grass; the sun, which had been fiercely flaming all the day, now rested for a moment the rim of its great brazen face upon the horizon, and then sank slowly down, leaving behind him clouds of every gorgeous dye—clouds which lingered for a little while, and then faded out into the duskiness of night.

Charles Woodson was somewhat of a poet and a dreamer. He lived in the hot and crowded city, where men jostle each other rudely, while chasing fame, wealth and power. He sometimes grew tired of tongues—the strife for place —the vanities and sins which clustered in the Babel that he called " home."

" By and by," he said mentally, as he contemplated the humble scene spread out before him, " when I get my fortune made, I will have a wife and a country seat. My wife shall be like the picture in Irving's Sketch Book—she shall dress in white, love strawberries and cream, and be the personification of sweetness, beauty and good humor. Heaven help the city dweller! He never gets the scent of a bank of violets, or sees the twinkling waters of a rivulet, from year's end to year's end. Nature, with all her blessed influences, is to him like a sealed book—no wonder his heart grows like adamant—no wonder that he forgets Nature and Nature's God! Here, all is real, sweet and pure. The place is humble, but who cares for that! Every good, true, vigorous feeling I have, is here refreshed and strengthened. Yes, I will have a country seat !"

He turned away and began his walk; but when he reached the trunk of the elm-tree, he stopped again and looked back. Finally, he threw himself down at full length upon the mossy carpet which covered the roots, and shut his eyes, in order to enjoy better the bird-music at its top. How long he lay thus he could not say. The urchin went by, following the cloud of dust raised by the cattle's feet—the air grew cool and filled with dew—Venus came out, and hung like a spark in the sky just over the ivy-clad chimney—and the bird finished her song, and sank into the nest which was hidden away among the light foliage beneath her.

But the young man was startled from his dreams at last. An old man, a traveller like himself, came slowly up the road ; and when he reached the elm, he threw his knapsack from his shoulder, and sat down on a large white rock, which jutted out of the ground, not far from where the dreamer's head rested. He took the hat from his forehead, and wiped his bald temples with a silk handkerchief. As

he did this, the young man observed his features narrowly.
He had a blue eye, which was remarkable for the serene
light that slept in its depths—indeed, over his whole face
there played a good and benevolent expression. The
young man instantly grew interested. The venerable figure
of the old traveller, sitting there like those angels the
patriarchs of old sometimes entertained at close of day
beneath their household trees, seemed to his poetical imagination to be in harmony with the scene. He removed
the hat with which he had been shadowing his eyes, and
looked at his venerable companion, long and earnestly.
The old man's eye was upon the cottage. He, too, seemed
attached by the quiet loveliness of the scene.

"That is a beautiful spot," said Woodson, at last making
bold to address him. "If an Eden had survived the fall,
I should suppose we might be in the vicinity of it. For
my part, I would rather live in a nook, leafy and quiet as
this is, than to occupy the proudest palace which lifts its
marble front in Broadway. I am sick of erring, proud,
contemptible and misguided humanity. Oftentimes I have
cried out with Cowper,

'O, for a lodge in some vast wilderness!'"

The old gentleman turned around, and looked at the
young man, in his turn, narrowly.

"You live in the city," he said abruptly.

"Ay," said the young man, half bitterly. "Faith has
shut me in with burning walls of bricks, where men live
like bees, and sting each other, oftentimes, to frensy
But one of these days I hope to live in a spot like this."

"And like Hanarus, the famous Eastern Cadi, you hope
to *escape* the vices and follies of your kind, I suppose,"
replied the old man, smiling. "Like him, you will find,
too, I opine, that you have undertaken a hard task.
There is no spot so cool and green, and quiet and retired,
that the Serpent, which invaded Eden itself, cannot find
its way into. Fallen human nature is everywhere the
same. Men in cities quarrel for supremacy. Why do you
marvel? Did not Christ's disciples—they who were led

by the Prince of Peace himself—fall out by the way, and strive, even while surrounded by the peaceful influence of nature in Judea, over that hackneyed theme of dispute, viz : *Who shall be the greatest ?* In such leafy nooks as this, wild, uncurbed and hateful passions reign. It matters less, young man, *where we are, than what we are.*"

If the dreamer had been at first attracted by the old man's countenance, he was now equally drawn towards him by the wisdom of his words. He sat upright, and seemed fearful of losing a syllable.

" You are a seer, I perceive, father," he said. " You have gained wisdom by travel and experience. I would fain sit a little while at your feet, and be taught."

Again the old man smiled.

" You have guessed rightly," he said. " I am very old —so old that my birth-day is lost amid the mist which enshrouds antiquity. Some date my existence from the building of Solomon's Temple—others maintain that I am co-eval with creation itself. At any rate, I have walked the earth a great while. I have been in almost all places haunted by man. I have wandered in tents—dwelt in palaces—slept in hovels—traversed wilds—dived in cities— and hovered, with tearful eyes and outstretched hands, around battle fields, while tides of blood crimsoned the green sod and filled the enamelled cups of flowers, made to be goblets for crystal dew alone. My mission has been one of mercy to mankind. I have tried to link in one vast brotherhood, men of every age and clime. I have preached Love—Love, which the Saviour himself made the greatest of christian discipleship, everywhere. Words of Brotherly Kindness have ever been upon my lips. I have sought, moreover, for Truth, as for hidden pearls ; but the strong hand of persecution has, nevertheless, been sometimes raised against me, and men have sought to banish me from the earth. Young man, you look surprised, but you see in the vigorous old man before you, the Genius of Masonry. I have met with you before. I have seen you in the lodge-room, for you are one of my professed disciples, and worship at my altars. Heed my words. Do not *fly from mankind.* Mingle everywhere freely with humanity; protect the weak; strengthen the wavering in virtue; minister alike to those who are sick in body and sick in soul; raise those that are cast down; live continually to bless your race. Then, in the hot and teeming hives of city existence, you will be happy; in the solitude of the country, you will find enjoyment, too. Wherever God, the Great Master Builder, apportions you your task, you will thrive, because you are living in conformity to His laws—loving 'man whom you *have* seen'—preparing, also, to love 'God whom you have *not* seen.' The great lessons of Christianity and Masonry harmonize. Both teach mankind contentment with their lot."

The Genius ceased speaking; and to the dreamer's astonishment, while he was gazing intently upon him, he seemed to melt away into thin, colorless air, and mingle with the silvery light which Venus and the Moon together were now shedding, like a mantle, over ivy and cottage—elm-tree and road.

The young man rubbed his eyes, and looked again.

"Is it possible," he queried, "that I have been dreaming all this? Was that old man a living, breathing reality, or a figure conjured up by my half-slumbering imagination?" A moment's thought convinced him that the latter supposition was correct, for no trace of the traveller was to be seen; even the white rock upon which he had reposed had melted, too, into moonlight—no knapsack was visible—no foot-mark was upon moss or sand.

"Well! well!" said the young man, musingly, as he got up and re-commenced his walk. "I have, for once in my life, 'had a dream, which was not all a dream!' '*Live continually to bless your race.*' Those were the old man's words; they ring in my ears now like the clarion call of a bugle. I will heed the admonition. Farewell, beautiful cottage—drooping elm trees—peaceful, rural scene! I may never enjoy a retreat such as you afford, but my mentor said, I recollect, that '*it matters less where we are, than what we are!*'"

20

THE GREYTON ROBBERY ; OR, THE MASON'S SON.

"Cast thy bread upon the waters."

DAME STEPHENS sat alone in her humble little cottage, at Greyton Hill. It was a sleepy afternoon in June. The bees hummed drowsily in the garden close by her, and her flax-wheel hummed drowsily in the neat but plain little room where she was sitting. Lulled by the sound of both, she was near falling asleep ; arousing herself at last, she re-arranged the flax upon her distaff, re-tied the strings of her close-fitting cambric cap, and began to move her foot, and turn the humble little instrument with renewed energy and vigor. The sun shone in, and lay like a flood of gold upon the well-scoured oaken floor. A large house cat sat on the hearth, with her face to the east, which she assiduously washed with her huge grey paw. The shelf dishes, which were ranged with great precision and care on the clean dressers at one end of the apartment, shone as brightly as clear water and hard rubbing could make them. The few split-bottomed chairs which the widow owned were placed in straight rows down the sides of the room. A well-worn Bible was on one end of the mantlepiece. It was carefully preserved. Not a leaf had been suffered to curl or become torn ; but bits of thread and scraps of paper and ribbon had been placed here and there between its sacred leaves, so that particular texts might be easily found when she had leisure to con them over. She was evidently one of those who believed with the poet in relation to that Book :

"Within this awful volume lies,
The mystery of mysteries—
Happiest they of human race,
To whom their God has given grace,
To read, to fear, to hope, to pray,
To lift the latch, to force the way ;
But better had they ne'er been born
Who read to doubt or read to scorn."

The dame was poor, and yet she was rich. Do you tell me that this is a paradox? I can only explain it as the wise man has done before me. "There *is* who maketh himself rich, and yet hath nothing; there *is* who maketh himself poor, and yet hath great riches." I do not imagine that the latter personage spoken of by the sacred writer had many dollars and cents to expend, or to hoard up—neither had the dame. In silver and gold she was poor, but in those rich affections which bless the fire side and neighborhood—in those gentle charities which shed light and cheerfulness around the sick and the afflicted—in those calm and peaceful thoughts and feelings which dwell only with the good and generous, the dame was wealthy, "blessed to overflowing."

She was all alone in the world. Her husband and her only child had slept so long in the church-yard at Greyton, that the rank grass was matted together on their graves, and hung in such a manner as to quite hide the head-stones. Her little cottage, which had just been built at the time of her husband's death, was now grey and weather-beaten; and the shingles on the roof were off in several places. She had but one relative in the world, and that was a nephew—a poor man who lived in the valley, with a wife and eight children to support. She herself made a livelihood by means of her flax-wheel and loom, both of which she had plied diligently all her life. She spun for the vicar's lady, who paid her very liberally—she spun for many of the neighboring gentry, and now and then the Freemasons helped her a trifle, in consideration of the honorable office her late worthy husband had held among them. One gentleman, now also deceased, had at the time of her husband's funeral given her a twenty-dollar bill. This money the old lady got changed into silver, and the silver she deposited in an old stocking leg, and carefully placed at the bottom of a chest. Nothing had ever tempted her to use a dime of it, or to hazard its safety by placing it out at interest. The sum was just the same which she had received from the mason—twenty dollars— no more, no less. Sometimes she got her hoard out and

counted over the precious pieces; the sum in her eyes
looked large; she wondered that John O'Creal, the donor,
had found in his heart to be so liberal. But then he was,
at the time of that donation, a wealthy Mason, though times
had changed sadly in his family. Within a short period
after her husband's demise, the Mason died, leaving his
affairs in a very unsettled state, and Jemmy O'Creal, his
only son had run, and was still running, a wild and desolate
career. His property had vanished away. The O'Creals
now were scarcely richer than dame Stephens herself.
But more of this anon.

As we were saying, on this particular afternoon dame
Stephens sat at work, but she was destined to be interrupted. A heavy foot was heard upon the sand, and soon
a rough-looking young man, with a gun upon his shoulder,
and a shot-pouch dangling by his side, came up to the door
and sank down most unceremoniously upon the threshold.
His face was red and somewhat bloated; his clothes had once
been fine, but they were torn and worn threadbare now;
his hat was slouched down over his forehead, as if he feared
there might be a Cainish sort of mark upon his brow,
which it would be best to conceal, if possible. He scarcely
nodded to the dame, by way of salutation, while taking his
seat, but she seemed to understand his mood, and did not
act as if she expected, or cared for, many tokens of recognition. She did not arise from her spinning-wheel, but
kept up with her foot the same monotonous hum.

"And so, Jeems,' said she, "I hear there has been a
freshet in the valley, and that part of Judge Ritcher's mill
dam is washed away. Has anything else occurred there
of late?"

The young man looked up at her, with a startled expression on his features, but he soon cast his eyes down
again on the sand before the door, and answered somewhat evasively:

"When did you hear from the valley, granny?"

"It has been several days since," continued the dame.
'Little Peter Pike went by here last Thursday, on his return from mill; he did not get his corn ground, owing, he

said, to the mill-dam being washed away. But why do you ask, Jeems?" Has anything unusual occurred there? I hope my nephew, Job Cotton, and his family are well."

The young man heaved a short convulsive sort of sigh, but did not reply. He got up, and placed his gun in an upright position against the wall; he took off his shot-pouch and laid it down upon the floor; he drew his hat down closer than ever over his eyes, and sat down again.

"I reckon," he said at length, "that Job Cotton and his family are well; but Job has been robbed, they say."

"Robbed!" shrieked the old lady. "Robbed!" did you say, Jemmy O'Creal?" and her wheel and foot both stopped their motion. "Who could have done it?" at length she exclaimed. "Greyton valley is one of the most moral, peaceble places in creation. I've lived here going on thirty-five years, and I have never heard of a murder or a robbery happening there before."

"No!" said the young man, "the like does'nt *often* happen."

"Who did it, and where was Job?" asked the old lady, still half-breathless through excitement. "Do tell me all about it!"

"He was riding on his grey pony from Harper's Creek to Greyton ferry when it happened, but it remains yet to be discovered who did it. His pockets were eased by a highwayman, of about fifteen dollars—not a very large sum, but still it was something for such a man as Cotton to lose."

"Ah! yes," exclaimed the old lady, "with his sick wife and his eight children to support! Who could have been hard-hearted enough to have done it? Is no one suspected, Jemmy?"

The young man coughed a short dry cough—he moved with a restless, excited motion, but he did not immediately reply. At length he said, glancing furtively into the old woman's face:

"I believe there *is* a youngster who is looked upon with some suspicion by the Greyton valley folks, but he may be innocent for all that."

"Who is it, Jemmy? Who is it?" asked the old woman eagerly; "he must be a graceless scamp, to make the best of him."

"A graceless scamp," repeated the hunter, nervously; "but yet, granny, there may be extenuating circumstances. The young man may have been drunk when he did it—so drunk as to be scarcely conscious of what he was about."

"But he had no business to get drunk," said the old woman, tartly. "I have no patience with those who try to hide or get excused for *one sin* by owning another—no patience in the world; *no* young man has any business to get drunk."

"You touch me then, granny," said the young man, in a low and sorrowful voice. "You know that that has been my failing from my childhood. I learned to love wine at my father's dinner table. The appetite grew upon me, until a burning thirst now at times rages in me like the fires of hell. The respectable part of the world long ago cast me off, but you have ever been a firm and steady friend to me. When I have felt hunger gnawing like a vulture at my vitals, after a three days' carousal, and have not had a dime in my pocket to satisfy it with, I have come here, and you have given me white bread and butter from the dresser yonder, and precious slices of meat. You have fed, warmed, and sobered me, and afterwards bade me depart in peace, granny, and lead a better life, but I, somehow have not done it—*cannot* do it. Heaven help a wretch like me!" and the young man covered up his face in his hands, and sobbed like a child.

The old woman, too, was much moved. She arose from her wheel, and came and sat down in a low chair near where the prodigal was sitting; she wiped her aged eyes repeatedly with the corner of her checked cotton apron.

"I wish you would do better, Jemmy," at last she said, in a voice choked with emotion. "You are almost like an own son to me. Many and many is the time, when your father has sat beside my dear man in the lodge-room; and on the afternoon after poor Mr. Stephens' burial, your father, who was a grand gentleman in those days, did not hesitate to come in here and talk to me, and advise me what to do; and when he was going away, he gave me a twenty-dollar bill, Jemmy. I shall never forget his kindness, and ever since then I have been glad to do what I could for you all, but it's little that a poor old body like me can do for anybody. But I am sure that I shall always do my utmost for you."

"Will you!" said the young man, hastily starting again to his feet, "will you do your utmost for me now, granny? You can, if you will, save me from the blackest ignominy and disgrace."

"What do you mean, Jemmy O'Creal?" said the woman, startled at his vehemence. "What have you been doing now, and from what can I save you?"

"I am that highway robber, granny. In an hour when I was more of a maniac than a sane person, I disguised myself, waylaid your nephew, and took from him and his family by violence, his honest earnings, and I spent that same night the accursed sum at the gaming-table. Some of the money I learn has been recognized, and the bloodhounds of the law are already scenting my track. Hide me, granny, shield me from the just punishment of my crimes, and the shade of my father will look down from Heaven and approve the deed. I promise after this, repentance. Ah! I am racked by that now—I promise, granny, upon your Bible yonder, reformation. So help me, heaven!"

It was the old woman's turn now to start up in alarm.

"How could you do it, Jemmy!" she said. "How could you do it? After all my kindness to you, is this the way you have repaid me, by robbing my nephew—the only relative I have in the world—of his little pittance? It was an ungrateful deed, Jemmy, as well as one punishable by the laws. How could you do it?"

"I did it, as I before told you, when my brain was on fire, when I was mad and not sane. Do you not pity as well as blame me? Will you forget now your promise to aid me?"

"How can I aid you?" said the old woman, doubtfully. "What can I do for you?"

"Five dollars," said the culprit, "will place me out of the immediate reach of my pursuers. Can't you give me five dollars, granny ? I promise to refund it with interest."

The old woman did not answer, but she went to an old chest and mechanically drew forth her hoard. She recounted the dollars into her horny palm.

She then went to a small drawer, and brought forward pen, ink and paper.

"I promise to aid you, Jemmy O'Creal," she said, "upon two conditions. One is, you are to pledge yourself from this hour to total abstinence from all that can intoxicate ; the other is, you must write a letter to Job Cotton, confessing your guilt, acknowledging your penitence, and enclosing a sum of money which I will give you, equal in value to that taken. These conditions complied with, I will give you a sum large enough to aid you to escape, and may that Divine Power, whose aid you just now so earnestly invoked, help you in deed and in truth to reform your life !"

The young man seized the pen with a tremulous hand. He scrawled, as best he could, the letter and the pledge. He afterwards received the five dollars promised, from the hand of the old woman, and before sundown that night he was in a fair way to escape all pursuit.

He did escape—he did reform his life.

One day, near two years afterwards, while dame Stephens was sitting by her door, employed in turning the heel of a sock, which she was knitting for the vicar, little Peter Pike stopped before her door, on his way home from Greyton mill, and after fumbling about with his mealy hands for awhile in both pockets, he drew from one of them a letter which he said was given to him for the dame at the post office.

The old lady never got letters, and the event was a remarkable era in her life. She went into her cottage, and nervously broke the seal. As she did so, there fell into her lap a hundred-dollar bill. She could scarcely believe her eyes. The sum looked to her to be such a prodigious one. But the letter explained it all

"Dear madam," it began, "I am prepared now to refund, with interest, the five dollars borrowed of you some time ago. I thank you for the loan. I am now a sober, respectable man, engaged in a good business, and am soon to be married to a lovely and worthy woman. I thank God *for having been born a Mason's son!* Ah! they little know what they are about when they sow beside all waters their precious gifts. They know not who will reap perchance the fruits of their benevolence. 'Bone of their bone, flesh of their flesh,' as in this instance, may do it. Well was it written in that old-fashioned book, called a Bible, lying on one end of your mantlepiece, granny, 'Cast thy bread upon the waters, thou shalt find it after many days.'—J. O'CREAL."

The old woman dropped a few quiet tears over this affecting scrawl. She then laid the letter carefully between the leaves of the precious volume over her head, and little was ever said by her or her nephew about the Greyton robbery, although the valley people often wondered that a poor man like Job Cotton should have taken the loss so quietly. Should they ever see this sketch, they will doubtless acknowledge the mystery to be now, for the first time, explained.

———◦◦◦◦◦———

THE LIFE OF MAN.—An ancient author thus moralizes on the life of a man: "His birth is as his morning; his strongest time, or middle life, is as his noon; and his night as that when he takes leave of the world, and is laid in the grave to sleep with his fathers. This hath been the state of every one since first the world had any on it. The day breaking, the sun ariseth; the sun arising, continues moving; the sun moving, noontide maketh; noontide made, the sun declines; the sun declining, threatens setting; the sun setting, night cometh; and night coming, our life is ended. Thus runs away our time."

THE BLUE HYACINTH;

OR,

THE MASONIC MEDAL.

CHAPTER I.

There are bright flowers of care bereft,
And hearts that languish more than flowers.
—*Willis.*

THE ice-king is here, binding creek and river with fetters which glitter in the sunshine like silver. If you stand, and gaze up through the morning air into the high, birdless and cloudless concave of blue above, nothing seems to intervene between you and that, but, as Willis has expressed it, "palpable cold."

If you glance off into the neighboring forest, you see the trees standing like great skeletons, stretching their long arms towards one another, as if they were sentient beings, with feelings of mutual sympathy stirring at their oaken hearts. At their feet lie brown withered leaves—leaves which last summer were green and glossy, dancing and fluttering on the bows, and wooing the birds to build nests within their shadows. Now they lie one half over the other, and coated with frost-work. Three months hence, and not a remnant of these will be found. The dying beauty of most things has a silvery glitter. The head of the old man grows white as wool beneath the frosts of age, and these dead leaves are white with the frosts of the year. The sheen will disappear from the forest when the sun has travelled further towards the zenith. When shall it melt from the brow of the veteran? Perchance when "the Sun of Righteousness shall arise with healing on His wings"—healing for all the infirmities of age, strength for its decrepitude, and immortal youth and beauty to supplant decay.

The frozen ground rings beneath the tread like the clatter of a metalic hoof over the pavement, and in the garden there is a grass-plot, every spear in which stands stiff and formidable as a bristling bayonet of steel. If you pluck one, and scrape the coating of frost away, you are surprised to find it wearing a clear tint of verdure still. It reminds you of the heart sometimes found in old age—a heart kept green and lively beneath time's hoary frosts by happy and kindly memories. Such a heart has forgotten to look at Old Time's hour-glass; nor has the sharpest point of his scythe, or the frostiest breathings of his wintry breath, touched it, withering its never-dying affections.

But it was not about the grass that I sat down to write, nor the skeleton trees, nor the blue concave above, nor the frozen stream. It was about a little blue hyacinth which, strange as it may seem, I found half an hour ago, lifting its clear blue eye towards the heavens, as bright, cheerful and fragrant, as though no frost glittered in the garden walks. I came near plucking it, but the little blossom looked so brave, so hardy, so upright, that I did not find it in my heart to uproot it. "Grow on," I said; "battle bravely with wintry blasts and chilling skies! Thou shouldst have been born among the bees, and honeysuckles, and rich rains, and clear golden sunbeams of spring. But wrestle with an adverse fate—look out with a clear eye from the glitter of the frost-work, and be, thou delicate thing, a type of childhood and of womanhood, as both are often found in this dreary world.

What an influence association has upon the memory, calling to it pictures seen in childhood—dreams that long ago rang through the brain, and then vanished as the ripple vanishes from the surface of a lake—thoughts, feelings, fancies and images which you deemed long ago buried and forgotten. It has been said that we never entirely forget—that at some point in our lives, every scene witnessed, comes rushing back upon memory, and these incidents are called up by some mysterious principles of association. It may be so. At any rate, the sight of that wintry blossom has brought back to me, as vividly as if it had been but yesterday, a face, a form, a figure, and a life, which, like a rounded bubble, burst and disappeared from earth. Beautiful little Madge Bryant! let me, in another chapter, narrate your history.

CHAPTER II.

"Ugh! how the wind blows, and the ice is fast forming by the door-steps," said farmer Nichols, one dreary December night, as he stirred the fire, and re-arranged his spectacles, preparatory to reading the newspaper that he held in his hand. "I should not at all wonder if somebody froze to death to-night; and, bless me! it is raining! I thought that it was too cold to rain; but hear the big drops beating against the windows! Hannah! I think we have great reason to be thankful for so comfortable a home, when many a poor wretch has not where to lay his head. Don't you think so?"

Hannah—the woman addressed—sat in the opposite corner of the fireplace, busily counting off the stitches for the heel of a sock which she was knitting. She was an old woman, wearing a thick cambric cap and a checked apron; in appearance she was rather rough, but she harmonized well with the farmer, and when referred to, looked up and nodded without speaking, for she had a knitting-needle between her lips.

"Yes," pursued the old man, "we have a great deal to be thankful for, but we've worked hard for it. It strikes me that there wouldn't be so much destitution and suffering in the world, if everybody would be as industrious and frugal as we have been since we married. You know, Hannah, that we had little to begin with, and we have raised a family of seven children, and seen all but one well settled in the world. Isaac will soon be a man, and a noble fellow he is going to be, or I'm no prophet. When he gets through college, I take it that he'll be somebody that we needn't feel ashamed to own."

"The Lord grant it!" ejaculated old Mrs. Nichols, in a tone that showed how strong the feelings of a mother were stirring at her heart. "The Lord grant that Isaac may do well, and be a great comfort to our old age, as I am sure he will be. But hark! I thought I heard the little gate open. It isn't possible that any of the neighbors will come to sit with us on such a night as this. It may be that old Mrs. Journagan is worse, and has sent for me to sit up with her again."

The farmer laid down his newspaper and listened intently, yet he heard nothing but the wind moaning round the window-panes.

"It was Tray, I dare say," he said at last, "sweeping the panels of the door; it sounds sometimes, when heard from the piazza, like the gate. But what ails you, Hannah; you have suddenly grown as white as a sheet."

The old lady's face did indeed betray fear. She sat with her eyes directed towards a dark, curtainless window which looked out upon the front lawn. Her knitting had fallen down in her lap, and a whole row of stitches had dropped from the needle. . What had suddenly happened to agitate quiet dame Nichols?

"Hush, John!" she said at last, in a hoarse whisper; "I fear there are bad folks about here to-night. I am sure I saw a face looking in upon us at that window half a second ago. My eyes could not have deceived me; it was a white face. I am afraid that there are robbers about the lot. All's not right, I'm sure."

"That cannot be," said the farmer. "Oaklands is a quiet place, and no robber ever showed himself in this neighborhood, to my knowledge. You must have been mistaken, Hannah; but in order to satisfy you, I'll go out of doors and see."

"Oh, no, John! don't go!" said Hannah, reaching out her hand to detain him. "Some ill will befall you, I'm certain. When there is no one in a house but two old folks like us, it is prudent to shun and guard against danger, rather than run out into it. Are you quite sure that you bolted the front door for the night? I shall not sleep soundly, unless both doors and windows are well fastened, I'm sure."

Just at that moment there was a heavy knock, as of somebody asking admittance from without. The farmer rose from his seat and went towards the door.

. "Don't go, John! don't go!" said the old lady imploringly. "I'm sure all's not right. No honest people would be out on such a night as this, and thieves had better stay out. I wouldn't open the door, John; pray don't."

"Nonsense, Hannah!" said the old man in a firm voice, and with an undaunted air. "I wouldn't let a dog stay out on such a night as this, if it was in my power to give him shelter; and as to any harm befalling us, I'm not afraid. I never injured anyone, so nobody can be seeking revenge; and as to being robbed, we are not rich enough for that. Give me the candle."

A knock, louder and more imperative than the first, now summoned the old farmer, and he proceeded to turn the key in the lock and swing open the door. A strong blast of wind and rain swept in as he did so, nearly extinguishing the candle, and quite blinding for a moment the worthy master of the house.

"Who's there?" at last he demanded in a stentorian voice.

"Will ye gie a night's shelter to a poor woman and chile?" said a female voice without. "The night is dark, and I'm cold; my baby, too, is suffering."

"Good heavens! a woman and her child out on such a night in the rain! Come here, Hannah, and hold the light so that I can see. In the name of goodness, woman, who are you, and where did you come from? But come in," he continued, as a second blast swept against him. "Don't stop to answer questions while standing there in the rain. Bring your child to the fire."

A dripping figure stepped over the threshold—a beggar-woman with a baby in her arms. The vagrant came to the fire, and sat down in a low kitchen chair, which Hannah placed for her. As strong ripples of light from the fire broke over her, she shaded her eyes for a moment with her rough, weather-beaten hand. She was dressed in a black *sacque* made of bombasin and trimmed with velvet. Her dress was of the same material, and torn in slits in several places. A faded calico sun-bonnet, with a remnant of green *barege* hanging to it, by the way of veil, partly concealed a face tanned by much exposure to the weather, and slightly wrinkled by age. Taken altogether, it must have been a handsome face, although foreign in its aspect. The forehead was low, and a good physiognomist would have detected a sinister expression in the eye; but as she removed her sun-bonnet, the farmer and his wife both thought that they had seen, in the course of their lives, many uglier faces than that.

Her child did not sleep, and yet it lay in her lap as if perfectly exhausted with cold and hunger. It was a beautiful child, and its dress, although wet and bedaubed, was such as was strange to find on the child of a foreign beggar. A soft hood of blue silk, nicely quilted and lined with straw-color, with a roll of swan's down surrounding its front, was on its head—a nice flannel blanket, richly wrought at the edge and the corners, was wrapped around its tiny form; while one little foot encased in a green morocco shoe, peeping from beneath its blanket, displayed a pretty little ankle, white as a snow-flake. Its face was perfectly white; indeed, it looked like a face which might have come from Canova's chisel, only the lips were slightly tinged with rose; two eyes of dark blue looked languidly yet wonderingly about, and soft golden curls strayed out from beneath the hood. All these things, the quick eyes of Hannah and John noted, as their guest sat and thawed her benumbed fingers before the genial blaze.

"Have you come very far to day?" at last said the farmer, stirring the coals with the poker, and then sitting down at no great distance from his guest. It is a black night for a woman and her baby to be abroad."

"Yes," said the beggar, "an uncanny night enough—but nobody wo' keep me before. Can I sleep in some outhouse to-night with my chile?"

"We'll find a bed for you somewhere," said Hannah, whose fear had banished at the sight of the vagrant. "Take

off your baby's bonnet, it is wet I think. Are you hungry?
I suppose you have not had your supper. A terrible life
you must lead. What makes you wander about the country so? Why don't you work instead of begging?"

"My little chile—my poor little chile," said the woman,
lifting her hand as if to brush a tear drop from the corner of her eye. "I canna work with this little chile;" and
so saying, she drew a paper—a bluish, well-thumbed,
greasy-looking document from her pocket, and presented
it to the farmer.

It was a printed copy of a history of wrongs and suffer-
ings which, from the frequency with which we meet with
them, we may well suppose to be stereotyped. But farmer
Nichols had a kind heart, and moreover, he had seldom
been visited at the Oaklands by beggars. As he read
and re-read the paper, and then looked up at the face of
the woman, who sat looking into the fire, he felt a sentiment of pity stirring at his heart. "It is a sad case!" he
said, mentally. "It must be very mortifying to beg about
the country as she is doing, and then having been brought
up in the old country, I dare say that she don't know how
to do our sort of work."

While the farmer was thus engaged, Mrs. Nichols had
brought from the pantry a plate of cold biscuit, some
butter, a bit of cheese, and a large piece of pastry. These
she placed upon the hearth before the vagrant.

"Can't you have a cup of something hot made for her,
mammy?" asked farmer Nichols. "A little tea, or coffee,
or something so? The poor thing must need it after such
an exposure, and then, perhaps, the child would like some
milk—it looks half-famished."

Mrs. Nichols obeyed her husband's suggestion, and
when the tea was made, and the milk warmed, she even
offered to take the baby into her own lap, and feed it with
a teaspoon from the cup of sweetened milk which she had
prepared. The little creature opened its hungry little
mouth, and eagerly swallowed what she gave it, while the
woman devoured with a ravenous appetite the biscuit
and pastry.

Inclement as the night was, the worthy farmer and his wife were destined to be again interrupted by a knock at the door. The old man went to open it, and this time admitted a stout young man, with a ruddy face, bright black eyes, heavy whiskers, and raven hair. He knocked the rain-drops from his fur cap, and shook hands with the farmer and his wife with the air of an old acquaintance.

"It's a rainy night, Squire," he said, "but I've been up to A—— to-day, and have brought you a letter from Isaac. So I thought that I'd come over to bring it, and spend the night with you, while I was about it." He came to-wards the fire as he spoke, and his eye fell upon the beggar. He looked surprised—slightly bowed, and then sat down in the seat that farmer Nichols placed for him. It was James Wallace, the schoolmaster. Such a school-master, too, the whole region round about thought him to be, as is not often vouchsafed to a neighborhood. Like Goldsmith's hero, it was certain that he could "write and cipher, too"—yea more, he talked Latin and Greek as if they were vernacular tongues, and was seldom found at fault on any subject.

A silence of some moments ensued. The farmer, who still held the paper in his hand, at length handed it to the schoolmaster. He perused it in silence, and then handed it to Mrs. Nichols, who reached out her hand to receive it. She in her turn gave it back to the vagrant.

"A sad story," said the farmer, looking at the school-master. The latter simply bowed. He was busy pulling from his coat-pocket Isaac's letter. This delivered, he commenced talking to the farmer's wife about sundry matters, but his eye often scrutinized the woman and her child; upon the face of the latter, especially, he looked long and piteously. The little creature was now lying across its mother's lap. Its soft blue eyes were closed in slumber; and the sodden blue cap having been removed, as beautiful a mass of curly hair was displayed as the young man remembered ever to have seen upon so young a child.

The woman did not seem to relish the scrutiny. She

nestled uneasily in her seat, and finally asked the farmer's wife to show her a place to sleep. As the good dame arose for the purpose of doing so, the vagrant got up too, and commenced rummaging in an enormous calico bag which she carried with her. Something metalic rang upon the floor; the farmer's wife looked down, and so did the beggar—nothing was to be seen, and they moved forward.

CHAPTER III.

AFTER the farmer had finished the perusal of his letter, and Hannah had returned to the room, and ascertained that her son was well and doing well, and had resumed her knitting, the conversation turned upon their guest.

"I can't help but pity a woman like that, to save my life," said the farmer. "When a *man* begs, I can refuse him, but a lone woman, with an infant, is such a pitiable object, that I can't find it in my heart to turn one away, without giving her something."

"The child," said the schoolmaster, "is indeed to be pitied. It looks above its parent. I cannot think that she is the mother of it. It is one that she has stolen perhaps."

"Stolen!" repeated Mrs. Nichols, in a tone of surprise. "You jest surely. No woman, especially no poor woman, who cannot get enough to eat herself, would think of stealing *a child*. Pray, what could she want of it?"

The schoolmaster smiled. "Children are often stolen in cities," he said, "by beggars, who think that the sight of infantile helplessness will aid them in working upon the sympathies of the community. If you notice this one, you will see that its clothing is all of rich materials and soft texture—such as no beggar-woman could well procure for her child. Moreover, she does not yield it a particle of nutriment, I presume, from its starved appearance. I do not like the looks of the woman, and shall not, on her departure in the morning, give her a dime."

"A stolen child!" repeated Mrs. Nichols again, in an undertone, as if to herself. "I never thought of such a thing. How restless the idea makes me. It must be a false conjecture."

"It may be," said the school-master; "but it was no longer ago than yesterday, that I was reading, in some paper, of a mother who was almost frantic at the loss of her child. I forget now where she lived, or how the child was dressed. I read the paragraph hastily. The most that I recollect about it is, that the baby had around its neck a gold masonic medal. It was some thing belonging to its mother, and had been carelessly placed about the neck by the nursery-maid. Perhaps it is because I am myself a Mason, that I remember this much. But surely it must be a dreadful thing to be robbed of a child. I think that the paper stated that this one had been left sleeping alone in its crib, near an open window on the street. When sought after, it was gone. No clue could be obtained of it, and the mother, who is a widow, is quite frantic."

"Good heavens!" exclaimed the farmer, starting up— " what if this should be the very infant?"

"A supposition, the truth of which we cannot well ascertain just now," said the teacher, thoughtfully. "We should hardly be justified in robbing a mother of her babe, on the strength of *mere conjecture*. There are thousands of beggars in the country, any one of whom might have taken it."

"True! true!" said the farmer—but he thumbed the arm of his chair with his heavy fingers, and looked straight into the fire, as if buried in thought.

The conversation was pursued for some time longer by Mrs. Nichols and the teacher, but finally the latter arose to retire for the night. As he did so, his foot hit something upon the floor. It was a shining object, and he stooped to pick it up. It proved to be a small and exquisitely wrought gold masonic medal. He started at the sight of it, and came near letting it fall from his hands.

"It must have fallen from the beggar's pocket," said Mrs. Nichols. "I heard something drop when she was rummaging there, and tried to find it for her."

"We have something tangible, now, upon which to ground supposition," said the teacher, holding the medal up to the candle in order to decipher its characters. "I do not think that we should be justified in letting this woman proceed without investigating the matter. I will go home and find the paper containing the paragraph to which I referred. I will bring it up here, and we can then consult together about what had best be done."

The schoolmaster was already putting on his overcoat and looking for his cap. "Stop!" said the farmer; "it is very late, and the night is stormy. We can manage to detain the beggar here as long as we please. It will be time enough to look up proofs in the morning. I do not believe, Mr. Wallace, that I would go out again on such a night as this."

The young man stepped to the door, and looked out into the darkness. The rain had ceased, but the air was keen and biting Here and there a star showed itself in the sky above. Something like the gate creaked. He looked in the direction, but saw nothing. He shivered with the cold, and turning back, determined to follow the farmer's suggestion, and not venture out until light dawned. But before any of them slept, Mrs. Nichols slipped to the door of the vagrant's apartment—a room, by the way, opening upon the piazza, and carefully turned the lock. "She is secure now," she thought. "No criminal in his dungeon is safer."

CHAPTER IV.

WITH the earliest gleam of light, the farmer's family were all astir. Indeed, none of them had slept well during the night. Mrs. Nichols had tossed to and fro upon her pillow, vainly trying to imagine the agony that must wring a mother's heart, when she finds her babe missing, and week after week passes, and still her lost one is not restored to her. Oh! is the human heart susceptible of a keener pang than must then rend a mother's bosom! Surely not. Death would be preferable to such a living death—to the knowledge that her child—perhaps her first-born, lives, but where, how, and with whom.

Several times the good farmer's wife strained her ear to catch a sound from the apartment of the vagrant. In vain; everything was as hushed as death. Does guilt know such a thing as still, dreamless and sweet repose? Did the vile vagrant sleep that night as sweetly as the stolen babe upon her bosom?

The farmer's wife at least heard no sound, and her conclusion was, that both were resting silently and well.

After breakfast had been prepared, and while it was smoking upon the table, Mrs. Nichols turned the key, and tapped gently at the door of her mendicant guest. No answer was returned—no sound was elicited. Again she knocked—again the same result. She softly turned the knob, and entered. Could she believe her eyes? *Mendicant and babe had both fled.*

Mrs. Nichols raised both hands in astonishment, and summoned her husband to the vacant room. There was the couch with its bed-clothes disturbed, showing that it had at some time during the night had an occupant—even the print of the baby's tiny form was there, pressed deeply down among the feathers. When and how could the beggar have fled with the child? This was an enigma. Wallace had left the farmer's house at an early hour in pursuit of the information that he sought, and was not expected back until nine o'clock or thereabout. All the worthy couple could now do, was to await his arrival. It was quite certain that the mendicant had escaped before Mrs. Nichols had locked the door. One supposition assumed the color of certainty. She must have overheard the conversation carried on by the schoolmaster the night before, and fearful of immediate apprehension, have fled. Both the farmer and his wife remembered now to have heard the creaking of the gate while the schoolmaster stood with his cap in his hand in the open door, discussing the necessity of immediate action. It was quite clear that at that moment, the woman with the babe, closely clasped to her bosom, was creeping under shadow of the fence, to

gain the road, and the creaking of the gate was caused by
her passing through it with her burden. Had the schoolmaster gone forth, as he at first thought of doing, he might
have encountered her at that very spot. But she had now
fled, no one could tell where. She had doubtless hidden
herself in some obscure corner, or perhaps travelled all
through that bitter night with the helpless infant in her
arms.

When the schoolmaster returned, and heard the recital, his face expressed the keenest disappointment. He
felt quite sure that the stolen child spoken of in the newspaper was the one the mendicant had in possession. The
dress and age of the child corresponded, and he yearned
to be the one who should restore to the arms of Mrs.
Bryant—for such it appears was the lady's name—her
beautiful, but half-famished babe. Animated by such
hopes, he proposed that the worthy farmer and himself
should take horses and institute an immediate and thorough
search for the woman. This they did, but returned at
night, wearied and disappointed. They had neither heard
or seen anything of the beggar. The next step to be
taken, was to send to the bereaved lady the medal, and to
ascertain from her whether it was the one worn by her
babe at the time it was taken from its crib.

This mission Wallace determined to execute in person.
Accordingly he took the medal, and journeyed to the city.
He sought the house of the bereaved family, and was admitted by a servant. As he passed through the hall into
the parlor, he saw around him all the insignia of wealth.
The floors were covered with the richest carpeting—heavy
chandeliers of cut-glass hung pendant from the ceiling—
tall massive mirrors threw back his figure from every side,
as he moved forward—heavy damask and lace curtains
shaded the windows.

"Poor, poor babe!" he muttered to himself, as he sat
down upon a sofa—"to be taken from such a home as this,
into the filthy, disgusting bosom of a foreign beggar!"

Mrs. Bryant, who had been summoned by the servant,
soon made her appearance. She was a lady in feeble

health, and now looked care-worn and very haggard. She was richly dressed, but seemed entirely unmindful of her person. She evidently was engrossed by one thought, and that a most wretched one. Her face looked like one in which wrinkles had been cut during a single night—her lips did not appear to have ever worn a smile—her complexion was sallow, and her form bowed. So powerful is grief, in the destruction of youth, health, and beauty.

She started when she saw a stranger in the room awaiting her, and a doubt whether he was the messenger of good or evil tidings seemed to pass in a moment over her face. She simply curtesied to him, and then sat down.

The teacher sat silent for a moment. He did not know how to introduce a topic painful to both, and he feared that, by showing her the medal, he should raise hopes in her bosom, only to have them rudely extinguished again. At length he said:

"I believe that I have the honor of addressing Mrs. Bryant, the lady of the house, have I not?"

The lady bowed. "Have you any intelligence to communicate to me in regard to my lost child?" she asked. "If so, your visit is not inopportune. Otherwise I cannot, converse with you, for in my great distress, no other theme ever comes into my thoughts. Tell me quickly, do you know aught of my child?"

The schoolmaster was moved almost to tears by the wretchedness of the woman before him—by her eager questioning in regard to her lost darling.

"My dear madam," he said, "compose yourself. I think that I have obtained a trace of your infant, but I cannot tell you at this moment where it is. I have in my possession, however, a medal, such as I find described in the public prints as worn by your child. Whether it is the same, I cannot tell. It fell from the package of a foreign beggar, who had in her care a beautiful infant, richly dressed. I have sought you this morning, for the purpose of showing you this trinket. If you are satisfied in regard to its identity, I pledge myself to search long and faithfully for your child." So saying, he drew from his vest pocket the golden medal.

Mrs. Bryant received it with trembling hands, and as she perused its characters, uttered a faint shriek.

"It is the same one worn by my lost, my dear, my darling Madge," she said. "I know it by these two initials of my name, traced upon the rim. O my child! O my child! where is she? restore her to me instantly, or my heart will burst."

"Be calm! be calm! my dear madam," the teacher exclaimed. "I will, as I before said, do my best, but you must wait patiently, and, perhaps, long. The woman fled with her charge before we could apprehend her. But should I meet with her, as I hope to do soon, I shall surely recognize her, even though I stumble upon her in the heart of China. I shall know that deep-cut, piercing eye, with its diabolical expression—I shall know the low, cunning forehead, and the shrill voice."

"O tell me no more about her," shrieked the lady wildly; "tell me not that my darling Madge—my first-born and only child—is in the possession of a wretch like that. Oh Heaven! how dark and inscrutable are thy ways!"— and the wretched mother covered her dry burning eyes with her thin pale hands, and groaned in the bitterest agony of soul.

Wallace saw that he had raised a storm which it was useless to try to calm. There could exist no balm for that wretched woman, save in the possession of her child. He therefore arose, and took her hand in the act of parting.

"Madam," he said, "I am a stranger to you, but I am a man with a heart in my bosom—a heart not yet grown callous, by rough contact with the world, to misery like yours. I pledge myself—I pledge *the honor of a Mason*— to aid you to the best of my ability in the recovery of your treasure. You shall hear from me often. Meanwhile, keep up good courage. The woman will not suffer your child to die."

CHAPTER V.

GENTLE reader, we must, from chapter fourth to chapter fifth, skip over a period of seven years—seven years of fruitless search on the part of Wallace and others for Madge Bryant

From the dark stormy night in which a vagrant had asked alms in the sitting room of farmer Nichols and his wife, nothing had been seen or heard of her. In vain, Wallace and others had instituted enquiries everywhere; in vain, cities all over the Union had been visited, in the vague hope of meeting the mendicant with her stolen child.

Poor Mrs. Bryant's head had, in the lapse of those years, grown white as snow. She had, however, entirely relinquished all hope in regard to her babe—she was a widow, and was childless.

John Nichols and his wife both slept beneath the green mounds of the neighboring churchyard. Strange, that people should ever forget death, when the grim tyrant so often sweeps from a house all of its occupants. Their son Isaac had, true to the old man's predictions, become a lawyer of some note, and was now practising his profession in a neighboring city. It was at the dwelling of the latter that James Wallace chanced to stop, when business called him to the city, seven years after his first visit to Mrs. Bryant.

He was sitting in his room one day during his sojourn there, when he heard the shrill tone of a female voice in the street beneath the window. There was something in the tone that arrested his attention. He had somewhere heard it before. It spoke now as if in great anger.

"I'll break every bone in your body, you wretch of a chile," it cried, "if you don't do as I bid you. You are gitting above your business I see clearly. Why didn't you follow the man, and beg as I bid you?" And the question was followed by a succession of quick heavy blows upon the person of some one.

Wallace became instantly on the alert. He stepped to the window, and threw up the sash. Below him was a beggar, beating most unmercifully her child. He knew that face at a glance. He knew the low forehead, and the dark angry eye. He thought that he saw, in the counte-

22

nance of the weeping girl, a resemblance to the beautiful babe. He took his hat and rushed out, and before the vagrant had finished chastising her child, she found herself in the strong grip of a police officer.

Little Madge Bryant then was at last found, but in what a wretched condition. Her beautiful curls were matted together with filth; rags hung loosely around her delicate form; and she bore heavy bruises all over her person. Her little blue eyes had wept until tears could no longer be wrung from their fountain, and she looked into every face, even into the most kindly, with a wild, scared expression.

Poor little Madge! like the blue hyacinth in the garden, she grew up amid wintry blasts, and was frozen by them to the inner core of her heart. She had tried to look bravely up at the wintry sky, but the blasts had been too bitter. She lived to be transplanted to her native *parterre*, to be clasped to her mother's bosom, to be clad in beautiful garments, and to be watched over with loving eyes for six brief months—but no longer. They then scooped out a narrow grave for her among the April flowers, and laid her in its bosom. Is not that wintry hyacinth a beautiful type of her? Like her, it will strive to face the cloud for a season, but when the genial influence of Spring revisits it, it will be found frozen I wot, at the root.

EFFECTS OF INDUSTRY.—All the performances of human art, at which we look with praise or wonder, are instances of the resistless force of perseverance. It is by this that the quarry becomes a pyramid, and that distant countries are united with canals. If a man were to compare the single stroke of a pickaxe, or of one impression with the spade, with the general design and last result, he would overwhelmed by the sense of their disproportion these petty operations incessantly continued, in mount the greatest difficulties, and mour and oceans bounded by the slender fo

CLAUDE FISHER;

OR,

THE SECRET MARRIAGE.

CHAPTER I.

"Doubt that the stars are fire,
  Doubt that the sun doth move,
Doubt truth to be a liar,
  But never doubt I love."

"I AM for a walk to the lake," said a fair-browed girl of sixteen, jumping up from a low stool on which she had been sitting for the last three hours, busily constructing a moss-basket. "I want some more moss, and there is plenty growing on the rocks there. I shall be back in a trice, mamma," she continued, as she glanced towards a pale, nervous-looking lady, who sat by a window, knitting a bead-bag; and reached up her hand and took a gingham sun-bonnet from the nail on which it was hanging, while she spoke.

"Claude, my love, you ought not to go alone," said the lady, with a good deal of anxiety in her tone. "Wait till Frank comes from school; he shall go with you."

"It will be too late to finish my basket then," replied the girl carelessly, "and I have set my heart upon getting it done to-night. There is no danger of anything happening to me, mamma—no danger in the world. I've often been to the lake alone, when you never knew a breath about it;" and laughing a merry laugh, she bounded down the steps, and was soon out of sight.

"If anything should happen to her," said her mother, as she laid down her work, and looked intently out of the window at the little bridle-path which the girl had taken; "if anything *should* happen to her, I should never forgive myself for permitting her to go alone. Claude is so venturesome—so daring and fearless. Poor child! she does not know that this world is full of

"Evil things that hate to look on happiness,"

and that her pathway is unusually beset. But she is happy in her ignorance, and

" If ignorance is bliss, 'tis folly to be wise."

Having finished her musings, the lady resumed her work, and wrought on in deep thought.

Greenwood Lake, to which the girl was bound, was a little silvery sheet of water, shut in by high hills, and skirted by tall grey rocks which drooped down in many places to the water's edge, and were covered, in Spring especially, with here and there beautiful little patches of emerald-green moss, spangled with star-like yellow blossoms and tiny white flowers. It was a beautiful place, for the water reflected in Summer the sapphire tints of the sky, and caught on their dawning wavelets the golden gleams of the sun. The king-fisher, too, haunted all day long the drooping bows of the trees which grew around, and every now and then dipped into the water after the speckled little finny tribes which sported through the liquid tide. But beautiful as this spot was, it was left alone in its loveliness. It was seldom visited by the inhabitants about Marsden. It lay out of the common track of travel, and somehow there were few who knew or cared anything about its beauties. Claude Fisher had, however, as she laughingly told her mamma, often stolen out, unobserved, to visit it, for she loved the quiet seclusion as well as the wild beauty of the scene ; and, moreover, it lay scarcely half a mile back of her father's residence.

On the afternoon on which we have introduced her to our readers, she trod lightly over the soft green turf, and along the well-beaten bridle-path, winding through a glen in the direction of the lake, carrying her sun-bonnet dangling by its strings in her hand, and humming to herself snatches of a song which she often sang :

" They told me not to love him,
  They said he was not true ;
  They bade me have a mind. lest I
  Should do what I might rue."

A breeze swept from the west, sweet with the scent of
brake and fern, and wild forest flower ; and the fair cheek
of the girl borrowed a blush from its cool, invigorating influences.   Her dark-blue speaking eye seemed, moreover,
to gain brightness, and her richly-colored auburn hair was
disordered by the wind.   But she was evidently entirely
regardless of personal appearance.   Her thoughts were
not upon what was passing—upon the moss she was soon
to gather—upon the breeze, the sky, or the sunshine.
They had wandered away—away—away ; and as she
sang, sometimes a pensive shade stole over her face, and
sometimes a pleasurable excitement illumined her eyes.

She reached at length the lake, and clambering up the
rocks, she soon filled a small basket, which she had
brought with her for the purpose, with moss.   This accomplished, she descended, and stood for a few moments
at the base of the rocks, on the white sand close to the
water's edge, contemplating the still and impressive beauty
of the scene.   The golden face of the sun was dropping
slowly down behind the trees which grew on the bank
opposite to her, and the shadows of the rocks stretched in
some places half across the water's dark yet shining surface.

While she thus stood, she was startled by a dog which
sprang through a thicket not far from her, and bounded
and capered around her, striving at the same time to lick
her hand.

"Down, Rouser ! down, I say !" she repeated in a startled, imperative tone ; and while she was vainly trying to
free herself from the officious and affectionate salutations
of what seemed to be a canine friend, she looked down the
lakelet's side, and saw a young man, clad in a green hunting suit, with a gun upon his shoulder, slowly coming up
a path which lay not far from the water's margin.   Claude
turned hastily when she made this discovery, and would

have retreated unperceived by the sportsman, if she could have done so, but it was already too late. He had raised his eyes when he first heard her voice, as she spoke to the dog, and was now attentively regarding her. As he came up within speaking distance, he touched his cap respectfully, and said in a low but manly voice:

"Good evening, Claude!"

"Good evening, Mr. Washburn!" she replied, while confusion deepened the blush which already burned upon her cheeks.

"*Mr. Washburn!*" repeated the youth half-reproachfully, "why don't you call me 'Allen,' as you used to do? Why have you gone to Mistering me of late, and treating me as though I were a thousand miles away from you. We went to school together, and you called me 'Allen' then—after school we often met, and you called me 'Allen' always. I liked the sound when pronounced by your lips; but now you pass me when you chance to meet, with as little token of recognition as possible, and call me '*Mr. Washburn*,' in a voice whose tones sound like the knell of Hope. Claude, what possesses you to treat me so coldly and distantly? Have I done anything to merit your displeasure? I am only conscious of having loved you too well for my own happiness. I am going to sit down here, and await an explanation from your lips, for I have bothered my brains over your enigmatical conduct long enough. If you don't love me, say so; make me this afternoon the happiest mortal in existence, by declaring it frankly and boldly." And the boy of eighteen threw himself down upon the turf, not far from where the girl was standing, and lifted his cap from the black, wavy hair which shadowed his fine open brow.

Claude did not reply at first, but reached out her hand, and strove to keep Rouser quiet, for the dog still frisked in joy and gladness about her.

"Come here, Rouser—come here, I say!—there, lay down, and be quiet. You see, Claude, that even my dog recognizes in you an old friend. He has not forgotten, I wot, how you used to go with me to feed him when he was a tiny thing. We were children then, but times have changed with us since, it seems, Claude. We have somehow got into estranged relative positions. How is it? Can you, will you, explain the matter? I used to fancy that you liked me—somehow I cannot relinquish the sweet hope, born of that idea, now."

"I did like you, Allen," said the maiden, "I like you still, but what is the use of fostering a passion—love—which must eventually be rooted out from the heart? It is suicidal to do so. I have tried to forget you, and in order to accomplish it, I have shunned you. I have treated you coldly, and distantly, because I wished to *feel* so towards you. It is not best, Spartan youth-like, to press the fox closely to our bosoms, when it is gnawing upon our vitals. Better cast it away and forget that it exists."

"And why is it a sin to love me, Claude? Why do you utter that ominous sentence, 'love must eventually be rooted out from the heart?' I am not altogether, I hope, unworthy of your regard. My family is, if anything, superior to yours in wealth and influence; but while they are, strange to say, willing, yea anxious for the match—since my happiness is involved in the issue—your family look coldly upon me and my suit, and have persuaded you to do the same. I cannot understand how it is."

"Neither can I," said the girl, "but my father's will has always been law to me. I have been accustomed, as you well know, from my earliest childhood to obey it unquestioningly. He has intimated to me that your suit is not to be encouraged, and I bow to his behest."

"And that is the alpha and omega of the matter, is it?" replied the youth; "the beginning and the end of your reasons for treating me thus? Your father doesn't approve of me. We are to submit to his decisions, are we, as serfs would bow to the will of the autocrat of Russia? No murmuring word must be heard—no reasons asked for —no explanations desired. Cringingly we must bow down, though the veins run fire and the heart weeps blood—coldly and distantly we must go, you one way, and I another, in life, scarcely looking an adieu, though heart leaps to heart, and soul yearns to mingle with soul!"

" Hush, hush, Allen!—do not speak in such an earnest, passionate manner! My father is a wise, grave, reasonable man. He never does anything without having it in his power to assign the best of reasons for thus acting. If he does not smile approbation upon our union, rest assured that there exists some cause why it should not be consummated."

" And why doesn't he assign it then, pray? Why does he discard me, without once deigning to give a why or a wherefore for the deed?"

" Ask him for the reason, Allen; see if he will not give it."

"I am too proud for that. Much as I love you, my sensitiveness might be stung to anger; and angry, I might do things unbecoming in one so young. I am hot headed, Claude—too hot-headed, passionate, and proud, to venture into such an interview with Judge Fisher, your father. But there is one thing I do desire—one thing I ask, yea beg at your hands. Seek an interview for my sake, Claude —ask the old gentleman why he looks thus coldly on my suit, and if his reasons are such as satisfy both you and me, I will turn my face to the wall, and, figuratively, die to you. No murmur shall escape my lips—the boy of eighteen will show his manhood. But to be frowned upon without a cause—to be repelled without a good and sufficient reason, is more than I can brook. Were *you* to say, Claude, that you did not love me—that your heart was elsewhere—that it never could be mine—that would be a seal upon the matter. But it is not so—you love me —and now the query is, why parental authority must come, like some dark menacing shadow, between us. Will you find out the Judge's reasons, and to-morrow afternoon come and tell them to me?"

The girl hesitated.

" Will you make an effort to find them out, Claude? Make the effort for my sake, if not for your own."

" I will do my best, Allen."

" And you will come and tell me the result of the trial, will you?"

" Yes, I think that I will meet you here, if it is best. If

I can and may tell you my father's reasons, I will reveal them to you. I cannot make a certain promise to you on that head."

"The cautious daughter of a cautious sire," said the youth in a voice half-impatient and half-ironical, at the same time rising from the bed of turf where he had thrown himself.

"The sun is almost down," he continued, coming towards her. "Suffer me on this night, at least, to be your guide and protector. It is too late for you to be out all alone. Shall I see you safe home?"

"I am much obliged to you for your kindness, Allen," said the girl, with a blush; "but it will be wisest for me to return as I came. I am not at all afraid. So good night," she continued, extending her hand, and looking up into his face with a frank expression in her eyes. "Good night, Allen. I believe you are half angry with me, as well as with my father and all the world."

"Am I, Claude?" said he, taking the extended hand in both of his, and looking down into her upturned face with inexpressible tenderness; "am I angry? Were I as jealous as a Spaniard, savage as a Turk, and revengeful as an Indian, one look from eyes as innocent and beautiful as these would entirely subdue me. One kiss—one kiss of reconciliation, if we must part here."

"Not one," said the girl, hastily withdrawing her hand, and lightly tripping up the bank; but at the top she paused, and looked back.

"Good night, *Mister* Washburn," she said, in a merry, mocking kind of voice; "I wish you good night!" and her laugh rang as silvery as the tones of a bell.

"Good night," *Miss* Fisher," replied the youth, in a mimicking tone; "good night, Claude, dearest," he continued, though in a changed voice; "remember your promise, and meet me here to-morrow afternoon."

"Shall I come or send?" said she, mischievously.

"Send at your peril," he replied. "I'll shoot your messenger," he continued, laughingly; "so you had better show your own pretty face, as you are in duty bound to."

23

"Well, I'll see about it, Lord Dictator," she said ; "but mercy on me! the sun is down, and mamma will be so much alarmed over my stay. I must hasten home."

"You had best let me go with you, Claude," said the youth, springing up the bank, and striding towards her; "it will be almost dark before you get home. The dew is beginning to fall now."

"I am not at all afraid," she said, motioning him back. "Don't come, Allen—good bye;" and she tripped away as lightly as though she trod on air.

The breeze which swept her face was indeed fast filling with the vapors of night, and the first pale star of evening was tremblingly lighting its lamp on high. Claude quickened her pace, first to a brisk walk, and afterwards to a run. She regretted having tarried so long—she scarcely knew what excuse she should render to her parents for her protracted stay.

"I will tell them the truth," she said at last, mentally; "deceit and subterfuge shall form no part of my character. I will do nothing—be beguiled into nothing, which I shall feel ashamed to have all the world know, that is, if it in the least concerned them, and is proper for them to know it—at any rate, nothing which I shall blush to have looked into by my good and reasonable parents."

Having formed this wise and noble resolution, she pressed forward, and was already in sight of her father's house, when she espied a dark object sitting beside the path, ahead of her.

She slackened her pace, and her heart beat violently.

"Who is that?" she queried mentally ; "nobody ever travels this by-path. Is it a man, or a woman, or a dog ? It is something alive, I know, for I saw it stir. I wish I had let Allen come with me. Why did I stay out so late?" But these reflections did not lessen her fears ; neither were they entirely allayed, when she perceived that the object before her was a woman, masculine in her proportions, rough, and dressed like a wandering vagrant.

"She will not hurt me, I reckon," she said mentally, drawing a longer breath, as she made the discovery. "I must, at any rate, pass her, and I will be very civil if she speaks to me."

The woman sat near the path, with a pack resting on the grass beside her. As Claude drew nigh, she lifted her heavy eyebrows, and scanned her person narrowly.

"You stay out late, my pretty miss," she said, in a voice as rough and masculine as her exterior, when Claude had reached the part of the walk opposite to her; "but I expect, like other night birds, you have a nest to fly to in an hour of danger!"

"Yes, I live in the house below here," said the girl, in a voice which she tried to render firm and steady, but which trembled in spite of her efforts as she hurried forward.

"And you come from the glen above?" continued the old woman.

"Yes."

"Well, stop a minute; is thar a 'ouse up yonder whar a poor old cretur like me could stay all night?"

"No house up that way, mother—this is the last one on the road."

"Would they let one stay at your 'ouse below here, think you?"

"I can't say how it would be," said Claude, starting on a run, and never once looking behind her, until she paused breathless upon the threshold of her mother's door.

"Where have you been, child? why have you stayed out so late?" said Mrs. Fisher, coming forward with a countenance full of anxiety. "I have been so wretchedly miserable about you."

"I stayed at the lake longer than I meant to, mamma; and there is an old woman back of the house, who came near frightening me out of my wits. She wants to know if she can stay here all night."

"An old woman, Claude? How does she look?"

"It was so dark that I could scarcely tell. She is a rough old creature, however—one whom you would not feel much like harboring. She has heavy eyebrows, brawny arms and hands, and a voice like a man's."

Mrs. Fisher trembled violently, and seemed very much agitated.

"Why, mamma," continued Claude, "you are really more afraid of her, here in the house, with papa for a protector, than I was when I met her alone in the dusk and darkness of twilight. Are you very much afraid of her, mamma? Will you allow her to stay all night if she comes here?"

"I am not at all afraid *now*, Claude—the danger is over for the present. She will not come here—she will not solicit food and shelter at our house. She has been with us too often for that. She begins to mistrust that her disguises are seen through."

Claude looked up in unfeigned astonishment.

"Pray, mamma," she said, "do you know her? Who is she, and where did she come from?"

"*I know her.* Fifteen years of close and constant contact, I think, will warrant me in making that assertion; but who she is, or where she comes from, I cannot so well answer."

"My curiosity is greatly excited, mamma. Why have I never seen her before? I do not know her from the man in the moon."

"Never mind, Claude—never mind. Curiosity is said to be the besetting sin of our sex. Put up your bonnet. Do not turn into a second Eve. On some future day the mystery may be explained to us all; at present, I am almost as much in the dark as you are. But shun this old woman—this *shape* that annually crosses, in some guise or other, our paths. I fear her presence bodes no good to any of us. Your father is in the library. He has been very anxious about you. You had best go in and let him know that you have returned."

Claude hung her bonnet upon the nail—set her basket of mosses upon the table, and smoothed her disordered locks with one hand, while with the other she turned the knob of the library door.

CHAPTER II.

Alas! I fear to love thee as I ought—
  I fear to strengthen ties already strong,
Since greater love with greater grief is fraught,
  And strongest ties their strength can not prolong ;
Oh, Life! oh, Love! oh, Friendship! ye are sought
  As blessings, and as blessings ye belong
Unto the blest—but there be hearts which feel
A growing wound that earth can never heal.—*Kaleidoscope.*

CLAUDE'S interview with her father was a protracted one. Thrice Mrs. Fisher went to the library door with the intention of opening it and entering, but the low, earnest tone of her husband deterred her from carrying her purpose into execution.

"Can it be," she said to herself, "that he is telling Claude *all!*" and the thought arrested her hand, and drove her back to her seat beside the fire.

A servant entered, announcing supper.

"Open the door and tell your master that supper is on the table," said Mrs. Fisher. The girl did so.

An hour passed away. The Judge did not heed the summoms—he had not even heard it. At length the door opened, and Claude re-appeared. But a change, a marvellous change had passed over the fair, hopeful face of the girl. The cheek which had three hours before glowed like a peach-blossom in early spring, was now as colorless as Parian marble—the open brow was collapsed with internal agony—the deep eyes had a faded look, and yet they had not been weeping—some painful, burning truth, had probably fallen upon the brain, and dried up the fountain of tears. Her lips, even, were blanched—they looked as if they never more could utter sound—glad, gushing heart-laughter would never more sing through them. Her hair, disordered by the evening wind at first, had now fallen loose, and shreds of it fell over her shoulders unheeded ; and yet her step was firm as she crossed the floor, and she mechanically took a candle from the table, and proceeded to light it.

"Claude, my love, you are not going to your room, are you? Supper has been waiting for you and your father for more than an hour," said Mrs. Fisher, in a troubled tone, and with an anxious glance into the fallen face of her child.

The white lips parted; the voice which came through them was steady and calm.

"I do not want any supper, mamma. I am going to my room."

"You are very pale, Claude. Are you sick? Was your walk too much for you? Let me send Betty up to help you undress and see you safe in bed. Shall I ring for her?"

"Not by any means, mamma. I do not want Betty; I only want to be alone in my chamber. I am perfectly well."

"If you are sick, and want anything in the night, you will be sure and let me know it, I hope. You are very pale; you cannot be quite well."

"Yes, I will let you know," said the girl, in a voice which she tried to render unfaltering to the end; but she hastened out of the room, as if conversation were a burden to her, and as if anxious also to escape the observation of every eye, even that of her gentle mother.

"I knew that this hour must come sometime," said Mrs. Fisher to herself, as she sank back into her chair, and shaded her pale face with her hands; "and I knew, too, how its revelations would wring the heart of one, sensitive and proud-spirited as Claude has always shown herself to be, and therefore I dreaded it, but it is wisest, best, that she should now know it. 'An ounce of prevention is said to be worth a pound of cure.' It is a homely adage, but I believe it to be a true one."

Claude's hand was so weak, when she reached the door of her apartment, that it was with difficulty she turned the well-polished brazen knob. Her trembling limbs could scarcely support her frame; the light wavered in her hand, and once came near falling to the floor. She, however, succeeded in getting in—closed the door, and mechanically locked it. She set the light upon the table, and sank down on a low chair not far from the side of her little white bed, completely exhausted. The moonlight stole in, and lay upon the floor, like flagging of silver, and the vine leaves at the window sent their shadows to speckle and dance, as they were stirred by the evening breeze in its soft lightness. The white muslin curtain, which was looped up on one side of the casement, hung with its pretty fringe to the floor.

The girl covered up her face with her hands. The starlight in the blue concave above—the mild face of the moon—the silvery mist stealing like some spiritual thing, born of the night, up the sides of the mountains, and the fragrant jessamine vine, starred with white dewy blossoms, all seemed to mock her with their peaceful, quiet beauty. She could not bear the sight; so she arose and went hastily towards the window for the purpose of closing it. As she was closing the apartment, however, she caught a glimpse of herself in a large mirror which hung against the wall. She was startled at the death-like paleness of the image reflected from its depths. She could hardly believe that it was her own face. The eye, generally so clear and happy in expression, seemed now to glitter with a strange brightness—the dishevelled locks and the white lips belonged to another, she thought. She stopped, and leisurely surveyed herself, lifting the candle from the table, as she did so.

"I am as white as death," she murmured half-aloud. "I do not look like myself. No wonder mamma—yes, mamma—I will still call her by that sweetest and dearest of names—no wonder that she declared I must be sick. I *am* sick. Oh heavens! how sick I am! Sick—dead— yes, *dead!* literally and figuratively *dead!* Claude Fisher of yesterday, the glad expectant girl, has ceased to exist. Into her place has come—what? The ghastly thing, with glittering eyes and white lips, which stares at me from the shining concave yonder. What a miserable-looking object it is! We call people dead, when the heart ceases to flutter—when the crimson current coagulates in the veins—when the breath freezes from the lips, and the spirit takes flight from its clay tenement—but people sometimes die, and still live, paradoxical as it sounds. They are dead; though the breath comes warmly through the lips—though the blood courses in crimson tides vigorously through the heart, stirring all the machinery of physical existence—though the pulsations of our being go calmly on, and will not stop in their measured beatings. They are dead to joy and happiness!"

She replaced the light, and essayed to close the window. As she did so, a shadow moving over the moonlit grass below arrested her attention. She put aside with her hand the rich emerald vine leaves, shaking a shower of snow blossoms all over her dress and the window-frame as she did so, and leaned her well-rounded but girlish form out of the casement, and gazed long and earnestly at what seemed to be a human form standing close in the shadow of the tall walls, the outlines of which stretched far out in the moonlight, surmounted with huge column-like chimneys, through which dense dark wreaths of smoke were curling up languidly into the star-lit heavens.

"It is that old woman," she said; and her heart instantly sprang through fear, into her mouth.

"What is she lingering about here for, at this time . o'night?" she mentally queried. "I will go below and tell papa. I am afraid of her." But a second thought reassured her.

"Why should *I* be afraid of *anything* now?" she continued mournfully. "Fear is for the young and happy—those who have characters which may be blasted—hopes that may be wrecked—treasures that may be stolen—valuable lives which may be lost. Claude Fisher of yesterday *might* harbor fear—timidity was becoming in her; but the creature who stands there"—she said, glancing into the glass—"the image confronting me with blanched lips, and disheveled hair—what has *she* to do with fear! she who has for ever shaken hands with happiness?"

Thus soliloquising, she deliberately put forth her hand;

drew the shutters together with a crash which must have startled the weird form beneath; let down the casement with a jar; dropped the soft muslin curtain over the shining panes; and felt that she had, for one night at least, shut out the world, with all of its glad natural beauties—its moonlight, its flowers, its mountain pass, and dewy glen. Would that she might as easily have shut out from memory and heart, all knowledge of those terrible moral sins, which make earth sometimes, even to the innocent and good—those whose only heritage, it would seem, should be gladness and joy—"a valley of tears," brooded over by the shadow of death!

"When people die," she continued, taking an elegant tortoise-shell casket from its place on the mantlepiece, and searching for a moment on a watch-guard, which was suspended around her neck, for a small golden key that could unlock it, "there is an executor appointed to administer upon the estate. Who better than I, can arrange Claude Fisher's affairs? I who have so long known her entire stock of hopes, fears, loves and sorrows! This little shrine contains something that must be looked into;" and with her trembling white hand, she gave the tiny golden key a twist, which caused the lid to fly open, and revealed the inside, lined with rose-colored pearl, that tinged with a pale-pink shade a package of letters lying on the bottom, tied together with a knot of white satin ribbon. She took them up, and looked upon the superscription. Her own name was written in clear, round, vigorous characters upon the face of each; the hand was decided and firm, like the purposes and virtues of the writer.

Claude took hold of one end of the ribbon, and untied the knot—the letters fell scatteringly over the surface of the table, and one or two dropped on the floor. These she picked up, and drawing the chair to the side of the table, she sat down, and unfolded them one after another, resting at the same time her pale forehead upon her hand, while she pored over their contents in silence.

"Beautiful dream!" she exclaimed at last, half-passion-

ately—" beautiful dream, born of Hope, and tinted with
the hues of Eden, why could ye not last! Fool that I
have been! I have whispered to my heart continually,
that ye *would* endure, and become a realization and a
blessing yet! I thought that my father's opposition had
its root in some foolish freak or whim, which might be
argued down and overcome. I avoided Allen, but at my
heart slept continually the sweet, sweet thought, that on
some future, nameless day, I should yet go to his side,
there to remain for ever in time. I did not know that
there was a gulf, deep as Hades and dark as Erebus,
yawning between us."

She got up, and paced the floor rapidly, but with a soft
and velvetty tread.

"Beautiful dream!" she murmured again, mournfully to
herself—" dream of youth who ever follows on willing
wing the soaring flight of Hope, must you now go out in
darkness, and dreariness, and death? What is life, after
thy departure, to me? Did I not say well, when I said
that I was dead? No—it is false. I am not dead. In
my bosom there is a living, quivering, agonizing *heart*, and
in that heart, deep enshrined in its innermost recesses,
there is a love, vital as vitality itself, ever asserting its
existence by convulsive throes—a thing which refuses to
be crushed, and if burned out, would, Phœnix-like, spring
to life again from its own smouldering ashes. But crushed
and burned out it must be."

She turned again to the table, and re-tying the satin
ribbon, she replaced the package of letters in the casket,
and sat down, with her hand upon her head. This position she maintained during the remainder of the night.
She never thought of seeking her couch for repose; but
the grey dawn of the morning found her with her pale
face upon her hand, looking more like some statue of
marble, than like a living, breathing soul.

But at length she aroused herself, and threw open the
casement. The cool fresh air of the morning came floating in, laden with the sweet scent of the jasmine blossoms,
at the windows; but there was no sign of the old woman

beneath. On the distant hills the cattle were rousing themselves from their smoking beds, where they had rested through the night, and were already beginning to crop the green and tender grass.

"Nature never sympathizes with human wo," she said, half-bitterly, as she turned away. "I love better the thick black darkness of night. I am sorry that it is morning, yet I believe I will go down."

She went to the door and unlocked it. For a moment she stood irresolutely upon the threshold.

"I cannot go," said she; and she turned and threw herself down upon the bed which stood near, with its white covering, as if inviting to repose. She buried up her face in the pillow, anxious to shut out from her aching eyes the beauty of the morning, and from her ears the voices of the singing birds.

Here her mother found her.

"Why, Claude," she began, "what does this mean? Surely you have not laid in this position all night—and the candle there is quite burned down into the socket. Breakfast is ready. I could not hear you stirring, and I came up to see if you were dressed. But from the appearance of things, you have not been otherwise during the night. Are you sick, child?"

Claude answered with a feeble groan.

"What ails you, Claude? Rouse yourself. Are you sick? I want to know that?"

"No, no, dearest, best of—of—mothers—not sick—so leave me alone. Do not distress yourself about me."

"But I am distressed about you. Your father, too, scarcely shut his eyes to sleep last night. *He* is distressed about you. He desired me to come up, as we could not hear you stirring. Will you come down to breakfast?"

"I do not want any. I have no appetite for eating."

"But you *must* eat, Claude. You did not swallow a mouthful of supper last night. You will starve to death if you go on in this way. Shall I send Betty up with a piece of toast and a cup of coffee for you?"

"I do not want it, mother."

"But you must try to eat, Claude. Will you try, if I send it up ?"

"Yes, I will try."

"And you must fix yourself more comfortable in bed. I believe you have a fever. No, your face is as cold as marble. Claude, do not, for Heaven's sake, let any trouble, be it what it may, so overpower you. On the contrary, be strong. We were made to strive and to endure."

The girl did not answer. She lay as quiet as death. Mrs. Fisher cast a mournful glance at her prostrate form, and then hurried down to send Betty up with the toast and coffee. But she might as well have kept them below. In spite of all Betty's persuasions, who was indeed and in truth greatly distressed at her young mistress's appearance, both remained untasted.

"Set the tray down, Betty. I will eat when I feel like it," was the only reply the faithful old domestic got to all her importunities.

"What *has* come over Miss Claude ?" muttered the old woman, as she turned to go below. "She was always so brisk and lively—the joy and the delight of the whole house! But now she looks as if she were dead, and nobody can get a word out of her about what's the matter. If she's sick, why don't she say so, and let master send for Dr. Chamomile, who knows how to cure everything under the sun. She looked well enough when she started for the lake last night, and now I think of it, she must have met Master Allen somewhere in the glen, for I seed him going that way, with his dog and gun, yesterday afternoon. Well! young folks is curious, and old folks too. Why don't master let Miss Claude marry Master Allen, if she wants to ? I'm sure they'd be the handsomest couple ever married in these parts. And Master Allen is rich enough for Miss Claude—richer than master himself is, if anything. I declare it's a pity—it's a thousand pities, when young folks is headstrong, and old folks is obstinate !"

Thus sagely soliloquising, Betty descended to the dining-room. Several times that morning, Mrs. Fisher ascended the stairs to look in upon Claude, but the only answer she got to all of her inquiries was the entreaty to be left alone. And alone at last the solicitous mother concluded to leave her. She gently closed the door, and went below. She gathered up Claude's basket of moss, and tried to complete the work for her; but the task baffled her skill. So she replaced it upon the table, half-mournfully, wishing, in her inner heart, that no shadow had passed over the sunny life of her child—that no burning iron had been sent to probe her soul.

" But, after all," she said mentally, " afflictions are great teachers. We are never strong, until *they* have developed the latent powers of the soul. We call them evil messengers. In the golden courts of the New Jerusalem, we may recognize them as angels, sent earthward on embassies of love. Then we may see

> 'How sublime a thing it is,
> To suffer and be strong.'"

Sometime, late in the afternoon Claude raised her head, and saw the westerly rays of the sun gilding the white wall of her apartment.

" Is it so late ?" she murmured. " He is already waiting for me. I must see him again for the last time."

She hastily arose, and going to the wash-stand, she bathed her face and smoothed her hair.

She re-opened the casket, and placed the package of letters in her pocket. She then stole carefully down stairs, and finding that her mother and Betty were busy in the garden, over a vine which the wind had blown down, she secured her sun-bonnet, and took again the little path leading up the glen.

She walked forward with rapid steps, every now and then glancing behind her to see if she was observed, and she felt a sense of relief, when a winding in the path hid her father's residence from view.

" I wonder if that old woman is about to-night," she said, for the first time remembering her, and remembering also her mother's mysterious words in relation to her, and she looked hastily about, half-fearful, lest the old crone might, spectre-like, rise up in the path before her. But she was nowhere visible, and so she hurried on.

"Yesterday afternoon," she said musingly, "I told Allen that I loved him. How will he be astonished to learn, that now with my own hand I drive him from me. *Alas! I fear to love him;* but I cannot shut this passionate feeling from my heart—this feeling that draws me towards him, and asserts continually that his star is also the star of my destiny. But it must not—cannot be."

CHAPTER III

But you came on behind, John,
    And drew my arm in yours,
And said—" you must not go alone
    Across the barren moors."—*Mrs. Mayo.*

WHEN Claude arrived at the lake, she found Allen there awaiting her arrival. He stood, clad in the same green hunting suit which he had worn the day before, leaning his back against the rocks, while his chin rested upon the muzzle of his gun. He seemed to be attentively regarding his dog, for Rouser lay crouched at his feet. But the canine ear is sharp, and Rouser detected Claude's light footsteps tripping over the turf and moss, before Allen became aware of her presence. The dog uttered a short, joyous bark, and bounded forward to meet her.—The young man smiled, and stepped a pace or two in advance to welcome her also. But he paused, and the smile died upon his lips, while he marked the deathly paleness of her countenance, and the faded color of her eyes.

"Why Claude, is this you?" he said. "I am glad you have come, for I have been waiting for you this half hour. But what ails you? Are you sick? You are pale, and—good Heavens! what a change has passed over you every way! You don't look like the same person I bade adieu to here last evening."

"I am not the same person, Mr. Washburn," she replied in a faint, inarticulate voice. "There, take back your letters. Go, be wise, and forget that you ever wrote them."

" *Take back my letters*, Claude! Take back my letters, and forget that I ever wrote them! Wise advice, indeed! Can you give me back, too, *the heart* that went with them? What has happened to bring this about? You distress as well as puzzle me. Have you had an interview with your father, and has he insisted upon your taking this step. I do not, will not believe the act to be a voluntary one."

"It *is* voluntary, Allen. Judge Fisher never commanded it. He does not even know that I am here. I, individually—I myself, of my own free will, give you back the package, and bid you to forget me."

"Forget you!" exclaimed the youth bitterly. "Forget you! Yes, when I forget my own existence—when I forget the mother whose smile was the first lesson to my infant soul—when I forget all that I have valued and prized in life, then I *may* forget you. Ask me to forget that sunlight is sweet to my eyes—ask me to forget the vital air I breathe—ask me to forget God, the author of every good and perfect gift we enjoy on earth; and then, as a finis to the command, bid me to forget you. The injunction will be alike reasonable in all its parts."

"You talk wildly, Allen. You do not realize what you are saying. You *will* forget me, I dare say. I pray Heaven that you may. Take the letters. I came expressly to bring them. I wanted to see them safe in your own hands. Take them. I cannot tarry here a moment. I must go back immediately."

"You shall not go, Claude, until you tell me what has brought this about," he said, extending his hand for the letters, and grasping also the fingers which held them. "Tell me, Claude, do you indeed and in truth, of your own free will, pronounce to me that word—*depart?*"

"I do, Mr. Washburn," said Claude, tremblingly, yet resolutely. "I say it of my own accord."

"Say it, Claude—let me hear it from your tongue. It may lessen the pain of separation."

Claude strove to obey. Her lips moved as if trying to frame the word, but the sound died away in a murmur.

"I do not hear it, Claude. Your *heart* is not in that word, else it would gush more readily to your lips. Last night, I said that were *you* to say that you did not love me—that your heart was elsewhere—that you never could be mine, I would never urge my suit further. Can you—do you say it?"

"I can never be yours, Allen Washburn. That ought, and must satisfy you."

"It does not satisfy me, Claude Fisher; say in addition to it, 'I do not love you—I hate, I abhor you.'"

"I cannot say it—it would not be true. I do not hate, and I never can abhor you.'"

"You love me. Separation from me gives you pain. The thought of it has driven the life-bloom from your face—the brightness from your eyes. Say, is it not so, Claude?"

The girl was silent.

"You sought that interview with your father. The old Judge was inexorable. He bade you forget me. Is not that true also?"

"No! no!" said Claude, wringing with a sudden and powerful effort her fingers from his clasp. "Judge Fisher stands acquitted of all blame in this matter. He has, on the contrary, acted generously, nobly. He has sought, and will see, by every means in his power, to advance my happiness—he has the highest opinion of *your* merits—he does not object to your family—you are all that a father, jealous for his daughter's happiness, could desire, he said, in a suitor; and yet Mr. Washburn, we must part here, *for ever.*"

"You yourself utter the decree."

"I utter it."

"People sometimes demand reasons for certain courses of action in others. Am I denied that privilege now? Must I hear my doom pronounced without being permitted to hear a *why* or a wherefore? Criminals of the blackest dye are not so summarily condemned, even though their guilt is apparent at the first glance."

"I cannot explain reasons to you. Rest assured they

are such as—as—as your own judgment would approve, did you know them."

"How do you know that ?"

"I am sure of it."

"Am I never to know the reasons, Claude ?"

"God forbid !" exclaimed Claude, catching her breath as she spoke, and growing even paler than before. "Go," she added in a calmer voice—"go, Allen—do as I bid you—forget me, or if you ever think of me, remember that I did not part with you without a pang ; but Destiny is mighty. She takes us in her hand at our birth, and buffets us about as she wills. She tramples our air castles under her feet, and laughs mockingly and derisively at our plans and wishes."

"You bid me forget you—will you forget me, Claude ?"

"I shall struggle to do so, rest assured of that. I shall struggle earnestly, Allen. My own peace of mind—duty —filial affection, all demand the effort, and if you love me, pray that it may be a successful one."

"I would as soon pray for the execution of my father on the gallows—sooner by far for my own death. Indeed, I begin to think that death just now might prove a blessing instead of a curse."

"I must not stand here talking to you, Allen. Good night."

"Stop one moment, Claude—I cannot let you go yet," and as the young man spoke, he stepped slowly forward and took her hand.

"There exist reasons—such is my inference from your conversation—which render our union for the present expedient. Nothing more."

"Which render it impossible," faintly murmured Claude.

"Well, admit it—reasons exist which render our union *at present* impossible. Time is a great remover of obstacles sometimes. On some future day you may yet be mine."

Claude shook her head mournfully.

"I do not question the wisdom of your present decision.

24

I was hot-headed here last night, and said things about
your father, the Judge, which perhaps I ought not to
have said. I fear that in my disappointment and vexation
this evening, I have urged you too much—spoken too
hastily to you, perhaps. But forgive me, Claude. I have
been urged on by a pure, undying affection for you. I
shall never love another, and if I do not marry you, I shall
never wed. I had hoped that your confidence in me was
as great as that which I repose in you—that you would
reveal to me whatever objections your father might entertain, and that those objections would be overruled or
removed. I find that I was mistaken. I believe that you
love, but you will not trust me. Be it so. I am not angry
at your obstinacy and distrust in me. I love you too much
to be lightly moved to anger. But one promise, Claude,
before we part. Should the time ever arrive when you
can be mine—when the obstacles, real or imaginary, which
now exist shall be removed, will you write and tell me so?
—will you take back the terrible words which you have
spoken to-night?"

"There is little or no prospect of such a period ever ar-
riving," said Claude. "Do not delude yourself with false
hopes, Allen; it is wisest, best, to know the truth, and to
lay no flattering unction to the soul."

"You would then quench all hope—not a spark of it
may exist?"

Claude bowed.

"But hope will not be quenched. Phœnix-like, it will
rise even from its own smouldering embers. Claude, *I
will not be discarded.* Never lover was so obstinate in
persisting against accepting the refusal of a lady's hand
as I am. No reasons exist, I *know*, of sufficient magnitude
to separate us always. I part with you to-night, with the
confident expectation of claiming, some future day, this
little hand now clasped in mine. I believe this hand, so
soft, and white, and delicate, will trace the letter which
shall recall me from this cruel, cruel banishment, again to
your side, and make me once more and for ever the happiest of men."

Claude did not reply. Her eyes had fallen beneath his gaze. She stood still, grave, and speechless.

"Yes, Claude," said he, "I shall be your husband yet. Destiny has so written it. What did I say? We rave about Destiny, but I mean by that word, God—a kind, good and merciful Providence—has, in other words, so arranged it. Thus believing, I claim to-night what you refused me last night, viz: the office of protector. I shall see you safely to your father's door." So saying, he gently drew her arm through his, and walked with a slow but firm step by her side.

"*You are weeping,*" he said at length, as Claude hung down her head, and pulled her bonnet further over her face, to conceal the tears which were beginning to gush down her cheeks. "Are you thinking that we may not soon again tread this path together. Cheer up. We *shall* tread it again together. I am sanguine in that belief. Claude, I press you again to tell me what *bug-bear* your folks managed last night to conjure up and place between us. If it would take a tangible shape, hue, garb and complexion here in the path before me, I would pledge myself to leap over it at a bound, or to shoot it down with the rifle which I left Rouser guarding by the rock. I would shoot it, though it proved to be as great in magnitude as an old woman whom I espied loitering here after you passed. By the way, did she frighten you? I heard her accosting you."

"You heard her! I left you at the lake. How did you hear her?"

"I followed on in your wake, as faithful guardian should. I did not like to trust my little one alone in the dark twilight, on such a dreary road as this. Had that old woman said two more words to you, I should have pounced on her like a hyena. As it was, I had a great mind to tumble her and her pack into the middle of next week. But you glided by her like a phantom, and were soon in your door. So I turned, and left the old lady to her meditations."

"What became of her?" asked Claude, with breathless interest. "Where did she spend the night?"

" With the crows and the rocks, I reckon. She seemed
in a fair way to do so when I left."

" Did you ever see her before ?" asked Claude.

" No, never. She is a fresh importation, I take it—fresh
from the Emerald Isle."

" She did not talk like an Irish woman," said Claude—
" at least I did not notice her brogue ; on the contrary, I
thought her remarkably clear-spoken. True, she said
'ouce for ' house,' and 'oman for ' woman,' but many of
our own country people do that."

" I suspect," said Allen, now for the first time laughing,
" that my little friend was too much agitated with fear to
hear distinctly in what dialect she was addressed. But
look ahead. There is something there now. This is
really turning into a public thoroughfare. What possesses travelers to leave the highway, and follow up this little
bridle-path, I wonder. It is lucky for you, Claude, that
you have such a persevering suitor—one who is a self-
constituted guide to a poor little lass on such a night as
this, else you stand in danger of a fresh colloquy with a
man to-night—yes—it is a man, I believe, with a pack on
his back. A pedlar, I take it. I wonder if the fellow sells
spectacles ?"

" Sells what ?"

" Sells spectacles. I want to buy a pair, Claude."

" Who for ?"

" For myself. I want a pair of magnifying concave lens
of immense power—glasses which will enable me to penetrate all mysteries, and to look ahead into futurity, clear to
my wedding day. If the fellow has a pair, look out for
secrets. I will don them immediately."

Claude did not laugh. On the contrary, she shuddered.

" Would you object to my putting them on, and reading
that which I so much wish to know ?" he continued.

" Rest assured, Mr. Washburn, you would not be made
happier by the knowledge gained, and I—I should be
made, if possible, more miserable."

" That could not be, dearest girl. I would stand between you and misery. Trust me for that. Oh that you

would trust me! Be a good girl, and say 'yes.' Then give me your confidence, nobly, generously."

The young man, in his earnestness, had now stopped, and was striving to gain a look into his companion's face, but her head still drooped, and her eyes were fixed upon the narrow and hard-beaten path which she was treading.

"Your requisitions are too hard," at length she said, looking up into his face. "If I *could* tell you, I would."

Just then the pedlar brushed by. He looked into Claude's face narrowly, almost impudently. Perhaps it was her eyes, red with weeping, and her pallid cheek, which attracted his attention. He was a low man, with a pack of Irish linens on his back. He touched his cap to Allen, and was hurrying forward, when the latter accosted him.

"You are out of your road, my friend," he said. "You will hardly sell any of your wares on this route. The path you are pursuing terminates at a little lake just above here. There is not a house for miles."

"Thank ye—thank ye, sir, for the information. I was jest a thinking that 'ouses were monstrous scarce up this way, and that I mought be wrong. Where do I get into the right road? Just below here, is it?"

"Just below," said Allen. "You had best turn and retrace your steps."

Again the man swept past. Again he eyed Claude narrowly.

"That is the same person I met here last night," said Claude.

"Impossible. That was a woman," replied her suitor.

"It is the same voice at any rate—the same face, too, although the garb is different. I should know those heavy eyebrows anywhere."

"I fear my little friend is so full of mysteries herself, to-night, that she conjures them up in every object she meets," said Allen, smilingly. "What object could any person have in dressing like a woman yesterday, and like a man to-day, and in hunting this unfrequented by-path?"

"I don't know, I'm sure," replied his companion.

"I can't imagine," continued Allen; "but it strikes me as being very singular that travelers should be met with here two nights in succession. But mystery is the order of the day, Claude. I want those spectacles worse than ever. But yonder are the lights at your house. How cheerfully they are beginning to stream through the window. The twilight is thickening fast. You ought not to be out here in the dew; but we shall soon be at the gate now. Once more, Claude, won't you tell me what menacing shadow stands between us?"

"I cannot, Mr. Washburn. Do not ask it."

"Well, remember, Claude," he said, pausing and resting his elbow upon the low gate, before opening it for her to pass through, and looking at the same time into her still downcast face; "remember that, although we part here in mystery and doubt, perchance in distrust, still—*you are mine.* You have discarded me, it is true. I will not stay discarded. When I give you up, I give up almost all I prize in life: I shall not relinquish hope—the sweetest and dearest boon given to man, because you say ' depart,' when the word only comes from the lip outward. It never yet rested a moment in your heart. We shall meet again under happier circumstances. Until then, adieu."

He bent his head, and kissed her forehead. She did not venture a reply, but glided through the little gate, which he held open, noiselessly.

She felt a sense of relief when she found the room, through which she had to pass, unoccupied. She went into her chamber, and sank down again upon her pillow, faint and exhausted.

CHAPTER IV.

"Happy the man that finds a bride,
Whose birth is to his own allied.
The sweetest joy of life!"—*Watts.*

WE must now beg our courteous reader to leave Claude to her sad reflections, while he accompanies us back to a period of time, sixteen years antecedent to the events related in the preceding chapters. The place to which we would conduct him is a cellar in New York—the personage to whom we would introduce him is a red-faced Irish woman, who, with sleeves rolled high above the elbows of her brawny arms, dashed the soap-suds about, until the snowy foam mounted high in the tub of soiled clothes which she was washing.

Biddy O'Artey's room did not at any time present a very inviting appearance. The dark cement floor was time-stained, and had scaled up in various places—the windows were narrow and dirty, and clouded with steam —tubs, barrels, wash-boards, boilers, soap, and buckets were all scattered about the floor, so as to render both egress and ingress a perilous adventure. But little did Biddy care for the disorder which she thus created around her. She sung at her work, or stood with her red arms akimbo, and watched the crowds of pedestrians who swept by the low door of her humble abode, and listened to the drays, omnibuses and cars, which at all hours were rattling through the stony streets. Biddy was, it must be confessed, somewhat of a gossip. She liked to hail every one whom she knew—sometimes she called out to those whom she did *not* know; she was not very particular about the matter of introduction, and she quite as often accosted strangers as friends, especially if they bore any tokens of being like herself, importations from the Emerald Isle.

"Och, and what may ye be afther wanting, my darlint?" she exclaimed one afternoon to a middle-aged woman, who stood with a bundle in her arms, not far from the entrance to her humble abode, and who was looking wistfully yet cautiously around her: "Is it anything that ye have lost, me honey?"

The woman thus accosted, drew nigh and peered with her keen black eyes into the washerwoman's establishment. She did not immeiately answer. Biddy felt constrained to follow up the conversation so abruptly began.

"And what may ye be looking up the strate and down the strate afther, me jewel, if one may make bold to en-

quire?" continued the garrulous old woman. "Is it any
of yer friends that ye are seeking, or are you a poor lone
'oman like myself, with not a chick nor child in the wide,
wide world to cling to, and nobody to say to ye, why do
ye so?"

"I was not looking for any one in particular," said the
woman, resting upon the step which descended into
Biddy's cellar; "and I am, as you say, a lone 'oman in the
world. I have just come into the city, and all this noise
and hubbub sort o' stuns me, you see; so its nat'ral that I
should look about me with a sharp eye. Indeed, a body's
obliged to do it, or else be run over by the drays."

"Och, and that is very true," said Biddy. "But come
down into the room and rest awhile. If ye're a stranger
in these parts, it's very likely you've walked far and long;
and it's after resting you would be glad to be. There—
turn that tub bottom upward and take a seat. My room
is never none of the cleanest, but such as it is, ye're welcome to a seat in it."

The keen-eyed woman hesitated.

"I'm a thousand times obliged to ye," she said, glancing
at the same time at her bundle; "but I promised to do a
little shopping for one of my neighbors while I was in the
city, and as the afternoon is wearing away, I can't stay to
rest. But with your leave, I'll lay my bundle upon your
table yonder, until I come this way again. I am only
going across the street. Would you be obliging enough
to take charge of it for me?"

"To be shure! to be shure!" exclaimed the gossip-loving, but truly accommodating Biddy—"I'll take it and lay
it there meself, and then I shall be shure that nobody has
been afther mislaying it;" and as she spoke, she reached
out her hand and would have taken it from its owner, but
the keen-eyed woman motioned her back, and said very
blandly:

"Nay, nay, it's not burdening you with it that I am
after. I can lay it yonder myself, and get it again on my
return; its only *room* on your table that I want. The
bundle won't need looking after at all, for nobody will be

meddling with it, I'm sure." So saying, the country-woman—for such it seemed she was—stepped forward and laid the light burden which she bore upon the table.

"I shall be back in half an hour at furthest," she added, as she stepped briskly to the door and remounted the granite step. "It's only across the street to where I am going;" and while she was speaking the last word, she plunged forward into the crowd which thronged the pavement, and was soon lost to sight.

"A very civil-spoken woman!" said Biddy to herself, musingly, as she turned back to her tub. "It's enough to do one's heart good to meet with the like o' her in a stranger land. I've been in Ameriky—let me see—it's going on seven year, and I don't remember ever having seen a cleaner-tongued, civiler 'oman than that. She's welcome to room on my table for her bundle. I hope it will be long before room can't be found there for the like o' her." So saying, Biddy plunged into the tub with both arms, and commenced spattering the suds about in a very praise-worthy manner. There was a little Dutch clock, which she had brought with her from Ireland, ticking above the mantlepiece opposite to her, but the noise of it was drowned in the confusion of sounds which floated in from the street without, and by the splashing operation of Biddy herself. So the hours stole away oftentimes unnoticed.

On this particular afternoon, the Irish woman washed and sung, unmindful alike of clock and bundle. She did not perceive that the hands of the former had traveled far beyond the half hour which the country-woman had spoken of as the utmost limit of her absence, neither did she observe—for her back was towards the table—that the loose-looking bundle which lay thereon was stirred now and then, as if it contained a living, but half strangled being. Once, Biddy's attention was arrested, however, by a short stifled wail, which seemed to come from or behind the table or some tub in that vicinity. She turned hastily around, and surveyed, for half a minute, the whole region. Nothing was observed to be amiss. The bundle could not

25

be very distinctly seen, for a high-backed chair intervened between her and the table, and partially screened it from view; but it was not supposable that the sound came from *that;* so Biddy did not trouble herself to go and examine it.

"Pshaw !" she exclaimed, half aloud. "It was afther being the wind, to be shure, which is always piping and shrieking about like a mad cr'atur of the air, as it is. It's very idle in me to be a minding it at all;" and turning her face again in the direction of her tub, she went on singing and washing as before.

The clock at length struck nine. Biddy never washed later in the day than this, so she commenced rolling her tubs into one corner, and "putting things to rights," as she termed it, throughout her domain. Just at this moment, her eye fell upon the country-woman's bundle. To her surprise, it had kicked itself—if we may be allowed the phrase—quite to the edge of the table, and was near falling on the floor. It evidently was inhabited by some animated existence.

What had the country-woman stowed away there in her bundle ? Why had she not returned for it according to promise ? Was it a cat, or a dog, or a monkey, which caused it to move thus upon the table's surface? The Irish woman's curiosity was excited. She remembered the strange sound which had arrested her attention. To step to the table and examine the bundle was the work of a minute. Biddy lifted both of her red hands in astonishment, for there, revealed to the gaze of her two wondering eyes, was a child—a *bonâ-fide* live, flesh and blood baby.

What a trick that keen-eyed country-woman had played upon honest, unsuspecting, simple, gossip-loving Biddy O'Artey ! It was entirely too bad to abuse hospitality thus. What a return had been made for an act of kindness !

Biddy ran to the door and gazed eagerly about in all directions. No country-woman, answering, in the least, in appearance to the one that had visited her on the afternoon, was anywhere to be seen. No country-woman of similar appearance was like to *ever* again darken Biddy's door. Our humble friend felt this truth in all of its astounding magnitude sinking in the depths of her heart. She shouted aloud in the first stages of her perplexity and chagrin. But no policeman happened to be near enough to hear her, and the crowd swept by with hurried tread, scarce casting an eye downward into her humble abode. Nothing remained for her to do, but to go back and take the new-born infant into her brawny arms, and hush, as best she could, its now bitter wailing.

Biddy was, as she oftentimes said, " a lone 'oman," but she did not fancy the kind of company she was now called upon to entertain. She wished, in her heart, that the poor little girl, thus thrust upon her care, was at Jericho—anywhere, in fact, rather than in her cellar on Fifth Row. What was she to do with it? Where was she to cradle it? In what was she to dress it? With what was she to feed it? How was she to hush its crying? These were serious questions. If she called in a public officer, how was she to prove that the babe had been left upon her hands in the manner above narrated? Nobody, save herself, had any cognition of her visitor—nobody had seen her deposite the bundle on the table—nobody could bear testimony in regard to her entrance or exit.

Biddy was in a quandary, but hosts of people have been in similar ones, and this reflection served to comfort her somewhat. She sweetened some milk which she had bought that morning from the milkman, and fed her charge. She wrapped it up as snugly as she could, in the shawl which had been left with it and had formed a part of the unsuspicious-looking bundle; and then she rocked it to sleep, and laid it upon her own pillow to rest.

Biddy had many friends. Her garrulous disposition, and her simple kind-heartedness, won upon almost all of her customers, sooner or later. With people, humble and hard-working as herself, she was, moreover, an especial favorite ; so she felt sure of sympathy and aid from many quarters, when her story should be known. But it was too late to go abroad that night; so Biddy cooked her supper, ate it, and prepared to look after her charge, as best she could, through the long and silent hours of the night. When the morning dawned, the Irish woman was astir. Indeed she had rested but indifferently, although she was generally a sonorous and beaver sleeper. She was afraid to turn over, for fear of inadvertently crushing the tiny thing beside her; she was afraid to go to sleep, for fear she might turn over in her dream—so she had a weary night of it.

The little Dutch clock ticked as it had never ticked before. Its striking was loud, and echoed through the cellar like the ringing of a bell. But, as we have before intimated, the last dusky hour wore away at last. Light came in through the little dirty window, as cheerly as light could struggle into so dismal a place. The clatter of horses' hoofs rang again over the pavement without. The milkman that morning was early upon his rounds; Biddy was early up; the watchman left their posts early ; and the lamps, one after another, flickered and went out, as if they were sentient beings, and were aware that the cold grey dawn of the morning had come, and their feeble light was no longer needed. But the *babe*— that unowned little voyager, whose tiny barque was just launched upon the tempestuous sea of human existence —slept sweetly on, and seemed to smile at times, as if its dreams had stolen a rose-tint hue from Eden. Poor little innocent ! the lamb led forth to slaughter could not have been more careless of the fate awaiting it at the shambles !

Biddy stopped twice, while she was in the act of dressing, to look at it. She wondered what it was thinking about, or, if a creature so young and with such short experiences in life, could think or reason at all. She surveyed its delicate little profile, as it lay upon her pillow, and wondered how any parent's heart could be strong enough to cast forth such a fragile, helpless, innocent little thing upon the wide, wide world. Its features were regular, and she mentally pronounced them to be—for so

young a child—beautiful. It's little dimpled hand was
closely clenched. Biddy gently took it into hers, and
straightened one after another the tiny taper fingers.
The poor and humble—those who carry on a warfare with
haggard want, day after day, and toil with strained nerve
and hardened sinew for the crust of daily bread, and the
drop of water which is to sustain fainting nature under
her burdens, have little time in which to be sentimental.
Biddy was not often in this mood, it must be acknowl-
eged, but she had a warm, simple, Irish heart—one which
was sometimes touched with the woes which humanity is
found so often heir to in the crowded, jostling thoroughfares of city existence.

But she did not stand long by the pillow of the sleeper.
She had a turn of clothes to take to the residence of Judge
Fisher, then a resident of the city. She had long counted
the Judge and his wife among her best friends and most
generous patrons. She resolved, on this morning, to tell
them the tale of the foundling, and consult with them in
regard to what had best be done with it. She accordingly took the basket of freshly-ironed linen upon her arm
and proceeded to the upper part of the city. Early as it
was, she found it to be an easy matter to gain an audience
with those whose advice she sought. The benevolent are
generally at all hours accessible. Biddy told her story in
her own straightforward Irish way. The Judge and Mrs.
Fisher listened and fully credited the tale. Both promised to go around to Biddy's cellar and see the foundling,
after they had partaken of their breakfast. This plan
they carried into execution, and the result of the visit
was, an adoption of the child. They took the poor little
nursling beneath their comfortable roof—they dressed it
in neat robes—they had it baptized in their own name—
they rejoiced, day after day, in its health, and strength,
and beauty. When they spoke of it, 'twas as being
"bone of their bone and flesh of their flesh;" and as
they moved not long afterwards away from the city,
where all these things occurred, it is not strange that
Claude Fisher grew to glad and beautiful girlhood, igno-

rant of the doubt, obscurity, and, perchance, *ignominy*
which hung, like a cloud, over her birth. But, as we have,
before quoted,

> " If ignorance is bliss, 'tis folly to be wise."

Mrs. Fisher fully subscribed to this sentiment, and let
Claude rest in the belief that she was their own cherished,
darling daughter. Sometimes they debated the question,
whether it was best to *ever* enlighten her ; but Judge
Fisher was a correct, honorable, and high-minded man.
He did not know what ignominy might have been attached
to the birth of the one now known as his daughter. He
did not know what subsequent events might bring to
light of crimes and darkness.

After Claude's acquaintance with young Washburn
took the hue and coloring we have seen it assuming, he
plainly saw that a revelation must be made. The Washburns were, and had been from time immemorial, a proud
and haughty race. Claude Fisher, the daughter of Judge
Fisher, they did not object to receiving among them as a
daughter, relative and friend ; but the poor foundling,
picked up in an old Irish washerwoman's cellar in New
York, was altogether a different personage. They would
scorn to touch her, the Judge well knew, with the hem
of their silken robes.

At first he discouraged Allen's attentions, but the boy,
as we have seen, would not be repulsed. Nothing remained but a disclosure to Claude of the incidents narrated
in this chapter. How the intelligence fell, more blasting
than the sirocco of the desert, upon her young and sensitive heart, we have already seen. What barriers wealth,
birth, rank and station can raise to happiness !

> " Happy the man that finds a bride,
> Whose birth is to his own allied !"

Thus sung the poet, and he sung truthfully and well.

————

CHAPTER V.

"Yes, we have answers oft—we know not whence."

OUR readers, we fancy, after having perused the last chapter, feel some curiosity in regard to our heroine's parentage. "Was she the child of shame and sin?" they will ask. "What mother's heart could be unfeeling enough to thrust her helpless babe upon the cold charities of an unfriendly world?"

Again and again, Claude, as she tossed upon her tearwet pillow after her last interview with Allen Washburn, asked herself these questions. Never was a woman, she saw plainly, more devotedly beloved; and him who thus idolized her, she, in her heart of hearts, actually adored. He had refused to be discarded. How gently he had dealt with her! How earnestly and nobly he had urged his suit, and declared that nothing on earth could wean him from the remembrance of her! She loved him at that moment better than she had ever loved him before, and with that love was mingled a certain pride, which made her shrink away from the idea of revealing to him the darkness, and perhaps ignominy, which hung like a dark cloud over her birth. Would that mist ever be removed? Would she *ever* know herself, her real name, and the names and social position of her parents? Where could she turn for information? Just then, she remembered the odd, strange being whom she had met twice of late during her walks to the lake. She felt sure that the old woman and the pack-pedlar were one. She remembered, also, Mrs. Fisher's mysterious words, when asked if she knew her: "*I know her. Fifteen years of close and constant contact will warrant me in making this assertion; but who she is, or where she comes from, I cannot well answer.*" What did her mother mean by those words? Had that strange being been for fifteen years haunting her daily paths, without her being conscious of the fact? What did she want with her? Was it a man or a woman? Sometimes the personage could assume one garb, it seems—sometimes the other.

Did he or she know aught pertaining to her birth? The thought made her brain whirl with excitement. She raised from the pillow, and clasped her forehead with both hands tightly, as if to steady thought and fancy. The effort did her good. She could recall many things clearly. She remembered how Mrs. Fisher had warned her, over and over, against staying out late and taking long rambles, unprotected. She had often intimated that some unusual danger lurked beside her ways. That danger was embodied in the shape of that old woman. Mrs. Fisher had spoken of her assuming disguises. She had herself, in company with Allen, penetrated one of them. Who was she? What was she? What did she want with her? These where exciting, but not easily-answered queries.

"I *will* know," she said at length, starting up. "If this strange being knows aught of my childhood, I will seek, instead of shunning her. I have never wronged her. To harm me would be fiendish. The next time I recognize her, let her garb be what it may, I will certainly accost her. She shall, if she can, unfold, as on a map, the hidden history of my early life. She shall name in my ear the mother—no she cannot have been worthy of so sacred a name—the *creature*, who, with less affection than the brutes display, cast me forth upon the stream of life, to sink or swim, survive or perish, as fate might ordain. But Allen! to think of *him* is madness. The wealthy and petted daughter of Judge Fisher might aspire to so honorable a connexion—the foundling of a wash-house is altogether a different person. What a strange light burned in his eye when he said, '*I will not be discarded.* No obstacle exists, I know, of sufficient magnitude to separate us always.' How little does he dream of the nature of the barrier which inexorable destiny has thrown between us!

Thus mused the unhappy Claude. She arose at last from her couch, but the joyousness of her early days was gone. Her form grew thin and shadow-like—her sweet, young face wore an expression of settled melancholy, and she moved about her daily avocations like one in a dream.

Betty one morning gave her a note. She trembled vio-

lently when she broke the seal, for she recognized at a
glance the firm and vigorous hand of Allen Washburn in
the superscription. It read as follows.

"DEAR CLAUDE:—I am going to a distant part of the
country on business. I shall be absent several months—
perhaps a year. But remember—*you are mine*. It is thus
written. Fire, water, malice, hate and envy, strong though
they be, when arrayed against any object, are insufficient to
erase this decree from the book of Fate. I speak with the
confidence of perfect knowledge. So take heart, and think
of me ever as your devoted—ALLEN."

Claude read and re-read this epistle. It was a mere
note, but it somehow seemed to her to contain the elixir
of life. It refreshed her mightily, as a giant is said to be
invigorated with wine. Her step had in it for a short
time the elasticity of other days, and Judge Fisher and
his wife were comforted at the returning animation of
their darling. But in a day or two the old languor came
back, and the same mournful light was in her eye.

"Allen does not know what *I know*," she said to herself, musingly. "Did he, his note would not breathe such
a life-inspiring spirit as this. Heaven grant that he may
never know what I know. I could not bear his altered mien.
I could not bear to think that he had ceased to love me,
hopelessly as I know his passion to be."

But assured of her suitor's absence now, she resumed
her solitary walks again. She strayed off almost daily to
the lake, and although Mrs. Fisher expostulated against
the measure, she not unfrequently stayed abroad until twilight had almost deepened into darkness. She often
paused on the spot where she had encountered the old woman and her pack, and where she had also seen the same
individual, she felt confident, disguised as a pedlar. But no
weird form, now that its presence was actually longed
for, would start up at nightfall beside her path. Thus it
ever is. When we wait, with throbbing heart and strained
ear, for the echo of some much wished-for footstep, it

comes not—but in an unexpected moment, it startles us
by its sudden rustling.

For weeks, Claude waited and watched. She questioned
Mrs. Fisher closely ; but all that she could learn was, that,
for the last fifteen years, this strange individual had
crossed and re-crossed the paths about Marchden, and
evidently regarded the foundling with a curious eye of
observation. What her object was, Mrs. Fisher could not
divine. Rendered nervous and apprehensive of evil, by
continued ill health, she had surmised a thousand things,
and had guarded Claude as the apple of her eye. At first
the uncanny being had entered, under various disguises,
Judge Fisher's house ; but finding of late years that it
was recognized as one and the same individual under all
subterfuges, it had shunned the mansion ; but as often as
once a year, it was somewhere to be met with in the neighborhood.

Claude, innocent and unsuspecting of evil, believing that
persons and things were always what they seemed, had
never detected that she was sought after and watched by
so vigilant an eye. She was now startled. She remembered how often she might have been overtaken and
harmed during her long rambles, had that phantom-like
shape willed aught of evil in regard to her ; but the more
she mused upon the theme, the more convinced she became,
that that woman or man, whoever or whatever she might
be, was, in some way, connected with the incidents which
transpired during her earliest existence. Knowledge was
what she was after—a knowledge of her parentage, and
she felt willing to brave almost anything, in order to obtain it. She thought of the night in which that strange
visitant had stolen up beneath her window. She looked
out again into the moonlight, and pushed aside the jessamine vine with a nervous hand, vainly wishing for the
re-appearance of what had then, at first, filled her with
alarm. But the shadows of the tall chimney slept undisturbed upon the green-sward, and the unbrushed dew drops
glittered like globules of silver upon the grass. Some
months passed away, and Claude had relinquished all hope

of ever again meeting with the old woman; but in an un-expected moment, she found her in the path.

It was bright noontide. Languid for want of exercise, our heroine tied on her bonnet, and taking a stone pitcher from the kitchen cupboard, proceeded to the spring for the purpose of filling it. The fountain of water was in a cool, romantic place. Tall oaks embowered it, long, green moss trailed over the rocks, and hung even to the water's surface. Claude had filled her pitcher, and poised it with both hands upon the brink of the fountain, for the purpose of resting. She was startled as a voice exclaimed close at her elbow:

"The pitcher is heavy, miss. Could an old, no-account creature like myself help you any with your load? Your hands don't look big and strong enough to handle it well."

Claude looked up, and there stood the one she had so long ardently desired to meet. But the interview was so unexpected, that she became violently agitated, and the huge stone vessel swayed to and fro beneath her trembling hands.

"You will not let it fall, miss," continued the old creature, eyeing the vessel; "can't I help you with it, my pretty lass?"

"No, mother—thank you! I can manage it very well. I have only stopped to rest. I am not very strong, as you have intimated."

"Mother!" repeated the old woman, starting at the sound. "Mother! I am not your mother. Why do you apply the word to me? It sounds strange, when one so young, beautiful and handsomely dressed as yourself, calls a wretched old creature like me by *that* name. Pray, who is your mother?" and the strange visitant bent her keen eyes into Claude's upturned, deeply agitated face.

"I live on the hill yonder," said Claude, pointing to the mansion above her. "I am Judge Fisher's only daughter;" and Claude, in her turn, looked into the old woman's face to see how this announcement was received.

"Judge Fisher's only daughter!" repeated the old woman, with a sort of brazen coolness in her manner.

"Only daughters are always petted and a good deal spoiled. Every body makes a great deal of them—it must be pleasant being an only daughter—and your father, too, is a great man."

"He is very much respected in this vicinity," continued the girl, with an eye, beneath whose steady, penetrating gaze the seeming vagrant's fell—"he is very well thought of here, if he *is my father*, and it is, moreover, as you have said, vastly agreeable being an only daughter."

"You have everything you want, I suppose," continued the old creature, with her eye fixed upon a tuft of daisies, which she was trying to crush beneath the toe of her heavy shoe. "Like the girl in the story-books, you have only to wish for a thing, and then some kind fairy lays it, at night, upon your pillow. You must be very happy."

"So far as material comforts go," answered Claude, "I have few ungratified desires; but I am not entirely satisfied. I have wants, mother, such as you never dream of; I have wishes, which I feel a surety amounting almost to a certainty, that you, and you only can gratify."

The sun-burned face of the old woman crimsoned to the roots of her grey hair. She raised her eyes hastily, and looked warily into the face of the girl. Her shriveled hand trembled as she extended it, as if for support, towards a wooden post which stood near.

"Why do you shake?—why do you grow agitated?" demanded the girl. "Do you intend to refuse to aid me? Would you do nothing to contribute to my happiness? It is not often that I thus ask favors of strangers?"

"I start because you persist in calling me mother. The name is ill-applied. How can *I* aid you? What do you want which *I* can give?"

"I want knowledge," said the girl, placing her pitcher upon the stone flagging, and coming forward to where the old woman was standing. "I want *knowledge*, and you, mother, ignorant as you may feign yourself to be, can, I am confident, impart it."

"Knowledge," said the old woman, now, for the first time, bursting into a short kind of laugh. "Aye, I un-

derstand now. You want your fortune told. You have
a suitor; I saw him supporting you, not a twelve-month
since, across the moor at nightfall. You see that I have
keen eyes, and can see a long way. You would know
whether he will prove to be true, or false. He is true
as steel, but for all that, you may never marry him, for I
see obstacles in the way which, perhaps, one less sharp-
sighted might not observe. But do not despond; *only*
daughters, as I have before said, are a petted class. Your
father will seem obdurate, I dare say, at first—your mother
too may object; but perseverance wins its ends."

"Cease, cease," said Claude, raising her finger menac-
ingly, as she sank down upon a rock at the old woman's
feet. "It is not the *future* which I care to scan—it is the
past. I am not what I seem to be. Whence came I?
Who are my parents? Where is the mother who was
stone-hearted enough to thrust her child out into a world,
which is at best a valley of tears and a thorny wilderness?
She must have been a wretch, destitute of——"

"Stop, stop!" said the old woman, while the pallor of
death overspread her wrinkled visage—"do not upbraid
the mother who bore you—she was innocent of crime; she
was as fair-browed and beautiful as yourself. If you curse
anybody, curse the withered old crone who has tottered
on feeble limbs to look once more upon your fair face before she dies, and who now stands in your presence."

"I was not going to curse anyone," said Claude,
hurriedly. "If I were disposed to do so, your grey hairs
would shield you from the anathema—but Oh! mother!
clear up, I beseech you, the mystery which hangs over my
birth. It is a fearful veil—it has come between me and all
happiness."

"Not now," said the old woman, in an agitated voice.
"I cannot tell you now; but meet me at the lake side to-
morrow, and I will reveal to you all that you want to
know."

"Will you be sure and fulfil your engagement?" said
the girl. "I fear that you are trying to delude me, and
that when you escape from my presence now, I never more

may behold you. I have been looking for you, oh, so anxiously, for many weeks."

"Who told you that I knew anything· about your parentage?" said the old crone, with a puzzled look.

"Nobody—I only guessed it."

"Did you ever see me before?"

"Yes—twice, to my certain knowledge. How often you may have crossed my path unknown, I cannot say."

"It is strange, strange," mused the old woman, as if to herself. "But fate is mighty, and truth is a powerful being, ever seeking the clear, sunlight, and despising subterfuge and darkness. But I must away now. Meet me to-morrow at the lake, and you shall know the truth, and may the truth make you free."

"Amen!" said Claude, scarcely conscious of what she was uttering.

The old woman turned on her heel, and threaded a small path, leading through the woods, with a step as stately and noiseless as an Indian's.

CHAPTER VI.

Light without darkness, without sorrow, joy,
On earth are all unknown to man.--*Montgomery*.

OUR heroine awaited, with an anxious heart, the dawn of the day on which she was to meet with that strange being who held in her possession a key which could unlock the secrets of her mysterious birth. The morning dew sparkled on the moss and fern leaves in the glen, not yet having been exhaled, when she started on her walk to Greenwood lake. Birds, perched high on waving treetops, were trilling their loudest, gladdest songs; herds of cattle·and flocks of sheep grazed quietly in the golden light of the morning. It seemed to Claude's excited mind that the freshness and fragrance which, in time's far beginning, hung over Eden's bowers, dwelt in earth and air.

Alas! that the serpent should have spread the malaria of death over a world which God originally made so fair!

that the asp of sin should now be found amid its choicest garlands! Will there not yet come to this poor sin-sick earth a millennium of beauty and rest? Did not the angels of Bethlehem — those rejoicing spirits who spread their white wings around the shepherds and their flocks on the memorable night of the Saviour s birth, give us the key-note of a song yet to be sung: "*Peace on earth and good will towards men!*" Will not time end, as it began, with a Paradise on earth? May not the voice of God yet be heard at eventide in the garden, while man walks erect, no longer hiding himself because he is afraid? But we are digressing.

Crouched down among the tall grey rocks, close by the side of the lake, Claude found, early as it was, the object of her search. The old crone would have been, in the eye of the painter, a picturesque feature in the landscape. A shawl of gay colors hung negligently over her shoulders; her heavy shoes touched the water, where it rippled up on its sandy margin; her elbows rested on her knees, and the chin of her sallow face was supported by her hand; while her keen eyes gazed vaguely over the broad expanse of water. She was evidently in a "brown study," and did not hear the light, tripping step of Claude until she stood beside her.

"You have come early," she said in her abrupt way, as she turned her head and looked up into Claude's face; "you are anxious to hear that which I have promised to reveal."

"You have judged me rightly, mother; I *am* anxious."

"Why do you persist in calling me *mother?*" said the old woman. "Call me Hortense Bandeau; that is my name. I was your mother's waiting-maid. I am no more like her than iron is like refined gold—than dirty earth is like etherial blue—than the flinty rock is like the delicate flower which grows up and overshadows it."

"You were a servant of my mother!" exclaimed Claude, in a voice of breathless interest, at the same time sinking down upon the green turf where Allen had once sank at her feet. "Oh, tell me, who *was* my mother? Why did she so cruelly forget her offspring? . Why was I never permitted to climb her knee in prattling childhood, or to entwine my arms lovingly about her neck, or to press my lips against her cheeks? Who was my father? Was he some fiend in human shape, who stole, treacherous as a serpent, into the Eden of an unsuspecting heart, and with fair words, like the tempter of old, lured his trustful victim on to ruin? Did he curse the babe, who, with a faint wail, opened its eyes upon the light of heaven, and bore witness to his shameful sins? Did he thrust it angrily from him, and spurn the existence he had dared to invoke from the hand of the Almighty? Even slimy monsters of the deep, and wild beasts who roam in untamed fury through the forest, seeking their prey, still guard, with a beautiful instinct, their young. My parents were more unfeeling than they?"

The old woman's face became ashy in hue.

"Hush, hush, child!" she said; "do not speak in such an excited, impassioned manner. You have been kindly cared for in life—the dead cannot guard their own. Your father died before you came upon the stage of life; your mother never looked but once upon your face. Why do you blame them so bitterly?"

"And were there none left to care for me?" asked Claude, in a more subdued voice. "Where were you, that you did not keep me from being thrust, a miserable foundling, upon the charities of a poor old Irish washerwoman? Was my mother so unamiable in disposition, that you felt no affection for the helpless babe which she left behind her when she died?"

The old woman groaned, as if the question stung her.

"Your mother had combined, in her character, all that is gentle and amiable," she said; "in her person, all that is charming and beautiful. But you are the offspring of a *secret marriage*. Your father was a man whom your rich old grandfather detested; and the ground of that hatred lay in the simple fact that your father was a *Freemason*, and, in a time of great excitement upon the subject, wrote ably and well in defense of his tenets, and supported his ground, in spite of all the vituperation and abuse with which the old gentleman assailed him."

"There is no *shame*, then, resting like a dark shadow over me and my parents," exclaimed Claude. "I am the legitimate child of parents, unfortunate, perhaps, but not sinful. Thank God! thank God!" and the girl, in her gratitude, clasped her hands upon her breast, and kneeling, raised her tearful eyes towards Heaven.

Old Hortense brushed a tear from her rough cheeks.

"Yonder water-lilies," she said, "are not more stainless than your mother's fame. The world holds not a gentler, braver spirit than your father possessed. But I came here to tell you the story of their love and grief. Listen:

"Isadore Bentley, your mother, was, at the age of seventeen, as fair a girl as the sun ever shone upon. She was an idolized child. Her father was a lawyer and violent politican. His wealth was equaled by his influence in society, and Isadore stepped upon the stage of fashionable life under the most flattering circumstances. She was the acknowledged belle of the "upper ten." Her society was everywhere sought after—on every hand she was flattered and caressed. Her mother had died during the infancy of her child, and Isadore was left without a maternal guardian. Had Mrs. Bentley lived, her child might have escaped some of the bitter experiences which beset her life. I was for many years an inmate of the family, and your mother's most constant attendant. I went with her in the capacity of servant, or French waiting-maid, to watering-places, and to routes and balls. Many and many a time have these rough, shriveiled hands, in my younger and better days, twined the silver wreath among the beautiful braids of her hair, and decked her out in the array which taste can dictate, and wealth so easily purchase. I have watched her in the gay assembly, gliding hither and thither, everywhere the beheld of all beholders, with a strange kind of pride. My mistress was the star of every company into which she deigned to set the satin slipper which encased her tiny foot. Her father was proud of her—she was the light of his eyes—his only darling

26

one. He took her with him to Washington—for he was
in those days a member of Congress—and Isadore lived a
butterfly existence, scarcely knowing, much less realizing,
that there was such a thing as anxious care in the world.
During our sojourn at the capital, she was one day introduced to Edgar Porter. He was from her native city, but
they had never before met. He was young, handsome
and talented ; she was lovely, graceful and winning. It is
not strange that they became, in the course of time, attached
to each other, and that that attachment ended in an engagement of marriage. Isadore's father did not, at that
time, object to the match. Porter was a promising fellow.
He bade fair to become some day a distinguished man ;
and although he was not Isadore's equal in point of fortune,
still the old gentleman did not seem disposed to object to
him upon that ground.

"Time passed away, and we all returned home. Soon
afterwards, the subject of *Freemasonry* became a sort of
test question in the political world. Judge Bentley was
violently opposed to the Order. Young Porter was as
earnestly attached to it. Judge Bentley wrote bitter
articles for some of the political papers against the masonic
party. These papers called out able replies from a vigorous pen—that pen was, as it was soon ascertained, wielded
by Porter. Every day the theme grew more exciting—
every hour the war of words waxed hotter and hotter.
At length the day for the election came round ; eager
faces crowded about the ballot-boxes, and hands, trembling with excitement, deposited votes. The returns at
last showed that Judge Bentley's party had been defeated
in that district, and that defeat was said to be owing, in a
great degree, to the influence which young Porter's articles had exerted over the public mind.

"From that hour, your grandfather became Porter's most
stern and uncompromising enemy. He forbade him the
house. He called Isadore to him, and told her that if she
ever again spoke to her affianced lover, she would do it
at the risk of his eternal displeasure. In vain the girl
knelt, with clasped hands, at his feet, and implored for

giveness fo: her too talented and too self-willed lover. The Judge was, in his hatred, as inexorable as death. Tears, prayers, entreaties, were alike unavailing. For the first time in his life, Judge Bentley sent his child from his presence with harsh words and bitter reproaches.

"Isadore came up into her chamber, where I was sitting over my work. She was crying, as if her heart would break. By a few words which she accidently uttered, I obtained a clue to what was passing; and all that love of *intrigue*, which is said to be so often found in the French woman's character, sprang up spontaneously in mine. I said words to her, that I had never uttered in her presence before. I called her father unreasonable and ungentlemanly. I declared that I would defy his authority—that I would at any rate overreach him, and marry clandestinely, if in no other way, the object of my attachment. She listened, and at first shook her head mournfully. But gradually I won her over to my plans and views. That day I carried a perfumed little *billet-doux* to her lover, and brought back an answer. I became the medium of communication between them, and five months afterwards, I disguised my mistress, by dressing her as a Swiss peasant girl; and in this garb she was married, by a Roman Catholic priest, in an old church at the lower end of the city, to Edgar Porter, your father. Left to herself, your mother never would have taken this step, but I urged her on, and did not rest until I had accomplished my wishes.

"About that time, Judge Bentley was called to Europe. He left his daughter in the care of the housekeeper at Bentley Place—as his residence was called—never mistrusting that another had the legal right of protecting her. Isadore parted from her father with many tears. Her conscience upbraided her for the duplicity of which she was guilty; indeed, she was always, after her marriage, sad and tearful—starting ever at the sound of a sudden footstep upon the stairs, and refusing always to mingle in society which she had once so admirably adorned. But she loved her husband with a love bordering on idolatry, and he was as tender with her as a mother is with her first-born. But neither were happy. They had transgressed the divine commandment, "*Honor thy father ;*" and this truth proved to be an asp in the garland of their joy, a poisonous dreg in the cup of their happiness.

"The ways of Providence are inscrutable. Judge Bentley had scarcely touched the shores of England, when Edgar Porter was thrown from his horse and instantly killed. I shall never forget that day. It is seared, as with a hot iron, into my memory. Isadore's anguish was bitter—too bitter to be described in words. Had her father been at home, there could have been no longer a concealment of facts. But he was on a foreign shore, and did not hear the wails and groans with which Bentley Place, for weeks, resounded. All night and day, for months, it seems to me, in succession, your wretched mother paced her apartment with disheveled hair, and eyes which were not tearful, because anguish had dried up the fountain of tears. She would not be comforted. One night I missed her at midnight. I sought for her everywhere. She was not in the house, in the yards, or in the garden. At length I went to your father's grave, and there, stretched on the ground, as senseless as the clods that covered him, lay your wretched mother. But I am saddening you. You are begining to weep. I will cut short my tale. I took her in my arms, and carried her to her chamber. I bathed her brow, and animation was restored. But she never again left her chamber. Six weeks afterwards, you were born. Your mother lived to look but once upon your face, and then expired. In three hours after your mother had breathed her last, Judge Bentley arrived from his foreign tour. I saw, from my window, the ship in which I knew he was a passenger, when it sailed majestically into the harbor. Dread, fear, dismay, all took possession of my soul. I feared that he would pour upon my head the vials of his anguish and wrath, when he learned the particulars of his daughter's marriage and death. Your existence in the household forbade concealment. My plan was hastily formed. I wrapped you in a shawl, and stole with a swift step into the busy street. I assumed, as nearly as I could, the gait and manners of a country woman on a shopping expedition. How I duped unsuspecting Biddy O'Arty, you already know. It was not my intention, at that time, to leave you long in her hands; neither did I intend returning to Bentley Place. It was my hastily formed purpose to secure for myself a home in some respectable family, and then to watch my opportunity and steal you away from Biddy as adroitly as I had palmed you off on her. I concluded to bring you up as my own child. I did not know what else to do with you. I was afraid to carry you to your grandfather. Your existence was unknown to him. I watched about the house, at Bentley Place, that night, and heard the groans of the strong man as he wept above his only child. I saw them when they carried your mother out to her burial. It was, to me, a never-to-be-forgotten scene.

"When I went back to look for you, you were no longer a resident of Biddy's cellar. I assumed various disguises, and looked for you long. At length my research was rewarded. Judge Fisher had adopted you. At first I intended to carry my original design into execution, and steal you from your crib some day when you might be left unwatched. But Mrs. Fisher was a vigilant nurse. Assume what disguise I might, she somehow seemed to penetrate it, and to have a suspicion that all was not right. At length I grew afraid to go into the house. But I kept, nevertheless, a sharp eye upon you. I wanted to ascertain if you were well treated—well fed, and nicely clothed. I saw that your lot had been cast in pleasant places, and you had a goodly heritage. Then I relinquished the idea of taking you from under their protection. But I have never lost sight of you. Once in a year, at least, I have managed to cross your path. Often, when you thought yourself alone, I was watching you. Yesterday I was thrown off my guard by your calling me so unexpectedly by that name "MOTHER." It seemed to me that you had, in some way, penetrated my former design of adopting you as my own, and that you spoke the word derisively. Say, was it so?"

"Not by any means," replied Claude; "I did not know who I was addressing, but something has been long whispering in my ear, that you knew and could reveal the secret of my parentage. For the last few months, I have been looking for you. You have now gratified my curiosity. I am satisfied. But tell me, is my grandfather alive ?"

"He lives," said the old woman, "a decrepit, broken-down old man, at Bentley Place. Since the death of his daughter, he has scarcely been beyond his own threshold."

"Is he still ignorant of my existence ? Has no one told him of my birth ?" asked Claude.

"I think that he is yet ignorant of the events which I have just related. The housekeeper, Mrs. Brown, is a close woman, and would scarcely tell him anything about it. The physician, who waited upon your mother in her last illness, would not be likely to reveal secrets, and I have feared to cross his threshold, for fifteen years. As we were the only ones knowing the facts just stated, very likely he is ignorant to this hour of your existence ; but I am determined he shall not die ignorant of it. I have made a clean breast to you. I already feel lighter, happier and better for the revelation. I intend to go to Bentley Place, and reveal to him all the facts in the case. I am getting feeble. I do not think that I shall live much longer. His anger cannot harm me much now. He may be persuaded to accept you as a child, and to will to you his vast estate at last. There is no one else to whom he can leave it."

Claude's heart leaped in her bosom.

"Allen was right," she thought. "I *may* yet be his. This hand may yet write the letter of his recall."

The old woman's eye was upon her flushed face, and it seemed to read her thoughts.

"I told you yesterday," she said, "that you had a suitor. I have seen you with him twice in the glen. He is a noble fellow, and I verily believe you will yet be happy with him. But the Washburns are a proud race. Should your grandfather refuse to acknowledge you, they may turn up their noses at you, too; but keep up a good heart. Old Hortense Bandeau will do her best for you."

*   *   *   *   *   *   *

Hortense Bandeau performed her promise. Judge Bentley was led, at last, through her influence and that of the physician and housekeeper, to recognize in Claude a grandchild and heir. He sent for her, and installed her mistress of his beautiful mansion. He delighted to trace in her face the features of his buried Isadore. Allen Washburn received from Claude's own hands, as he had prophesied, a letter, which called him home from his wanderings. He became a happy bridegroom, and Claude a joyful bride. Even Biddy O'Arty was present at the wedding, and was seen to shake hands with the keen-eyed country woman, who had once abused her unsuspecting good-nature. At this interesting point, we beg leave to close our history of CLAUDE FISHER, OR THE SECRET MARRIAGE.

------- ∞◇∞ -------

DEATHLESSNESS OF WHAT IS GOOD AND BEAUTIFUL.— There is nothing, no, nothing innocent or good, that dies, and is forgotten; let us hold to that faith, or none. An infant, a prattling child, dying in its cradle, will live again in the better thoughts of those who loved it; and play its part, through them, in the redeeming actions of the world, though its body be burned to ashes, or drowned in the deep sea. Forgotten! Oh, if the good deeds of human creatures could be traced to their source, how beautiful would even death appear; for how much charity, mercy, and purified affection would be seen to have their growth in dusty graves. While wealth, and fame, and beauty, and even earth itself shall fade, the deathless spirit will bloom immortal beyond the tomb.

ONCE MORE, MOTHER!

Once more, mother, let me rest,
  With my head upon thy breast—
Once more see the lilac-tree,
  Which in childhood shadow'd me—
Once more find the silvery stream,
  Where the speckled trout doth gleam,—
Once more climb the mountains grand,
  Mountains of my native land.

Twelve long years have come and past,
  Mother, since I saw thee last;
I have older, graver, grown,
  And a sadness in my tone,
E'en may speak of the human wo,
  All must see who onward go.

But I shall grow gladsome there,
  By thy well-remembered chair,
When I set me down by thee,
  And lay my head upon thy knee,
When I feel thy fingers press,
  On my brow with soft caress,
And can smell the fragrant hay
  Where I used to toss and play.

Once more, mother, do I dream?
  Thou hast cross'd death's icy stream—
I shall see thy face no more,
  Till I tread heaven's radiant shore;
I may never clasp thy hand,
  Upon time's receding strand—
Mother, from thy home afar,
  Guide thy darling like a star.

HOW THEY CAME TO MARRY;

OR,

THE SMITHS AND ALLENS.

"There's such a glory on thy cheek.
And such a magic power around thee,
That, if I would, I could not break
The spell with which thine eyes have bound me."
— *Mrs. Hemans.*

"Oh, I am very tired."

The speaker was a pale girl, with dark, expressive eyes, lips firmly set together, and a small frail figure. She now threw her white arms over her head, and continued, "I'm very weary—my throat, too, is sore. Will there ever be an end to all this talking, and weariness of the flesh?"

She got up and paced the floor with short, but uneven steps. She had breathed with gentleness and love upon obduracy itself, until it melted—she had heard recitation after recitation—explained, demonstrated, and gone over fundamental truths, again and again—she had watched the hot hours of noontide come out of the dewy freshness of the morning, and the long shadows of evening creep on, precursors of the solemn night. She had not flagged or faltered at her tasks, but now they were over—she had locked her desk—seen every little scholar safe on the road homeward, closed the door of the seminary, and sought the quietude of her own room.

But, as she said herself, she was very weary. Her physical strength was spent—her brain ached with excess of thought, and a bronchial affection, to which she was subject, had been aggravated that day by ceaseless talking. No wonder the poor girl said mentally, "will it ever end?" For a long time she paced the narrow confines of her little apartment. But at length a curly head was thrust through the open door, and a clear voice said,

27

"Sister Nell, brother Herbert wants to know if you are never coming down ?"

"Yes, yes, Maude; say that I will be with him directly;" and Nell Smith went to the wash-basin, bathed her face and hands, and smoothed her disordered hair. She then went below.

In a large rocking-chair, before one of the front windows, sat a pale, intellectual-looking young man. He turned his head, as if eagerly listening for the light footfall now approaching him, and a smile came over his .before pensive face.

"Nell," he said, "you are such a long time coming. You have been at home from school these two hours. Why have you not been in here before to see me?"

"I was tired, Herbert," said the girl; and she went and stood by the arm of his chair, quietly and silently.

"Tired!" he repeated, at the same time reaching up his hand, and laying it on her forehead—"tired, and feverish too. Nell, this is too bad—too bad. I almost feel at times, like murmuring. You have to work like a .... , while I sit so quietly—so uselessly here."

The girl laid her soft hand over his lips. "Stop, Herbert," she said—"do not talk like that; I suffer the least of the two. I can see, but you are blind, and cannot work. One of these days, perhaps, your eye-sight will be restored, and then you can go abroad and visit the haunts of commerce and of trade, and mingle with your fellow-men, and take part in all the exciting, stirring events of the day. Till then, you must sit quietly here, and let me support you. I can do it very well. Sometimes I get weary, but a few hours' rest restores me. As the Psalmist has beautifully said, 'I will fear no evil; His rod and His staff shall comfort me.' Believe me, it is a privilege to work for those I love."

Tears forced themselves out of the sightless eyes turned up towards her—large briny tears, such as men shed when they suffer deeply; but with a gentle hand she wiped them away, and with a braver heart than she had brought in with her a few hours before from the school-room, she sat about her nightly task of reading to him.

There was a sweet-pea vine, which little Maude had planted beneath the window. It was now winding its tendrils about the casement, and showing its wealth of green leaves in the soft moonlight, silvering the landscape without. A breath of fragrance came in with the night air. Its perfume was exceedingly grateful to the afflicted man. He spoke of it, and asked Nell to move his chair nearer to the window. He could not see the neat room, with its snowy counterpane upon the bed—the bright mirror, and mahogany bureau standing against the wall—the well-scoured chairs—the little toilet-table, with Nell's work-box and a vase of wild flowers, standing in the middle of it—the sky without, now thickly studded with stars, and the pink and white clusters upon the casement—all these were denied his vision. But it has been beautifully said, that "compensation is the law of our earthly existence." When God takes from us one enjoyment, He gives to us another source of pleasure—when He blunts one sense, He enables us to drink in a double amount of gratification through the others; and so the blind hear, and feel, and taste, with perhaps a keener relish than do others who have sustained no such loss.

Herbert Smith, as he sat there on the night referred to, was a picture worthy an artist's pencil. Tall, slight and pale, with thick raven hair, slightly inclined to curl, he would have graced alike the pulpit, the bar, the counter, or the physician's office.

A stranger, coming in suddenly, would never have dreamed of his being blind. His eyes were very black, and the defective sight was such, that it could not be detected by glancing at the eye. But bright and beautiful as those visual organs seemed, they had been sources of exquisite suffering to the young man. Sight had failed at last, and he sat now at broad noonday, enshrouded by the darkness of midnight. When total extinction of vision came on, he was just from college. He had there graduated with the highest honors. Nell and Maude were his sisters, and both parents were beneath the green sod of the village burying-ground. Old Mr. Smith had died, leaving

three penniless orphans behind him. Herbert had struggled manfully to get his education, and Nell, his sweet
young sister Nell, had striven hard, too, in the village
school-room, to aid him. He had taken the money she
from time to time proffered, reluctantly, but he had said
to himself, when she almost forced it upon his acceptance,
"Never mind, I will pay this back with compound interest one of these days."

Alas! for human calculations. Before he was able to
refund a cent, blindness came on, and now he sat like a
piece of statuary, in the very household which he had
hoped to maintain by the strength of his strong right
arm.

They still lived at the old homestead. Neither Nell or
Herbert had felt that they could part with that spot—the
humble little spot where their parents spent all their married lives—where they themselves had been born, and
where both father and mother had taken the pale king
of terrors by the hand, and gone down into the silent
land, peacefully and trustfully, and without a shadow
of fear.

There was one hired servant in the kitchen—old Bess.
She was maid-of-all-work—a perfect Amazon—and she
kept the house in order, and looked after Herbert and little
Maude, when Nell was away at her task.

On this evening, while Nell read, Bess spread their frugal
supper, and little Maude climbed upon Herbert's knee.
She soon laid her curley head against his bosom, and slept
the sweet and refreshing slumber of childhood.

It was a pretty sight, although a sad family picture—
three orphans thus clustered together at nightfall, all
frail, all weak, and yet yielding to each other great love
and tenderness.

It was eleven o'clock when Nell left Herbert for the
night. She was weary still; but peace, great peace, had
been born in her soul. A day, made almost holy by good
deeds, had been woven, like a golden thread, into the
warp of her life. It lay there now, glittering and precious
in the sight of angels. It could not be taken out of the

web—it would assuredly go with it to the judgment seat of God.

Oh! it is a great thing *to live*—to be "patient and long suffering" like Him who, long ago, filled the world with the fragrance and melody of His beautiful life. He was, in all things, "our example;" and He stands, even now, upon the far heights of the White City, looking down upon us with tender, benignant compassion; and, as we walk in much weariness, and weakness, and with many burdens of sin in the path appointed, cries out continually unto us:

"Come unto *me*, all ye that labor and are heavy laden, and I will give you rest."

Nell felt this, as she walked to the casement and looked out upon the star-spangled night. She felt it as she laid her head, with its wealth of brown tresses, upon the snowy pillow, and closed her eyes to pay her evening devotions. She rejoiced that she had been able to live through one day, sweetly and patiently, and her prayer went upward, converted almost into a song of praise.

The next morning she went into the school-room with a stronger step than she had left it the night before; and, when the pupils came in, one with a bunch of roses for her desk, another with a choice bit of cake, and a third with a beautiful book, she felt, again, that it was sometimes a sweet, as well as glorious thing to live.

Country school children! God bless them, every one! What different creatures they are from the prematurely developed little bundles of pride, and haughtiness, and sauciness, which we find, too often, in our village and city school-rooms. They commune with Nature, until they borrow from her radient face sunshine and warmth, beauty and life, and their hearts are as guileless as their tongues. God bless them! with their berry-stained fingers, home-made dresses, sun-burnt faces, and tangled hair. They can tell you where every bird builds her nest for miles around, but nothing could tempt them to rob her of her treasures of speckled eggs—they know where pennyroyal beds are most fragrant at nightfall—where the spearmint grows the rankest under the shadow of the old mill wall—where the blackberries ripen first—where the cows herd, and can distinguish their bells apart, though they are a mile away.

It was among such beings as these that Nell Smith's lot was cast, and she was often thankful for the rural scenes by which she was surrounded. She had, however, a pupil from one of the highest families in the State. This was the daughter of an ex-member of Congress—a Col. Allen, who, won by the wild beauty of the region where she resided, had built a country seat in the neighborhood, and his daughter Ruth had teased him into the idea of patronizing Miss Nell's school, by sending thither her very sweet and beautiful little self.

The Colonel's residence was so far away from the seminary, that she was obliged to ride. A nice little pony was accordingly purchased, and Ruth, escorted by an elder brother, came galloping up, morning after morning, to the school.

The little rustics, at first, were full of wonder at her long purple riding dress, plumed cap, well-filled satchel, and shining kid gauntlets. But when Ruth had thrown all these aside, and shown them that she could swing as high as any of them, in the old grape vine south of the seminary—that she was kind-hearted and gentle, and ready to associate with the humblest of them—that she was not at all given to " putting on airs," but was simple and child-like in all her ways, the affections of the whole school clustered spontaneously around her, and they would greet her advent among them in the morning with a shout of joy. Nell, too, soon got to loving this girl. She was so bright-eyed and smiling—so easily made satisfied and happy—so careful not to give her teacher unnecessary trouble—so sunny-faced and affectionate, that it would have been quite foreign to Nell's nature to have overlooked or neglected her.

As to Ruth, she loved her teacher enthusiastically. Soon after her father came to Edenton, she had chanced to see the sweet-faced young mistress, in company with her blind brother, at a little chapel where the Edenton people attended divine worship every Sabbath.

The pale student, with his blind eyes, instantly became an object of interest to her; and, as she watched Miss Nell's never-tiring care of him, her interest grew into admiration and love. It was soon after this that she one morning encountered her father in the library, and the following scene took place:

"Papa," said the girl, gliding up to him, and twining her snowy arm about his neck, "I want to go to school."

"There is none here that you can go to, daughter," he said, scarcely raising his eyes from the paper; "moreover, I thought you had quite enough of books and teachers, last year, at Madame Toulard's boarding school. You told me, when I took you from there, that, as to Algebra, you detested it—for Geometry, you had no use—Latin and French you abhorred; and, of music, you were heartily tired. You chatted incessantly about the freedom of a country life—about horseback rides, and raising chickens, and planting rose bushes, and I don't know what all. What in the world has possessed you with the idea of school again? I am at a loss to divine."

Ruth laughed.

"Papa," she said, "there is such a sweet-faced teacher up at the old seminary. I am quite in love with her. Then I can have such charming horseback rides, coming and going, and it will be so pleasant going to school in the country; and—and—I want to go. Papa, mayn't I go?" and the little hand patted his rough cheek coaxingly and carelessly.

"Nonsense, Ruth! I expect you can teach any school mistress in this neighborhood. With your advantages, you ought to have a smattering of everything. I paid a thousand dollars for you last year, at the least calculation. Sixteen dollars for flower making; twenty dollars for fruit lessons; nobody knows what all for French, and German, and Italian, and music, and monochromatic painting, and use of piano, and board, and store bills, and tuition, and washing, and lights, and hack hire, and stage fare, and car tickets. Ruth, you've already cost me a small fortune, and ought to know everything; and now you want to go to a little country school. Who ever heard the like?"

"But, papa, you are rich, and don't mind the expense, I am sure; and, as to knowing *everything*, why, I've just come to the conclusion that I don't know anything as I ought to know it. So I want to begin at the beginning, and learn some things thoroughly and well. Don't say a word, papa! I want to go to school;" and the girl put her rose-bud mouth down to his, and kissed him fondly.

"Well, go, Ruth," said the strong man, winding his vigorous arm around her slender waist. "Do just as you please about it—that's the way you have done all your life. Confound me! before I had children, I thought I'd govern 'em, but they rule me. This girl here understands charming the gold out of my pocket by a wink of her eyes. I'll send her to Patagonia, if she don't mind," and the Hon. ex-member just at that moment brushed something very much like a tear from the corner of his left eye with his coat sleeve.

But Ruth had gained, as she always did, her point; and now you know, kind reader, how such a fairy-like, half-grown creature, with an aristocratic toss of golden curls, and cheek like a flushed lily, came into Nell Smith's school. She not only went to school, but to the cottage also, and got acquainted with Maude and Herbert. Sometimes, on her way to the seminary, she brought baskets of fruits and flowers, and left them in old Bess's hand for "Master Herbert," and "Miss Maude." Sometimes she went there on Saturdays, and relieved Nell in her task of reading to Herbert. In short, the inmates of the little cottage of Edenton, and the scholars at the seminary in the valley, felt as if a golden sunbeam had come dancing into their midst, whenever Ruth Allen crossed their thresholds.

The summer went by. Col. Allen, so that Ruth seemed satisfied and happy, thought little about her "childish freak," as he termed it. He did not for a moment imagine that she was learning anything worth knowing.

October kindled its watch-fires on the hills and in the western skies. The emerald leaves of summer were painted, too, by his frosty breath, and silently in the dense forests were falling one by one. The harvest of the year had come. Men sat down by their granaries of golden grain, and looked proudly upon the fruitage of their toil. They had sowed and reaped—gone forth " bearing precious seed, and found it coming back to them in ten-fold measure "after many days." Their hearts were glad, and so was the heart of Ruth Allen. While for Herbert Smith's amusement, she had been silently garnering up golden stores of rich thought, bright fancies, historical facts, and great lessons from the Book of Life.

Herbert was in the habit of commenting more or less upon everything read to him. He possessed intellectual powers of the highest order, united with a calm, indomitable energy, which, under happier circumstances, would have marked him out as one born for greatness. His favorite study was religious philosophy, and he poured into Ruth Allen's soul the high thoughts of God and immortality which burned in his own. His calm, kind smile—his clear, unhesitating voice—his pale and noble face—his commanding figure, as he discussed at times the momentous question of life and its responsibilities, of death and the mysteries of eternity—awed the girl's soul within her.

Her youth had been spent in the fashionable circles of Washington, New York, Saratoga, and her native city. Such themes are considered unfashionable topics in these places; and Ruth Allen had scarcely, in all her life before, given a passing thought to the immortal.

Herbert now, as well as Nell, became her teacher; and sitting there at the feet of these orphan children, far away from the gay scenes of her earlier days, the daughter of the proud senator listened, her heart burning within her, as did the disciples, when the Master talked with them by the way.

She sought through her father's extensive library for books treating upon the themes that Herbert loved. Carlyle's works were there; Channings also; Göethe's

"Wilhelm Meister," and "Festus"—that strange poem which is always so suggestive of thoughts and fancies. There, too, were the divines of almost every faith—ponderous volumes which had laid unopened for years—books that had come to Colonel Allen from a pious ancestry, of whose faith he knew little. One after another, during the bright summer months, those books had been read in the cottage of the Smith's; the wheat had been sifted from the chaff—the gold separated from the dross. The former had been carefully stored up in the treasury of their souls, and the latter cast away. Ruth Allen had, as her father intimated, been the pupil of *famous* teachers—she now felt herself to be at the feet of wise ones; and her blue eye grew calm and serene, and revealed, in its clear depths some of the precious things hidden away in the soul.

But, as we have said, October came on, and Ruth was, one clear, bright morning, standing with her riding-cap dangling by one string from her hand, while with her other she hunted through the library shelves, previous to starting to school. Her father came and stood beside her.

"What are you looking for, daughter?" he said, as he watched her tiny white fingers gliding from volume to volume. "You don't study any of these ponderous tomes in that precious country school of yours, do you?"

"Not exactly at school, but we have read a great many of them at the cottage," she said gravely, without removing her eyes from the shelves. "I want now a treatise on Freemasonry. I promised to carry it this morning to Herbert; and where can it be? I know I have seen it here often; it is an old book, full of pictures, and it tells about Solomon, and Hiram, and the old Charges, and I don't know what all," she said impatiently. "I want it, for Herbert is very anxious to hear it read. His father was a Mason. Oh, where can it be?"

"Sister, are you *never* coming?" called out Webster Allen, stepping that moment to the threshold, and looking in at her. "The pony has been ready this half hour, and my horse is as restless as he can be. Why don't you let

those old musty books alone, and come along to school ?
It's too bad to make Miss Nell wait for you in this way."
And the tall, fine-looking young man, standing there, spoke
as if in *his* eyes, at least, Miss Nell's comfort, and con-
venience, and approbation, were of vast amount.

Colonel Allen looked at his children like one half-be-
wildered.

" Who are these country people ?" he said, laying a detaining hand on Ruth's arm ; " who is this country school-
mistress and her brother, that you and my son yonder
seek them continually ? I cannot make it out. There is
Webster, now ; he, of late, has grown wonderfully interested in this country teacher ; as for you, you cannot be
kept at home, rain or shine. I thought, when you first
spoke of going to that school, that you would tire of it in
three weeks."

A crimson blush stole to the cheek of Webster Allen, as
his father's questioning eye sought his face, but Ruth's
blue eyes were clear, and earnest, and truthful, as she
turned around, and said : " They are among the most interesting people in the world, father. If you were to know
Mr. Herbert Smith, you would certainly like him. He
knows everything, it seems to me, although he is quite
blind. Won't you go up there, father, some day, and
see him ?"

" Me, child ? How could he possibly interest *me ?*
Does he know anything about history, politics, or science,
that *I* should seek him ?" and the Honorable gentleman
straightened himself up with a sort of conscious pride, that
was amusing to behold.

" Yes, father, he knows about politics, and history, and
science, and religion, and now he wants to know about
Freemasonry ; perhaps you could instruct him, father, for
you are a Mason, ain't you ?" and the girl looked question-
ingly into the old man's face.

" Yes, daughter," he said, " I have the honor of being
P. D. G. M. among that noble fraternity. Do you say that
these orphans are the children of a Freemason ?"

" Yes, father ; I heard Herbert say so last night. Their

father was a bright Mason: one among the highest in the craft. But here's that book! Now, Bud, I'm ready." And the girls natched it up, and ran out to the horse-block. Webster followed her with a musing kind of face, and the two were soon on their way to Edenton Seminary.

After they were gone, Colonel Allen paced, with a thoughtful brow, his library floor, for the space of an hour. His wife came and looked at him through the half-open door, but seeing him deeply lost in thought, she went back without interrupting him. It could not be that the Honorable ex-Member was bestowing so much thought upon that blind boy and his toiling sister! We shall see.

I do nor know how it was, but that evening, when Nell went home from school, accompanied as usual by Ruth, she was startled to find a proud, aristocratic-looking stranger chatting very sociably with Herbert, near the front window. She could not, at first, surmise who it was; but Ruth went straight up to him, called him "Papa," and kissed him. The matter was made clear then to her astonished vision.

Almost every day afterwards, Colonel Allen visited the humble little cottage. He conversed with Herbert upon many topics. To his great surprise, he found that the blind boy was one of the most extraordinary men he had ever met. His eye, at the same time, was a good deal upon his own daughter. He saw how that blind young man had, all unconsciously, to quote the beautiful language of another, "with delicate touch, opened the door of her heart, and gone into a stately room, set with fluted columns, and richly adorned for his reception." The first love of a young heart is generally little less than idolatry; and Ruth Allen—heaven help her—the spell was upon her!

The Colonel was a shrewd man of the world. He had intended that his bright-eyed pet should wed among the noblest in the land; but, for all that, he shared the interest she manifested in that blind man.

"Smith," he said one day, as he sat under the pea vine, now fast withering, "your eyes can be cured; I feel confident of it. There is a skilful oculist in the city—a cousin of my wife's. It is getting almost time for us to return. I want you to go home with us, and let us all see what he can do for you. It seems to me that he has cured worse cases than yours."

Herbert started.

"Oh," he said, "the blessing of sight looks, to me, too great to be enjoyed. I have about made up my mind that I shall have to *grope* my way to the grave. I don't mind it so much for myself; but Nelly—I feel anxious on her account."

The Colonel glanced at her pale, soul-lit face.

"She has been a good sister," he said. And seeing that the conversation was taking too grave a turn, he added, laughingly: "She will make somebody, one of these days, a good wife. Good sisters make good wives."

Just at that moment, Webster stepped over the threshold. His face glowed for a moment, as if he fully endorsed the sentiment.

To be brief, Herbert Smith went with the Allens to the city. The operation upon his eyes was eminently successful. After weeks of weakness and suffering, he looked once more upon the blue sky, the green fields, the noisy city, and quiet country. Meanwhile, Nelly patiently carried on, at home, her school. But there came a change. She was not to be there always.

In a proud city at the South, there now stands up before admiring crowds, Sabbath after Sabbath, a grave, pale man, with brilliant eyes, graceful mein, earnest, heartfelt tones, and commanding eloquence. Were you to go into that church, you would recognize him immediately. It is Herbert Smith. Ruth Allen is his wife, and before him sits sweet-faced, patient Nell. Her country work is ended. She is the wife of an eminent lawyer—Webster Allen. The old man is there, serene and satisfied. He is not chafed because his ambitious scheme ended thus. He remembers

that he, in part, aided in bringing all this about; and, as
he listens to Herbert Smith's eloquence, and watches Nell's
graceful form, and patient endurance of life's stern trials—
those that come to all—he says, mentally—

"*It is well!*"

And little Maude! what became of her? I will tell
you. Once she laid her burning cheek upon Herbert's
breast, at nightfall, and went to sleep. There was fever
in her eyes, and wildness in her brain. She slept on, however, and when she awoke, she was not on earth; neither
was she an orphan. She was amid the angels, and God
was her father. In the church-yard, back of Herbert's
city residence, there is a marble slab and urn. On the
smooth white surface are carved the words:

"ALAS! MY SISTER!"

How brief, yet expressive, her epitaph.

Gentle reader, do you ask what Freemasonry has had to
do with my story? I can simply say, *I do not know.*
Freemasons are mystical beings. I cannot tell how far
Colonel Allen was led on by the principles of his Order;
but I somehow feel a conviction that, had the Smiths been
anything but the children of a Mason, all these pleasant
after events would not, through his agency, have happened
to them.

FLOWERS.—How the universal heart of man blesses
flowers! They are wreathed around the cradle, the marriage altar, and the tomb. The Cupid of the ancient Hin-
doos tipped his arrows with flowers; and orange-flowers
are a bridal crown with us—a nation of yesterday. Flowers garlanded the Grecian altar, and hung in votive
wreaths before the Christian shrine.

THE SOOTHSAYER'S MALEDICTION.

MAN is a strange being. Sometimes we find him gifted
and noble, but without, it would seem, the power of re-
sisting temptation, and consequently he soon becomes
debased like the brute. Edward Arthur was a young
lawyer. He graduated at an institution in the North, where
he took the highest honors, and on his return to his native
village, was received by his friends with every mark of
approbation and esteem. But during his college life, his
social disposition led him to contract convivial habits, and
long before he was aware of himself, he was in the broad
road to ruin. He loved the wine-cup—he loved the song
—the revelry which borders on madness, and the party
which tarries long at the board.

"Where is Arthur? We cannot have 'a wake-up'
without him," were expressions that were often heard
from young men of his own age, whose characters were
not the most irreproachable in the world. But these
things remained for a long time hidden from the public
gaze. Arthur was everywhere spoken of as a young man
of great talents—of extraordinary promise. Parlors were
readily thrown open to him. Prudent mammas smiled
approvingly upon him, and gay girls boasted to each other
of tokens of esteem—the kindly glance, the delicate
attention, or the little flower won from him at public and
private parties.

But there was one pale-faced, gentle young being, who
never mentioned his name, although she met him frequently, and had learned to blush at his approach. She was
the clergyman's daughter, and was the fairest of all the
village maidens.

But although the young lawyer's *name* seldom came to
Gertrude Atherton's lips, his *image*, nevertheless, dwelt
continually in her heart; and many a little token of his

regard was carefully laid away from prying, inquisitive eyes, by her hands. There was between the leaves of one of her choicest books, a withered rose-bud; in another, a faded sprig of *arbor vitæ*. And she repeated to herself, again and again, the sentiment which she found written on a small strip of paper, attached to the evergreen's stem, when she received it from his hand—"*I live for thee!*" "Is that the language of mere compliment?" she queried mentally, "or does one, noble and gifted, bow at my feet and sue for a smile?" Then she sat down, and dreamed those dreams which a young and ardent imagination can color so highly.

She was thus engaged one evening, when she was startled by a footstep; she looked up, and saw an old woman —one whom she well knew to be a straggling, gipsy-like fortune-teller, standing directly in the path before her. She started to her feet, and a feeling akin to fear crept to her heart. "What do you want with me, mother Agnes?" she said hastily; "what do you want with me?"

The old woman took a short pipe from between her lips, and bent an eye of snaky blackness upon the maiden's face.

"*You* want *me*," she said at last, "instead of my wanting you. You want your fortune told!"

"Indeed, mother, I do not," she replied—"my father, you well know, disapproves of your occupation, and would be very angry with me, were I to listen to any of your revelations. I do not want my fortune told. What God has hidden deep in the future, I do not care to scan. I must not listen to you. Excuse me, mother Agnes; I *must go.*"

"God?" said the old woman, without heeding the last remark; and she held up her long, bony finger, and shook it violently to and fro. "Is there a God? Do you believe in the existence of such a Being? If so, where is He, and why does He live so unmindful of the creatures He has made? I used to believe in Him once, but I do not now."

Gertrude trembled, for the old woman's vehemence

frightened her. She, however, summoned resolution to
reply. "Mother Agnes," she said solemnly, "you are yourself an immortal being, endowed with ever-expanding
capacities for good or evil. Do not talk thus! How dare
you talk in that way?"

"How dare I?" said the old crone. "How dare I tell
the truth? Prove to me that I am immortal! Prove to
me that there is a God! Prove to me that I am not the
offspring of chance, and the plaything of events!"

"I cannot reason upon such points," said Gertrude
timidly; "but if you will go into the house, my father, who
is in his study, will take pleasure in pointing out to you
the evidences of Christianity. Pray, mother Agnes, what
made you ever grow sceptical. A woman who is an infi-
del, my father has often told me, is the most hideous
monster in nature."

The old woman 'wickered' a short, sarcastic laugh.
"My faith," she said, "is the offspring of despair. At
your age I was as hopeful, and for aught I know, as religious as yourself. But the wheel of fortune has ground
me into the dust. I have had my paternal inheritance
wasted—my confidence betrayed—my children cruelly
murdered by their father. I have been myself the subject
of brutal personal violence from one who promised, at the
altar, to love, cherish and protect me. My faith in man
has been destroyed; my faith in God uprooted. I now
earn a precarious, and your father thinks, an unhallowed
livelihood by fortune-telling. When fate, or destiny, or
fortune, or whatever you please to call it, has sifted you
about as it has me, then you too may doubt the existence
of one supremely wise and infinitely good: one who can
shield the unfortunate and protect the creatures He has
made."

Gertrude Atherton shuddered. "Whatever my misfortunes may be in life, mother Agnes," she said. "I hope
that I shall never be driven to Atheism. Let me at least
exercise a sweet and trustful hope in Him, who has said,
'ask and ye shall receive; seek and ye shall find; knock
and it shall be opened unto you.' She who casts away
28

her faith in God—in Christ, the ever present Saviour—casts away the prop which will sustain her in adversity, and scorns High Heaven's most precious consolation. Heaven save me from being ever driven to such a dreadful extremity."

The old woman laughed, but less scornfully than before. "Well, if you will not be converted," she said, "to my creed, you might at least have your fortune told—it shall not cost you a dime, whereas most people are willing to pay me a quarter of a dollar. What is given, ought to be thankfully received."

Gertrude shook her head. "I do not care to hear it, mother Agnes," she said. "I fear your croakings, like the raven's, will bode me no good. My father would disapprove of it."

"But others listen to me eagerly," continued the old soothsayer. "Are you wiser or better than young lawyer Arthur? I have just told his."

At the mention of that name, she started and blushed deeply. The old woman saw the vantage ground gained, and eagerly improved it.

"*He* crossed my palm with silver, and afterwards, when I told him of a sweet-faced bride yet to be won, he laughed with great delight, and declared that he had not paid too highly for the information gained. I told him a great deal; but there is a page I did not read in the mortal's destiny. I have sought you out for an auditor! Shall I read it to you?"

"I thought," said Gertrude, still blushing, "that it was *my* fortune you wanted to tell—not Mr. Arthur's. He is nothing to me. Why should I be anxious, or care to hear his fortune?"

"Why should you, indeed?" said the old woman, with a mocking air. "I know of but one reason why you should; as that is an interesting one, though, I'll make bold to mention it. It has been revealed to me that your fortunes may, on some future day, intermingle, intertwine and cross each other strangely. You were in short, both born under the same star. The same card of destiny turns up for both."

"You jest," said the maiden hastily. "You prate about things you do not understand. Surely you did not tell Mr. Arthur this? If you did, I am very angry with you."

"I told him all that. I chose to tell him," said the provoking old soothsayer, "all that it was meet for him to know. But I have that to tell *you*, which I did not reveal to him. Will you listen, or are you too puritanical to give me your hand?"

Gertrude, when the old woman first began to speak, had half-way extended her open palm, but she drew it back as the sentence closed, and shut it as quickly as if a live coal had been dropped into it.

"No!" she said resolutely. "My father—my wise, good, reasonable father—does not approve of you or your trade. I will not listen to you. Stand aside and let me pass. I would not listen to your jargon for a world."

"Stop!" said the old woman, stepping before her more directly than before. "What I have to say, touches your future peace. Hear and heed my revelations and advice, or you will rue in dust and ashes and tears of blood. Will you stop and listen?"

"No, I will not!" said she, still pressing forward. "I would not listen, though you wore the garb of an angel of light, for my father disapproves of you and your practice. It is in vain to tempt me further;" and the girl glided up the granite steps leading into her father's mansion, as if afraid of being pursued by some mocking spirit of darkness.

The old woman watched her light form, until she ascended the porch. There was grim disappointment written on her wrinkled visage.

"Stop, Gertrude Atherton!" she cried. "You may fly from me, but, mark well my words, you cannot fly from destiny—that will pursue and hunt you down, as the wolf pursues its prey in the dense wilderness. There is an abyss, wide and dark as Erebus, yawning beneath your feet. I would have saved you from falling into it. I sought you out for that very purpose, but you have scorned my revelations. Go on now—go on; and may the fate from

which I would have saved you, come upon you. A darker
destiny I cannot wish you. When you are fallen, remember the old soothsayer's malediction!"

The old woman then replaced her pipe, drew her tatter-
ed hood down so as to shade her smoke-colored visage,
and wrapping the fragment of a small red cloak, which
she wore, closely about her, swept from the yard.

Gertrude, who had paused by the railing until the conclusion of the elf's words, felt weak, and for a moment
sick, but she turned and sought her chamber. Here she
threw herself down into a chair, and mentally congratu-
lated herself upon having shown great firmness and decision of character, and that too when strongly tempted to
do wrong. But in spite of all her efforts, the old crone's
malediction rang in her ears, and she could not shut it
out.

"That old woman," she said mentally, "has an eye like
the spirit of evil, and her words haunt me like prophesy.
But what does *she* know of the future? She does, she
can know nothing. It is not right to encourage such people ; and yet I had rather, outcast as she is, have won her
blessing than her curse. But it is too late to repent now.
If she does know aught of evil awaiting my footsteps, I
must e'en abide my fate. My father says that we were
made to struggle and endure. A portion of unmixed
good never fell yet to the lot of mortal."

Thus reasoned Gertrude Atherton, as she smoothed her
hair and bathed her face previous to going below. While
she was completing the last operation, the door-bell rang.
She stopped, arrested by the tones of a familiar voice in
the hall. It was Edward Arthur's. She heard the servant ushering him into the parlor, and heard Mr. Arthur
inquiring for her. Her heart beat violently. Her interview with old Agnes made her almost afraid to meet him.
But after having re-arranged her neck-ribbon, and re-
smoothed her hair, she hastened down. To make a long
story short, when the door of the clergyman closed that
night upon Arthur's retreating form, Gertrude was his
affianced bride.

We hasten over the wedding. But one thing occurred to disturb the serenity of the young bride's mind. That was the visage of old Agnes, looking out from behind a tombstone in the church-yard as the marriage procession swept forward to the altar. She trembled at the sight of her, and clung closer to Arthur's arm. He looked down to see what had agitated her.

"It is nothing and nobody but that canny old being, mother Agnes, the fortune-teller," said he, smiling at Gertrude. "Are you afraid of her, my love? By the way, I believe she *can* foretell future events; for a month or two ago, she pictured to me, in strong and vivid colors, this very scene. But she is an ugly-looking being, crouched down there behind the tombstone. She has an eye like an Indian's, and I do not blame you for trembling in her presence. I hope that she will not be there on our return."

The train swept on, and paused before the altar. The clergyman was there in his surplice, prayer-book in hand. The bride bowed her veiled and flower-crowned head, and the bridegroom looked up with an exultant air, as the few brief words were said which linked them together for weal or woe—linked, until death should come, with skeleton fingers, to unclasp the chain. In the confusion attendant upon these solemn rites, Gertrude forgot the fortune-teller; but as she passed the tombstone, a hollow voice murmured in her ear: "Remember! yet, go on—you are in the pathway I foresaw!"

She shuddered more violently than before, and Arthur uttered something like an imprecation on the old hag who hid herself in that manner behind grave-stones to frighten people in passing. But the old woman and her malediction were soon forgotten by both before they reached the parsonage on their return.

Two years went by on rapid wings. The worthy village clergyman died, and Gertrude soon afterwards followed her mother to the grave. Being an only child, she was now left dependant on her husband alone for comfort and support. The faces which had smiled over her cradle were both hid away beneath the coffin-lid, and she was

brotherless and sisterless in the world! But a new link
bound her to life. A lovely babe opened upon her its soft,
bright eyes, and smiled. She felt, as she looked upon it,
like adopting the words of another:

> "This beautiful mysterious thing
>   This seeming visitant from heaven,
> This bird with an immortal wing.
>   To me—to me Thy hand hath given.
>
> The pulse first caught its tiny stroke,
>   The blood its crimson hue from mine;
> This life which I have dared invoke,
>   Henceforth is parallel with Vhine.
>
> A silent awe is in my room;
>   I tremble with delicious fear;
> The future with its light and gloom—
>   Time and Eternity are here.
>
> Doubts—hopes in eager tumult rise,
>   Hear, oh my God! one earnest prayer,
> Room for my bird in Paradise,
>   And give her angel plumage there."

And Edward Arthur looked too, with all of a father's
pride, upon his first-born. To him the little round face was
the sweetest he had ever gazed on. He forsook for a
while his jovial companions in the club-room and at the
restaurant, and confined himself, when not professionally
engaged, to his wife's chamber.

Gertrude, who had often wearied for his presence, in his
absence, felt glad and grateful for his attentions. She had,
however, never dreamed what a course—what a *downward*
course her husband was pursuing. She did not know
that he had begun to frequent horse-races and gambling
saloons, and many other of the ante-chambers of Hell.
Had she, how would her heart have died within her!

There was a fraternity of noble men to which Arthur,
in his palmiest days, had attached himself. We allude to
Freemasons. They saw, with great regret, the frequency
with which he trampled under foot one of the most sacred
of their cardinal virtues, viz: *Temperance;* and strove, by

every means in their power, to avert the cloud which they saw slowly gathering and lowering in the future. They counseled him—they advised him—they entreated him, for the sake of his family, if not for his own, to reform, but in vain. His business dwindled—his respectable friends— men who had honored him for his talents and for his so- cial virtues, after having tried, by every means in their power, to reform him, began, like the Priest and Levite, to "pass by on the other side."

Poor Gertrude! When she realized how desperate mat- ters were gathering, she could hardly believe it. She had never dreamed of her heart's chosen becoming a drunkard. But there he was, with all his noble talents and splendid endowments, sinking into a sot—the weak victim of every temptation. She began to suffer too, as drunkards' wives do, alas! too often suffer. Poverty, with his grim, hyena- like visage, stood looking her in the face. Those who in more prosperous days had courted her smiles, now passed by with a slight nod of recognition, or stared rudely in her face.

Her child grew in grace and beauty, and, under other circumstances, would have filled her house with joy. But alas! she was an inebriate's child, and destined to drain the cup of bitter dregs which a father's trembling hand held with fiendish cruelty to her lips.

Arthur, when he found his wife had gained some knowl- edge of his excess, from a feeling of shame shunned her presence more than ever; but this feeling gradually wore away, and sometimes he came stumbling home, drunk.

But why need we dwell on an inebriate's progress? Who does not know that when intemperance is finished, "it bringeth forth death"—death to every moral excel- lence—death to every social affection—death to every spi- ritual aspiration—death, alas! to the immortal soul?

Edward Arthur's house and furniture were sold for debt. He moved his family into a rude tenement in the outskirts of the village, but his whole time was passed among the low and vile. His face became blotched and purple—his eyes blood-shot, and his form bloated. Gertrude did what she could to earn a subsistence with her needle, but shirt-making is proverbially a poor business. The Freemasons did a great deal for her about this time. One of them, during the cold winter, sent her wood—another, meat—a third, flour. But Arthur's offences had caused him to be cast out long before from the lodge, and she felt that she was not, in any way, entitled to their kindness and consideration.

Oh! this is to many a poor mortal a bitter world. "Remember the days of darkness," says the Psalmist, "for they shall be many." And to know that they are owing, as Gertrude did, to the sinfulness of those we have loved and trusted, adds to the blackness of their gloom.

But there was a darker day coming to the inebriate's wife than any she had yet experienced. One day her husband came home half-intoxicated. Of late he had grown brutal towards her and her child, when in that state. Little Ida, who had not learned to fear him, ran toward him, with outstretched arms, crying, "Papa, take the baby—take me!"

"Curse the brat!" said the angry fiend. "Can a man have no peace in his own house? Gertrude, you are a fool, and the child is like its mother. Take *that*, you miss, for your sauciness;" and he dealt the little prattler a violent blow on one side of its head, quite lifting it to the other end of the room.

"Oh, Edward!" said Gertrude, springing forward. "What have you done?"

"Knocked the brat's brains out, I hope; and I'll knock yours out, if you whimper about it. It's a pity a man can't correct his child, without his wife taking its part. Curse you and the child, too."

Gertrude said nothing. She gathered her smitten, dying child to her bosom, and tried to hush its wailing and mourning, lest its father's anger should be again directed towards it. The child slept at last. It was a fearful sleep, and the mother knew too well that it was the precursor of death; but she stilled her agony, and rocked it silently to and fro. The drunken wretch, feeling the need of another potion of liquid fire, went off to seek it, leaving the poor woman alone. No sooner had he disappeared from the threshold, than she laid the child from her arms, and strove, by every means, to arouse it, and warm its livid hands and feet. Her efforts were partially successful. It opened its little eyes heavily, but soon closed them again. "Mamma," it said, in its sweet little accents, "baby sick—baby sleep now," and then ceased breathing for ever. Edward Arthur had become a murderer.

One wail of agony—one scream of mortal anguish, such as, if uttered amid the Andes, would have frightened the wildest-winged condor from his cloud-shrouded eyry, went up to heaven with that ascending spirit. It was followed by a long death-like swoon. When Gertrude next opened her eyes, they fell upon the ghastly features of her dearest one, over which a few house flies were slowly crawling. The sight aroused her. "They shall not trample over Ida's pure brow thus," said she, hastily brushing them away. "I must arouse and shroud my dead. I know no one in this part of the village who can help me. If they would, they shall not do it. I will shroud the child. It will be no more unnatural for me to do that, than for Arthur to kill it. The wife of a murderer should be strong!"

She brought water with her own hands, and washed its little waxen limbs. She combed over its high, polished brow the yellow, silken curls. She folded the plump little hands over the pulseless bosom. She brought from a drawer a nice white robe, which she had made for her babe out of a remnant of her wedding dress, and clothed it in it. She then took her little work-table, and spreading a sheet and pillow upon it, laid there her murdered darling, close by an open window, where a cool and pleasant breeze stole in. The table, with its white covering, looked like an altar. She knelt beside it, and clasped her hands in prayer. Unseen wings seemed to fan her aching brow. A calm, such as God gives to those over whose souls the hot lava tide has rolled and seethed and hissed—souls that feel that, come what may, the worst has passed—fell upon her spirits. She felt that she had little more to dread.

29

The bitterness of death had passed. What was to follow, she neither knew nor cared for. Heaven's pearly
gates opened as she gazed ; and amid an innumerable company, who had washed their robes white in the blood of
the Lamb, she thought that she recognized her venerable
sire, welcoming her child to the abodes of the blessed.
Among the brightest cherubim on high, her darling stood.
In her hand she held a golden harp, and around her beautiful head there was a halo of glory. Her robe was even
whiter than the one in which she had just clothed her poor
earthly remains, and from her smiling lips flowed the sacred song of God's redeemed : "Unto Him who hath
loved us, and given Himself for us, be praise, and power,
and dominion, for ever and ever." "Oh, happy group!"
murmured the inebriate's wife. "Would that I were with
you! 'They shall hunger no more, neither thirst any
more, neither shall the sun light on them, nor any heat.
For the Lamb, which is in the midst of the throne, shall
feed them, and shall lead them unto living fountains of water; and God shall wipe away all tears from their eyes.'"

She was startled by a footstep near her. She looked
with a brow as calm and passionless as an angel's. Old
Agnes, the fortune-teller, was there.

"The evil which I foresaw, and would have warned you
against, had you listened to my words, has fallen on you,"
she said, in her harsh, taunting way. "The malediction
which I afterwards uttered is fulfilled. You are going
through the fiery ordeal which drove me to Atheism and
madness. I knew Edward Arthur's habits, and would
have saved you from the gloomy flood that wrecked me ;
but you would not heed my words. Are you ready now
to curse God and die ?"

"No!" said the clergyman's daughter, rising up with the
dignity of insulted majesty, and with the light of a martyr
glowing in her eyes. "'Though He slay me, yet will I
trust in Him.' Never was the religion that my father
preached, half as precious to me as at this moment. God,
my father's God, will never forsake me. Begone, tempter
of my soul. Leave me alone with my sainted child. 'It

shall hunger no more;' and I shall go to it, though it can return no more to me."

Old Agnes started backwards, as if awed into silence. "Good Heavens!" at length she said; "does the Christian faith comfort like this, and have I rejected it? May God yet have mercy on me a sinner."

Freemasons brought in a coffin; dug a grave, and laid into it Gertrude Arthur's only child. Its guilty father fled, as soon as the astounding intelligence fell upon his sobered senses that he had murdered his child. He wandered, Cain-like, for a long time over the face of the earth, and fell at last in a deadly affray which occurred in a lottery-office.

But Gertrude's faith was not misplaced. Kind friends clustered around her—friends who strove to heal the wounds in her bleeding heart—and gave her generous meeds of sympathy. She passed on her pilgrimage, calm and serene, and at last went home to her child in the "Better Land." Who shall say the religion of Christ has no sustaining power?

———◦◇◦———

TRUE—TOO TRUE!—Fanny Fern never said a truer thing than when she said the following:—" Chiefest of all sublunary abominations, is a slatternly woman. I blame no man who rushes from a home, whose mistress habitually, and through choice, pours out his coffee in curlpapers or tumbled hair, dingy, collarless morning gown, and slip-shod feet. If there is any time when a woman looks prettier than at any hour in the twenty-four, it is in a neat breakfast toilette, with her shining bands of hair, and nice white petticoat peeping from a breakfast robe, —calico, if you will, provided it fits well, and the color be well chosen—and if there is a time when a plain woman comes nearest to being handsome, it is in this same loveable, domestic dress."

THE YOUNG BACHELOR'S FIRST LOVE.

Accursed Pride! what harp may tell,
Since first by thee even angels fell,
The miseries that are entailed
On human hearts by thee assailed.—*Gold Hunter.*

"Who is that beautiful girl?" asked Marshall of his
friend Philips, as they stood in the centre of Mrs. Boughton's parlor, and watched on a *fête* night, the ladies who
moved hither and thither about them. "Who is she,
Dick? She came in with the Hortons."

Philips looked in the direction pointed out, and saw,
standing near an arch in the room, a magnificent creature.
The lighted lustre overhead poured down upon her a
flood of brilliancy, and revealed a form half-oriental in its
style of beauty—a fine oval face, as clear as marble, and
lit by eyes, dark, piercing, and full of intelligence ; at least
they seemed to the captivated sense of Marshall, at that
moment, to be full of thought and expression.

"I don't know her, Hal. I never saw her before.
There is about her a good deal of innate loftiness of spirit,
I should judge. By George! she is a perfect queen, and
she feels her dignity, too. Deliver me from coming in
contact with such a lofty personage!" and Philips sought
out a little blue-eyed girl, modest as a spring violet, who
had shrunk away from observation into a corner, and was
examining with little Fanny Boughton—their hostess'
daughter—the mysteries of a Noah's Ark, which her uncle
had brought for her the day before from town.

"Who can she be?" he mused mentally. "That is the
form and kind of face I like. A perfect Juno, and no mistake about it. Born to command respect! I take it, she
is a brilliant and accomplished woman, and I must manage
to get an introduction."

Marshall moved away to join the group, who were

already clustering about the fair stranger, and he soon obtained his desire. He was introduced to Miss Margaret Rogers, an heiress, who was on a visit to the Hortons— one of the wealthiest and most respectable families in the village where he resided.

He stayed beside, or not far from her chair, during the remainder of the evening. He was charmed by her wit, as well as captivated by her beauty. True, there was something very haughty in her bearing—something which seemed to indicate continually to all around her, that she scorned to touch the humble and lowly with the hem of her robes as she passed. Yet she had a fine person, and sang and played delightfully. Her attainments were so brilliant, that her admirers never once suspected that the heart of so fair a being could be cold and barren by nature —never throbbing with a benevolent pulsation, but frigid in its selfishness. Yet such was the case.

Hal Marshall was considered by all 'managing mammas' to be, to say the least, a very 'respectable match' for any of their daughters. Little was known of his parentage or family. He had made his *debut* at Fairhaven, where he now resided, when a mere lad. He had been employed as an under clerk and errand boy in the fashionable establishment of Muslin & Co. Time passed on, and he became head clerk, and enjoyed the entire confidence of his employers, and after a while was taken as a partner in the business. The sign over the door now read, "Muslin, Marshall & Co." He was a very promising young man, although, perhaps, not yet actually wealthy. Shrewd, calculating men took his note, and considered it as good as gold. He was everywhere received into what is called genteel society—where he figured about like an Adonis, but he had never seriously thought of love and marriage. He had never, in fact, met with his *beau-ideal*—one who answered to the heroines about which he read in novels; for it must be confessed that Hal Marshall *would* sometimes pore over that foolish kind of literature. His companions liked him. He was frank, earnest and warm-hearted. A little *dandyish*, perhaps, in dress, but he was fine looking, and the weakness was pardonable. It did not, by any means, prevent him from having many friends among the young and light-hearted of his own sex; and he and Philips especially were considered inseparable friends. They were not alike, however, in person, taste or disposition. Persons sometimes wondered over their friendship. It was one of those enigmas in social life, so often met with, where *dissimilarity* seems, in some way, to become in itself a bond of union between hearts. But then again, they were both Freemasons. Persons said that perhaps *that* had something to do with their remarkable cordiality of manner towards each other. Perhaps it had, for Masons are generally queer fellows, and there is no understanding their idiosyncracies. But, after all, this fact has little to do with our tale. It would be more to the purpose, were we to inform our readers that, although Hal Marshall entered Mrs. Boughton's parlors on the aforesaid night, heart-free—heart-hardened, he almost fancied—he was, nevertheless, in a very different condition when he made his exit at two o'clock on the next morning. In other words, Hal Marshall's was that pitiable case—*in love*.

He did not try to reason himself out of the entanglement of the affections; for who that is seriously smitten, can be made to think that there is any object worth thinking about on earth, but his *dulcinea*—anything worth striving for, but the attainment of her hand? Marshall's was a first passion. Novel writers have long maintained that this is the only one ever seriously entertained, although the experience of nine-tenths of the human race declares the falsehood of the assertion. But Marshall loved Miss Rogers, if ever a man loved a woman—or, at any rate, he fancied he did.

He cultivated her acquaintance most assiduously. He became a weekly visitor at Mr. Horton's. A house, by the way, which, before her appearance in the village, he had never entered. He sang duetts, played, flirted and waltzed with no one else.

People everywhere said that there was an engagement

between the two—it would probably end in a marriage.
People were, as they often are, half correct in their guessing. There was an engagement; and Marshall would
almost have staked his life upon it, that there *would* eventually follow a marriage; but humanity is proverbially
short-sighted, and Marshall was but human.

As to Miss Rogers, she was evidently proud of the
conquest she had made. She was proud of her lover's
person, for he was full a head taller than any other young
man in the village. His dress was elegant, and he sported
an unexceptionable black moustache. They were a proud,
happy-looking couple, as they moved side by side, through
the parlors on a *fete* night, and felt conscious continually
—a consciousness in which they both secretly exulted—of
being "the observed of all observers." But,

> "Alas! how light a cause may move,
> Dissension between hearts that love?"
>
> *   *   *   *   *   *
>
> "Oh, you that have the charge of Love,
>   Keep him in rosy bondage bound,
> As in the fields of bliss above,
>   He sits with flow'rets fetter'd round;
> Loose not a tie that round him clings,
> Nor ever let him use his wings,
> For even an hour—a minute's flight,
> Will rob his plumes of half their light."

Hal Marshall never married Margaret Rogers, and the
way it happened was in this wise:—There was a musical
soirée at Mrs. Sawyer's. Miss Rogers had set her heart
upon being present, and as usual she expected to be escorted thither by her affianced lover. But it so happened
that it was the night on which the Fairhaven Lodge met;
and Marshall, who held a high office among his brethren,
and knew, moreover, that on that particular night important business was to be transacted, did not well see how
he was going to manage so as to meet both demands upon
her attention.

"It will make no difference with Margaret," he said
mentally, as he took his hat one night after supper, and
deliberately drew on his back kid gloves. "It will mak-

little difference with Margaret, whether I go to the *soirèe* or not, but it will make the greatest difference in the world, if I fail in being present in the lodge-room to-morrow night. I will go up and explain to the dear girl why I cannot go, however; I want to see her anyhow."
And he took his walking-stick, and stepped out into the night air, suffering the hall door to slam to behind him with no very gentle crash.

A brisk walk brought him to Mr. Horton's. He rang the bell, and was immediately afterwards shown into the parlor.

"Is Miss Rogers in ?" he asked of the servant in waiting.

"I will go for her," said the girl, and disappeared.

In a few minutes afterwards Margaret entered. She was dressed with exquisite taste, and had a cheerful smile upon her lips. Marshall thought that he had seldom seen even her when she looked so charmingly pretty.

"It is a beautiful moonlight night," she said, after the usual salutations had passed. "I hope that Mrs. Sawyer will be favored with a good time for her entertainment to-morrow night. I have set my heart upon going to it."

"I am sorry that *I* cannot be present, too," said the young man, with a careless smile; "but it is our lodge night, and I shall be compelled to go there. *You* must go, however, and enjoy yourself, and hold yourself in readiness to give me a minute description of all that transpires. I feel quite disappointed, I assure you."

Margaret's brow darkened. Marshall had never seen it look so black before.

"Why! this is a very strange arrangement, Mr. Marshall," she said in a vexed tone. "You really must go. Let the lodge take care of itself. I did not know before that you were a Freemason."

"Oh, yes!" said Marshall in a surprised tone. "I have been a member of the fraternity for several years. I thought you knew it. I have great love for the Order, and hold an important office just now. I cannot by any means fail in being present to-morrow night; but it will

make no difference with you, dearest. You can go in
Mrs. Horton's carriage, or, if you prefer it, I will call and
wait upon you, as far as the door, on my way to the lodge-
room."

But Miss Rogers' brow did not brighten. A cloud,
dense and dark, seemed suddenly to have settled over it.

"Strange, that I never heard a lisp about all this before,
Mr. Marshall!" she said in a haughty tone. "I never
dreamed of such a thing. I have a decided and rooted
aversion to the Freemasons. I have said that I would
never marry one, and I meant what I said. I cannot be
chained for life to a man who goes off periodically to the
lodge-room—who sets aside everything else in order to
accomplish this—who will have secrets which no persua-
sion can induce him to impart to me. No, no! my dear
Hal, you must give up Masonry, or give up me."

Young Marshall felt at that moment as if a thunder-
bolt had fallen at his feet, and suddenly exploded. He
looked into the girl's face to see if she were indeed in earnest. The shadow that rested there, convinced him that
she was firm and decided in what she had uttered. There
was no jesting in the matter.

"Why, dear Margaret!" he said, as he drew his chair
up beside her, and attempted to take her hand. "You
surely do *not* mean what you say. You cannot be silly
and weak enough to entertain hatred against a benevolent
association of men, who choose to follow the Scripture injunction, and not let the right hand know what the left
one does in the way of charity. You are far too sensible—
too noble-minded for that. I never mistrusted that you
would care whether I was a Freemason or not."

"But I *do*, nevertheless," said the beauty, in the same
chilling tone. "I do care, though you are pleased to pronounce me silly and weak for doing so. I can never marry
one of the Order. If you take me, you will have to with-
draw. You may as well begin by staying away from the
lodge-room to-morrow night."

Marshall sat for hours, patiently trying to overcome this
singular resolution on the part of his lady-love, but all in

vain. She was as inexorable as death. She was wholly, and to Marshall's eyes, fearfully in earnest. Not a muscle relaxed in her face—not a smile came to eye or lips. She sat upright, and stubbornly maintained her cause.

"Margaret," said the young man after he had exhausted every argument, and talked himself almost hoarse. "Margaret! I did not apprehend any such encounter as this—any such clashing of wills and sentiments, when I came here to-night. I thought, at first, that you were jesting—that you could not be in earnest, but I see my mistake. I love you better almost than life itself. For three months past, you have been continually in my thoughts. Your image has been painted on the 'God-woven canvass in my heart.' I love you, but I cannot leave the Masons. I am indebted to them, in part at least, for my present position in society. Listen while I tell you a tale:

"There was a poor widow who lived in an humble cottage, and spun and wove cloth for her daily bread. She had but one child—a little feeble boy, and she was herself an invalid—not by any means able to undergo the physical toil to which she daily and nightly subjected herself; but she kept on at her tasks, and sung cheerful songs to cheer the sad heart of her boy. She was pious, and piety is, observation has taught me, in all its lineaments, cheerful and beautiful. But finally, she sickened to helplessness. A fearful paralysis seized her. The hum of her wheel, and the busy stroke of her loom, no longer resounded throughout her cabin. Her poor boy crept to her bedside and wept as if his heart would burst. But she was too far gone to speak the soothing words with which she had many times before stilled his grief. In that hour of gloom and darkness, Masons entered, like angels of mercy, the widow's humble dwelling. They provided for all of her necessities. They took care of, and comforted her sensitive child. When the widow died, they buried her, and they placed her boy in a situation, where he could, by active exertion, rise in the scale of social and physical well-being. That boy grew rapidly to manhood, watched over and protected on every hand. He took an honorable stand among his fellow-men; but he has not forgotten his friends—he has not forgotten those Masons, who ministered to his mother's dying wants, and shielded her child. God willing, he never *will* forget or desert their ranks. Margaret, that poor widow's child sits now by your side. Do you still ask him to relinquish that to which he owes so great a debt of gratitude?"

"I did not know before," said the girl, rising, "that I had engaged myself to one belonging to so low a family. I did not know that I was near marrying a beggar's son, but such it seems was the case. You will please excuse me, Mr. Marshall. Our intercourse may as well end here. I shall return in the course of a few days to my friends. I wish you good night!" and Margaret Rogers swept haughtily from the room.

Marshall sat like one petrified. He did not respond to her "good night." He did not move. He scarcely breathed. It seemed to him that his heart stood still in its pulsations.

"Yes," said he at last, in a bitter tone, rising and taking his hat, "I can excuse you, Margaret Rogers. I *do* excuse you for life. I thank Heaven that my eyes have been opened before it was too late!"

He went out, closed the door gently and noiselessly behind him, and walked with a firm step homeward. The next night found him at an early hour in the lodge-room, with a brow as calm and unruffled as if no golden hope had a few hours before fallen, like some precious vase, and become shattered at his feet.

In a few days after Mrs. Sawyer's *soiree*, Miss Rogers left for her home in the South, and Marshall said mentally, "I shall never see her again!"

*   *   *   *   *   *   *   *

Time flew on rapid wings, as time, alas! *will* fly, and Marshall forgot his *first* love, and married his *second*—the little blue-eyed creature whom Philips had essayed to entertain on the night of Mrs. Boughton's party. She was a gentle, loving being—a violet, half hidden in the retired nook where it chose to expand and send out its breath of fragrance on the air. Our hero's home was a happy one. Fair golden heads sprang up about his table, and there was no trace left in his heart of the queen figure of his first idol. But life for him had another chapter.

"I hear," said Philips one day, coming hastily into the counting-room, and stopping beside him, while he was adding up a long string of figures, "that there is a poor woman, living three miles out of the village, on the Byington road, who is suffering for the necessaries of life. She is not, in any way, connected with the Freemasons, so no help can be looked for in that quarter; but it has struck me, Hal, that although she may not be claimant on our liberality, still we had best not let her die there without aid. We are too good Christian for that. Suppose you take your little wife, Hal, and ride out there this afternoon! You can find out what she needs, and if it is more than we two feel able to provide out of our private pockets, we will take up a subscription, and apply the money to her relief."

Marshall acceded very cheerfully to this arrangement, for he had a kind, benevolent heart. He accordingly that evening handed his wife into the buggy, and started out on his mission of mercy.

The Byington road lay in a wild, neglected spot, and they had some difficulty in finding the object of their search. They stopped, however, in front of a miserable tenement at last, and entered. A middle-aged woman lay helplessly upon a rude pallet in one corner. She was an inebriate's wife. That most sorrowful of all conditions had overtaken her. An inebriate wife! those words rightly understood, and thought upon, are enough to melt a rock to tears. But this it seemed in her case was not enough. Pale disease had come to tug at the heart-strings, and sap away the fountain of life.

Mrs. Marshall went towards her, and inquired of her wants. It did not occur to her that she had ever seen her before; but Hal, somehow, after the first glance at the deathly face, and at the large, bright, proud-looking eyes, grow pale and sick at heart. He, too, had started to approach her bed, but he paused midway in the room, and finally went back to the open door, and stood there irresolutely for some minutes.

He heard his wife, while she inquired into the invalid's wants. Heard her promising to send a servant with a basket of necessaries that afternoon. Heard the woman's feeble, inarticulate replies, and wondered if he was not in a dream. But he roused himself at last.

"Emma, my love," he said to his wife, as she came towards where he was standing in the open door—"order what you think proper for the woman; it shall be sent up this evening. But the dew will be falling presently, and I think we had best go home, love. Let me assist you into the buggy. Good evening, madam!" and Hal turned away. During all his homeward ride, and, for months afterwards, he never whispered to his wife, or to any other human being, that he had recognized, at a glance, in that wretched hovel, the yet proud face of his FIRST LOVE.

———◦◇◦———

A FEELING is not to be regarded as enthusiastic, because a man experiences it in its full power only in hours of peculiar elevation. Such hours are rather to be regarded as those in which a man is most truly himself.

A BRAVE man thinks no one is his superior who does him an injury; for he has it then in his power to make himself superior to the other by forgiving it.

THE SABBATH.—The streams of religion in a country, or in an individual soul, run deeper or shallower as the banks of the Sabbath are kept up or neglected.

AN act by which we make one friend, and one enemy, is a losing game, because revenge is a much stronger passion than gratitude.

THE SPARKLING WIFE.

"A nobler flame shall warm thy breast,
    A brighter maiden faithful prove;
Thy youth, thine age, shall yet be blessed,
    In woman's love."

"ALMOND CRAMPTON! It's astonishing you can't hear me; I've spoken to you three times already."

"What is it, auntie—what is it? Pardon me for not listening. I was reading a thrilling incident in California, and did not at first hear you."

"I was going to tell you of something I heard this afternoon. I don't know whether to believe it or not. It is really very astonishing. I never should have dreamed of such a thing; and yet people, who ought to know, say that it's a fact."

"What is it, auntie? Perhaps I can enlighten you."

"Well, you ought to be able to do so, but whether you will or not, is another question. It's something about you."

"Heard something about *me*, auntie? Really what can it be?" And the young man now laid down his paper, and moved his chair close to that of his aunt Tabiatha Spratling's, who sat, spectacles on nose, mending a pair of dilapidated stockings.

"If you've heard aught about me, aunt Tabby, I want to know it. Is it good or bad?"

"Well, that is what puzzles me. I can't decide, for the life of me, whether it's good news or bad news that I've heard, Almond. Sometimes I think it's one, and then again, I'm quite certain it's the other. When I've heard what you've got to say about it, perhaps I may be able to decide."

"What have you heard?"

"That you are going to be married!"

The old lady, at this point, raised her keen grey eyes,

and fixed them upon her nephew's face. The tell-tale blood mounted to his cheek. He cast his eyes down, and played with the tassel of a cloak, which hung over the back of his chair.

"Going to be married," she continued, "and scarcely twenty-one years of age! A clerk's salary is your only hope at present for a maintenance. You have not at best very firm health. I don't know what to think of it. I am afraid it's a foolish step, Almond—one you may possibly rue in future time. But I'm not opposed, as some folks are, to early marriages. If young people would choose discreetly, and then settle down, determined to live frugally, self-denyingly, and industriously, I think, in nine cases out of ten, it would be best for them to wed young. But the girls, now-a-days, are brought up, and live on one idea, namely, *to catch a husband.* No matter whether they are fitted, mentally, physically and morally, for the position of wives and housekeepers—a husband they are bound to have. They learn to play a little on the piano—to dance and flirt at parties—to paint and dress; few of them are fit to be the companion of a poor and industrious, but aspiring man. Few of them have a discreetness of action, a depth of affection, a domestic education, or a piety of heart, such as I should want to see in my dear boy's wife; and that is why I say that I don't know whether to be glad or sorry over this event."

Aunt Tabiatha having thus delivered herself, took a new thread of darning-cotton, and proceeded with her work. Almond Crampton ceased playing with the tassel, and drummed with the end of his fingers on the arm of his chair.

"Mollie Edwards," he said at last, after clearing his throat, "strikes me as being a very fine girl."

"I don't doubt it," said the old woman; "I don't doubt it in the least. But the question that arises is, *is* she as good as she seems to be?"

"You must see her, and judge of her for yourself, aunt."

"But if she has deceived you, she might also deceive me. I do not pretend to be infallible in judgment."

"No, I suppose not," said the young man, musingly. "Few of us can lay claim to that. Mollie has a sparkling eye, a sweet laugh, and a step as bounding as a deer's. Perhaps I have been fascinated by these too much. Perhaps I have not examined the qualities of her mind and heart as I ought."

"Where did you first meet with her, Almond?"

"Well, let me see. It was sometime last winter. I was introduced to her at a party. But I was not particularly struck with her at that time. On the contrary, I was, if I remember rightly, somewhat repulsed by her boldness. She was carrying on a flirtation with a gentleman who was with her, and who seemed to be a stranger to every body else in the room. After that I saw her frequently. I met her in the street; saw her at the singing-school; observed her at the church, and met with her at parties. She was always the same; bright, sparkling, but bold. She feared nothing—was abashed at nothing. I never thought of falling in love with her, until one afternoon, when she came into my store. She flattered my vanity, and in many ways showed me that she had ' set her cap for me.' From that hour, aunt, strange and inexplicable as it may seem to you, I have loved her. My judgment does not approve of my choice. Perhaps I have ruled sober reason off the stage; but I cannot help it. I love her, and am engaged to be married to her. I have no doubt that she will many times, in future, render my life unhappy. Now have'nt I been bold, and made a clean breast of it to you. What have you got to say in reply?"

"If this is the state of affairs, my child, little that I can say will do any good. But I do not fancy that I shall like your lady love very much. There is little Helen Hannahs! I would much rather you would marry her. She is a poor girl, I know, and is supported and educated entirely by the Masons, but she has gentle ways, a pleasant disposition, and an affectionate heart. Miss Eateman, one of the teachers of the Masonic College, told me no longer ago than yesterday, that Helen Hannahs was the favorite of the school. Teachers and scholars unite in their tributes of admiration. I think, moreover, she likes you, Almond; but she has never, by word or deed, declared to me that preference. Indeed, the love that a young girl will show to the world—a delicately-minded, and high-principled young girl—is at best, I am thinking, a shallow sentiment. It is not natural or becoming in them, to turn their hearts inside out for the inspectoin of every jesting idler; and when I see one playing this game, I doubt very sincerely the depth of that love which she thus boasts of to the world."

"So do I, aunt; but I love Molly Edwards, and am going to marry her. I believe I am bewitched, but it is a sweet infatuation."

The old lady sighed, and stuck her darning-needle into her ball preparatory to putting up her work.

Almond arose, and remembering that he had an engagement, went out.

Three months from that very evening, the sparkling Mollie Edwards became Mollie Crampton. She moved immediately into a nice little cottage that her husband had rented; and for a time, she was brighter and gayer than ever.

High up in one of the rooms of the Masonic College, there sat a slight girl, apparently busy with her textbooks; but her cheek somehow was very pale, and there was an abstract air of weariness about her, as though hope had suddenly died, and life become a burden. Still she never spoke of disappointment or heart-sickness. She strove to perform her task more perfectly than ever. And when the President went his daily rounds through the recitation-rooms, his attention was arrested by her clear voice and kindling eye, as she went through, with unerring accuracy, some long and difficult problem.

"Helen," he said affectionately, pausing beside her, and taking the book from her thin white hand, "that was beautifully demonstrated; but you are studying too hard. You need rest and relaxation. You had better go and stay with your friend, aunt Tabiatha, awhile. She will give you root-beer, and strengthen you up amazingly."

30

A slight spasm contracted the girl's mouth, as she listened.

"Oh no," she said, "not there; do not send me there, I pray."

"I thought you liked her very much, and she has ever taken a deep interest in you. She has sent for you to stay with her many a time, and you always went with alacrity, and came back with a cheek full and dimpled, and glowing like a rose-leaf. Don't you like her now?"

"Yes, better than ever; but I am not in want of recreation. I am getting along very well indeed. I do not need her root-beer, I am sure."

"You need something," said the President, rumpling the book-leaves with his fingers. "My wife is going to start for Niagara next week. How would you like to go with her?"

"Oh, very much, indeed—very much, indeed; only I fear I might be an incumbrance, Mr. White?"

"I will see to that," said the benevolent-minded old man; and he did see to it. The next week, Mrs. White's carriage stopped before the college door. A trunk was brought out, and strapped on behind; and then a slender girl, in a brown traveling dress and green veil, was led out by the old President, and handed in among the blue-velvet cushions. Rosy-cheeked, dimpled, laughing girls came out with kisses and adieus, and little pale-faced Ellen Hannahs was whirled towards that world's wonder—Niagara. It was a feast to see her, ten days later, standing near "that ever-swaying temple of waters—that vast sheet of silver embossing, whose strange devices are woven into the black loom of the waters overhead." Her beautiful spiritual face was upturned towards the rushing flood, and all aglow with wonder and admiration. The silvery spray rolled in mighty clouds, and finally enveloped her form. She felt her damp hair blown about by the wind kissing her cheek. Drops of water gathered in silver globules on her india-rubber robe. She felt that she was receiving a fresh baptism from the fount of Almighty power; and she inwardly prayed, as she stood there, that she might ever be found submissive to His will, whose voice, in awful majesty, there proclaimed himself: " The Eternal of Days —the I am that I am."

She went back to the school-room, glad and rejoicing. She knew that there must be " One who doeth all things well." And the old President said, as his keen eye read her face with fatherly interest, " I knew it was rest and recreation that my little one wanted." Oh, yes! it was rest; rest for a weary, disappointed heart. How many voices in the world, could they all be collected into one mighty utterance, would roll out at this very moment that solemn diapason: " Rest—give me rest!"

Almond Crampton had owned to his aunt that he did not expect to be at *all* times a happy man. He began to think after he had been married a twelvemonth or so, that it mattered very little to Mollie, whether he was at *any* time a happy man or not. He often, when he came home, found not only an unswept, but a solitary hearth. His sparkling wife could not sparkle well alone ; it was hardly worth her while to do it. She was fond of admiration ; and so she sparkled out on shopping expeditions, much to the detriment of her husband's pocket-book, much to the injury of his credit, and much to the discomfort of his home and heart.

When aunt Tabiatha paid him a visit, he was mortified that she should find the house " at sixes and sevens" from top to bottom, as she termed it. Woman's great work— her mission, if you are pleased to call it such—was, by Mollie, ill understood, and entirely unpractised. The old lady was distressed beyond measure, and took it upon herself to give her niece a few kindly words of advice. Mollie, at this, chose to sparkle altogether in a new way. She sparkled with anger ; and finally aunt Tabby, finding the atmosphere of her nephew's home not condusive to her well-being, went away, with no likelihood of ever returning. In fact, the old lady was sick, and took to her bed. She sent for Helen Hannahs to come and see her. The girl went with sprightly step and a sweet smile. A voice has spoken to the deep waters of her soul, " peace be still."

She bound up the old lady's head, and read her to sleep, and then she went back to the college. As she closed the door of her little room behind her, her lips moved in a prayer of thanksgiving; thanks that the anguish had died out from her soul.

*   *   *   *   *   *   *   *   *

Two years went by. Almond Crampton went with a slow step and a pale cheek, and stood in an inner room, by the corpse of his wife. It was twilight, and the summer wind was swaying the long curtains to and fro. The cold dead eyes before him no longer sparkled either with anger or merriment; they were curtained by their blue-veined lids. The tongue was still; the whole form stretched in ghastly rigidity, and draperied in the white habiliments of the grave. A feeble step came in, and stole to her side. He looked down, and saw aunt Tabby's white muslin capped head bowed in tears. "I have been to her, aunt, a true husband," he said. 'I have never upbraided her; never spoken an ill word to her in my life. I am glad of it now. Towards the last, she was much changed. She clung to me affectionately, and desired me to point her away to the cross of Calvary. I did my best for her, and the lion seemed to become the lamb. Perhaps to me it has been given, through much perplexity, through many heart-burnings, through darkness and cloud, to lead a soul to Heaven. God accomplishes his wonderful purposes through our blind instrumentality."

"God grant it!" murmured aunt Tabby; and then he drew her arm through his, and they went out together soon afterwards, and stood side by side on the grave's virge, in the little cemetery of C——.

It was the Commencement of the Masonic College in C——. The spacious house was filled with a gay and expectant assembly. A band of music in the gallery was pouring forth delightful strains; and all at once it ceased, and a pale girl stepped forth and read her graduating composition. Her theme was, "I HAVE DONE WHAT I COULD." Almond Crampton was in the crowd, and somehow he held his breath with a new feeling of delight, as the orphan daughter of a Mason, the pet of that proud institution, spoke of the trials which beset a student's life, and then added in her simple, appealing way, "*I have done what I could.*" But he did not know *all* that she had done. Not one in that brilliant assembly dreamed how a battle had been fought in that delicate girl's soul, which left the victor at one time, almost as weak as the vanquished. None but the eye of the Almighty had witnessed the struggle.

That night, when Almond Crampton sought aunt Tabby's social circle, he found Helen Hannahs there. He came forward with a smiling face, and an extended hand, to offer her his congratulations.

Why did the blood mount in the pale girl's cheeks?

I do not know, I am sure. She fancied, and had said to herself continually, "his approbation or dislike is nothing to me now." Perhaps it was not—perhaps.

There was a promenade at a party projected one night, and somehow, Almond was by Helen's side.

During the walk, he said something to her, which made her turn her face quickly towards him in the moonlight. It looked paler and more spiritual than ever at first, but the flash stole up and overspread her whole countenance. "I used to fancy at one time that, perhaps, you looked upon me kindly, to say the least; something as a little sister might look upon an older brother," he said tremulously. "I would that feeling were revived, or rather a stronger one might take its place. Tell me, Helen, is there hope for me." She hesitated, and then said, as if in an undertone to herself, "yes, there is hope."

"The love that I offer," said the young man, "is founded in reason, and approved by judgment. It is not the wild outgushing of youthful passion. The heart that has been given you, has been disciplined sharply in the school of affliction, and has looked even into the pale face of death. Can you be satisfied with an affection like this?"

"I can," murmured the girl.

"Then," said the young man fervently, "we will go hand in hand together, studious ever of each other's welfare."

The girl simply said " yes" to this, but she felt at that moment, that the stars of Heaven, beneath which they wandered, had witnessed in all their shining rounds, since the world began, no happier betrothal.

AN AUTUMNAL THOUGHT.

SUMMER roses—they are dying
   Summer birds are southward flying,
And there is a soft breeze sighing
   In the rosy-tinted west.
Autumn's here with golden sheaving,
   And with busy shuttle's, leaving,
Rainbows, like a fairy's weaving,
   Wheresoe'er his foot had pressed.

Soon will sound the bird's last twitter—
   Soon will howl the blast so bitter!
Soon the frost, with silvery glitter,
   In the garden paths will lie.
Winter winds will come a sighing,
   Where the roses now are dying,
And the storm-god will be flying,
   On black wings through all the sky.

How shall I, in that bleak hour,
   When there is no bird or flower,
And the winter storm doth lower,
   Keep glad sunshine in my heart?
I will manage that another,
   Some poor, sick and weary brother,
On whom yet had smiled no other,
   Of my gold may share a part.

HENRY WHARTON.

CHAPTER I.

"A man shall not be established by wickedness, but the root of the righteous shall not be moved."--*Solomon.*

THE branches of two old oak trees, standing near the residence of Tom Thayer, rattled against the windows, and scraped over the roof. The wind was high, the sky was leaden, but not a drop of rain had fallen during the live-long day. The faded yellow autumn leaves had drifted into piles against the fence enclosing the front yard, and the apartment wherein the master of the mansion sat, was dark and gloomy. The ceiling was smoked brown, and so was a solitary picture of "Napoleon crossing the Alps," which hung in a cheap frame of wood over the fire-place. The furniture belonged to a remote age, and showed the marks of time and wear; the floor had been painted brown, but the paint had worn off, and had left patches of dingy white before the cracked mirror, between the windows, and by the hearth-stone, where the owner now sat before a blazing fire of wood.

Tom Thayer looked like a Spaniard. His hair was as black as night—his eyebrows were heavy—his eyes deep-set, yet piercing in expression—his complexion was sallow—his face long, and his skin was shrivelled. His clothes, moreover, hung about him loosely, although they had originally been made of good materials, and perhaps fitted the wearer. He sat, on that gloomy October night we have described above, alone in moody silence, with his elbows propped upon his knee, his chin supported by his hands, and his eyes fixed steadily upon the bed of glowing coal before him. His thoughts could not have been pleasant or innocent; now and then a frown passed over his forehead; he started upright, and ground his teeth

together, as if meditating revenge, or summoning courage
for some villainous deed. While he was thus occupied,
the door was pushed open, and the grizzled, capless head
of old Polly Rudd, his housekeeper, was thrust in. Her
faded calico dress, was pinned up in front, as if to preserve
it from contact with the earth; her heavy leather shoes
were miry and well worn; and she carried a milk-pail, with
a puddle of milk swimming about over the bottom. She
was evidently somewhat flustered and provoked.

"Mister Tom," she began, in a squeaking, cracked
voice, "if you don't keep Ike Brown at home to help me
o' nights, I'll give up my place, and go to service somewhere else. That confounded brown heifer has kicked
over the milk-pail thee times to-night, and knocked me
over, and almost broke my neck, just because there is nobody to keep that pesky red calf of hers where it ought to
be, while I am milking."

"Why don't you tie it up?" queried the master, without raising his chin from his hands, or removing his eyes
from the fire. "I've sent Ike up to Bill Waters, after a
load of fodder. I should think that you might manage
to milk one cow, without Ike at your heels. You
think you can't do anything, without he is tugging after
you."

"*I can't do anything, Mister Tom!* when I do everything that *is* done about this house and lot! That shows
how much consideration some folks have. Don't I milk
the cow, and feed the hogs, and nail on the palings, and
cook every mouthful that is eaten here; and half of the
time chop my own wood, because that lazy rascal of a
boy won't do a thing, when he is out of your sight, and
next to nothing when he is in it? Ike Brown don't earn
the salt that it takes to season his victuals, but he has the
knack of making *you* think that he does every thing that
is done here."

"Well, well! why don't you tie the calf up, Polly, if it
provokes you so?" said the master, now raising himself up,
and adopting a soothing tone. "Why don't you tie the
thing up, before you begin to milk, where the brown heifer

can't see it, or get to it? I should think you might manage some way to save the milk."

"I have tried it again and again, and that is all the good
it does. The string is rotten and tender, and there isn't
another cord about the lot. It Ike staid at home, as he
ought to do o' nights, he might make a rope of cotton,
strong enough to hold it; but no, he is running hither
and thither, nobody knows where, all day and all night.
I'm tired of living such a dog's life. The well-pole has
fallen off, and the bucket is in the well, and there is no
drawing water for supper. If he was here, he might go
down after it; but he's gone, as usual. It looks likely to
storm, and there isn't a stick of wood cut on the place. It
is expected that I will tote a pile on my head, from the
south wood—that I can hold the calf, and milk the cow—
that I can go down into the well and get the bucket, and
cook supper, and have it all done by seven o'clock; and
then I shall be told that I can't do anything without Ike
at my heels."

So saying, the old woman slammed the door, and disappeared from the threshold. Five minutes afterwards,
her grey head, and slim witch-like form, were seen at the
stable, in earnest combat with the brown heifer's calf. The
nursling was made fast at last, and the business of milking
was summarily dispatched.

Tom Thayer watched her until she was safely seated on
a low stool beside the cow.

"Confound these women folks!" he muttered, as he
leaned his face back again on his hands. "Wherever you
see one of them, the devil's to pay. I'll be shot if I ever
marry. That old hag of a housekeeper is more than I
can manage—inferior in social position though she is. But
it's time Ike and Billy were coming. I hope old Snowden
won't see them; he might smell a rat, for he is devilish
keen on the track. But there are some folks keener. If
that fool of a Meachem comes to-night, as he promised, I
shall be glad. But he is as slippery as an eel, and nobody
knows where to find him. If it was'nt for *some things*, he
shouldn't be into this business with me. I'll quicker em-

31

ploy a hyena, or trust a pirate. But it is, and it can't be
any *tiser*, as old man Carlisle used to say. I'm into it,
and can't get out."

Tom Thayer stopped talking aloud at this point in his
soliloquy, and the wrinkles on his sallow forehead seemed
to deepen, in the flickering fire-light.

Polly Rudd had just managed to hook the well-bucket
on the pole, and was drawing it dripping to the curb,
when she looked up and saw Ike Brown, accompanied by
Billy Waters—a neighbor of theirs—entering the yard.
If there was a man on *terra firma* who she despised above
all others, that man was Billy Waters. Of late, he had
been a constant visitor. He was a short, thick man, with
a bullet head, set up close to his shoulders ; a head covered externally with a crop of stiff yellowish hair, worn
short, and bristled up like an Arab's. His hands and feet
were thick and heavy, and he moved them clumsily ; his
tongue, after a visit to a neighboring grocery, oftentimes
partook of the same infirmity, and moved as if it was too
large for his mouth. He wore a light drab overcoat and
a low-crowned hat. His jests were vulgar, and his words,
at times, " sharper than the piercing of a sword." Polly
Rudd was never too good-natured with anyone—to Billy
Waters, she was bitterness and gall. But she feared, as
well as hated ; and consequently when called, she went
hastily, and waited upon him as demurely as a nun. She
now muttered epithets of abuse to herself, as she emptied
the bucket, and then went to quarrel with Ike about
building the kitchen fire.

Tom Thayer received his guest with much cordiality
of manner, and placed a kitchen chair for him, before the
decaying fire. They soon were buried in a low earnest
conversation, which was instantly suspended, when Polly,
an hour afterwards, entered to announce supper.

The sky, which had been dark all day, now sent down
an avalanche of sleet and snow. The wind wailed louder
than ever, and the oaks wrestled like two huge giants
with the stormy blast.

The supper was not a very inviting repast, but such as

it suited Polly's irritated temper to procure. A few slices of fried meat, swimming in a large quantity of grease; a few fried potatoes, burned almost to a cinder; a cup of strong coffee, and some smoking corn-bread, completed the meal. A dim oil lamp shed an uncertain light from the centre of the table, and the two men sat down, one on on each side, with Ike Brown at the foot of the board, and Polly Rudd at the head, to enjoy the fare which the bachelor's establishment furnished. But little was said during the meal. Polly and Ike cast looks of defiance at each other, and the men ate the meat and bread, and piled the potato cinders by their plates, without apparently knowing or caring what they devoured. They could not have eaten for the enjoyment of the epicure. Their thoughts were far, far away, from what was going on before their eyes, or passing into their mouths. Perhaps they wandered abroad into the dark and stormy night, and conjured up scenes of guilt and crime. Perhaps— I know not *where* they were—I shrink from the task of following them, for into the secrets of the sinful, my soul, come thou not, and " unto their assemblies, mine honor, be not united," for " *sin, when it is finished, bringeth forth death.*"

CHAPTER II.—DOCTOR MEACHEM.

" From the bottom stirs the hell within me."

THE unsocial supper at Tom Thayer's was hardly completed, before a heavy knock was heard at the door, and Polly, snatching the lamp from the table, went to obey the summons. A man, clad to the ears in a thick fur overcoat, with a cap drawn closely to meet the collar, stood with a riding ratan in his gloved hand, on the snow-whitened door-step without. He was covered with the feathery flakes, until he looked, in the dim light cast from the lamp in Polly's hand, like a drift made by the storm. He, however, nodded his head to the domestic, by way of recognition, and then asked if her master, Mr. Thayer, was at home. The old woman answered in the affirmative, and led the way into the apartment, where the men had resumed their seats before the fire. Both started up at the entrance of the new comer, and shook him heartily by the hand. They called him Doctor Meachem, and aided him in divesting himself of his heavy overcoat and cap. Polly took the articles into her hand, and carried them with her to the kitchen, where she proceeded to shake the snow off, and place them on chairs before the fire to dry; but her temper was by no means pleasant. She muttered to herself between her half-closed teeth. Perhaps she feared that a supperless guest had come into the house, and that there would be a fresh trial to her patience. But if so, her fears were groundless. Doctor Meachem had supped, and when he had sat down before the blaze, and thawed his fingers in the genial heat, he looked ready to proceed with the business which had called him, on that inclement night, to the remote, and not very cheerful, establishment of the bachelor.

He was a young man; and now, that he was rid of his overcoat, was by no means formidable in size. On the contrary, he was slender, and not very healthy in appearance. His dress was fashionable in the extreme, and rich in texture. He wore a heavy gold chain and watch—a faultless bosom of linen—a diamond breastpin—and a ring of massive gold sparkled upon his white and lady-like hand. His countenance was far from being frank. He had one of those cold-blue eyes which we sometimes see—an eye that is transparent as glass; one can look clear through it, without discovering any soul behind. His face was red and blotched, but his hair was as smooth and silken as an infant's. His manner was courteous, even bland, as he turned to address his companions. But his air lacked sincerity. One, shrewd at guessing character, would probably have hit at his, by calling him "a snake in the grass"—"a soulless man"—"almost a desperado." Tom Thayer, in his soliloquy, had called him "as slippery as an eel;" and Tom Thayer knew, for he had dealt with him long and closely.

Gentle reader. would you know in the begining, for

what purpose these bad men, so dissimilar in appearance, had convened on that dark October night? They had met, by preconcerted arrangement, to plan the destruction of young Henry Wharton—a youth of family respectability—a youth of guileless heart, and gentle purposes—who knew not, dreamed not, that the spoiler was abroad. But we will look in upon him in another chapter.

Dr. Meachem finished warming his hands, and Tom Thayer went to bar the outer door and lock the inner one. Every thing was made secure from intruding footsteps—even the precaution was taken of stuffing some cotton into the key-hole, lest some inquisitive ear might strive to catch their words. Tom Thayer was a cautious man. It was well that he was such, for he was steeped in iniquity, and the word of Jehovah is pledged, that "the wicked shall fall by his own wickedness." With such a tremendous fiat hanging over his head, it becometh the unrighteous to walk cautiously, and speak guardedly, lest "a bird in the air carry his voice, and that which hath wings tell the matter."

This important preliminary attended to, Tom Thayer went back to the fire. The three drew their chairs into a row before the hearth-stone, and talked low and earnestly, until the night was far spent.

"For my part," said Tom Thayer, "it is a portion of Wharton's *money* that I want, and money I will have. I have spent all that the old man left me. There is not a red cent left. There is a mortgage on this place, and I am obliged to raise the needful before many days. Wharton has got money, and money I mean to have."

The thin lips of Meachem curled into a significant expression.

"I care nothing for the money," he said, at the same time drumming with his delicate fingers upon the back of Waters chair; "money is a good thing in its place, and the more a fellow has, the better the world thinks of him, but I always manage some way to get all that I want. If I can't get it by fair means, I can by foul; but I have reasons for hating this Wharton—for heartily detesting him from the bottom of my soul. I have sworn to accomplish his ruin, and when I undertake anything, I generally accomplish it. A man had better not cross me in my plans; I am the very devil when I get started."

Tom Thayer looked gratified. "Aye", he thought, "I knew all this before; and it is well that I do know the cause of your wrath, and the sincerity of your hatred. You never would have been let into my confidence, if I hadn't known and studied you well beforehand. Old Snowden's pretty daughter, Mary, managed to touch a soft place in your heart, but Wharton proved a rival. He married the girl. I knew that all the fiend in your nature was aroused by that—else, my sharp boy, you would not have been here."

Billy Waters looked simple. "I believe, Doctor," he said, "that you used to think a good deal of that little gal that Wharton married—little Mary Snowden. That gal *was* pretty, and that's the fact. I didn't blame you for swearing vengeance on Wharton, when I learned that he had carried her off. But there is an old saying, that 'there are as good fish in the sea as ever were caught out.' If I was as good-looking as you are, I shouldn't fear being cut often by the women."

Doctor Meachem's face flushed to a crimson. "It was not the girl's beauty that captivated me so much," he said, "I never could tell why I liked her, but like her I did better than I ever expect to love anybody else. But that's neither here nor there—it was enough for me to fancy her sufficiently to address her, and to have Wharton supplant me in her eyes. If I hadn't have cared a pea-nut for the girl, I wouldn't have borne that."

Tom Thayer laughed a short, sarcastic laugh. "You may take all the women and go to the devil for me," he said. "I've a got a housekeeper, and she manages to keep me on the coals all day long. Heaven knows what I should do with a wife. Old Poll is enough to try the patience of saint or sinner."

"If I had old Poll to deal with," said Billy Waters, "she'd learn better than to cut up such antics about me,

as she does about you, T 'yer. 1 whip my wife when
she needs it, and I'd lay Poll straight, or make her stop
her clatter, one of the two, if she lived with me."

Just then the two were startled by a rustling noise outside of the door, and a half-suppressed exclamation of
anger. Tom Thayer jumped to his feet, turned the lock
and swung open the door. There was nobody there.
The entry was dark, and long, and silent. Violent gusts
of wind shook the outer door to and fro, and rattled the
bars which were thrown across to secure it. The noise
of the outer door might have disturbed them, or the whin-
ing of Ike Brown's puppy in the yard. But Tom was not
satisfied. He took a light, and went into the kitchen.
Polly Rudd sat before the fire, with her head dropped on
her bosom, snoring audibly. Her knitting had dropped
into her lap, at the same time letting down a whole row
of stitches, and her ball was half consumed in the ashes.
It could not have been Polly Rudd who was listening, and
Ike Brown had gone to spend the night with Jim Waters.
Tom Thayer aroused his housekeeper, and bade her ex-
tinguish the kitchen fire, and retire for the night. He
then returned to his guests, and secured the door as before. Here we will leave them for the present. How
they planned and schemed for the destruction of a fellow
mortal, remaineth yet to be written.

CHAPTER III.

On the dark, forbidding October night, which we have
spoken of, a very different scene was occurring at the
residence of Henry Wharton, from that at Tom Thayer's.
The storm raged without, but within the young merchant's
house all was rosy warmth, innocent hilarity, and brilliant
light. The merchant was seated by an elegantly carved
table, from the centre of which an astral lamp shed a starry
radiance over richly bound volumes, beautifully tinted
carpets, and shining rosewood furniture. At his feet,
Mary, his wife, sat on a low chair, busily at work over a
cluster of paper flowers. The merchant looked noble, even

handsome. He had a frank, open face, and cheerful, genial
manners. His wife was a delicate creature, with a slender
form, soft violet eyes, shaded by long brown eyelashes,
and a cheek, which in the warmth of the heated room,
glowed like the crimson heart of a rose. A half-open
volume lay upon the marble surface of the table before the
young man, but he was not reading. Every now and then
he reached down his hand, to aid his wife in the adjust-
ment of some leaf or petal in the flowers which she was
weaving, and his dark eye grew tender and thoughtful, as
it rested upon the face of undimmed beauty at his feet.

A small clock upon the mantlepiece, every hour gave
out a silvery chime, and so rapidly did time fly by, that
the two married lovers declared that the reverberation
never ceased—that that clock was always striking.

Henry Wharton had been left an orphan in early boyhood, and Col. Snowden, Mary's father, had been appointed the guardian of his estate. The boy grew up to manhood under the Colonel's eye, and had always depended
more upon *his* judgment than upon his own. Henry and
Mary loved each other while children, and when they grew
to maturity, their look took a more impassioned character,
and so they joined hands, and vowed before high Heaven
to live together, as clergymen say, "in the holy estate of
matrimony."

At that period in existence, life looked to them as fair
as Eden did to our first parents before the fall. They saw
the flowers—they heard the music of singing birds—they
felt a thrill of happiness at the heart, and never dreamed
that a serpent *could* lay coiled beneath the clustering vines.
But experience teaches that this is a world of stern realities. The vivid imaginings of youth are never fully realized.
The sky at the outset may be as shadowless as midsummer, but clouds soon begin to darken the prospect, and
almost before we are aware, we find that a snow-storm
has whirled over the foliage of June. Those who have
trodden to the utmost verge of human existence, declare
that earth is a valley of shadows and tears. Why then
do the young so fondly imagine that only roses are matur-

ing, for them to pluck, and weep afterwards, when they feel the piercing of the thorns? Man begins life with a plaintive wail, and ends it with a groan. Anguish is his vernacular tongue. Around the tower of Babel all languages were confounded; but the groan, the sigh, and the tear, each have a language that was not lost. They are universally understood, because they are common to all mankind. But why are we led into such a melancholy digression?

Henry Wharton laid his book down at last, and lifted the heavy lace and crimson curtains from the window behind him.

"It is a dark night," he said musingly. "One would hardly suppose, from the cheerful aspect of things within, that it could be so dark without. The wind is high, fairly boisterous, and I believe that it is beginning to snow. Are you quite certain, Mary, that the nurse will keep the baby warm? She had better bring it in here, or put some more wood on the fire in the nursery. Shall I ring the bell for her?"

Mary smiled by the way of reply, and reaching up her hand, touched the ivory handle of a small bell. The tingle of it was answered by a respectable-looking colored woman, who soon opened the parlor door, and, as plainly as words could have done, said, "what is wanting?"

"Is Rosamond asleep, Susan; and have you got a good fire in the nursery?"

"No, *Miss* Mary," said Susan, "the child aint asleep, and it looks like she never is going to be again. Her eyes are wide open, and she has been dancing in my lap, and springing towards the blaze of the candle for the last hour. She come pretty nigh burning her hand once, but I didn't let her quite *toch* it. Miss Rosamond is a mighty wakeful child, anyhow. I can't get her to sleep. The fire has gone down, and Dan won't fotch any light wood."

"She had better bring the child in here," said the young merchant to his wife, while an expression akin to concern came over his expansive forehead. "I don't like Rosamond being left so much alone with the servants. I am afraid she will be left to suffer sometimes through their carelessness."

"What a careful somebody you are, Henry," said the young wife, again smiling. "Susan takes as good care of the baby as I could take myself, I am sure. But bring her in, Susan," she continued, turning to the nurse. "There is plenty of room here, and a good fire. But you will have to stay and look after her. I want to finish my roses."

Susan disappeared, but soon came back with a blanketed bundle in her arms. When the covering was removed, as sweet a baby as ever smiled, threw out its little hands and gave a merry spring towards its father. It was dressed in a white frock, the sleeves of which were looped up from its little dimpled arms, by strings of coral, fastened on the outside with heavy clasps of gold. Its large blue eyes brightened at the sight of the parlor lamp, and then turned upon the gay colored paper in its mother's lap. Its little fat snowy fingers were thrust at first into its mouth, and then grasped at all the pretty objects about it.

Henry took the treasure, and gazed upon it with all the pride and fondness which a father feels for his first-born. Mary laughed, as only a mother can laugh, at all its cunning ways, and felt quite sure that there was never another such a baby in the world.

While they were thus engaged, there was a ring at the door-bell. Both of the parents started, at first, at the unexpected interruption; but Mary soon recognized her father's footsteps in the hall. The door opened, and showed that she was correct. The tall form of Col. Snowden entered, divested of cloak and hat, which he had left white with snow, and moist from exposure, in the hall. He glanced quickly over the pleasant scene before him, and then seated himself in a large rocking-chair, which Mary had placed near her own more humble stool, at the time of his entrance. He was a noble-looking man—one of Nature's nobility. His features were angular, and some of them sharp. This was especially true of his chin, but his forehead was high, and sprinkled over with thin locks of grey hair.

"We were not expecting you down to-night, father," said Mary, reseating herself, and resuming her scissors and paper. "You see that we have got nurse and baby in here, making in all quite a family group. It was such a black night, that Henry insisted upon having Rosamond brought into the parlor. He is more careful of the child than I am."

"You both think enough, quite enough of her, I dare say," said the grand-parent, snapping his fingers at the blue-eyed little creature, now restored to its nurse's arms. "People always think enough of the first-born. Come, Rosa, and see your old grandfather;" and the Colonel reached out his hands, and took the tiny thing into his lap. "The child is growing marvellously like you, Henry, of late," continued the Colonel. "She is going to be a pure Wharton."

"I'd rather she would be like her mother," said Henry, almost sadly.

"Why?" said Mary, archly. "You are the handsomest of the two. That is universally conceded."

"I don't think so, Molly," said the merchant. "The Snowdens were remarkable for their beauty, and I always thought you to be the prettiest of the race. But, compliments aside, the Whartons were rather an unfortunate pack, and I would rather the child would be like your folks."

Mary laughed outright. "You were fortunate once in your life, were you not?" she asked. "Fortunate when you married me, the very prettiest one in all the handsome, beautiful Snowden family. I should count myself a lucky fellow, were I in your place."

"It would be a dark sky, indeed, Molly, that had no streak of sunshine in it," said the young man, musingly. "But I did not refer to myself, individually, when I spoke of the Whartons. I have had a good deal of luck, I am free to acknowledge; but there were my ancestors, some of them sick, and some of them crazy, some of them bankrupt, and so forth and so on, to the end of the chapter."

"There were none of them hanged, I hope, for the honor of us all," said the Colonel, laughing.

"No, not exactly hanged," said Henry, "although some of them, I dare say, deserved to be hanged. But however unfortunate and culpable my ancestors may have been, I have always thought myself very lucky in having found, orphan as I was left, so good a guardian, and so good a wife. At the time of my marriage, Dr. Meachem thought me fortunate, I am sure. He had my sympathies, because he did not get my wife. I had much rather give him the former than the latter;" and the merchant laughed, while a deep blush suffused the cheek of Mary.

Colonel Snowden's brow darkened. "That fellow is the greatest scamp now on the face of the globe. That is my candid opinion," said he, setting Rosamond down upon his knee, and drawing out his pocket-handkerchief. "There is no knowing of what meanness he is capable. I never meet him, without feeling very much like caning him. Of late, he and Tom Thayer are together a great deal. I saw Billy Waters going down there, also, to-night, although he tried to escape my observation. The three together make a desperate trio—a trio who will do no good to any human being, I can promise. I cannot account for it, but of late, they watch my movements as a cat would watch a mouse. They are purposing no good. Dr. Meachem has never been friendly since Mary discarded him, and if he can work mischief, he will. The sight of him to-night ruffled my temper so much, that I came down here to wear away my vexation. It is such a dark night, that had I felt comfortable at home, I should hardly have ventured out. Here, Susan, take the baby, she is fast asleep;" and the Colonel resigned his charge, and sank back into the large rocking-chair in which he was so comfortably ensconced, at the same time drawing his pocket-handkerchief across its arm. Mary worked on in silence, and Henry looked down upon the book-cover before him, musingly.

<hr>

CHAPTER IV.

"Domestic love! to thy white hand is given
Of happiness the golden key."

THE evening had begun and advanced, thus far, plea

santly; but after the Colonel uttered the above words, a feeling of uneasiness, that could not be accounted for, crept to both Henry's and Mary's hearts. Presentiments of evil are strange things; they cling to the soul, saddening its lowest depths, and clouding the brow oftentimes, although the coming misfortune cannot be discerned, or at best, is dim and disguised in the future.

Mary had never liked Dr. Meachem. She had always avoided his society. In her girlhood she had shunned him, and for a long time, strove to prevent a declaration of his sentiments towards her; but her efforts had proved in vain, and when, at last, he made a formal offer of his heart and hand, she politely but firmly refused to accept either. She knew his disposition well, enough, to be aware that she had wounded him deeply; but she did not dream that an Indian-like hatred towards Henry, his fortunate rival, had been born in his heart. On the night in question, she never surmised, as she sat there surrounded by those whom she loved, with her infant smiling in its nurse's arms, that the avenger was abroad, with scorpion tongue and blasting breath.

> "Oh, blindness to the future kindly given,
> That each may fill the circle marked by Heaven."

"I seldom meet Doctor Meachem now," said Henry, at length breaking the silence; "but Billy Waters, strange old mortal that he is, is always thrusting himself in my way, with a word or two of advice—advice which I oftentimes adopt, even in opposition to my better judgment, just for the sake of getting rid of him. He is one of the most officious men I ever met with. He can have but little business of his own, or else he is of a most generous disposition, for he attends faithfully to that of his neighbors. Old Polly Rudd despises him above ground. She never comes into the store without muttering something about his meanness. He and Ike Brown both share her hatred. Neither does she entertain, one would suppose, the highest opinion of Tom Thayer; but she rules him, and where she can rule, I suppose she is content—as most women are," he added, in a laughing under-tone to Mary.

The Colonel did not reply.   On the contrary, he drummed moodily with his fingers upon his outspread handkerchief over the arms of his chair.   At length he arose, as
if to depart, but seeing the piano open, he sat down again,
and requested Mary to play for him.   She laid down her
work, and going to the instrument, ran her fingers over the
keys.   Her husband came and stood behind her, and
turned the leaves of her music for her; Susan, who was
half asleep, opened her eyes and listened.   Even little
Rosamond, in her lap, opened, at first, her wide blue eyes
dreamily, but closed them again, as flowers close at sunset
in summer.

Somehow or other, Mary played, without intending to
do so at first, pieces that she had learned and practiced in
her girlhood.   Memories of *old lang syne* came over all
three.   The Colonel leaned back his head, closed his eyes,
and gave a half hour to reverie.   Henry seemed to himself to be the fond lover of other days, and Mary, herself,
lived over again the freshest and best period of her
existence.

Blessed memory! it hath, at times, the comforting,
soothing office of an angel.

Before any of them were aware, the clock upon the
mantlepiece struck eleven.   All started in surprise.   The
Colonel shook hands with his children, and then went into
the hall after his hat and cloak.   Both Henry and Mary
followed him to the door, with a candle in their hand,
regretting his determination of venturing again into the
black storm raging without.   Mary clasped his cloak close
about his throat, and drew it, with loving hands, into
close folds about his person.   Both stood in the sweeping
blast, admitted through the outer door, until they heard
the clasp go to after the Colonel's retreating form, and then
they barred the door, and retired.   Darkness and silence
reigned throughout the before well-lighted mansion, and
God gave another family of "His beloved, sleep."

CHAPTER V.—THE MYSTERIOUS NOTE.

" Disasters on disasters grow,
    And those which are not sent we make.

SEVERAL months went by, after the night spoken of above, without any change. either in the business or prospects of the young merchant. Customers came in throngs to his counters; his sales were heavy, his profits good; and he never dreamed that slander might be whetting her scorpion tongue, and making ready for her victim. One day he came into dinner with an open letter in his hand. He seemed very much absorbed in its contents; so much so, that Mary forbore to make her usual remarks, but continued to rock the cradle with her foot, and went on with the book that she was reading. He sat down on one end of the sofa, and threw his feet carelessly over a chair that stood by. He re-read the letter from beginning to end. When he got through, he folded it, and taking a key from his pocket, arose and went into the library. Mary did not see him again until they met at the table.

" Were there any letters in the office for me to-day?" she asked ; " or any news of importance from any quarter of the globe? You seemed very much occupied when you first came in ?"

" No letters for you, my love—hardly one for me—nothing but a business note," he said in a careless tone ; but, nevertheless, he seemed thoughtful beyond his wont—excited and absent-minded. He ate anything and everything that the servants handed to him, evidently bestowing no thought upon the matter; and, before the dessert was served. pushed back his chair, remarking that his business was pressing, and that he should go back immediately to his store. He did not stop on his way to bestow a caress upon his child, although the little creature crowed and stretched out her dimpled hands as he passed by her cradle. That business note, lightly as he had spoken of it, had robbed him of ease at home for that day, it seemed. Mary was surprised, but she finished her dinner, and then went back to her babe and book.

"Men have strange moods, I have always heard," she said mentally, as she turned the leaves of her volume, without knowing for the first few minutes what she was reading; "but I had supposed Henry to be an exception. I do wonder what that business note was about. Perhaps somebody has ordered a larger bill of goods than usual; but he would have said so, had such been the case, I should have thought. Well, I don't know what *has* happened. Nothing bad, I hope. Where did I leave off? Oh, here, at the horseman coming up the hill;" and the young wife soon forgot, in the interest awakened by the tale that she was reading, her husband and his frugal dinner.

But she was doomed to be interrupted. She heard a heavy step in the hall, and presently some one knocked at the door of the room where she was sitting. She arose and opened it. Old Polly Rudd stood on the mat outside, with a bag over one shoulder. Mrs. Wharton started. It was the first time that Tom Thayer's housekeeper had ever honored her with a visit. She was hesitating whether to invite her in or not, when the old woman addressed her.

"*Miss* Wharton, I dare say," she began, by way of introduction. "I've often seed ye, and I know ye very well by sight, but I never spoke with ye, as I remember afore. Don't mind about my coming in. My shoes aint fitten no how to step on the carpet; but I was coming by this way, and as I thought mought be you hadn't got any fine winter apples, I'd bring ye a few, seeing we's got more than we knows what to do with; and if you'll accept of them, you's welcome to 'em;" and Polly, stooping down, emptied the contents of her bag on the floor. The large red apples rolled every way over the smooth straw carpeting.

Mrs. Wharton hardly knew in what manner to receive a present so gratuitously offered. She had no great desire for cultivating an acquaintance with Polly Rudd. But the apples were really very nice, and she did not know how to refuse them. She therefore told old Polly that she was much obliged to her for the gift; and called for Susan to gather up the apples, and convey them to the store-

room. The old woman smiled, and began fumbling in the
pocket of her dress. She soon drew forth a dry, brown-
looking ginger-cake and a sugar toy.

" May be your baby will like these, too," she continued,
holding out her brown, withered hand. " I've seed your
baby a heap o' times, when Susan had it, of mild days, out
a walking ; and somehow, the little one has quite got my
heart. I always did fancy babies, but yours is prettier
than common, and I hopes you'll take an old 'oman's gift,
though it's neither grand nor uncommon. I'm a lonely
old cretur, and have few things to love. It's nat'ral for
all of us to love something, and I hopes you won't be offended if I loves your baby, and comes sometimes to see
it, and brings it such little things as I gathers up."

Mrs. Wharton bowed, and took the cake and toy. The
tones of the strange uncouth being before her touched her
heart, now that she spoke of her darling. Old Polly had
wittingly or unwittingly found the " open sessame" leading
to every mother's heart. Perhaps she saw the tears that
sprang to Mary's eyes, for she kept on, as if conscious that
she at that moment stood on vantage ground.

" I'm a poor lonely old 'oman, and I works mighty hard
for them that neither knows nor cares for me. When I
sees a little baby looking so innocent-like and happy, it
makes me think of my little Sally Ann, who died with the
measles, when she was a year older, it mought be, than
yourn here. She was all I had to love and work for in the
world ; and since she died, I hasn't cared much which
way the world's went with me."

Old Polly brushed away a tear with the back of her
rough hand, and took up the bag lying at her feet.

" When Sally Ann lived," she continued, " I thought I
should like to stay with the quality, in such a fine house
as this, and learn their genteel ways, so that I mought
teach them to my little gal, but I made, may be, too much
of an idol of her, and so God took her away. I'm mighty
lonely, and it's only now and then that anything or any
body gets much of my thoughts; but your little baby, as
I was saying, looks so innocent-like and pretty, that I could

32

not help loving it, and that's one reason why I took the apples, and made bold to come here to-day. I hope you won't think me impudent nor saucy, nor nothing of the kind. I'm a rough old cretur, but I've got some soft and tender places left in my heart yet ; and though I quarrels more, may be, with Tom Thayer, and that scape-gallows of a wretch, Ike Brown, than I ought to, yet they's mightily to blame, I tell ye."

The old woman scraped her foot over the mat, and sallied back, with a swinging motion, as if she would feign have made a courtesy. Mrs. Wharton gave her a respectful parting salutation, and told her that she must come again ; that she should feel truly obliged to her for any little present which she might be disposed to make. The words were few and simple, and easily said, on the part of Mary, but they fell like oil on poor old Poll's rough and troubled nature. Kind words ! Oh, speak them oft. They are cheap, but precious things. No matter how simple, how rough, how low, how mean and abject, may be the one with whom you come in contact, speak gently. You do not know what wild blasts of temptation may, simoom-like, have passed over and scathed the soul. You do not know how want and vice, twin sisters often in this world of misery, may have come with skeleton form and sensual leer, and dragged their victim down, down to horrible depths of degradation, almost before it was aware of their approach. You cannot see how some prop to pride and virtue was wrested away, leaving a heart withered and worthless; a soul sick and famishing for the bread of love. Polly Rudd said truly. She was a rough old creature ; but the world saw the worst side of her character.

Mary Wharton went back to her seat by the cradle, but her book had lost its interest. She had been reading a more interesting page, than it could show, in the great volume of human life—that book which is everywhere open for inspection—which has so many varied passages in it, that almost anyone, it would seem, might be interested, but which is seldom perused by the great mass of mankind at large; or if perused, its most important and

solemn lessons fail, perhaps, to impress themselves upon
the heart. The babe was asleep, and Mary bent over and
contemplated, in silent admiration, its calm, delicate and
beautiful little face. "Sweet little innocent!" she thought.
"No wonder that even old Polly Rudd—the most graceless woman in the neighborhood—was touched by infantile
innocence, and your matchless loveliness! If she loved
her flaxen headed, sun-burned and uncultivated little Sally
Ann half as much as I love you, no marvel that the world
looks dark and dreary in her eyes now. No wonder that
her pride is dead—that her interest in life is abated, for
she is alone, and she feels that few care for her. I will
care for her—I will be kind to her. I will love her, because she first loved you, my darling."

The young mother kissed the ruby little lips before
her; and when the child stirred at her touch, she sung a
soothing lullaby. There is not in all this wide world, a
sentiment so pure and deep, and beautiful, and unselfish,
as maternal love.

CHAPTER VI.—A KEY FOUND TO THE MYSTIC LETTER.

"In social converse sped the eve."

THAT night, when Henry came in, Mary thought that
she would tell him, first of all, about her strange visitor,
but he did not stop in the parlor. He passed instantly
into the library, where he was soon deeply buried in the
folds of that mysterious "business note." Mary, in spite
of herself, felt annoyed, slighted and uneasy.

"He might have stopped and spoken to the baby, for
the first time to-day, one would have thought," she said
mentally; "but that little bit of paper has quite won his
affections. What can be in it? I have a great mind to
go in and ask him if anything has occured to trouble him
—but he don't look troubled—he looks excited, absorbed,
and rather restless. I think from his countenance, that
the wonderful 'business note' conveys pleasing intelligence,
rather than otherwise. Has anybody left him a patri-

mony? If so, why is he so silent about it? Has there
been a rise in cotton, or a fall in tobacco?"

Just then her eye fell upon a masonic paper on the
table. The sight of it brought to remembrance the fact
that her husband had recently been installed Master of his
Lodge.

"Pshaw!" she exclaimed, half aloud. "There is after
all a key to the mystery. That letter is something about
Masonry. I shouldn't wonder, from the profound gravity
and absorbed interest with which he peruses it, if it contained *the very secret itself.* Well! he may study it to
his heart's content for what I care. I knew that he was
a Mason, when I married him, and I resolved never to
worry my head about his wonderful *secrets* in that line of
business. He may have as many of them as he chooses,
but it's too bad for him to treat his wife and baby with so
much indifference. Heigh ho! I've always heard it said,
that husbands cease to be lovers after awhile—that we
needn't expect anything else of them; it's true I suppose."

Mary here ended her soliloquy, and went out to summon
the cook, and give directions respecting supper. While
she was gone, the clock upon the mantlepiece gave out
its silvery chime, and aroused the infant. Henry locked
up his letter in his writing-desk, and coming out, took
the little girl in his arms, and sat down in Mary's seat by
the cradle. Col. Snowden entered soon afterwards.
Wharton arose to give him a chair. "Never mind," said
the Colonel, "about a chair, for I cannot stay to sit long.
I was passing, and thought that I would run in, and see if
Mary had heard from her cousin Walter this morning."

"No father," said Mary, who had come in, in time to
catch his words; "there were no letters to-day—only a
short business note for Henry." As she spoke she glanced
mischievously into her husband's face. "He *told* me that
it was a business note," she continued laughingly, "but
had he been unmarried, I should long have pronounced it
a love-letter."

Henry blushed slightly, but he did not reply. "I shrewdly suspect," said his wife teasingly, "that it was some

masonic document—at any rate, I am sure it must have reached him under the seal of privacy."

"A seal which I suppose my prudent little wife has no desire to break," said Wharton, smiling in his turn. "The ladies have no curiosity in regard to the secrets of Masonry! None of them would turn Eve, and taste the apple, if they could!"

"I can only speak for myself," said Mary. "I am quite willing that you should keep that secret as closely as you can. I shrewdly suspect that it is hardly *worth* knowing, else it would have leaked out long ago. Valuable things do not remain long undiscovered."

"The reason that it has been kept so well, Mary," said the Colonel, laughing, "is altogether owing to there being *no women* in the scrape. The ladies were never known to keep a secret."

"That is because we are so benevolent in our feelings," said Mrs. Wharton. "If *we* were in possession of any knowledge calculated to benefit the world, as the Masons pretend that they are, we would grow instantly anxious to put it into wide and extensive practice. *The more who knew it the better*, and so we would take to telling it to each other with all speed. We should go in for the greatest good to the greatest number; but men, or Masons, at least, hide the light, so that one has to get under the bushel in order to see it. No wonder that those who are kept on the outside, often imagine and declare it to be no light at all."

"But because there is a bushel intervening between you and the lamp, Mary, *you* don't, I hope, feel disposed to deny the existence of the light," said her husband. "You are willing to believe the testimony of others—those who have been under the measure, and seen for themselves."

"I suppose," said Mary, "that there is something there which they term 'light,' but I believe that it would be better to remove the bushel, and let the rays go out to illuminate the whole earth. I must confess that, secretly, I have but little love for secret societies. The time may come, when I shall believe in them more strongly."

"If you ever need aid, Molly," said Henry, "you will perhaps get a glimpse of the light under the bushel. Until that time arrives, I think that you are right in concerning yourself but little about the matter."

"God grant that no female member of my family may ever have occasion to test the virtues of the institution," said the Colonel, with a slight shudder. "But I must go home. Good-night, Molly; good-night, Wharton," he said, moving towards the door. But he paused before he reached the threshold, and said: "Henry, I hope you don't leave much money in the store at night. There have been several robberies of late in the neighborhood, and I thought a word of caution to you might not come amiss. Have you got that iron chest which I gave you, in your room."

"Yes," said Henry, "and every dollar and cent in the establishment is safely deposited in it at night. I sleep with the key tied around my neck. I think that it would be a hard matter to get into it, without my knowing something about it, and it is too heavy to be easily carried off. So I have few apprehensions of being robbed, although the rogues, it is said, are very bold."

"Robbers about," said Mary, with a troubled look. "I am sure I shouldn't know what to do, if I were to awake at night, and find thieves in the house. I shouldn't know whether to scream, or to be still, and let them have what they could get without any interruption."

"I am *very* sure," said the Colonel, laughing, "that I should feel like disturbing the light-fingered gentlemen, by shooting them if possible. I have no opinion of people who appropriate to themselves, so coolly and noiselessly, the hard-earned savings of many a year. But I agree with Henry. There's little to be feared from them here, if the iron safe is kept safe and secure—so good-night again."

As the Colonel issued out into the cold, dark street, somebody brushed rudely by him, as if in haste to get out of the way—to be free from his observation. As near as he could discover, it was Ike Brown. "That boy is as contemptible as his master," muttered the Colonel to himself. "I never chance to be out at night, without stumbling upon him. He is prowling about like a wolf, and Billy Waters is generally with him. The fellow is a good candidate for the gallows."

CHAPTER VII.—THE FIRE.

> " Come, gentle sleep !
> Balm of my wounds, and soft'ner of my woes,
> And lull my weary heart in sweet repose,
> And bid my saddened soul forget to weep."

THE Whartons were enjoying the first sweet slumbers of the night. The little velvet cheek of the babe was pressed closely to the face of its mother, and the clock counted off the dark hours unheard and uncared for. But soon Henry was aroused by a voice in the street below, and a cry of "fire," mingled with the ringing of the bells, and the clattering of engines. He sprang to his feet, and rushed first to the window. · The air was filled with heavy volumes of smoke, and he could not see distinctly what was passing below; but he heard a confusion of voices, and feet running to and fro. He sprang to the door, and was surprised to find it unbolted and ajar. Blue wreaths of smoke came curling through it, visible by the night-taper burning upon the hearth, and suffocating when inhaled. His senses began to awake to the astounding discovery that his dwelling was on fire, and from appearances without and within, it was already, he concluded, almost consumed. He rushed back to the bed, and shook his wife until he aroused her. Both threw around them the first covering that they could appropriate ; and then Henry, taking Rosamond in his arms, and Mary by the hand, proceeded to grope his way, as best he could, through the darkness and smoke and blasts of hot suffocating air, which came mingled with sparks at times through the open door. He passed into the hall and sought the front stairway. It was no longer dark—the roof over his head, and the floor beneath his feet, blazed and glowed and crackled like a furnace. He paused, uncertain how he was to proceed. He felt his thin clothes almost turning to ashes upon his back, and Mary fell prostrate, overpowered by terror and heat. Just at that moment, somebody wrested his child from him, and a rough voice at his elbow whispered, "take your wife in your arms and jump the whole length of the stairway, or you are lost." To obey was but the work of a moment. He gathered Mary to his heart, and gave one fearful plunge headlong through the fire and smoke, down the crumbling stairs, and amid falling timbers. He did not stop until he found himself in the midst of a thick concourse of people in the open street. The fresh night air, aided by a pitcher of water, which somebody turned upon her head, restored Mary to her senses, and springing to her feet, she shrieked for her child. In the confusion of the moment, Henry could not recollect what had become of Rosamond. He remembered that somebody had snatched her from his arms at the head of the stairway; but half blinded by smoke, and terrified at the condition of his wife, he had not seen *who* it was, or whither the child had been borne.

"My babe is perishing in the flames," shrieked Mary. "Let me go in search of her—I would rather die with Rosamond, than to live without her."

"You must not go, Mary—*you must not go*," said her agonized husband, circling her with his arm, and detaining her by force from entering the burning building: "better that one than two perish; and if Rosamond is in there, her destruction is inevitable—no mortal power can save her; she must die, there is no help for it. O, my baby, my darling child!"

It was fearful to hear the sharp, shrill, piercing cry of anguish which burst, at that moment, from the frenzied mother's lips—it was heard far above the voice of the multitude, and the working of the engines—it was such a cry as none but a mother's lips can utter, in such an hour. Earth has no sound of misery so intense. But while Henry was striving, to the uttermost of his strength, to detain his wife from certain and immediate destruction, somebody at his elbow uttered a low, fiendish *laugh*. He looked up to see who or what it was, whether a human being or a devil incarnate, and caught a glance from the cold blue eye of Dr. Meachem. There was a scornful smile upon his lips—an expression of gratified malice and revenge pervading every feature. Henry turned away, and as he did so, a capless, grizzled head made its appearance at an open window above, and Polly Rudd stretched out her long arms, and exhibited to the multitude beneath, the fully aroused but unstartled, half-wondering visage of the lost babe.

"Who will come for the child?—who will come for the child?" screamed old Polly, at the top of her voice. "The fire is so hot I can't get down any way. Somebody must bring a ladder quick, or the building will fall in Ike Brown—Tom Thayer—I say, bring me a ladder."

Neither of the individuals addressed, stirred. The crowd thought that they were stupified by terror, and did not hear the appeal. The task of rescuing old Polly was indeed a perilous one, for the whole fabric might fall in, and the ladder, together with those upon it, would be precipitated forward, and crushed beneath the half-burnt timber. No one, at first, seemed to go; but all at once, more than twenty voices were heard to exclaim—"to the rescue! to the rescue! a ladder! a ladder!—the child is the child of our brother!" What magic impulse stirred them at that moment, and made the dense crowd sway to and fro with excitement, like a forest smitten by a powerful wind? Henry Wharton was a Mason, and needed aid.

"Steady! steady there!" said old Polly; "not too fast, and yet agin be quick! I don't care so much for myself, as for this 'ere child in my arms! I'm a poor lonely old cretur, that few cares for, but this 'ere child is different. Steady there—now come on, and snatch the baby, and I'll follow on as best I can;" and old Polly leaned more than half of her body out of the window, and gave the child into the hands of a sailor, who had sprung up the rounds with the agility of a cat, as soon as the ladder was upright against the building. In a moment the sailor was safe again on *terra firma*, and Polly was following on, as best

33

she could.   But crash went the walls—the ladder fell, for
no mortal hand could hold it up, the heat was so intense ;
and the unfortunate woman went headlong forward among
the burning coals.

"Save her! save her!" was heard on every side, but
there were none who were not driven back by the smoke and
heat.   At that moment a red shawl was seen to dart forward from the crowd, and soon a young Irish girl came
out, with burnt hands and blistered face, bearing the in-
sensible form of Polly in her arms.

"Are all out?" shrieked Henry, at the top of his voice ;
"are the servants all safe?   Where is Susan?"

"Yonder she stands," said Mary.

"Thank God!" exclaimed Henry, sinking down, overpowered by his emotions. "Thank God! let the flames
burn on, and my possessions perish."

The flames spread in spite of all the firemen could do.
A strong wind was blowing from the north-east, and the
whole block of buildings, including Henry's store, was
soon enveloped in flames.

Colonel Snowden did not reach the spot until Wharton's
house was a pile of ashes.   He found Mary sitting amid
the snow, with her child clasped, with almost frantic
strength, to her bosom.   Neither of them wore any but
the lightest clothing, and the sparks of fire had half consumed the night-dress of the child.   The Colonel stopped
a moment in amazement, and surveyed the fire and the
group before him.   He then took his cloak, without
saying a word, from his shoulders, and throwing it around
his daughter, assisted her to her feet, and almost bore
her and her child to his own house.   Henry, at first,
essayed to assist him, but the Colonel motioned him back.
"Stay," he said, "and look after your burning goods. I
will take care of Mary and the child."

"Where is old Polly?" asked Mary, as she was leaving
the spot.   "She must go, too—my home must be *her*
home henceforth, let it be under what roof it may. Oh,
father! turn back, and find Polly."

The Colonel did not understand why old Polly was

thought of at that moment—indeed, he had seen nothing
of her, and did not know that she was upon the ground,
but he turned back and made inquiries in regard to her
whereabouts, but nobody had seen her since the Irish
girl brought her out from the flames—nobody could tell
where she was.

"She is not here," said the Colonel, going back to where
he had left his daughter; "somebody has taken care of
her. We will look her up some other time. But tell me,
Mary, how did all this happen?"

"Heaven only knows, father, I do not. The fire could
not have originated in the house. The last thing I did,
after you left, was to see that every spark was extinguished in the parlor, nursery, and servants' rooms. It must
be the work of an incendiary." Just then, she thought
of the fiendish laugh which she had heard in the midst
of her misery about her child. She had not turned, as
Henry had, to see *who* laughed—at that moment she had
not cared, for her whole soul was absorbed in the safety
of her child, but now she wondered who it could have
been; and, somehow, the conviction fastened itself upon
her heart, that the author of all her misery had been very
near her, and triumphed in her anguish.

After seeing Mary safely at home, and comfortably fixed
there, Col. Snowden threw around him his cloak, and went
down again to where the fire was raging, like some wild
beast starving for blood. Henry stood looking upon the
smouldering embers of his once happy home.

"The store is gone, father," he said, "every piece of
goods that was in it is gone. The wind was too high to
save anything, but somehow I do not mourn the loss of
that, as I do of this dwelling, where Mary and I have lived
ever since we were married, and where we have been so
happy together. My property is nearly all consumed,
but I thank Heaven that my wife and child are spared
to me."

"Where is the chest?" asked the Colonel. "Has it
been removed? I do not see it here among the embers.
Iron does not burn easily, and some of your money must

be safe in that, even if your papers are destroyed. We will look into it."

For the first time, the remembrance of the great iron chest, in which he was in the habit of depositing all the money and valuable papers belonging to the firm with which he was connected, flashed across his mind. He had not seen it—he had not thought of it before. It had not been removed from the ruins; he felt confident of that, and he remembered that he had not stumbled over it on his return to the bed after his wife, or even observed it, and its situation in the room was such that he did not know how he could have done otherwise, had it been in the room. He remembered, too, that he had locked the door on retiring, and found it open on arising. He felt in his pocket—the door key was there, but the chest key was gone from around his neck. He was puzzled, and knew not what to think.

"What is the matter?" said the Colonel, who saw consternation pictured in his face. "Don't you know what has become of the chest!"

"The chest was stolen from my room, and then the house was fired—that is my solemn conviction," said Henry in reply. "I locked my door on going to bed, and found it open on awaking. The chest was not in the room when I got up, else I should have fallen over it, for it was fully in my way; the house must have been robbed of its valuables. I do not find a vestige of any of the silver that there was in the house here, and silver would have melted and not perished."

"Very likely," said the Colonel, "that the house was entered by means of false keys; the chest was taken out, and then the whole establishment was fired. Mary says that it must have been the work of an incendiary. A sad business it was, too, a sad business!" And the Colonel sat down on a little rock, from which the snow had melted, and leaned his head thoughtfully upon his hands.

"If the chest had only contained my own property," said Henry, sorrowfully, "I would not have cared so much; but there were large sums in it belonging to others—sums which I only held in trust. Well, this is an uncertain world, to make the best of it. I thought that all was perfectly secure and safe, when you mentioned the subject last night, but there is no knowing what an hour may bring forth. But day is beginning to dawn; I see streaks of light in the east. We may as well go home, and look after Mary and Rosamond, as anyway. There is nothing to be saved here, and the air is as sharp as a sword."

"What became of Polly Rudd?" said the Colonel, rising and drawing his cloak still closer around him. "Mary would not be satisfied until I promised to find her, and bring her home with me. What has she done to earn Mary's gratitude? I did not have time to ask, but the child was very earnest in her request. Did she save any of you from burning?"

"Sure enough!" said Henry, starting again; "where is old Poll? She saved us all from burning, for what I know; at any rate, Rosamond would have been lost if it had not been for her. Hetty Sanders had her in her arms. I suppose that Hetty took her home with her, but the house where she was at service is burned. I am sure that I do not know where to look for them."

"Somebody has probably taken care of them," said the Colonel. "The fire is nearly extinguished, I judge, by appearances. We may as well go home." So saying, Col. Snowden and Henry walked rapidly forward, and soon arrived at the house, where Mary sat before the fire, weeping and soothing her child.

"Was anything saved?" said Mary, as her husband came and stood beside her.

"Yes, my most valuable things are safe I find, thank God!" said Wharton, stooping over, and taking the hand of Rosamond. "My wife and child are safe. The spoiler came near taking even them, and I should have been desolate indeed." He drew a low stool beside his wife's chair, and sat down almost at her feet.

"Did I not tell you, Mary," he said, "that the Whartons have always been an unfortunate race? This proves that I, the last leaf upon the ancestral tree, am not to be exempted from the fate of my race."

"Last night we were in possession of a pleasant home, and of almost every luxury that the heart can crave; this morning, the light finds us without a roof of our own to shelter us. 'So passes away the glory of the world,' as the spelling-book used to say in Latin. Still, as I said before, I am thankful, Molly, that it is no worse."

"Did you find Polly Rudd?" said Mary, still weeping. "Poor old Poll! how much we owe her! What did become of her?"

"Hetty Sanders has her safe somewhere, I presume," said Henry. "The last I saw of her, she was in her niece's arms. Hetty will see that she is well taken care of; but I shall take the earliest opportunity of going to see her, when I can find out where she is."

"Hetty Sanders!" said Mary. "I did not know that there was such a being in the world before to-day. Pray, where does she live? and how came you to be made acquainted with her name?"

"I have often seen her," said Henry. "She was housegirl at Landrum's. They were burned out; but Hetty has found a shelter, I dare say, somewhere. Mary, my chest is nowhere to be seen; it was certainly in the room when we retired. You are quite sure of that?"

"Quite sure, Henry, quite sure. I sat down on it, and lifted the curtain and looked out at the clouds trooping through the sky, and half obscuring the moon. You know that I have always been fond of watching the clouds at night; and while I sat there, I thought that I heard somebody jumping over the fence, and running around the corner, into the front yard. I did not say anything about it, for I thought that what papa had said about the robbers had made me weak and childless, full of nameless terrors and ill-defined apprehensions. So I undressed and went quietly to bed. Now I think that it must have been the incendiary whom I heard; and Henry, did you hear that laugh at my elbow when I was shrieking for my child? Was it a ghost, or goblin, or spirit damned? I cannot get rid of that laugh; it rings in my ear like a knell over the grave of Hope. Oh! Henry, it was dreadful. I have been weeping more at the memory of that, than the destruction of our property. I believe that my senses are destroyed by the shock which they have sustained to-night, and that I have become more of a child than Rosamond."

Mary's face was indeed as pale as snow, and her eyes had in them an excited light. Henry went to a medicine closet, and taking a vial containing ether, mingled with some opiate, from a nail where it was hanging, he dropped a small quantity into a tumbler, and gave it to his wife. He then took the babe from her arms, and wheeled the sofa before the fire. She laid down upon it, and closed her eyes wearily, like one desirous to sleep. But she soon started up, and looked wildly around her.

"What is the matter, Mary?" asked her husband.

"I thought," said she, "that I heard that fiendish laugh here at my head."

"Sleep," said Henry, for I guard your pillow, and no fiend shall come near."

CHAPTER VIII.—CLOUDS AND TEMPESTS.

> "In her eye and faded cheek,
> Is read the grief she will not speak."

ALL search for the iron chest and its contents proved in vain. Henry Wharton and his family had suffered the wreck of home and fortune; but a heavier cloud than this was lowering in the horizon above their heads. On the morning after the fire, little knots of citizens were seen standing at the corners of the streets, discussing the conflagration—its origin, its progress, and its effects.

"It must have originated in culpable carelessness," said a bullet-headed old fellow, who sat down on a rock, and twisted the corner of his silk handkerchief carlessly around his fingers. "Fires are awful things, and I think the people, where they first break out, ought to be taken to task for their carelessness. If I had my way, I'd make folks answer for fires as well as murders."

"The fire broke out at Wharton's," said another. "They pretend to say that it was the work of an incendiary."

"Poh! no such thing," said Dr. Meachem, wiping the head of his gold-headed walking-stick at the same time with his black kid glove. "If there was an incendiary, he slept inside of the house. People sometimes set their own houses on fire, especially if there is a good quantity of gold, as there was in this instance, I learn, to secure. Wharton had a chest full of other folks' money up in his room. The house was burned, but nothing has been seen of the chest or its contents. Those he owed can whistle for their pay now."

"Yes, indeed," said Tom Thayer; "but it's a tune I shouldn't like to learn. I never did have much confidence in Wharton anyhow, though he has a fine face, and can be as polite as a dancing-master. It isn't every one who knows how to palaver and talk nice, that it will do to tie to, as the saying is."

"No, indeed," chimed in Billy Waters. "I was passing there at twelve o'clock, and there was no signs of fire then; but I thought that I heard a lumbering sound overhead, as though somebody was moving something amazing heavy. Ike Brown was with me. So said I, 'Ike, it sounds mighty suspicious to hear folks fumbling about at this time of night.' Ike said that he supposed folks had liberty to do what they pleased in their own houses—to move furniture about at night, if they chose to do so; although to him it looked like a strange fancy to be doing it; and I said nothing more about the matter. It's my opinion that that chest was getting out of sight about that time. Furniture takes legs and walks off sometimes. Spiritualists make tables turn and move about, and that iron chest was up to the game, I'm thinking. I'm mighty glad that it wasn't my money that was in it."

"But I had money in it," said one of the firm to which Wharton belonged; "and I don't relish the idea of losing it much. I've always taken Wharton to be a clever fellow—the fair thing. In all my dealings with him, he has been just and honest."

"Oh, to be sure! to be sure!" said Billy Waters. "Wharton has always seemed to be a perfect gentleman; and it isn't I that's going to accuse him of being anything else now. But it was a monstrous temptation—a monstrous temptation, I tell ye, to have a chest full of gold setting at a fellow's feet, and the fellow knowing all the time, that all he had to do was just to slip out of the way, and then drop a spark of fire down a crack, and soon there was a big blaze. Every thing would be burned up, and nobody would know what become of the money. It was a monstrous temptation, I tell ye. Human natur is weak; and I wouldn't trust anybody, not even myself, too far." And Billy Waters winked his eyes, and looked wise.

Injurious suspicions are subtle things. They find rooting where the people at first least look for them to grow, and, like poisonous weeds, soon affect the whole atmosphere with blighting miasma. There were three evil spirits at work in the community where Wharton resided; yes, four, for Ike Brown was quite as busy as Tom Thayer, Dr. Meachem, or Billy Waters. Wherever there was a cluster of men to be seen, one of the four were sure to be found standing in the centre of the circle, doing his best to lead public opinion. Dark insinuations were continually thrown out, and the minds of those who had suffered by the destruction of their property and the loss of Wharton's chest, were wrought upon by every means, until they became exasperated against one as innocent and unoffending as themselves.

Meanwhile, Wharton was watching, with anxiety akin to despair, beside the bed of his sick wife. Mary had grown delirious; and when she awoke from an unsound sleep upon her sofa, her eye glowed with a strange light, and her cheek was red with burning fever. She did not recognize her husband, her father, or her child. In imagination she seemed to be living over the horrors of the past night. She shrieked, and stretched out her arms towards what she fancied to be her burning child—she called on Henry wildly, like one infuriated, to let her go, so that she might perish in the flames—she threw herself from the bed, with a startled look, and declared that a devil was laughing in her ear—that a whole host of goblins were after her, triumphing at her anguish.

It was a heart-rending task to watch such utter misery, hour after hour, without the ability to relieve it; and Henry never once set foot in the street to learn what was transpiring without. He little thought that there were agencies at work all around him, endeavoring to crush his fair fame. He never mistrusted that his name was being linked with fraud and incendiarism. So completely was he absorbed by the situation of his wife, that he almost forgot the loss of property, home, and business. When he again went forth, men looked upon him coldly, and watched his movements with prying, suspicious, inquisitive eyes.

It is a terrible thing to be guilty of crime and wrong-doing—to flee away, like a hunted hind, a fugitive from justice; feeling all the while that the mark of Cain is branded on the forehead, and fearing, at every step, that the eyes of all you meet are fastened on the foul blot, and may read its full signification. Men, under such circumstances, have carried life like a load into the haunts of strangers, into foreign lands, into thick forests and impenetrable wilds—on the ocean, amid the clangor of arms and the blood-red strife of the battle-field; and failing in any and every situation to obtain relief from the upbraidings of a guilty conscience—from the gnawings of the undying worm within them—have at last, with their own hands, taken their own lives. Next to the wretchedness of feeling guilty, is the knowledge that you are suspected of being so; and this knowledge came to Henry Wharton like a clap of thunder from the serene sky of midsummer.

CHAPTER IX.—THE MASONS.

"Masonic charity! draw near to aid."

But there was one class of men who strove to vindicate Wharton's honor—a class who declared that they would not believe a brother to be guilty of crime, until the case was too clear to admit of a doubt. The Masons rallied around Henry, and tried, by every means in their power, to root up the seeds of distrust and mischief, which his enemies were so busily sowing throughout the entire community. But they who were against him were richer and more powerful than they who were for him. Day after day, the cloud of suspicion, which was gathering around his head, grew blacker and more menacing in shape; and those who watched the aspect of affairs, saw plainly that it must burst, and they feared that the fortune and fair fame of Wharton were destined to be swallowed up in irretrievable ruin. None of the firm to which the young merchant had belonged were Freemasons. Their minds were disturbed, when they thought of the golden sums that thay had lost by him. And there were three persons forever following, like so many shadows, in their footsteps, and by artful words, stirring up all that was avaricious and distrustful in their nature. Henry sat down beside the couch of his scarcely convalescent wife, in anguish and dismay. He had not thought of such a result—he had not dreamed of it. When the fire was at its worst, he had comforted himself with the reflection, that he enjoyed the confidence and respect of all who knew him, and that they would yield him, to say the least, the sorrowful meed of sympathy. He had thought that perhaps they would do more—that they would contribute of their substance to supply, in part at least, that portion of his goods which the insatiate flames were devouring, but oh! how wrongly he had reckoned—how strangely had he miscalculated! Those whom he had been in the habit of looking upon as his best friends, now turned aside to let him pass, with scarce a token of recognition; indeed, some of them frowned at him, as they would upon a viper crawling across their paths. He almost felt like the mean, guilty thing that he was suspected of being; he leaned his face upon his hands, and the veins upon his broad white forehead swelled almost to bursting. Mary was too ill to bear such cural tidings. Both Col. Snowden and

Henry strove, by every means in their power, to prevent
an echo of the wild tempest now raging without from
reaching her chamber. When her eye looked upon their
faces, they tried to appear calm, unconcerned and un-
troubled; but ah! what an effort it cost to veil the dismay
and grief that had fallen upon their souls.

But the storm at last reached its height—the cloud
broke, and the thunders fell in stunning violence upon
Wharton's ears. He was arrested and thrown into jail.
The Mason attempted to bail him out, but his enemies
were too vigilant, and too numerous to suffer it to be done.
All that they could do was to cluster about Mary, and
speak to her, as best they could, the sorrowful, heart-rending tidings, that her husband had been apprehended for a
thief and an incendiary. The result was that she again
became delirious, and raved as incoherently as a maniac.

It has been said, and wisely perhaps, with some degree
of truth, that "troubles never come singly." Col. Snowden had once or twice, during periods of great excitement
in his life, been threatened with apoplexy. One morning,
soon after Henry's arrest, he went out from the sick
chamber of his child, to whose wild delirium he had been
all night listening, and stopped for a moment to gaze
through the drawing-room windows, at the beautiful dawn
of light which was dappling the east. Spring, with her
gentle influences, was bursting over the earth—the first
robin of the season was swaying to and fro, and singing
his matin song upon a tree-top in the yard. Bulbous
roots were sending their green tender shoots up, through
the lately frozen earth, to greet the gold sunlight, and the
shrubs were putting forth rapidly their soft and velvety
leaves. Fragrance was abroad in the mild morning air,
and life, freshly renovated, seemed to be gladly astir
everywhere. It was a strange time to think of death,
when everything so recently seemed to have begun to
live; and yet death, with his skeleton form—with his hollow eyes and sepulchral voice—was there, whispering,
"away! away!" The Colonel alone heard the summons.
He threw his hand with nervous quickness to his blacken-

ing brow, and fell prostrate on the floor. His servant, who happened to be passing, at that moment, through the hall, heard the sound, and ran in to ascertain the cause. He soon cried out for assistance, saying that his master was dying in a fit of apoplexy. His words, alas! were too true. When the rich golden sunbeams came in through the windows, they streamed in bright, glad beauty over a tall, prostrate, blackened, and yet noble looking body, from which the immortal spirit had for ever taken its flight. Col. Snowden was a corpse. Thus suddenly sometimes is the silver cord loosed—the golden bowl and the pitcher broken at the fountain. Who was to carry the tidings to his daughter? What voice was there in the wide world whose accents were gentle enough to tell the sorrowful tale of her bereavement to poor, delirious Mary Wharton? Who was to tell her, that the only earthly prop left for her to lean upon in her wretchedness, had been suddenly and violently wrested away by the king of terrors? Oh! life has hours o fterrible weariness —strange visitations come from the hand of Providence —periods arrive, in which it seems that all the gods conspire against the mortal's happiness and life. Such a time had come to the young merchant and his wife.

Henry had once said to Mary, half jesting, it is true, and yet with a great degree of truthfulness, that if there ever arrived a period in *her* life, in which she needed aid, she would catch a stray beam, perhaps that full blaze, of Masonic charity, which is so carefully hidden beneath the bushel. That time had come—that dark dreaded time— which Col. Snowden had so fervently prayed might be averted from him and his. It was several weeks before Mary fully comprehended that her father was dead. She was too insane at first to pay any attention to the news, had it been conveyed to her; and when, at length, reason once more resumed its empire in her brain, she was so weak, so pale, so languid, so utterly miserable, that it was deemed inexpedient, if not hazardous, to tell her of her loss. She lay, and wondered, sometime aloud, why her father did not come to her--she alleged that she had had a terri-

ble dream, and that she would rather die than have a
similar night-mare come over her faculties. Alas! the
father she called for had become a mass of corruption in a
neighboring grave-yard, and the dream, that she had
dreamed was not more fearful than the realities which
surrounded her. Masons looked after her and her child.
Masons had shrouded her father, and borne him with masonic honors to his grave. Masons visited her husband in
his lonely cell, and spoke to his heart words of cheer and
consolation. And yet there were many evils that Masons
could not avert.

It was ascertained that Col. Snowden's property was
not what it had been supposed to be; and the home
where Mary had spent her childhood—the asylum toward
which her father had led her weary, frozen feet, on the
night of the fire—was advertised for sale by his creditors,
and was purchased by Dr. Meachem and Tom Thayer. It
seemed that this was the last drop of misery that could be
added to Mary's cup of misery—it was already full and
overflowing. She was now without a husband or a father
to protect her, or a roof to shield her from storm or sunshine. But when she ascertained how matters stood, she
became prompt and decisive in action. Her spirit seemed
to gather strength. She had at first been crushed into the
very earth by the iron heel of destiny, but the principle of
vanity was stirring strong at her heart, and she lifted up
her head, as woman often does, when the storm was blackest and most terrible, and seemed to defy its fury. She
said at once, that she would leave the house—that she
would not remain in it, if it passed into the hands of her
husband's enemies. She had become nearly well in body,
and was able to walk from room to room, and look after
her child.

It was the first bright day in summer, when she prepared to leave for ever the home of her girlhood. Some
Masons had offered her an asylum beneath their roofs, till
some other means could be provided for her shelter by the
fraternity. But before she went out to return no more to
all those haunts made sacred by the hallowed memories of

friendship and love, she went into the flower-garden, and
flung herself down on a bench that her father had caused
to be erected near a summer-house, now completely over-
shadowed by a rose-vine in full bloom. At her feet there
was a bed of small white violets. Their fragrance came
to her, loaded with the memories of other days. She remembered how, on one spring day, long, long before—
when she was quite a school girl—before she had ever
seen Henry Wharton—before she ever knew Dr. Meachem
—an aged friend of her father's had sent a small cluster of
sweet-scented violets to her, with the roots attached. She
remembered how Charles, the gardener, had laughed when
she asked him to plant them for her, and had said that
they were so much withered, that they could not live;
but she, nothing disheartened by his words, had dug with
her own delicate and jeweled fingers in the fresh dirt, and
there deposited the roots. For awhile, they drooped like
shreds upon the soil, but by aid of water and sunshine, developed a latent principle of vitality—lifted up their heads
bravely—put forth heart-shaped leaves, and grew vigorously; and now those few roots had multiplied into a legion, and those green leaves were matted together over a
wide spot of ground.

"Ye did well, brave flowers," she said, half aloud.
"They dug you up, they bruised and removed you; but,
when once removed, you struck a root downward, and
showed that ye _would not_ be crushed. Ye are emblems
of what I will be. A few friendly hands are left yet, willing to apportion to me the dew and sunbeam, as I once
gave them to you. I am bruised, but I am not entirely
worthless."

She bent over to gather a few of the delicate blossoms
to press and take with her, not only as a memento of the
spot, but as an encouragement, should she ever grow despondent; and as she did so, a foot crakled the gravel in the
walk leading from the gate. She looked up, and saw
Polly Rudd approaching. The old woman came forward
slowly, as if it were a difficult matter for her to hobble
along; and once or twice she stopped near some beds

edged with box, as if she would inhale the mingled breath of the sweetwilliams, pansies, primroses, and southern wood, which grew together in luxuriant profusion.

Mary had not seen her since the night of the fire; she had not been able even to discover the place of her residence, and had begun to fear that she was dead. But the being before her was certainly Polly Rudd, although there were horrible scars upon her hands and cheeks, and she had evidently been in some way crippled for life—probably at the fire.

Mrs. Wharton dropped her violets, and arose to meet her unexpected, but not unwelcome guest. Polly Rudd was the being, of all others, whom she was gladdest to see.

"Keep still, Miss Wharton, keep still!" said the old woman, motioning her back with her crooked hand; "I'm coming to you, as fast as I can, but it's mighty slow that I gits along now-a-days. But I'm abler—a powerful sight abler—to come to you, than you is to me. Poor thing! you do look pale. I've heard about your being sick and crazy, and the like o' all that, and I'se wanted to come to see you powerful bad, but this is the first time Hetty Sanders has let me touch foot to earth, since your house burned down over your heads, last winter. And a powerful sight o' trouble you's seen since then. Poor thing! it makes my heart sad enough to cry to look at you. You looked so plump and pretty, and lady-like; and spoke in such a sweet, happy voice, when I carried your baby the apples; and now you look so pale, and shadowy, and sorrowful, nobody would think it was the same high born lady. And *they* have done it all," muttered the old woman to herself, as if she had grown altogether unconscious of Mary's presence. "They have done it all. The wretches! Heaven will blast them yet!"

"Of whom do you speak, my dear friend?" said Mary, extending her hand, and leading the old woman to the seat from which she had arisen.

"Of your husband's enemies, child; your husband is as guiltless as your baby—and that, bless its little heart, always did look so innocent-like, nobody could mistrust it of evil. Where is the child? I come almost on purpose to see it. I've never seed a child like it, since the death of my Sally Ann, and it aint any other child that could reconcile me to walk on crutches, and carry about such scars on my face and hands as these here. It's a monstrous pretty child, and I always said so."

"Rosamond is in the house asleep," said Mrs. Wharton, much moved by the old woman's words; "you did, indeed, do for us what our language does not afford words strong enough to thank you for—you saved the child's life almost at the expense of your own. Pray, where did you go? What became of you on that dreadful night? My father and husband searched for you everywhere, but could not find you. I said then that my home should always be your home, that I would wait and watch over you with the untiring affection of a child, if I could ever find you. But alas! you have come at a moment when I have no home to offer you—no roof to cover my own head, save one that is given by the hand of masonic charity. How little did I dream then of coming to this!" and Mary burst into tears.

"Don't cry, child—don't cry!" said the old woman, soothingly. "It's their time now to triumph, and jeer, and buy houses, but it'll be *his* by-and-by. I knows what I's saying. I know a thing or two—I understand what's what."

"You deal in enigmas, good mother," said Mary. "I cannot understand you; but if you speak of my husband and his enemies, our Heavenly Father grant that your words may prove true. We have been hardly, wickedly dealt by."

"That you has, that you has!" said the old woman, producing the stump of a pipe from a pocket in her dress, and preparing to smoke. "I knows more about it than anybody else, and when Mr. Wharton has his trial, I'se going as a witness for him, but don't say nothing about it. I wouldn't have *them* smell the rat for nothin' in the world. Billy Waters said once, at Tom Thayer's, that he

34

could manage me—that he'd lay me straight, or make me
stop my clatter. He! he! he! He'll see how it will be.
Some folks' clatter can't be stopped by Billy Waters;
though, I dare say, when the time comes in court, for me,
and Hetty Sanders, and John O'Ryan, and a parcel of us
humble folks to tell what we knows, Billy Waters will be
powerful glad to make us stop our clatter! The insolent
puppy! And then, Ike Brown! he'll get paid, I'm thinking, for some o' his smart tricks, at Tom Thayer's—always
making me do everything, and then pretending like *he* did
it;" and the old woman became so excited during her
soliloquy, that she got up, and attempted to walk without
her crutch.

Deeper than any other feeling or passion in Polly Rudd's
nature, was her hatred of Billy Waters and Ike Brown.
Mary looked at her in astonishment. She did not comprehend the drift of her remarks, but she hoped that if she
knew anything favorable to her husband's case, she
would make it known.

The old woman refused to enlighten her further, and so
she wisely concluded to let the matter rest until the day
of her husband's trial. She called to Susan to bring Rosamond into the garden, and when the child came, she gave
her into old Polly's arms. The child seemed to remember
the face of her deliverer, and laid her soft rosy cheek lovingly against the old woman's scarified face.

"Bless its little heart!" said old Polly; "bless its little
heart! I'd almost go my death for it agin. But I must
be going. I promised Hetty Sanders that I would not
stay long. I heard that you were going to leave this
house to-day; and I wanted to see you, and to tell you not
to be faint-hearted and sorrowful. This 'ere is sold, and I
knows where the money came from that it was bought
with. I knows, too, that you'll git it back agin, so don't
set down and cry over those violets, as though your heart
was clean broke. I've lived a great many years in the
world, and I knows that when folks try to do right, and
keeps a clear conscience, they needn't fear nobody nor
nothin' in the world. Folks may try, and folks *will* try,

to pick a fuss with them, for this is a quarrelsome good-for-nothing world; but a good Being, that some folks calls God, I believe, watches over every body and every-thing."

So saying, Polly Rudd picked up her crutches, and prepared to take her departure. The last reflection was comforting, and she deemed it eminently religious. "I shall come to see you often," she continued, as she shook hands with Mary at parting; "and I hope to see your pale face looking better, one of these days. Yes, I'm sartain that I shall see it looking better—quite as well as it did when I brought your little gal the apples." Old Polly Rudd turned and hobbled off on her crutches; but her last words had a prophetic sound, and Mary would gladly have believed them to be true.

As Mrs. Wharton was closing the door of her paternal mansion for the last time that night, and upon her re-treating, she was startled by hearing the same *low, fiendish laugh*, that had greeted her ears on the night of the fire. She started, and almost fell prostrate upon the door-steps. She knew now its source. Dr. Meachem stood directly in the path before her. His thin lips wore a curl of triumph—his eye was not soulless now—it showed one as dark and revolting as a fallen spirit's. There was that in his air which said, "*the sweet, sweet hour of revenge has come—this is what I have been plotting for, and scheming over. You are going out into the world, wretched in future and ruined in reputation. I am avenged.*"

Mary was afraid of him; she shrank back, and her first impulse was to return into her late father's house; but then came the astounding reflection, that the knob which she held in her hand—the tall and stately edifice before her—even the marble step upon which her feet rested, were the property of the wretch before her. She dropped her hand from the knob, and sprang past her former suitor, with the agility of an antelope. Susan and Rosa-mond were before, and she hastened on, never once look-ing back, until she had overtaken them. "Farewell, once loved, but now gladly quitted home!" she said, as she covered her face with her hands, and let the hot tear-drop trickle between her fingers. "Dr. Meachem's presence would turn a paradise into a desert."

CHAPTER X.—THE CONCLUSION.

" The hopes of the wicked shall be cut off."

THE time for Henry's trial drew near. Witnesses were summoned, and able counsel was employed. Nothing was left undone in his behalf, that masonic friendship could suggest. Mary visited her husband, and tried to infuse into his soul a portion of the calmness which had been born in her innermost spirit. She repeated to him what Polly Rudd had said in the garden; she told him that she felt quite sure that old Polly had a tale to tell, which would throw light upon the missing chest and its contents. She begged that Polly might be immediately summoned as a witness in the case. Her suggestion was acted upon; and on the day of the trial, the old woman, accompanied by Hetty Sanders upon one side, and John O'Ryan, the active sailor, who had taken Rosamond from Polly's hands on the night of the fire, upon the other, entered the court-house.

At sight of this unexpected trio, even the dark cheek of Tom Thayer, the Spaniard, grew a little pale. Dr. Meachem looked sly and suspicious; and Billy Waters wrathful. Old Polly took her seat, and looked calmly and quietly around over the crowded benches—at the crafty lawyers, at the prisoner, and even into the stern, commanding face of the judge, and at the deeply interested jurors. She had never been in such an assemblage before, but she was not intimidated. She pulled Hetty Sanders' red shawl, and told her not to be afraid, but to tell the truth, when she should be called upon, bravely and in spite of all the puzzling questions that them pesky lawyers might put to her. Hetty promised that she would, and John O'Ryan declared, that if anybody was saucy to Hetty, or to her aunt, he would knock them down. The three were duly sworn, and called upon the stand.

Old Polly was the first to testify. When asked what she knew relative to the matter undergoing judicial investigation, she began her story, evidently determined to tell it her own way—to tell the truth, and the whole truth. She began by saying that she had been at service at Tom Thayer's for quite a number of years—that Hetty Sanders was her niece, but that John O'Ryan was in no ways related to her. Here she was stopped, and requested to stick closely to the subject under consideration; but the old woman, who had always had her way with Tom Thayer, determined to have it with the court also. She kept on in spite of all that could be said to her, to tell what she had sworn on the good book to tell—viz; the whole truth, and nothing but the truth; the purport of which was—that Hetty had told her that all was not right—that she had heard Tom Thayer, Billy Waters, and Dr. Meachem contriving how they could remove the iron chest, obtain the money, and burn the building—that she and Hetty secreted themselves in the vicinity, and then saw the three steal quietly up to the door, when the Doctor drew a key from his pocket, and opened it—that she saw them enter Henry's apartments, and carry away the chest—and that while leaving the house, they had set fire to the stairway.

She was through with her recital, and then patiently waited to reply to any questions that might be asked her; but consternation seized her adversaries. Her evidence was too clear, too positive in its nature, to admit of much wrangling, and she sat down, while John O'Ryan was called to her place, and requested to inform the court what he knew about the matter.

John O'Ryan was an Irishman, and had followed the seas from his earliest boyhood. He got acquainted with Hetty Sanders during her passage to America, he said, and "a *swater cratur*" he thought that he had never seen. Her surprising beauty had induced him to abandon for awhile his occupation, and he had concluded to remain

"a land lubber" until he had wooed and won her for his
bride. Whatever interested Hetty, interested him; and
when the girl came to him that night, with the tale of a
robbery in the neighborhood, he had gone with her instantly, to aid in knocking down and arresting the rogues.
But while they were hastening through the wood, they
caught a glimpse of the dark lantern, and found that the
rascals were depositing their treasure. for safe k eeping in
a place which they had dug out of the gravel near a large
rock. They waited and watched until all things were made
secure; and then they hastened on, and reached Wharton's
house just in time to save old Poll and Rosamond from
the flames. O'Ryan went on to say, that if any of the
gentleman present would go with him, he would show the
place where the chest was still to be found, but as to the
money that it once contained, he couldn't say that they
would find that there. It was his opinion that Tom Thayer
had used some of it to pay a mortgage on his estate, and
a good deal of it had gone to pay for the late Colonel
Snowden's residence, which he understood two of the
robbers had purchased, thereby turning "a swate lady
and her blessed child out o' doors".

At this point in the trial, the court was thrown into
confusion by Dr. Meachem's falling from his seat in a
spasm. A small blue paper, which evidently had, at one
time, contained a white powder, was found convulsively
grasped in his hand. The physician present examined a
particle or two of the drug, which was adhering to the
paper, and declared it to be strychnine. Dr. Meachem
had poisoned himself. Half an hour afterwards he was a
blackened, swollen corpse. Surely the words of the wise
man, with which we prefaced this tale are true : "*A man
shall not be established by wickedness !*" His sin is sure
"to find him out." At some time, in some place, perhaps
when he is least expecting it, the transgression will rise
hydra headed from the silence and darkness in which he
has fancied it to be secretly buried, and every head will
have found a scorpion's tongue, and every tongue will
sting him on to madness—perhaps, as in this instance, to

suicide. The hour of retribution may be long coming. but come it will.

Of course, much confusion ensued, and the court was unable to proceed immediately with the trial; but Tom Thayer and Billy Waters were arrested instantly, and thrown into jail. Ike Brown was not to be found. The boy had somehow escaped from the court-house, unperceived, and his whereabouts has never been ascertained from that day to this. It is supposed by most persons that he fled diguised as a female to Cuba. Rumor went so far as to say, that he stole one of Polly Rudd's calicc dresses, in which to make his exit from his native land, but the old woman stoutly denies the charge. She affirms that her wardrobe remains whole and complete—not an article is missing. But that has little to do with the sequel of this story.

The iron chest was subsequently found in the spot pointed out by O'Ryan. The money had all been expended, but some of the bills paid out by Tom Thayer, Billy Waters, and Dr. Meacham, were identified by Wharton, and other members of the firm, as among those once enclosed in the chest. The result of all further judicial investigation went to establish the innocence of Wharton, and the guilt of his accusers. Billy Waters and Tom Thayer were sentenced to ten years' hard labor in the State prison, while the young merchant was set at liberty, and aided by strong, powerful, and sympathizing friends, soon regained posssession of Col. Snowden's house and estates. Those who had been loudest in accusing him, now became his best friends, and aided by them, he was soon firmly re-established in business, and stood higher in the estimation of his fellow citizens, than he had ever done before. Ay! "*the root of the righteous shall not be moved.*" Strong winds may speep over it—hot blasts may visit it—the sirocco of the desert may strive to blast and overturn it; but "it standeth sure." It is upheld by the hand of infinite love—it is watered and made vigorous by the dews of divine grace.

Mary went back to the home of her childhood, and

wept for joy, as she sat down again by the rose-clad arbor and the fragrant violet bed in the garden. Her husband was now by her side and her babe prattled, by her knee. Her happiness would have been complete, if old Poll had formed one of her family group; but John O'Ryan and Hetty Sanders had been 'to the priest, and become bound together by the silken tie of matrimony, and they declared that "aunt Polly" never should live with anybody else, as long as they had a roof to shelter her. Mary was constrained to relinquish her claim, but the old woman often came, on warm summer days, and smoked her short stump of a pipe, and fed Rosamond on apples and gingerbread, and uttered her short pithy sayings, while Mary sat in the shadow of the arbor, and busily plied her needle.

There was one subject, however, upon which the merchant's wife sometimes mused alone, and that was the "mysterious note." She had never found out its contents, and she did not like to ask about that which her husband had once appeared unwilling to reveal, But she found out, before a year had elapsed, from old Poll, the nature of its contents. It was a letter that Hetty Sanders had written to Henry, after he had shielded her from Bill Waters' insults, and obtained a good situation for her in the family of a brother Mason—a Mr. Landrum. Hetty's gratitude had been greatly awakened by this act of masonic charity, and she had, in her uncouth way, poured out her thanks to her protector in "a short scrap of a letter," as she expressed it.

Mary was satisfied ; and so we hope our readers will be with this sequel to their story.